Metamorphoses of Science Fiction

METAMORPHOSES
OF SCIENCE FICTION

On the Poetics and History
of a Literary Genre

Darko Suvin

New Haven and London   Yale University Press

To friends and comrades from *Science-Fiction Studies*
Marc, Fred, Ursula, Dale, Patrick, Bob, and Don:
they helped.

Second printing, 1980.

Printed in the United States of America by The Murray Printing Company, Westford, Massachusetts.

Published in Great Britain, Europe, Africa, and Asia (except Japan) by Yale University Press, Ltd., London. Distributed in Australia and New Zealand by Book & Film Services, Artarmon, N.S.W., Australia; and in Japan by Harper & Row, Publishers, Tokyo Office.

Library of Congress Cataloging in Publication Data

Suvin, Darko, 1930–
    Metamorphoses of science fiction.

Bibliography
Includes index.
    1. Science fiction—History and criticism.
I. Title.
PN3448.S45S897   809.3′876   78-6265
ISBN 0-300-02250-6 (cloth)
ISBN 0-300-02375-8 (paper)

Contents

Les choses pourraient être autrement. . . .
                    Raymond Ruyer

I remember that in Spain during the civil war I had a revelation of
"the other man." . . . The Spanish dream was broken and defiled
later, . . . the faces I saw have become as they were before they were
transformed by that elated sureness. . . . But the memory will never
leave me. Anyone who has looked Hope in the face will never
forget it. He will search for it everywhere he goes, among all kinds
of men. And he will dream of finding it again someday, somewhere, perhaps among those closest to him. In every man there is a
possibility of his being—or, to be more exact, of his becoming once
again—another man.
                    Octavio Paz

What is at issue is not (merely) relating the works of literary art to
the historical context of their origin, but representing the time of
interpretation (i.e. our time) in the time of their genesis. Thus
literature becomes an organon of history. . . .
                    Walter Benjamin

I have been a sorehead occupant of a file drawer labelled "science
fiction" ever since [my first novel], and I would like out, particularly
since so many critics regularly mistake the drawer for a urinal.
                    Kurt Vonnegut, Jr.

But then are we in order when we are most out of order.
                    William Shakespeare

Preface

1. A justification for paying serious attention to science fiction may by now be necessary only for other literary critics and scholars. Still, the question of why a book addressing itself to science fiction, and furthermore one that does not deal with what is admittedly the focal point of the genre and the convergence point of this book too—modern English-language SF—has to be faced briefly. I cannot even begin here to discuss the reasons for studying paraliterature—the popular, "low," or plebeian literary production of various times, particularly since the Industrial Revolution. Let me merely note that a discipline which refuses to take into account 90 percent or more of what constitutes its domain seems to me not only to have large zones of blindness but also to run serious risks of distorted vision in the small zone it focuses on (so-called high lit.). The noncanonic, repressed twin of Literature which, for want of another name, one calls Paraliterature is (for better or worse) the literature that is really read—as opposed to most literature taught in schools. Within it, SF is one of the largest genres, and to my mind the most interesting and cognitively most significant one. This is not at all to say that an average SF text is "good," that is, aesthetically significant. On the contrary, 90 or even 95 percent of SF production is strictly perishable stuff, produced in view of instant obsolescence for the publisher's profit and the writer's acquisition of other perishable commodities. But even this 90 or 95 percent is highly significant from the sociological point of view, since it is read by the young generation, the university graduates, and other key strata of contemporary society, and is thus only less important than the 5 to 10 percent of SF that *is* aesthetically significant: in our days the writings of Lem, Le Guin, Dick, Disch, Delany, the Strugatsky brothers, Jeury, Aldiss, Ballard, and others.

2.1 If the interest for this genre has flowed out from the expansion and influence of that category of commercial publication called "science fiction," this interest should not be confined to the last 50 (or even 100) years, a period in which the SF production has been predominantly determined and strongly inflected by the capitalist market with its alienating and degrading tendencies. On the contrary, the no doubt very important *empirical realities* of SF must—if we are to pass any value-judgment on them—be obstinately confronted with the as important *historical potentialities* of the genre. These potentialities are necessarily in part speculative, but no more so than any reasonable hypothesis based on observable facts and probable laws. For laws, we can use the characteristics inherent in this genre and its generic *telos*, determined by homology with the characteristics of other, more developed genres, be they the psychological novel or the fairy tale. For facts, we can use the best productions in this genre, as redefined by these laws in a proper, spiralling hermeneutic feedback. In this perspective, SF should not be seen (as I will argue at length in the theoretical part of this book) in terms of science, the future, or any other element of its potentially unlimited thematic field. Rather, it should be defined as a fictional tale determined by the hegemonic literary device of a *locus* and/or *dramatis personae* that (1) are *radically or at least significantly different from the empirical times, places, and characters* of "mimetic" or "naturalist" fiction, but (2) are nonetheless—to the extent that SF differs from other "fantastic" genres, that is, ensembles of fictional tales without empirical validation—simultaneously perceived as *not impossible* within the cognitive (cosmological and anthropological) norms of the author's epoch. Basically, SF is a developed oxymoron, a realistic irreality, with humanized nonhumans, this-worldly Other Worlds, and so forth. Which means that it is—potentially—the space of a potent *estrangement*, validated by the pathos and prestige of the basic cognitive norms of our times.

As always, theoretical delimitation calls for a historical corpus (and vice versa): if one does refuse the one-dimensionality of most current commercial SF, then I do not see any logical possibility of a delimitation that would not be at least akin to the one in the preceding paragraph. In that case, all the not impossible other worlds and voyages thereto, from Lucian and More on, must be included into SF on the same basis as Verne and Wells. Thus it is not for directly ideological reasons but for formal ones that I have included utopias (and marvelous voyages) in SF. Admittedly, formal principles are themselves ultimately bound to given conceptual horizons and are in that sense "ideological," but in an indirect or mediated way (by way of the notion of "lateral possibilities," which is touched on in the first three chapters); and to my mind this makes all the difference.

2.2   The general working hypothesis in this book has been that the history of SF is the result of two conflicting tendencies. A potential cognitive tendency, quite evident in all the significant writers dealt with (More, Lucian, Cyrano, Swift, Verne, Wells, Čapek, etc.), is allied to the rise of subversive social classes and their development of more sophisticated productive forces and cognitions. However, an opposed tendency toward mystifying escapism dominates in second-rate SF and shows even in the masters (the statics of More or Swift, the catastrophism of Mary Shelley and Wells, the positivism of Verne), formed as it is by the practical and cognitive limitations of fiction steeped in the alienation of class society and in particular by the stagnation of a whilom subversive class. Such is the case with the bourgeoisie which, in its decline from the leader of a general plebeian progression to an isolated exploiter of nature and people, comes to treat productivity and cognition not as fundamentals of creativeness but as means of profit, and reverts in the process to all kinds of mystifications, from theism to astrology. The ascendancy of a cognitive approach makes for its fertile blend with the ludic pleasure of estrangement. Obversely, the predominance of anticognitive impulses degrades estrangement to a formal, surface sensationalism that first shocks the bourgeois but then rejoins him—already very apparent in Verne and the mediocre Wells. In the first case, estrangement is a creative approach, an organon (as Bloch said of utopia) for exploring the novum, but in the second case it is an opium for the people: if one should not forget that opiates may be necessary for momentary relief from great pain, one should not forget either the venerable adage *corruptio optimi pessima*.

All such considerations should, no doubt, also be the starting point for any serious examination of English-language SF of the last 50 years. I have tried my hand at such examination elsewhere;[1] and I hope to have here at least indicated why this

1.   The reader is respectfully referred to my articles "The Significant Context of SF," "P. K. Dick's Opus: Artifice as Refuge and World View," and "Parables of De-Alienation: Le Guin's Widdershins Dance," in R. D. Mullen and Darko Suvin, eds. (Bibliography I); "The Science Fiction Novel in 1969," in James Blish, ed., *Nebula Award Stories Five* (New York, 1972); and, in spite of its title, "Stanislaw Lem und das mitteleuropäische Bewusst-

is, in my opinion, impossible without a previous theoretico-historical reflection such as is attempted—but certainly not concluded—in the present book. The preceding very brief and partial sketch of the book's rationale may provide some first arguments as to why and how the lack of such a reflection makes for what one must regretfully call the one-dimensionality of much SF criticism—measured not so much by a priori ideological criteria (which can nonetheless, just as the ethical and formal criteria, serve as a first alarm bell) as by the practical criteria of the stupefying consequences for the matter at hand, contemporary SF. Hence my belief in the necessity of *reculer pour mieux sauter*, of beginning from the beginnings.

3.   It remains to sketch a few considerations about the shape of the book at hand: how did it come about, why does it contain two kinds of essays, theoretical and historical, and why do they deal with what they do rather than with other possible matters?

3.1   *Habent sua fata libelli*: and though the historical vicissitudes of this book do not make it better or worse, they may help to explain it. For the book has been gestating (on and off) for about 20 years. A first sketch of its historical part—no doubt crude and excessively lacunary, but in its attitudes, subdivisions, and choice of subjects a "baby figure of the mass to come"—was published as "The Sailor on the Mast" in the Zagreb monthly *Naše teme* (*Our Themes*) in 1958. Edited by Ivo Bojanić fresh from the chairmanship of the Zagreb student union, this was an exciting periodical which brought together and largely revealed the young post-revolutionary generation of philosophers, social scientists, and cultural and literary critics arising from Yugoslavia's dual anti-capitalist and anti-Stalinist struggle; even the somewhat pathetic title of my article, taken from an essay of Zamyatin's as characterizing the role of modern literature in general and SF in particular, testifies to the excitement of that moment in time and space. In more academically mediated ways, a similar orientation and pathos informed at least the most significant contributions which blended a "warm" Marxist attention to historical specificity with the Formalist attention to material forms of textuality in *Umjetnost riječi* (*The Verbal Art*). This quarterly was published at

---

sein der Science-fiction," in Werner Berthel, ed., *Insel-Almanach auf das Jahr 1976: Stanislaw Lem* . . . (Frankfurt, 1976).

the Faculty of Philosophy in Zagreb, where I began teaching in 1959, and in it a first approach to the theoretical part of this book appeared in 1963 as "SF and Utopianism." I will not recount the further stages of gestation, which led through a number of essays, published in Yugoslav periodicals, on major figures in SF history, from Lucian to Morris, to my history-cum-anthology *Od Lukijana do Lunjika* (*From Lucian to the Lunik*, Zagreb, 1965) and to English-language publications from 1969 on, except to say that though all these texts were completely rewritten in the 1970s the main orientation has, I trust, remained constant. It can perhaps be followed in the epigraphs to this book.

   3.2   As to the book's coverage, I am acutely aware how difficult it is to present a fully convincing case about practically anything, much less a whole historical tradition, within the scope of an individual's effort. True, in the last decades much scholarship and criticism of the first order has been devoted both to the major works in this tradition and to the general theory of culture and fiction that underlies my approach, and (even when I had to differ with established opinion in particular fields) I have thought it possible to deal with both the historical and theoretical part in the spirit of *was mich nicht umbringt, macht mich stärker*: a spirit of summary, connection, and incorporation into whatever new concepts I had arrived at. Nonetheless, the only proper, truly modern approach to all such matters would have been an organized collective effort by a team with identical horizons that included not only people who would know much better the various literary times and places dealt with, but also an economist, a psychologist, a philosopher; and in the case of SF also a politicologist, a historian of science and technology, and so forth. Indeed, an individual overview of a whole historical process, however one slices it up, has by now become an impossibility for any single scholar (for a socialist it is, furthermore, a conscious *contradictio in adiecto*). Even this work of mine would have been quite impossible without the generous material help of collective bodies and moral and intellectual help of a number of friendly colleagues, mentioned in the acknowledgements and dedication. But this poor individual approach to or variant of teamwork has still left me with the necessity of a number of compromises and maneuvers. One is a certain rhetorical boldness and foreshorten-

ing, especially in the theoretical chapters, without which nothing
of interest could have been said at all. Another is a not merely
linear but also spiral progression of the argument in the theoretical section of the book, where matters already touched upon are
looked at again in a wider context and (I hope) with better
results—as, for example, the discussions of naturalistic versus
estranged genres or of extrapolation. A third is the adoption of a
systematic—but implicit rather than explicit—convergence toward the locus from which any reflection on modern SF must
start out, the contemporary mass production, as a principle of
unity. One or two other stratagems will be touched on below; let
me mention here only one further problem (not peculiar, of
course, to this book) posed by culture being at any moment a
conflictual unity of the historically concrete particular and the
equally historically given possibilities of the general. A cultural
process such as a literary tradition can therefore only be grasped
with help of the general: the horizons and tendencies of a cultural locus—its historical semantics, to begin with—have to be
used to interpret any production of that time, place, and society.
Yet, paradoxically, no such general approach can afford to
forget that, while in the antinomic class culture the atomized
particular—the actual text as isolated monad—is stunted, the
undifferentiated general—the theoretical approach as pure
ideation—is dehumanized. Thus, for a vivifying and meaningful
result, a (hopefully) wise interaction between these two poles is
constantly needed. This is why in my opinion further valid
theoretical elaboration will have to pass through investigations
into a social theory of literature—a long, arduous, and expensive
pursuit obviously impossible without teamwork. It is to be hoped
that such work might be carried out around the journal *Science-
Fiction Studies* in Montreal.[2]

2.   The "Sociology of SF" issue of *Science-Fiction Studies* (No. 13 [1977]), reprinted in R.
D. Mullen and Darko Suvin, eds., *Science-Fiction Studies: Selected Articles on Science Fiction
1976–1977* (published in 1978 by Gregg Press/G. K. Hall, Boston) could be considered
as a prelude to such investigations. A general basis for them is given by the items annotated in Marc Angenot's bibliography of the sociology of literature in that issue and in
the book. In particular, Fredric Jameson's *Marxism and Form* (Princeton, 1972) and Raymond Williams's *Marxism and Literature* (Oxford, 1977) provide both excellent summa-
tions and significant developments of a social theory of literature and culture. Though
the latter title appeared too late for this book, I am methodologically much indebted to
both of these critics, as well as—obviously—to quite a number of others either mentioned

3.3 The historical part is arranged chronologically, from More to Wells with a retrospective from More to at least some kindred earlier forms in the Middle Ages and antiquity, and with two forays from Wells into twentieth-century domains, forays which are if not chronologically then logically anterior to English-language SF of the 1940s and 50s. But as I have said, this book is an essay in definition, appreciation, and evaluation; although it takes a historical view and attempts to identify key epochs of achievement and development, it is not—nor could it within a reasonable compass even approach—detailed literary history. Even where it most closely approaches an overview, I found it inevitable to focus at some length on a small number of tales, trusting that the reader will infer their representative status from my analyses rather than from cumbersome special metadiscussions of reasons for it. More, Rabelais, Bacon, Campanella, Cyrano, Swift, Mary Shelley, Verne, Bellamy, Morris, Twain, Wells, and Zamyatin are names that may be expected to appear in a study of the SF tradition as delimited in my theoretical part, and I have included them. Obversely, however, the nature of the field demanded also that such "intensive" representativeness or vertical cross-cutting be in a number of cases accompanied by horizontal cross-cutting or "extensive" representativeness. Some analytico-synthetical assumptions about the equivalence of these two types of representativeness or cutting, difference from assumptions classically used for "high lit.," are perhaps hidden in this methodology, but the book does not explicitly delve into this. A number of further points about the historical section will be indicated in the introductions to "Newer History" and "Older History."

In particular, I am painfully conscious that ideal circumstances of time, resources, teamwork, and the like might have mitigated my curtness on subjects, authors, even works that in their richness deserve by themselves to be (and have often been) dealt with at book length. This holds true for almost all major authors or works glanced at in this book (and indeed for a number of minor

---

in this introduction, in the notes and bibliography to the book, in my introduction to the "Sociology of SF" issue cited above, or left unmentioned on the assumption that it was better to run the risk of some readers not noticing my debts than to swamp other readers with unnecessary references to them.

ones); perhaps the two most obvious ones might be Blake and
The Tempest. I am here not referring primarily to my possibly
heretical approach to some works: after much soul-searching I
find myself, for example, much less favorably disposed toward
New Atlantis and much more critical of *The Tempest* than the
present majority (though not unanimous) opinion, much more
appreciative of Cyrano, and guilty of theoretical imperialism by
annexing to SF not only the fictional utopia but also *Gulliver's
Travels*. An accusation of subversiveness or heresy would, however, be quite congruous to my heretic subject matter, the genre
showing how "things could be different," and thus in a way a
great compliment. What I have in mind is rather what seems
prima facie the sheer inadequacy of dealing with Blake or *The
Tempest* in a few pages each. Admitted: and the accompanying
Bibliography is at any rate an indication that any sins were pre-
meditated. But what I wanted to provide a first argument and
sketch for was not *the* central thing that could be said about a
number of cultural phenomena *in abstracto*, but how each of
those representative phenomena in some significant—central or
eccentric—aspects arises out of, flows into, or otherwise contributes to my purposes—the tradition I am sketching and arguing
for; and on that basis I would like to think I shall be judged. I
am attempting, in other words, to apply a by now fairly classical
procedure—in the wake of the concepts of Eliot, Lukács, Auerbach, Bloch, and Brecht, possibly best formulated by the latter's
friend Benjamin in writings such as that from which one of the
epigraphs to this book was taken—to a new (but only seemingly
newfangled) subject. Furthermore, as different from the "high"
or elite tradition of most (though not all) Eliot and Lukács, possibly the Russian Formalists, Brecht, Bloch, and Benjamin have
by now taught us that a tradition is not necessarily—or even that
any healthy tradition is necessarily not—only a canonic or "high
lit." one. On the contrary, a healthy tradition is a diachronic
texture of what Raymond Williams has lately called the dominant, the emergent, and the residual in any cultural synchrony
(for a synchronic moment is simply an analytic convenience for
marking a process, a pause between systole and diastole rather
than Faust's beautiful cardiac arrest). Nearest to SF, I still vividly
remember the revelation that, in my student days, Empson's
sometimes perhaps perverse but always beautifully bold *Some*

Versions of Pastoral was to me, to the point that I seriously considered calling this book, alliteratively, *Some Versions of SF*—a title that might still be appropriate. However, the pleasing blend of protean formal-cum-substantial process identified by the (Lucretian rather than Ovidian) metaphor of metamorphosis kept recurring in my typewriter so often that I finally, as a materialist should, surrendered to my matter, *hominum deorumque genitrix*.

4.   No doubt one could envisage various ways of supplementing this book: not only chronologically but also in depth. Thus the history of SF could—once we had it—usefully be discussed as a history of some invariant problems in its storytelling: plot, chronotopes, the inextricable link between *societas hominum* and *societas rerum*, and so on. This study is confined to working out the rationale and the main lines of an SF tradition. It has the ambition to be pathbreaking, and the limitation of pathbreakers: once the path has been chosen, one cannot glance right or left very often. But on the whole, I would hope the book might show the interested reader that side by side with the "canonic" genres there is a great number of works of fiction which have so far been neglected, or considered solely as nonfiction (history of ideas, unmediated ideology, etc.), or considered as marginal aberrations from another properly canonic tradition; and that, as a consequence, the specific pleasure which a reader has the right to expect and find in them has been too largely ignored. In a way, this book is an exercise in cleansing our perception; and what we could perceive is this material dialectics of human history and its possibilities: "the development of the five senses is a labor of the whole previous history of the world."[3] Never was it so necessary as it is today to iluminate this history of ours, with its works and dreams, triumphs and servitudes. The formalized daydreams of science fiction can be claimed as a privileged *pars pro toto* or vibration of this history.

---

3.   Karl Marx, "Private Property and Communism," in Loyd D. Easton and Kurt Guddat, eds., *Writings of the Young Marx on Philosophy and Society* (Garden City, NY, 1967), p. 309.

Acknowledgments

Various versions and parts of this work have benefited from the financial assistance of the University of Massachusetts at Amherst, the Humanities Research fund at McGill University, and especially of several Canada Council research grants. The bulk of the book was prepared during the 1973–74 sabbatical leave granted me by McGill University and partly supported by a Canada Council Leave Fellowship. My sincere thanks go to all these institutions, whose encouragement was not merely material, as well as to the main libraries whose staff facilitated my research: the McLennan Library at McGill University (and in particular its Inter-Library Loans department, unfailingly helpful above and beyond the call of duty), the New York Public Library, the Library of Congress, the libraries of Yale, Indiana, and Cambridge universities, the British Library in London, the national Libraries at Paris and Florence, and the National University Library at Zagreb.

Earlier reasonably recognizable versions of various chapters—as a rule significantly changed or enlarged in the present book—were first published in the following periodicals: chapter 1 in *College English* No. 3 (1972) (Copyright © 1972 by the National Council of Teachers of English. Reprinted by permission), and in a differing version in *Foundation* No. 2 (1972); chapter 2 in *Genre* No. 3 (1973); chapter 3 in *Studies in the Literary Imagination* No. 2 (1973); the first part of chapter 5 and chapter 6 in *Science-Fiction Studies* No. 4 (1974) and No. 10 (1976); the first part of chapter 7 in *Clio* No. 1 (1974); chapter 9 in *The Minnesota Review* No. 4 (1975); chapter 10 in *Comparative Literature Studies* No. 4 (1973) and in a differing version in *Strumenti critici* No. 18 (1972); and chapter 11 in *The Modern Language Review* No. 1 (1971). My thanks are due to the editors of all these periodicals for permission to use the above materials.

I have incurred debts of gratitude larger than usual, I suspect. First and foremost, to the friends to whom the book is dedicated, and to whose names that of Nena should (as always: *come prima, più di prima*) be joined. Second, to many other people who have encouraged my work, from whom I have surely learned and absorbed much, but who are too numerous to mention here. I would at least like to single out my McGill students, whom I have slyly induced to teach me more often than they suspected; the Department of English chaired by Donald F. Theall and later by Peter Ohlin, who allowed and indeed incited me to teach SF to those students; and my friends and colleagues, the late Jim Blish, Mike Bristol, Mike Holquist, Charles Le Guin, and Judy Merrill in North America, as well as—much earlier—Ivo Bojanić, Ivan V. Lalić, Milan Mirić, and Zdenko Škreb in Yugoslavia. I am also indebted to Barbara L. Campbell for the typing and indexing, and especially to Ellen Graham and Lynn Walterick, my editors at Yale University Press.

As for the reasons, factors, thrones, dominations, and powers that prevented me from writing a better book, I hint at some in my preface . . . : and to spell them out in a kind of "Anti-Acknowledgements" might have been quite illuminating, but it would be too long.

D. S.

Montreal, April 1978

I

POETICS

1

Estrangement and Cognition

1. SCIENCE FICTION AS FICTION (ESTRANGEMENT)

1.1. The importance of science fiction (SF) in our time is on the increase. First, there are strong indications that its popularity in the leading industrial nations (United States, USSR, United Kingdom, Japan) has risen sharply over the last 100 years, despite all the local and short-range fluctuations. SF has particularly affected such key strata or groups of modern society as college graduates, young writers, and the avant-garde of general readers appreciative of new sets of values. This is a significant cultural effect which goes beyond any merely quantitative census. Second, if one takes the minimal generic difference of SF the presence of a narrative novum (the dramatis personae and/or their context) significantly different from what is the norm in "naturalistic" or empiricist fiction, it will be found that SF has an interesting and close kinship with other literary subgenres that flourished at different times and places of literary history: the classical and medieval "fortunate island" story, the "fabulous voyage" story from antiquity on, the Renaissance and Baroque "utopia" and "planetary novel," the Enlightenment "state [political] novel," the modern "anticipation" and "anti-utopia." Moreover, although SF shares with myth, fantasy, fairy tale, and pastoral an opposition to naturalistic or empiricist liter-

The first version of this essay emerged from a lecture given in Spring 1968 in J. M. Holquist's seminar on fantastic literature in the Yale University Slavic Languages and Literatures Department. I have derived much profit from discussions with him, with the late Jacques Ehrmann, my UMass colleague David Porter, and my McGill colleagues Irwin and Myrna Gopnik, over and above a number of persons mentioned in my general acknowledgements. The final version owes much to Stanislaw Lem's *Fantastyka i futurologia* (see Bibliography I), which considerably emboldened me in further pursuits within this protean field, even where I differed from some of Lem's emphases and conclusions. Notes to all chapters are supplemented by the bibliographic sections to be found at the end of the book.

ary genres, it differs very significantly in approach and social function from such adjoining non-naturalistic or metaempirical genres. Both these complementary aspects, the sociological and the methodological, are being vigorously debated by writers and critics in several countries, evidence of lively interest in a genre that should undergo scholarly discussion too.

In this chapter, I will argue for an understanding of SF as the *literature of cognitive estrangement*. This definition seems to possess the unique advantage of rendering justice to a literary tradition which is coherent through the ages and within itself, yet distinct from nonfictional utopianism, from naturalistic literature, and from other non-naturalistic fiction. It thus makes it possible to lay the basis for a coherent poetics of SF.

1.2. I want to begin by postulating a spectrum or spread of literary subject matter which extends from the ideal extreme of exact recreation of the author's empirical environment[1] to exclusive interest in a strange newness, a *novum*. From the 18th to the 20th centuries, the literary mainstream of our civilization has been nearer to the first of these two extremes. However, at the beginnings of a literature, the concern with a domestication of the amazing is very strong. Early tale-tellers relate amazing voyages into the next valley, where they found dog-headed people,

---

1. A benefit of discussing the seemingly peripheral subject of "science fiction" is that one has to go back to first principles, one cannot really assume them as given. One must ask, for example, what is literature? Usually, when discussing literature one determines what it says (its subject matter) and how it says what it says (the approach to its themes). If we are talking about literature in the sense of significant works possessing certain minimal aesthetic qualities rather than in the sociological sense of everything that gets published at a certain time or in the ideological sense of all the writings on certain themes, this principle can more precisely be formulated as a double question. First, epistemologically, what possibility for aesthetic qualities is offered by different thematic fields ("subjects")? The answer given by the aesthetics prevalent at the moment is: an absolutely equal possibility. With this answer the question is booted out of the field of aesthetics and into the lap of ideologists, who pick it up by our default and proceed to bungle it. Second, historically, how has such a possibility in fact been used? Once one begins with such considerations, one comes quickly up against the rather unclear concept of *realism* (not the prose literary movement in the nineteenth century but a metahistorical stylistic principle), since this genre is often pigeonholed as nonrealistic. I would not object but would heartily welcome such labels if one had first persuasively defined what is "real" and what is "reality." True, this genre raises basic philosophical issues, but it is perhaps not necessary to face them in an initial approach. Therefore I shall here substitute for "reality" (whose existence independent of any observer or group of observers I do not at all doubt, in fact) the concept of "the author's empirical environment," which seems as immediately clear as any.

also good rock salt which could be stolen or at the worst bartered for. Their stories are a syncretic travelogue and *voyage imaginaire*, daydream and intelligence report. This implies a curiosity about the unknown beyond the next mountain range (sea, ocean, solar system), where the thrill of knowledge joined the thrill of adventure.

From Iambulus and Euhemerus through the classical utopia to Verne's island of Captain Nemo and Wells's island of Dr. Moreau, an island in the far-off ocean is the paradigm of the aesthetically most satisfying goal of the SF voyage. This is particularly true if we subsume under this the planetary island in the aether ocean—usually the Moon—which we encounter from Lucian through Cyrano to Swift's mini-Moon of Laputa, and on into the nineteenth century. Yet the parallel paradigm of the valley, "over the range" (the subtitle of Butler's SF novel *Erewhon*) which shuts it in as a wall, is perhaps as revealing. It recurs almost as frequently, from the earliest folktales about the sparkling valley of Terrestrial Paradise and the dark valley of the Dead, both already in *Gilgamesh*. Eden is the mythological localization of utiopian longing, just as Wells's valley in "The Country of the Blind" is still within the liberating tradition which contends that the world is not necessarily the way our present empirical valley happens to be, and that whoever thinks his valley is the world is blind. Whether island or valley, whether in space or (from the industrial and bourgeois revolutions on) in time, the new framework is correlative to the new inhabitants. The aliens—utopians, monsters, or simply differing strangers—are a mirror to man just as the differing country is a mirror for his world. But the mirror is not only a reflecting one, it is also a transforming one, virgin womb and alchemical dynamo: the mirror is a crucible.

Thus it is not only the basic human and humanizing curiosity that gives birth to SF. Beyond an undirected inquisitiveness, which makes for a semantic game without clear referent, this genre has always been wedded to a hope of finding in the unknown the ideal environment, tribe, state, intelligence, or other aspect of the Supreme Good (or to a fear of and revulsion from its contrary). At all events, the *possibility* of other strange, covariant coordinate systems and semantic fields is assumed.

1.3. The approach to the imaginary locality, or localized daydream, practiced by the genre of SF is a supposedly factual one. Columbus's (technically or genologically nonfictional) letter on the Eden he glimpsed beyond the Orinoco mouth, and Swift's (technically nonfactual) voyage to Laputa, Balnibarbi, Glubbdubbdrib, Luggnagg, "and Japan" represent two extremes in the constant intermingling of imaginary and empirical possibilities. Thus SF takes off from a fictional ("literary") hypothesis and develops it with totalizing ("scientific") rigor—the specific difference between Columbus and Swift is smaller than their generic proximity. The effect of such factual reporting of fictions is one of confronting a set normative system—a Ptolemaic-type closed world picture—with a point of view or look implying a new set of norms; in literary theory this is known as the attitude of *estrangement*. This concept was first developed on non-naturalistic texts by the Russian Formalists ("ostranenie," Viktor Shklovsky) and most successfully underpinned by an anthropological and historical approach in the work of Bertolt Brecht, who wanted to write "plays for a scientific age." While working on a play about the prototypical scientist, Galileo, he defined this attitude ("Verfremdungseffekt") in his *Short Organon for the Theatre*: "A representation which estranges is one which allows us to recognize its subject, but at the same time makes it seem unfamiliar." And further: for somebody to see all normal happenings in a dubious light, "he would need to develop that detached eye with which the great Galileo observed a swinging chandelier. He was amazed by that pendulum motion as if he had not expected it and could not understand its occurring, and this enabled him to come at the rules by which it was governed." Thus, the look of estrangement is both cognitive and creative; and as Brecht goes on to say, "one cannot simply exclaim that such an attitude pertains to science, but not to art. Why should not art, in its own way, try to serve the great social task of mastering Life?"[2] (Later, Brecht

2.   Viktor Shklovsky, "Iskusstvo kak priem," in *Sborniki po teorii poèticheskogo iazyka*, 2 (Petrograd, 1917). In the translation "Art as Technique," in Lee T. Lemon and Marion J. Reis, eds., *Russian Formalist Criticism* (Lincoln, NE, 1965), *ostranenie* is rendered somewhat clumsily as "defamiliarization." See also Victor Erlich's classical survey, *Russian Formalism* (The Hague, 1955).

Bertolt Brecht, "Kleines Organon für das Theater," in his *Gesammelte Werke*, 16 (Frankfurt, 1973), translated in John Willett, ed., *Brecht On Theatre* (New York, 1964). My quotations are from pp. 192 and 196 of this translation, but I have changed Mr. Willett's

would note that it might be time to stop speaking in terms of masters and servants altogether.)

In SF the attitude of estrangement—used by Brecht in a different way, within a still predominantly "realistic" context—has grown into the *formal framework* of the genre.

2. SCIENCE FICTION AS COGNITION
(CRITIQUE AND SCIENCE)

2.1. The use of estrangement both as underlying attitude and dominant formal device is found also in the *myth*, a "timeless" and religious approach looking in its own way beneath (or above) the empiric surface. However, SF sees the norms of any age, including emphatically its own, as unique, changeable, and therefore subject to a *cognitive* view. The myth is diametrically opposed to the cognitive approach since it conceives human relations as fixed and supernaturally determined, emphatically denying Montaigne's "la constance même n'est qu'un branle plus languissant." The myth absolutizes and even personifies apparently constant motifs from sluggish societies. Conversely, SF, which focuses on the variable and future-bearing elements from the empirical environment, is found predominantly in the great whirlpool periods of history, such as the sixteenth-seventeenth and nineteenth-twentieth centuries. Where the myth claims to explain once and for all the essence of phenomena, SF first posits them as problems and then explores where they lead; it sees the mythical static identity as an illusion, usually as fraud, at best only as a temporary realization of potentially limitless contingencies. It does not ask about The Man or The World, but which man?: in which kind of world?: and why such a man in such a kind of world? As a literary genre, SF is fully as opposed to supernatural or metaphysical estrangement as it is to naturalism or empiricism.

2.2. SF is, then, a literary genre whose necessary and sufficient conditions are the presence and interaction of estrangement and cogni-

---

translation of *Verfremdung* as "alienation" into my "estrangement," since "alienation" evokes incorrect, indeed opposite, connotations: estrangement was for Brecht an approach militating directly against social and cognitive alienation. See Ernst Bloch, *"Entfremdung, Verfremdung*: Alienation, Estrangement," in Erika Munk, ed., *Brecht* (New York, 1972).

tion, and whose main formal device is an imaginative framework alternative to the author's empirical environment.

Estrangement differentiates SF from the "realistic" literary mainstream extending from the eighteenth century into the twentieth. Cognition differentiates it not only from myth, but also from the folk (fairy) tale and the fantasy. The *folktale* also doubts the laws of the author's empirical world, but it escapes out of its horizons and into a closed collateral world indifferent to cognitive possibilities. It does not use imagination as a means of understanding the tendencies latent in reality, but as an end sufficient unto itself and cut off from the real contingencies. The stock folktale accessory, such as the flying carpet, evades the empirical law of physical gravity—as the hero evades social gravity—by imagining its opposite. This wish-fulfilling element is its strength and its weakness, for it never pretends that a carpet could be expected to fly—that a humble third son could be expected to become king—while there is gravity. It simply posits another world beside yours where some carpets do, magically, fly, and some paupers do, magically, become princes, and into which you cross purely by an act of faith and fancy. Anything is possible in a folktale, because a folktale is manifestly impossible. Furthermore, the lower-class genre of folktale was from the seventeenth-eighteenth centuries on transformed into the more compensatory, and often simplistic, individualist *fairy* tale. Therefore, SF retrogressing into fairy tale (for example, "space opera" with a hero-princess-monster triangle in astronautic costume) is committing creative suicide.

Even less congenial to SF is the *fantasy* (ghost, horror, Gothic, weird) tale, a genre committed to the interposition of anti-cognitive laws into the empirical environment. Where the folktale is indifferent, the fantasy is inimical to the empirical world and its laws. The thesis could be defended that the fantasy is significant insofar as it is impure and fails to establish a superordinated maleficent world of its own, causing a grotesque tension between arbitrary supernatural phenomena and the empirical norms they infiltrate. Gogol's Nose is significant because it is walking down the Nevski Prospect, with a certain rank in the civil service, and so on; if the Nose were in a completely fantastic world—say H. P. Lovecraft's—it would be just another ghoulish thrill. When fantasy does not make for such a tension between the supernatural and the author's empirical environment, its monotonous reduction of all possible horizons to Death makes of it just a subliterature of mystification. Commercial lumping of it into the same category as SF is thus a grave disservice and rampantly socio-pathological phenomenon.

2.3. The *pastoral*, on the other hand, is essentially closer to SF. Its imaginary framework of a world without money-economy, state apparatus, and depersonalizing urbanization allows it to isolate, as in a laboratory, two human motivations: erotics and power-hunger. This approach relates to SF as alchemy does to chemistry and nuclear physics: an early try in the right direction with insufficient foundations. SF has much to learn from the pastoral tradition, primarily from its directly sensual relationships which do not manifest class alienation. This lesson has in fact often been absorbed, whenever SF has sounded the theme of the triumph of the humble (Restif, Morris, and others, up to Simak, Christopher, Yefremov, etc.). Unfortunately, the baroque pastoral abandoned this theme and jelled into a conventional sentimentality, discrediting the genre; but when pastoral escapes preciosity, its hope can fertilize the SF field as an antidote to pragmatism, commercialism, other-directedness, and technocracy.

2.4. Claiming a Galilean estrangement for SF does not at all mean committing it to scientific vulgarization or even technological prognostication, which it was engaged in at various times (Verne, the United States in the 1920s and 30s, USSR under Stalinism). The needful and meritorious task of popularization can be a useful element of SF works at a juvenile level. But even the *roman scientifique*, such as Verne's *From the Earth to the Moon*—or the surface level of Wells's *Invisible Man*—though a legitimate SF form, is a lower stage in its development. It is very popular with audiences just approaching SF, such as the juvenile, because it introduces into the old empirical context only *one* easily digestible new technological variable (Moon missile, or rays which lower the refractive index of organic matter).[3] The euphoria provoked by this approach is real but limited, better

3. Note the functional difference from the anti-gravity metal in Wells's *First Men in the Moon*, which is an introductory or "plausibility-validating" device and not the be-all of a much richer novel. Devices of plausibility are further discussed in chapter 4.

suited to the short story and a new audience. It evaporates much quicker as positivistic natural science loses prestige in the humanistic sphere after the world wars (compare Nemo's *Nautilus* as against the United States Navy's atomic submarine of the same name), and surges back with prestigious peacetime applications in new methodologies (astronautics, cybernetics). As I will argue in chapter 7, even in Verne the "science novel" has a structure of transient estrangement, which is specific to murder mysteries, not to a mature SF.

2.5.   After such delimitations, it is perhaps possible at least to indicate some differentiations within the concept of "cognitive-ness" or "cognition." As used here, this term implies not only a reflecting *of* but also *on* reality. It implies a creative approach tending toward a dynamic transformation rather than toward a static mirroring of the author's environment. Such typical SF methodology—from Lucian, More, Rabelais, Cyrano, and Swift to Wells, London, Zamyatin, and writers of the last decades—is a *critical* one, often satirical, combining a belief in the potentialities of reason with methodical doubt in the most significant cases. The kinship of this cognitive critique with the philosophical fundaments of modern science is evident.

3.   THE WORLD OF THE SCIENCE FICTION GENRE (CONCEPT AND SOME FUNCTIONS)

3.0.   As a full-fledged literary genre, SF has its own repertory of functions, conventions, and devices. Many of them are highly interesting and might prove very revealing for literary history and theory in general. I shall discuss some of these—such as the historically crucial shift of the locus of estrangement from space to time—in the chapters that follow. I shall not, however, attempt a systematic survey of such functions and devices, which would properly be the subject of another book, one that encompassed modern SF as well. I should only like to mention that all the estranging devices in SF are related to the cognition espoused, and that, together with the historical venerability of the genre's tradition, this seems to me a second, methodological reason for according SF much more importance than is usual in academe. However, it might here be possible to sketch some determining parameters of the genre.

3.1.   In a typology of literary genres for our cognitive age, one basic parameter would take into account the relationship of the world(s) each genre presents and the "zero world" of empirically verifiable properties around the author (this being "zero" in the sense of a central reference point in a coordinate system, or of the control group in an experiment). Let us call this empirical world *naturalistic*. In it, and in the corresponding "naturalistic" or "realistic" literature, ethics is in no significant relation to physics. Modern mainstream fiction is forbidden the pathetic fallacy of earthquakes announcing the assassination of rulers or drizzles accompanying the sadness of the heroine. It is the activity of the protagonists, interacting with other, physically equally unprivileged figures, that determines the outcome. However superior technologically or sociologically one side in the conflict may be, any predetermination as to its outcome is felt as an ideological imposition and genological impurity: the basic rule of naturalistic literature is that man's destiny is man.[4] On the contrary, in the non-naturalistic, *metaphysical* literary genres discussed in 2.1. and 2.2., circumstances around the hero are neither passive nor neutral. In the folktale and the fantasy, ethics coincides with (positive or negative) physics, in the tragic myth it compensates the physics, in the "optimistic" myth it supplies the coincidence with a systematic framework.

The world of a work of SF is not a priori intentionally oriented toward its protagonists, either positively or negatively; the protagonists may succeed or fail in their objectives, but nothing in the basic contract with the reader, in the physical laws of their worlds, guarantees either. SF thus shares with the dominant literature of our civilization a mature approach analogous to that of modern science and philosophy, as well as the omnitemporal horizons of such an approach—aspects which will be discussed in the following chapters.

3.2. As a matter of historical record, SF has started from a

---

4. In such cases as certain novels by Hardy and plays by Ibsen, or some of the more doctrinaire works of the historical school of Naturalism, where determinism strongly stresses circumstance at the expense of the main figures' activity, we have, underneath a surface appearance of "naturalism," an approach to tragic myth using a shamefaced validation for an unbelieving age. As contrary to Shakespeare or the Romantics, in this case ethics follows physics in a supposedly causal chain (most often through biology). An analogous approach to fairy tale is to be found in, say, the mimicry of "naturalism" in which Hollywood happy-end movies engage.

prescientific or protoscientific approach of debunking satire and naive social critique and moved closer to the increasingly sophisticated natural and human sciences. The natural sciences caught up and surpassed the literary imagination in the nineteenth century; the sciences dealing with human relationships might be argued to have caught up with it in their highest theoretical achievements but have certainly not done so in their alienated social practice. In the twentieth century SF has moved into the sphere of anthropological and cosmological thought, becoming a diagnosis, a warning, a call to understanding and action, and— most important—a mapping of possible alternatives. This historical movement of SF can be envisaged as an enrichment of and shift from a basic direct model to an indirect model (both to be analyzed at greater length in chapter 2). What matters here is that the concept of a science fiction tradition or genre is a logical corollary of the recognition of SF as the literature of cognitive estrangement. It can be gleaned from my approach and examples that I think the literary genre which I am trying to define embraces the subgenres mentioned in 1.1, from Greek and earlier times until today (the Islands of the Blessed, utopias, fabulous voyages, planetary novels, *Staatsromane*, anticipations, and dystopias—as well as the Verne-type *romans scientifiques*, the Wellsian scientific romance variant, and the twentieth-century magazine- and anthology-based SF *sensu stricto*). If the argument of this chapter holds, the inner kinship of these subgenres is stronger than their obvious autonomous, differentiating features. Some historical discussion of these kinships and differences will be attempted later on in this book; here I want only to observe that the significant writers in this line were quite aware of their coherent tradition and explicitly testified to it (the axis Lucian-More-Rabelais-Cyrano-Swift-M. Shelley-Verne-Wells is a main example). Also, certain among the most perspicacious surveyors of aspects of the field, like Ernst Bloch, Lewis Mumford, or Northrop Frye, can be construed as assuming this unity.

3.3.   The novelty of such a concept shows most distinctly when one attempts to find a name for the genre as it is here conceived. Ideally this name should clearly set it apart from (1) nonliterature, (2) the empiricist literary mainstream, and (3) noncognitive estrangings such as fantasy; furthermore (4) it should try to add as little as possible to the already prevailing confusion of tongues in this region. The academically most acceptable de-signation has been that of a literature of *utopian thought*. The concept is no doubt partly relevant, but fails to meet the first criterion above; logically, such an approach was usually taught and considered within the scope of either the history of ideas or political and sociological theory. Although I would agree that literature (and especially this genre) is most intimately involved with life—indeed, that the destiny of humanity is its *telos*—I think one should quickly add that literature is also more than an idea-tional or sociological document. Since this is the rationale for any systematic literary study and scholarship, I may not need to labor the point.

The only proper way of searching for a solution seems to require starting from the qualities defining the genre, since this would take care of the criteria 1 to 3 at least. Taking the kindred thesaurus concepts of *science* for cognition, and *fiction* for es-trangement, I believe there is a sound reason for calling this whole new genre Science Fiction (*sensu lato*).

There are two main objections to such a solution. First, cogni-tion is wider than science; I argued as much myself in 2.5. It is much less weighty, however, if one takes "science" in a sense closer to the German *Wissenschaft*, French *science*, or Russian *nauka*, which include not only natural but also all the cultural or historical sciences and even scholarship (cf. *Literaturwissenschaft*, *sciences humaines*). As a matter of fact, that is what science has been taken to stand for in the practice of SF: not only More or Zamyatin, but the writings of Americans such as Asimov, Hein-lein, Pohl, Dick, etc. would be completely impossible without sociological, psychological, historical, anthropological, and other parallels. Further, an element of convention enters into all names (compare "comparative literature"), but it has proved harmless as long as the name is handy, approximate enough, and above all applied to a clearly defined body of works. The second objection is that the use of "science fiction" confuses the whole genre with the twentieth-century SF from which the name was taken. Given the advantages of the only term at hand fulfilling the above criteria, I would argue that this is at worst a minor drawback: nobody has serious trouble in distinguishing between More's book, the country described in it, and the subgenre of "utopia." The trouble begins with the variety of unrelated interdisciplinary and ideological interpretations foisted upon such a term; "science fiction" might perhaps escape the interdisciplinary part of that obstacle race. Furthermore, theré are always advantages to acknowledging clearly one's methodological premises. As both Lukács and Eliot would agree, any tradition is modified and reestablished by a sufficiently significant new development, from whose vantage point it can be reinterpreted. This is, I would maintain, the case with the mentioned *ci-devant* traditions, for example, of "utopian literature," in the age of science fiction. If that is accepted, the new name is no drawback at all, but simply an onomastic consummation.

4. For a Poetics of Science Fiction (Anticipation)

4.1. The above sketch should, no doubt, be supplemented by a sociological analysis of the "inner environment" of SF, exiled since the beginning of the twentieth century into a reservation or ghetto which was protective and is now constrictive, cutting off new developments from healthy competition and the highest critical standards. Such a sociological discussion would enable us to point out the important differences between the highest reaches of the genre, glanced at here in order to define functions and standards of SF, and its debilitating average.[5]

4.2. If the whole above argumentation is found acceptable, it will be possible to supplement it also by a survey of forms and subgenres. Along with some which recur in an updated form— such as the utopia and fabulous voyage—the anticipation, the superman story, the artificial intelligence story (robots, androids, and so on), time-travel, catastrophe, the meeting with aliens, and others, would have to be analyzed. The various forms and subgenres of SF could then be checked for their relationships to other literary genres, to each other, and to various sciences. For example, the utopias are—whatever else they may be—clearly sociological fictions or social-science-fiction, whereas modern SF is analogous to modern polycentric cosmology, uniting time and space in Einsteinian worlds with different but covariant dimensions and time scales. Significant modern SF, with deeper and more lasting sources of enjoyment, also presupposes more com-

5. A first approach to the sociology of SF may be found in the special issue of *Science-Fiction Studies*, November 1977, edited and with an introduction by me.

plex and wider cognitions: it discusses primarily the political, psychological, and anthropological *use and effect of knowledge, of philosophy of science*, and the becoming of failure of new realities as a result of it. The consistency of extrapolation, precision of analogy, and width of reference in such a cognitive discussion turn into aesthetic factors. (That is why the "scientific novel" discussed in 2.3. is not deemed completely satisfactory—it is aesthetically poor because it is scientifically meager.) Once the elastic criteria of literary structuring have been met, *a cognitive—in most cases strictly scientific—element becomes a measure of aesthetic quality, of the specific pleasure to be sought in SF*. In other words, the cognitive nucleus of the plot codetermines the fictional estrangement itself.

2

SF and the Genological Jungle

Thanks to the Greeks, we can distinguish tragedy from comedy in drama. . . . When we come to deal with such forms as the masque, opera, movie, ballet, puppet-play, mystery-play, morality, commedia dell'arte, and Zauberspiel, we find ourselves in the position of Renaissance doctors who refused to treat syphilis because Galen said nothing about it.

Northrop Frye

1. A View from the Mountain: Taxonomy and a System

1.0. As Northrop Frye has rightly remarked, "just as there is nothing which the philosopher cannot consider philosophically, and nothing which the historian cannot consider historically, so the critic should be able to construct and dwell in a conceptual universe of his own."[1] For the purposes of constructing the universe of this discussion, I take it (1) that no field of studies and rational inquiry can be investigated unless and until it is at least roughly delimited; (2) that there exist literary genres, as socioaesthetic and not metaphysical entities; (3) that these entities have an inner life and logic of their own, which do not exclude but on the contrary presuppose a dialectical permeability to themes, attitudes, and paradigms from other literary genres, science, philosophy, and everyday socioeconomic life; (4) that the genres pertinent to this discussion are naturalistic fiction, fantasy, myth, folk tale, pastoral, and science fiction. I am assuming that these four axioms will be justified by their cognitive yield, by the light that they might throw upon the field of inquiry. Should this assumption prove justified, it would go a long way toward indicating that the basic and possibly central task of SF theory and criticism at this historical moment is the construction of a

---

1. Northrop Frye, *Anatomy of Criticism* (New York, 1966), p. 12.

heuristic model or models for "Science Fiction"—which is also the hypothesis of this chapter.

A heuristic model is a theoretical structure based on analogy, which does not claim to be transcendentally or illusionistically "real" in the sense of mystically representing a palpable material entity, but whose use is scientifically and scholarly permissible, desirable, and necessary because of its practical results. An example might be the construct according to which the molecules of a gas behave like minuscule elastic billiard balls in random motion. Though very little may be known or indeed knowable about what gas molecules are "really" like, both at the time this construct was promulgated and now it was certain beyond reasonable doubt that they were *not* elastic billiard balls of a microscopic size. Yet this heuristic model was among the decisive factors in the development of the whole discipline of thermodynamics. It had immense theoretical and practical consequences, among others a giant step forward in human understanding of natural and perhaps even social processes. It seems therefore unnecessary to reopen the debates of the medieval nominalists and realists about the "real" existence of entities such as SF or any other genre; such debates hinge on a pseudo-question. An acceptable heuristic model or set of models for a literary genre is as necessary for its understanding, for the setting up of standards pertaining to it, as the theory of ideal gases was for its time and discipline. In other words, however fragmented, laborious, or foolhardy this particular endeavor of mine might be, the critical community concerned with SF will have to evolve a theory of the genre which can serve as a framework for its history and criticism. Anyway, poets—including the poets among SF writers—have often reminded us that what the positivistic or philistine mentality considers foolhardy is, in Gorky's words, "the wisdom of life."

1.1 Conscious of the monsters and incubi lurking just beyond my path, and averting piously my eyes from the bleached bones of the pioneers fallen by its side, I proceed to recall my starting point, the identifications which I worked out for the aforementioned genres in the preceding chapter. I brought forward some arguments for their delimitation, which I shall here supply with further argumentation and subsume under the following taxonomic system:

Fiction is differentiated from other verbal structures by the presence of a *fable, plot,* or *narrative,* through which the writer endeavors to illuminate human relations to other people and the universe. (At this point the normal poetological distinctions of epic, dramatic, and lyric fiction could ensue, based on the different stresses in the relationship of the narrator and the characters or world of the fable, but such distinguishing does not fall within my scope in this book. I will assume it—as well as certain other distinctions, such as that between verse and prose—as given or at least as for practical purposes discernible in literary theory from Aristotle to Brecht, Frye, and Barthes, and in the literary practice which preceded the setting up of theories. My presentation has in mind at the moment epic prose—novels and stories—only, though for all I know the resulting heuristic model or models might have a wider scope.) Fiction, then, can be divided according to the manner in which men's relationships to other men and their surroundings are illuminated. If this is accomplished by endeavoring faithfully to reproduce empirical textures and surfaces vouched for by human senses and common sense, I propose to call it *naturalistic fiction.* If, on the contrary, an endeavor is made to illuminate such relations by creating a radically or significantly different formal framework—a different space/time location or central figures for the fable, unverifiable by common sense—I propose to call it *estranged fiction.* The normative trend of fiction after Boccaccio and Shakespeare has been naturalistic in the above sense, though this does not at all hold true for earlier stages of literature in our civilization nor in other civilizations.

The world of naturalistic fiction has thus a straightforward relationship to the "zero world" of empirically verifiable properties around the author. The ideal of *Tom Jones, The Red and the Black, Madame Bovary, War and Peace, The Idiot, Huckleberry Finn,* or *Intruder in the Dust* is to create a significant statement about the human condition by holding a mirror to nature. In naturalistic fiction, as in the zero world, physics stands in no significant relation to ethics. It is the activity of the protagonists, interacting with other equally unprivileged figures, that determines the course of narration and outcome of fable. In naturalistic fiction, the basic rule is that man's destiny is other humans and man-made institutions. In such a model, relating ethics to physics

(Hollywoodian happy-end, say) signifies a descent into sentimentalism, into what is properly called sub-literature.

However, estranged fiction can quite legitimately postulate that circumstances around the hero—according to the basic "literary contract" making up a particular estranged genre—either *are* or *are not* passive and neutral. One, larger group of estranged literary genres, which embraces various kinds of myths and their later descendants—fantasy and folktale—is indeed defined by a contract inverse to that of naturalistic fiction: their world is actively oriented toward the hero. The folktale (*Märchen*, later fairy tale) world is oriented positively toward its protagonist; a folktale is defined by the hero's triumph: magic weapons and helpers are, with the necessary narrative retardations, at his beck and call. Inversely, the fantasy world is oriented negatively toward its protagonist; a fantasy is defined by the hero's horrible helplessness. Both fantasy and folktale derive from mythology: the folktale from the victorious-hero myth and the fantasy from the tragic myth. Thus, in the folktale and the fantasy, ethics coincides with physics—positive (hero-furthering) in the first case, and (hero-denying) in the second. In the tragic myth ethics compensates the physics; Oedipus, Osiris or Christ have to fail because of the empirical world they live in, but the failure is then ethically exalted and put to religious use, usually by postulating a metaphysical world beyond the empirical one in which the narrative finds its true, compensatory ending. Parallel to that, in the "optimistic" myth of Perseus, Saint George and other light-bearing heroes, ethics not only coincides with hero-furthering physics but also supplies a systematic cosmosociological framework to normalize the coincidence.

The literary genres in which physics is in some magical or religious way determined by ethics, instead of being neutral toward the hero or the total human population of the presented world, deny the autonomy of physics and can properly be called *metaphysical*. But not all estranged genres enter into such a contract with their reader. Notably, the pastoral and SF worlds offer no assurances as to the outcome of their protagonists' endeavors. (Phenomena such as the sentimentalized Baroque pastoral or the "new maps of hell" of American SF represent particular, limited historical and ideological uses which do not necessarily flow out of the basic contract of the genre but are superadded to it.)

Together with some prefigurations in the pastoral, *SF is thus a metaempirical and non-naturalistic, that is, an estranged, literary genre which is not at the same time metaphysical*. On the contrary, SF shares with naturalistic literature, naturalistic science, and naturalistic or materialist philosophy a common sophisticated, dialectical, and cognitive *epistemé*.

The genological system discussed above can be presented schematically by using the two parameters or binary oppositions of naturalistic/estranged, and cognitive/noncognitive:

	NATURALISTIC	ESTRANGED
COGNITIVE	"realistic" literature	SF (& pastoral)
NONCOGNITIVE	sub-literature of "realism"	*metaphysical*: myth, folktale, fantasy

1.2.   In order to test the above taxonomy, let us introduce a new basic parameter of *time* and see whether the system can make sense of it. Naturalistic literature ranges through all empirical times. Though concentrating on the present, it has, parallel with the rise of historical sciences and dialectical philosophy, evolved the historical novel and drama, and it can even to some degree (admittedly not to the same degree as non-naturalistic literature) deal with the future in the form of hopes, fears, premonitions, and dreams, as in the psychological novel beginning with, say, Stendhal and Dostoevsky. Carelessness about precise time location or restriction to a one-dimensional point-consciousness in the present—both of which do not critically question prevailing anthropological modes of behavior—is the mark of the subliterature of mainstream "realism," from Renaissance street-ballads to contemporary *kitsch*. The metaphysical genres shun historical time: myth is located above time, folktale in a conventional grammatical past which is really outside time, and fantasy in the hero's abnormally disturbed, historiosophically dislocated present into which irrupts a "black" timelessness or another extrahistorical time. Inversely, SF shares the omnitemporal horizons of naturalistic literature, ranging through all possible times. Though concentrating on the cognitively plausible futures and their spatial equivalents, it can deal with the present and the past as special cases of a possible historical sequence seen from an estranged point of view—since any empirical historical point or flow can be thought of as one realization among practically innumerable possibilities. The scheme from 1.1. *sub specie temporis* would thus look like this:

	HISTORICAL	ESTRANGED
PLURIDIMENSIONAL	"realistic" literature	SF
ONE DIMENSIONAL	sub-literature of "realism"	myth, folktale, fantasy

It is not surprising to anybody who has read Marx, Hegel, or Augustine of Hippo that *naturalistic* in the temporal sphere means *historical*. It is more interesting to note that temporal cognition is allied to a free movement back and forth in time. Myth in its timeless suffering or bliss, folktale in its world apart allied to the empirical world by a grammatical past, and fantasy as the present lifted out of time into black transcendency—all share the impossibility of such a humanizing movement. Out of their several shortcomings they have, as is known, made tremendous virtues; yet the limitations remain.

2. AN ECOLOGICAL JUNGLE TRIP:
SYMBIOSIS, PARASITISM, MIMICRY, AND SUNDRY

2.0. So far my analysis has been conducted on a level which, no doubt, was abstracted from actual historical literary genres but one which endeavored to treat them as ideal types or pure heuristic models. In actuality, a particular work, literary opus, trend, or school is almost never entirely pure. Literary genres exist in historically precise and curious ecological units, interacting and intermixing, imitating and cannibalizing each other. To understand what one really has in mind when talking about SF, it is necessary to continue the analysis on the level of actual happenings in the noncanonic literature or paraliterature of this century. Only such a path, descending from the clear mountain sights and its wide horizons into the luxuriant and steamy jungle of literary genres, and supplementing an aerial survey with actual botanizing in the field, has a chance of leading to useful results.

2.1.   The relationship of SF to naturalistic literature, usually to the species of adventure-journey, is by now relatively clear and can be dealt with briefly. It is a relationship of filiation, best evidenced in the work of Jules Verne: SF has historically had one of its roots in the compost heap of such juvenile or popular subliterature, and in order to develop properly it has had to subsume and outgrow it—the quicker the better for its generic affirmation. It found congenial or congeneric elements in the cognitive and marvelous bias of the voyage extraordinaire and its catalogues of wonders seen along Ulysses' or Captain Nemo's way. The sea haunts this filiation, the island story is its microparadigm or root situation, and locomotion the connecting thread of its narration. All the marvelous interstellar SF voyages and quests in Heinlein, Blish, Van Vogt, and a thousand others, the Nietzschean, Columbian, or Sindbadian poetry of navigation—navigare necesse, vivere non necesse—belong here. Such voyaging is an honorable, though in retrospect one can scarcely fail to note that it is an initial (and for the reader initiatory), function of SF. It acts much in the way that a true long voyage does in the zero world, dialytically—estranging the reader from familiar and usually contemptible shores, dissolving his umbilical connections with old and firm earth (or Earth), preparing him to accept the marvelous beyond seven seas or galaxies. When unduly prolonged, this adolescence of SF means arrested development. It should be kept in its proper humbly useful place in the ontogenetic development of the reader as well as in the phylogenetic development of the genre.

In close proximity to the didactic aspect of the journey is the popular science compost heap which can be found next to the adventure-journey heap in the early phylogenetic stages of SF from technologically developed countries. Verne used both, adding a dash of puzzle in the manner of Poe and a barrelful of Saint-Simonian romanticism. Unalloyed, or alloyed with the

baser metal of subliterary conflict and sentiment, this leads no
further than to a primitive technological or at best technocratic
extrapolation, as evidenced in Bacon's *New Atlantis*, then in
Gernsback and the "SF reservation" between the two world wars.
A hybrid results that is neither good fiction nor interesting science; it is dislodged the first time the shapers of public and
publishing opinion happen to read Wells—or, indeed, a good
straightforward essay of scientific popularization, which has from
the time of Friedrich Engels and Thomas Huxley been im-
measurably more exciting and less reactionary than *Ralph 124C
41 +*. Of course, it usually takes those shapers a generation or
two to acquire the necessary taste in reading. In the meantime,
the Gernsbacks keep SF alive at the cost of starving, stunting,
and deforming it; comparing *The Iron Heel* with the output in the
United States between the World Wars, one strongly suspects the
cost is too high.

2.2. In 2.1. it was discussed how older paradigms of marvelous voyage, popular science essay, and individualist subliterature
(the Western and the sentimental story) interfere with the formation of an autonomous SF paradigm or model if their grip is not
loosened quickly. Unfortunately, a majority of what is published
as SF is still in that prenatal or, better, regression-to-womb stage:
it is simply the Western or some kindred sub-literary species
masquerading its structures—generally for venal and ideological
reasons—under the externals of SF: rockets, ray-guns, monsters,
or in the last dozen years their slightly more sophisticated equivalents. Usually the symbiosis of popular science and juvenile adventure finds it impossible to mimic SF without regressing into
their homologue of the *fairy tale*, with its victorious hero, foiled
villain, damsel in distress, and quaint helpers or marvelous help-
ing objects. Such sub-Vernean or Gernsbackian SF does not
change the fairy tale structure but only the motivation of its
devices: it pretends to explain away the supernatural by reassign-
ing it to natural science and noble scientists (who are energetic
and sentimental if young and in love with, absent-minded if old
and fathers of, the eternal feminine). However, the science is
treated as a metaphysical and not physical, supernatural and not
natural activity, as gobbledygook instead of rational procedure.
From Ralph, Buck Rogers, and the post-Stapledonian supermen
to Asimov's psychohistory (which has at least the advantage of

identifying the proper field of modern destiny, social relations), such metaphysical gobbledygook vitiates some of the best-known SF works. Neither cognitive nor magical but shamefacedly passing off a juvenile idea of magic for cognition, equating the photon rocket with the flying carpet and global social destinies with the victory of the third son, such a mimicry is like the newly fashionable pop wines: a hyping-up of the old grape juice into the new wine. In the perfectly just world of taste and poetic creativity, this procedure reaps the reward of hypocrisy: fairy tale readers rightly prefer the classics, sophisticated SF readers disbelieve the fairy tale. Inversely, in the very imperfectly retributive world of social taste and commercial SF, such a procedure breeds generations of readers with juvenile taste, unable to develop the standards by which to judge SF (not to mention empirical human relations).

2.3.   The more ambitious reader and writer cannot for long be satisfied with such pap. Yet trying to find a fresh tack in the cruel world of instant obsolescence, SF often veers from Scylla to Charybdis. A further step down into pseudo-sophistication—correlative, no doubt, to a marked decadence of cultural taste in bourgeois society and its literary markets—is the parasitism of Gothic, horror, and weird *fantasy* upon SF. Such fantasy is characterized, as I have said, by the irruption of an anti-cognitive world into the world of empirical cognition. One can understand some readers' panic flight from a science which produces nuclear bombs, napalm, and nerve gases, from a reason which justifies class societies in mutual balances of terror, condemning two-thirds of the world to hunger and disease, and the remaining third—"hypocrite lecteur, mon semblable, mon frère"—to the boredom of a nine-to-five drudgery relieved by flashes of TV commercials. Maybe such readers ought to have an escapist enclave of sword-and-sorcery or Cthulhu cosmologies—I cannot say. But surely SF, built upon the premise that nature is neither a childishly wicked stepmother ("As flies to wanton boys are we to gods / They kill us for their sport") nor inscrutably alien to man—surely SF cannot allow its contract with the reader to be contaminated by the Great Pumpkin antics of fantasy. Even more perniciously than is the case with the bland fairy tale structure, the black ectoplasms of fantasy stifle SF completely. Its time shrinks to the point-consciousness of horror, gloom, and doom, its daydreams turn into an inchoate nightmare, and under the guise of cognition the ancient obscurantist enemy infiltrates its citadel. Fossilized fragments of reasoning are used to inculcate irrationality, and the social energy of readers is expended on Witches' Sabbaths instead of focusing it on the causes for our alienating, murderous, and stultifying existences: the power structures holding back the hominization of the sapiens, the true demonology of war and market breeding pride and prejudice. At its best, in Swift and Cyrano, in Jack London and the dystopian "new maps of hell," in Lucian and Wells, in the great utopians and Zamyatin, SF has with different degrees of precision, but with unerring precision of orientation, focused on these power structures, on such demonology. It is at its worst, at its most alienated and alienating, when it honors the parasitism and vampirism of fantasy.

2.4. There has also been a great deal of talk about affinities between SF and the *mythological tale*. Though also a story about supernatural events involving superhuman figures, as different from other metaphysical fiction (folktale and fantasy), the events and figures of this genre form a systematic whole, *a mythological edifice of tales whose norms are supposed to have supertemporally (timelessly or continuously) determined man's basic relations to man and nature*. Obviously, all religious systems are in this sense mythological. On the contrary, plays and stories are neither myth nor ritual but fictional literature, although myths and rituals may underlie their forms, plots, and sometimes their characters. For example, Murray has convincingly shown that the forms of Attic tragedy derive from Dionysian sacrificial rituals, and Cornford has done an analogous job for Attic comedy.[2] The Hellenic tragic characters derive primarily from Homer, but through him from other sacrificial rituals, which is why Homerian themes fitted so well into the mythic pattern of tragedy. Thus, *fiction can be formally or morphologically analogous to myth, but it is not itself myth*. It uses mythical morphemes for nonmythic and—except in

2. Gilbert Murray, "Hamlet and Orestes," in his *The Classical Tradition of Poetry* (New York, 1968), and "Excursus on the Ritual Forms preserved in Greek Tragedy," in Jane Ellen Harrison, *Epilegomena to the Study of Greek Religion—Themis* (New York, 1966); F. M. Cornford, *The Origin of Attic Comedy* (Gloucester, MA, 1966). See also other anthropological works by the Cambridge School that, as far as literary studies are concerned, culminate in George Thomson's elegant *Aeschylus and Athens* (New York, 1968).

folktale, fantasy, and subliterature—for anti-mythic ends. "Myth and literature are separate and autonomous entities, though any specific myth text can and should be considered as folk-literature."[3] However—and this is in itself highly important and largely justifies the attention that modern scholars have devoted to myth—bearing in mind the caveats and distinctions discussed earlier, it should be acknowledged that important aspects of literature (primarily, many basic and possibly most significant plots) are *mythomorphic*. What a writer like Faulkner or Kafka creates is not a myth but a personal fictional statement formally analogous to myth in a radically different and indeed incompatible cosmological or ideological context. In other words, a realistic parable such as *The Bear* or an SF parable such as *The Metamorphosis*, although it uses a mythological bestiary as well as the mythological pattern of trial and death with or without resurrection, is in its message and final impact very different from, often diametrically opposed to the religious myth expressing a collective static vision. Kafka and Faulkner are—they cannot but be—*historical* writers.

Obviously, SF will be as mythomorphic in some basic patterns as other fictional genres are. Beyond that, SF shares with myth the fictional estrangement, the "outer limits of desire" as Professor Frye aptly formulated it,[4] and its formal closeness to myth will extend beyond plots to many characters and situations. But all attempts to transplant the metaphysical orientation of mythology and religion into SF, in a crudely overt way as in C.S. Lewis, Van Vogt, or Zelazny, or in more covert ways in very many others, will result only in private pseudomyths, in fragmentary fantasies or fairy tales.[5] As I mentioned in my first chapter, myth absolutizes and even personifies apparently constant motifs from periods with sluggish social dynamics, and claims to explain the eternal essence of phenomena. On the contary, SF claims to organize variable spatiotemporal, biological, social, and other characteristics and constellations into specific fictional worlds and

3. Stanley Edgar Hyman, "The Ritual View of Myth and the Mythic," in Thomas A. Sebeok, ed., *Myth* (Bloomington, 1970), p. 151.

4. Frye, p. 136.

5. See Harry Levin, "Some Meanings of Myth," in Henry A. Murray, ed., *Myth and Mythmaking* (Boston, 1969), pp. 111–12.

figures. Mathematically speaking, myth is oriented toward constants and SF toward variables.

On a different level of fictional structuring, however, is the treatment of religious beliefs or mythic situations as historical material. When such mythic elements are—by transposition, as it were, into the demystifying key of SF—extracted from a mythological paradigm and fitted into an SF one, what results is perfectly legitimate, often first-class SF. As always, the critic will in any particular instance have to rely on his literary tact and sense of measure to pierce this intricate double mimicry and parasitism, to decide with which type of interaction between SF and myth he is faced. To mention only two favorites of mine, Stapledon and Walter Miller, Jr., I believe that at a certain point (say in *The Flames*) Stapledon crosses the divide into pseudomyth, that is, into fantasy, and that Miller does the same at the resolution of *A Canticle for Leibowitz* with the character of Mrs. Grales. At such points the ideological attraction to myth as world view and not as formal pattern got the best of the SF writer.

3. To Greener Fields and Pastures New: The Extrapolative and the Analogical Models of SF

3.0. I would like now to try emerging from the jungle into the cultivated territory of selected SF, and analyze what look to be its two main species or models, the extrapolative and the analogical one.

3.1. SF written from, say, the period of the French Revolution on (though not necessarily in preceding epochs) has come to be considered as starting from certain cognitive hypotheses and ideas incarnated in the fictional framework and nucleus of the tale. This extrapolative model—of Mercier's *L'An 2440*, London's *Iron Heel*, Wells's *When the Sleeper Wakes* and *Men Like Gods*, Zamyatin's *We*, Stapledon's *Last and First Men*, Yefremov's *Andromeda*, Pohl and Kornbluth's *Space Merchants*, or Brunner's *The Jagged Orbit*—seems based on direct, temporal extrapolation and centered on sociological (that is, utopian and anti-utopian) modeling. This is where the great majority of the "new maps of hell" is taken to belong for which postwar SF is justly famous, in all its manifold combinations of sociotechnological scientific cognition and social oppression (global catastrophes, cybernetics, dictatorships).

Yet already in Wells's *Time Machine* and in Stapledon, this extrapolating transcended the sociological spectrum (from everyday practice through economics to erotics) and spilled into "billion-year" biology and cosmology. The ensuing radical estrangements can, no doubt, be *anticipated* in a chronological future, but they cannot, scientifically speaking, be *extrapolated*. By this token, futuristic anticipation reveals that extrapolating is a fictional device and ideological horizon rather than the basis for a cognitive model. It is thus dubious—as will be discussed further in chapter 4—that significant SF could be simply extrapolation. Nonetheless, whatever its ostensible location (future, "fourth dimension," other planets, alternate universes), the self-understanding of much SF—as shown in the historical section of this book—was uneasily futurological. Being written in a historical epoch dominated by anticipatory expectations, this SF demanded to be judged by the "scientific" import of the tale's premises and the consistency with which such premises (usually one or very few in number) were narratively developed to their logical end, to a "scientifically valid" conclusion.

SF could thus be used as a handmaiden of futurological foresight in technology, ecology, sociology, and so on. Whereas this may at times have been a legitimate secondary function the genre could be made to bear, any forgetfulness of its strict secondariness leads to confusion and indeed danger. Ontologically, art is not pragmatic truth nor is fiction fact. To expect from SF more than a stimulus for independent thinking, more than a system of stylized narrative devices understandable only in their mutual relationships within a fictional whole and not as isolated realities, leads insensibly to the demand for scientific accuracy in the extrapolated *realia*. Editors and publishers of such "hard" persuasion, from U.S. pulp magazines to the Soviet Agitprop, have been inclined to depress the handmaiden of SF into the slavey of the reigning theology of the day (technocratic, psionic, utopian, catastrophic, or whatever). Yet this fundamentally subversive genre languishes in straitjackets more quickly than most others, responding with atrophy, escapism, or both. Laying no claim to prophecies except for its statistically probable share, SF should not be treated as a prophet: it should neither be enthroned when apparently successful nor beheaded when apparently unsuccessful. As Plato found out in the court of Dionysius and Hythloday at Cardinal Morton's, SF figures better devote themselves to their own literary republics, which, to be sure, lead back—but in their own way—to the Republic of Man. SF is finally concerned with the tensions between *Civitas Dei* and *Civitas Terrena*, and it cannot be uncritically committed to any momentary city.

3.2. The analogic model of SF is based on analogy rather than extrapolation. Its figures may but do not have to be anthropomorphic or its localities geomorphic. The objects, figures, and up to a point the relationships from which this indirectly modeled world starts can be quite fantastic (in the sense of empirically unverifiable) as long as they are logically, philosophically, and mutually consistent. The analytic model can thus comprehend the extrapolative one, but it is not bound to the extrapolative horizon.

The lowest form of analogic modeling is that in which an extrapolation backwards is in fact a crude analogy to the past of the Earth, from geological through biological to ethnological and historical. The worlds more or less openly modeled on the Carboniferous Age, on tribal prehistory, on barbaric and feudal empires—in fact modeled on handbooks of geology and anthropology, on Spengler's *Decline of the West* and Dumas *père*'s *Three Musketeers*—are unfortunately abundant in the foothills of SF. Some of this may be useful adolescent leisure reading, which one should not begrudge; however, the uneasy coexistence of such worlds with a superscience, which is supposed to provide an SF alibi, largely or wholly destroys the story's cognitive credibility. The E.R. Burroughs-to-Asimov space opera, cropping up in almost all U.S. writers right down to Samuel Delany, belongs to the uneasy territory between inferior SF and non-SF—to forms that, as I argued earlier, mimic SF scenery but are modeled on the structures of the Western and other avatars of fairy tale and fantasy.

The purest form of analogic modeling would be the analogy to a mathematical model, such as the fairly primary one explicated in Abbott's *Flatland*, as well as the ontological analogies found in a compressed overview form in some stories by Borges and Lem. A somewhat more humane narration with a suffering protagonist is to be found in, say, Čapek's *Krakatit* or Le Guin's *Left Hand of Darkness*, and even more clearly in Kafka's *Metamorphosis* or *In the Penal Colony* and Lem's *Solaris*. Such highly sophisticated philosophico-anthropological analogies are today perhaps the most significant region of SF, indistinguishable in quality from other superior contemporary writing. Situated between Borges and the upper reaches into which shade the best utopias, anti-utopias, and satires, this semantic field is a modern variant of the "conte philosophique" of the eighteenth century. Similar to Swift, Voltaire, or Diderot, these *modern parables* fuse new visions of the world with an applicability—usually satirical and grotesque—to the shortcomings of our workaday world. Departing from the older rationalism, a modern parable must be open-ended by analogy to modern cosmology, epistemology, and philosophy of science.[6]

The analogic model of SF falls, however, clearly within cognitive horizons insofar as its conclusions or import is concerned. The cognition gained may not be immediately applicable, it may be simply the enabling of the mind to receive new wavelengths, but it eventually contributes to the understanding of the most mundane matters. This is testified by the works of Kafka and Twain, Rosny and Anatole France, as well as of the best of Wells and the "SF reservation" writers.

4. The Jungle Explorer: Medicine Man or Darwinist

4.0. Thus far I have not explicitly referred to the theory and practice of SF criticism, since it is impossible to discuss an intellectual activity before its field has been determined. The field of SF criticism is SF, and this truism becomes significant when we pause to consider how little agreement there is about the basic parameters of SF. Having discussed them, in the remainder of this chapter I would like to essay some remarks on SF criticism. They will have to be as disjointed, tentative, and unsystematic as that criticism, since the basic lesson one can draw from the history of literary criticism is that it is difficult for criticism to be more significant than the works it criticizes.

---

6. I have attempted to analyze some representative examples of such modern SF parables in chapters 10 and 12 of this book, *à propos* of Wells's *Time Machine* and Čapek's *War With the Newts*, in my afterword to Stanislaw Lem, *Solaris* (New York, 1971 and 1976), enlarged into a parallel to US and Russian examples in "Stanislaw Lem und das mitteleuropäische soziale Bewusstsein der Science-fiction," in Werner Berthel, ed., *Insel Al-*

4.1. Beyond the necessary but subsidiary critical activity of reviewing and chronicling, it seems that the most fashionable critical approach to SF is that of *mythical analysis*. In order to comment upon it, I shall have to try to disentangle the main meanings of this protean and tantalizing term.

Few writers considering myth in the last third of a century have failed to lament the divergent and indeed incompatible meanings given to this term in different professional and ideological fields of discourse. Though everyone—including myself—has to try to group these meanings for purposes of an overview, it is sometimes difficult to escape the conclusion of a philologist that there are as many interpretations of myth as there are critics. In ethnology "myth" is indistinguishable from "legend" or "folklore." Cultural historians "employ 'myth' with the quite separate meaning of a popularly accepted cluster of images."[7] The term can also be loosely used to mean "tale, fantasy, mass delusion, popular belief and illusion, and plain lie"; an essay as early as 1947 reduced this confusion of tongues to the absurd by adopting the title of "The Modern Myth of the Modern Myth."[8] But, cutting a long story short, it seems to me that the literary theoretician has presently to deal with three principal views of the field: that of Cassirer and his followers, that of literary scholars who consider all literature to be some kind of myth—a view most ably and influentially formulated by Northrop Frye—and that of a third group which would insist, as I argued earlier (see note 2), that literary artifacts are not myths and yet that many of them are significantly marked by genetic and morphological connections with myths.

4.1.1. Cassirer treats myth as a kind of symbolic vision correlative to the mythopoeic mode of consciousness, "mythopoeia" meaning the world view and forms of expression characteristic of a hypothetical early stage of culture "when language is still largely ritualistic and prelogical in character." In this view, myth

---

manach auf das Jahr 1976—Stanislaw Lem (Frankfurt, 1976); and in essays on Philip K. Dick and Ursula K. Le Guin, reprinted in Mullen and Suvin, eds. (see Bibliography I).

7. Richard M. Dorson, "Theories of Myth and the Folklorist," in Murray, ed., p. 84.

8. First quotation from Hyman, in Sebeok, ed., p. 153; see also, for a psychologist's attack on loose definitions of myth, Henry A. Murray, "The Possible Nature of a 'Mythology' to Come," in Murray, ed., p. 303. The second quotation is the title of Donald A. Stauffer's essay in *English Institute Essays 1947* (New York, 1948).

"is simply a basic way of envisaging experience and carries no necessary connotation of storytelling."[9] Rather, all creative, poetic, metaphoric thinking is "mythical." To this it must be briefly objected that metaphor is feasible only when some cognitively defined terms with fixed meanings are available as points of comparison, and that as far as literature is concerned poetic metaphor and language begin exactly where mythology ends. In the best mythical fashion, if poetry springs from the mother-soil of mythology, it does so only by spurning or destroying its parent. Finally, if everything (including science, philosophy, the arts, and all other aspects and motives of social practice) is myth or mythopoeia, if in myth, as Cassirer says, "everything may be turned into everything,"[10] then this term loses all usefulness for distinguishing literature from anything else, let alone for any distinctions within literature itself. Historically hypothetical, philosophically idealistic, and aesthetically useless, Cassirer's hypothesis for all its influences in the American cultural climate after World War II (for example, Susanne Langer) cannot contribute to our present needs.

   4.1.2. At the opposite extreme—but *les extrèmes se rejoignent*—is the position which preserves the autonomy of literary studies but affirms that myth is story and any story is myth. It possesses a heroic paradigm in Frye's *Anatomy of Criticism*. Though mentioning the secondary sense of myth as "untruth,"[11] and of "myth in the narrower and more technical sense" as stories about "divine or quasi-divine beings and powers,"[12] and then discussing a mythical *phase* or context of literary art which is primarily concerned with "poetry as the focus of a community,"[13] Frye concentrates on a Cassirerian "mythical *view* of literature" which leads "to the conception of an order of nature as a whole being imitated by a corresponding order of words."[14] This is based on

   9. P[hilip] W[heelwright], "Myth," in Alex Preminger, ed., *Encyclopedia of Poetry and Poetics* (Princeton, 1965), pp. 538–39; see Ernst Cassirer, *An Essay on Man* (New Haven, 1962) and *The Philosophy of Symbolic Forms*, vol. 2 (New Haven, 1955).
   10. Cassirer, *Essay*, p. 81.
   11. Frye, p. 75.
   12. Frye, p. 116; see also, on "the mythical or theogonic mode," pp. 120, 33–36, et passim.
   13. Frye, p. 99; see the whole section, pp. 95–99.
   14. Frye, p. 118.

his belief, explicated in the section subtitled "Theory of Myths," that "in myth we see the structural principles of literature isolated."[15] If structural principles are to mean isolatable formal narrative patterns, this is acceptable as a basis of discussion subject to historical verification. However, if they are also meant to subsume the motivation of a literary work, what the *Theory of Literature* calls "the inner structure of psychological, social, or philosophical theory of why men behave as they do—some theory of causation, ultimately,"[16] then I do not see how myth can contain the structural principles of all literature or be the "total creative act" which could account for all basic components of the final impact or message of all literary modes and genres.

In other words, among many brilliant insights in *Anatomy of Criticism* there is one about mythical patterns not only being formally analogous to basic patterns in other literary modes—which one would a priori expect in the imaginative products of the same human species—but also being more clearly identifiable in supernatural stories "at the limits of desire"[17] than in stories cluttered with surface naturalism. However, there is an essential difference between this and treating the fourfold seasonal mythos of Spring, Summer, Autumn, and Winter as the basic organization of all literature and indeed all verbal structures imaginable, including science and history.[18] Here the formal similarity has been left behind, and literature has (by way of a semantically redefined mythos) been identified to myth *tout court*, since its original meaning of superhuman story has not been abandoned.[19] Unfortunately, this is the most easily vulgarized and therefore possibly the best-known part of Frye's book. Logically, literature and verbal structures in general are finally reduced to a central unifying myth, adumbrated in Milton and Dante but fully manifest in the Bible, which is a "definitive" myth.[20] All writing, one might therefore expect, has in the past aspired to

15. Frye, p. 136.
16. René Wellek and Austin Warren, *Theory of Literature* (Harmondsworth, 1973), p. 207 et passim.
17. Frye, p. 134.
18. Frye, p. 341 et passim.
19. Frye: redefining *mythos*, pp. 134–40 and 158 ff.; retaining the meaning of superhuman tale, e.g., p. 317.
20. Frye, pp. 120–21; also p. 315, 325 et passim.

and will in the future be confined to variations on smaller or larger bits of the Christian myth of salvation. Obviously such a conclusion will finally be shared only by those who acknowledge the hegemony of a cyclical theory of history and a closed cosmology—that is, by anti-utopians. Therefore, this brilliant work can persuade us that much literature is morphologically informed by patterns which we might perhaps call mythical. However, "mythical" then proves to be simply shorthand for "basic narrative patterns which are seen at their clearest in some myths."

4.1.3. For, when we have rendered unto myth what is of the myth, we must recognize that finally, for a cognitive pursuit such as literary theory and criticism, myth as an instrument is fairly limited. Philosophically, myth is an evasion of precise distinctions and of full intellectual commitment: a myth is not true or false but believable or unbelievable, vital or dead. On its own grounds it is irrefutable, for as soon as it is queried as to its truth it is not treated as myth but as historical cognition or formal hypothesis. In other words, it seems to me that Frye has rendered a signal service to poetics by his formal hypothesis, but I find myself unpersuaded by his historical premises and his semantical gliding between myth as a historical genre, mythos as a formal paradigm, and both of them as a "structural principle or attitude."[21] I am unable to accept the conclusion that "in literary criticism, myth ultimately means *mythos*, a structural organizing principle of literary form,"[22] which does not differentiate between the formal and structural functions of myth.

As distinct from Cassirer and the Cassirerian aspect of Frye, it seems to me that myth cannot constitute a useful theory of history in general, and artistic or literary history in particular. Myth is parascientific and sometimes prescientific in its interpretations of nature and society. Although some among its numerous configurations are statistically bound to become precursors of scientific ones, it is essentially an insufficiently critical human experience which, for all its ideological and artistic uses, cannot be dignified as anything more than a first significant step on the human way to a cognition of reality. Speaking of the myth's "unity of feel-

21.   Frye, p. 310.
22.   Frye, p. 341.

ing," Cassirer rightly concludes that its pragmatic function is to promote social solidarity through feelings of cosmic sympathy at the time of social crisis.[23] Myth embodies and sanctions authoritarian social norms and the basic institutions which determine the life of each member of a certain collective authority-structure. It is intrinsically—whatever its surface innovations in this age where every new car fashion is "revolutionary"—a conservative force, a guarantee of the status quo (say of the mass existence of private cars). In the forceful words of David Bidney:

> To my mind, contemporary philosophers and theologians, as well as students of literature in general, who speak of the indispensable myth in the name of philosophy and religion, and anthropologists and sociologists who cynically approve of myth because of its pragmatic social function, are undermining faith in their own disciplines and are contributing unwittingly to the very degradation of man and his culture which they otherwise seriously deplore. Myth must be taken seriously as a cultural force but it must be taken seriously precisely in order that it may be gradually superseded in the interests of the advancement of truth and the growth of human intelligence. Normative, critical, and scientific thought provides the only self-correcting means of combating the diffusion of myth, but it may do so only on condition that we retain a firm and uncompromising faith in the integrity of reason and in the trans-cultural validity of the scientific enterprise.[24]

Thus, the literary scholar and critic, building his autonomous and yet rational conceptual world, must honor myth, in the Frygian "narrow sense" of stories about superhuman beings, as both occasionally fetching folk poetry and a reservoir of literary forms. At the same time, the critic—and in particular the critic of SF—must, I believe, abandon the belief that he has done much more than his formal homework when he has identified Yefremov's *Andromeda* as containing the myth of Perseus or Delany's *Einstein Intersection* and Verne's *Château des Carpates* as containing the myth of Orpheus. He is still left face to face with the

---

23. Cassirer, *Essay*, pp. 79–84.
24. David Bidney, "Myth, Symbolism, and Truth," in Sebeok, ed., p. 23.

basic questions of his trade, namely, is the myth or mytheme transmuted (1) into valid fiction; (2) into valid science fiction? "Mythical analysis" as a self-sufficient critical method collapses at this point; as an ideology it remains a contributing factor to the Babylonian confusion of tongues, a particularly lethal quicksand region on the path to SF.

4.2. Finally, it might be possible to sketch the basic premises of a significant criticism, history, and theory of this literary genre. From Edgar Allan Poe to Damon Knight and Stanislaw Lem, including some notable work on the other subgenres from the utopias to Wells and some general approaches to literature by people awake to methodological interest, much spadework has been done. If one may speculate on some fundamental features or indeed axioms of such criticism, the *first* might be that the genre has to be and can be evaluated proceeding from its heights down, applying the standards gained by the analysis of its masterpieces. We find in SF, as we do in most other genres of fiction, that 80 to 90 percent of the works in it are sheer confectionery. However, contrary to subliterature, the criteria for the insufficiency of most SF are to be found in the genre itself. This makes SF in principle, if not yet in practice, equivalent to any other "major" literary genre. The *second* axiom of SF criticism might be to demand of SF a level of cognition higher than that of its average reader: the strange novelty is its *raison d'être*. As a minimum, we must demand from SF that it be wiser than the world it speaks to.

In other words, this is an educational literature, hopefully less deadening than most compulsory education in our split national and class societies, but irreversibly shaped by the pathos of preaching the good word of human curiosity, fear, and hope. Significant SF denies thus the "two-cultures gap" more efficiently than any other literary genre I know of. Even more importantly, it demands from the author and reader, teacher and critic, not merely specialized, quantified positivistic knowledge (*scientia*) but a social imagination whose quality of wisdom (*sapientia*) testifies to the maturity of his critical and creative thought. It demands—to conclude the botanical marvelous voyage of this chapter—that the critic be a Darwinist and not a medicine-man.

3

Defining the Literary Genre of Utopia: Some Historical Semantics, Some Genology, a Proposal, and a Plea

For if the matter be attentively considered, a sound argument may be drawn from Poesy, to show that there is agreeable to the spirit of man a more ample greatness, a more perfect order, and a more beautiful variety than it can anywhere (since the Fall) find in nature. . . . it [Poesy] raises the mind and carries it aloft, accommodating the shows of things to be desires of the mind, not (like reason and history) buckling and bowing down the mind to the nature of things.

Francis Bacon

"Utopia," the neologism of Thomas More's, has had a singularly rich semantic career in our time. Having at its root the simultaneous indication of a space and a state (itself ambiguously hovering between, for example, French *état* and *condition*) that are nonexisting (*ou*) as well as good (*eu*), it has become a territory athwart the roads of all travelers pursuing the implications of the question formulated by Plato as "What is the best form of organization for a community and how can a person best arrange his life?"[1] And have not the urgencies of the situation in which the human community finds itself made of us all such travelers?

Utopia operates by example and demonstration, deictically. At the basis of all utopian debates, in its open or hidden dialogues, is a gesture of pointing, a wide-eyed glance from here to there, a "traveling shot" moving from the author's everyday lookout to the wondrous panorama of a far-off land:

But you should have been with me in Utopia and personally seen their manner and customs as I did. . . . [More, *Utopia*, book 1]

1. *Laws* 3, 702b. See Plato, *The Laws*, trans. with introduction by A. E. Taylor (London, 1960), p. 85.

37

> . . . it was winter when I went to bed last night, and now, by witness of the river-side trees, it was summer, a beautiful bright morning seemingly of early June. [Morris, *News from Nowhere*, chapter 2]

> We should both discover that the little towns below had changed—but how, we should not have marked them well enough to know. It would be indefinable, a change in the quality of their grouping, a change in the quality of their remote, small shapes. . . . a mighty difference had come to the world of men. [Wells, *A Modern Utopia*, chapter 1]

Morris's abruptly beautiful trees can be taken (as they were meant to be) for an emblem of this space and state: utopia is a vivid witness to desperately needed alternative possibilities of "the world of men," of human life. No wonder the debate has waxed hot whether any particular alternative is viable and whether it has already been found, especially in the various socialist attempts at a radically different social system. In the heat of the debate, detractors of this particular set of alternative conclusions—often shell-shocked refugees from it—have tried to deny the possibility and/or humanity of the utopian concept as such. Other imprudent apologists—often intellectuals with a solid position within the defended system—have taken the symmetrically inverse but equally counterutopian tack of proclaiming that *Civitas Dei* has already been realized on Earth by their particular sect or nation, in "God's own country" of North America or the laicized Marxist (or pseudo-Marxist) experiments from Lenin to Castro and Mao. Historians have transferred these debates into the past: were Periclean Athens, Aqbar's India, Emperor Friedrich's Sicily, Münzer's Mühlhausen, the Inca state, or Jeffersonian U.S.A. utopian?

Such fascinating and tempting questions cannot fail to influence us in an underground fashion—defining our semantics —in any approach to a definition of utopia. But I propose to confine myself here to a consideration of utopia *as a literary genre*. No doubt this is not the *first* point about utopias—that would pertain to collective psychology: why and how do they arise?—nor is it the *last* one—that would pertain to the politics of the human species and perhaps even to its cosmology: how is *Homo sapiens* to survive and humanize its segment of the universe?

Such a politico-eschatological question has understandably arisen out of twentieth-century heretic reinterpretations of the two most systematic bodies of thought about man in our civilization: the Judaeo-Christian one (in spite of its usual pat transfers of the answer into the blue yonder of otherworldly post-mortems) and the Marxist one (in spite of Marx's and Engels's scorn of subjective theorizing about ideal futures in their predecessors, the "utopian socialists"). Ernst Bloch's monumental philosophical opus, culminating in *Hope the Principle*, has reinterpreted utopia (as have some theologians such as Martin Buber and Paul Tillich) as being any overstepping of the boundaries given to man, hence a quality inherent in all creative thought and action. In a narrower and more academic version, a similar reinterpretation of "utopia" as any orientation that transcends reality and breaks the bounds of existing order, as opposed to "ideology," which expresses the existing order, was introduced by Karl Mannheim.[2] But all these horizons, interesting and even inspiring as they are, are beyond my scope here. I propose that an acknowledgment that utopias are verbal artifacts before they are anything else, and that the source of this concept is a literary genre and its parameters, might be, if not the first and the last, nonetheless a *central* point in today's debate on utopias. If this is so, one cannot properly explore the signification of utopia by considering its body (texts) simply as a transparency transmitting a Platonic idea: the *signifiant* must be understood as well as the *signifié*. Thus, especially at this time of failing eschatologies, it might even be in the interests of utopia (however widely redefined) if we acted as physiologists asking about a species' functions and structure before we went on to behave as moralists prescribing codes of existence to it: perhaps such codes ought to take into account the makeup of the organism? And since discussions of utopias are an excellent demonstration of the saying that people who do not master history are condemned to relive it, the physiological stance will have to be combined with an anamnesic one, recalling the historical semantics (in sections 1 and 2) of

---

2. See Tillich (a representative essay from which is reprinted in Manuel, ed.), Buber, Bloch, and Mannheim—all in Bibliography II; also the rich anthology on the concept of utopia: Neusüss, ed. (Bibliography II).

utopia while trying to tease out its elements (in section 3) and genological context (in sections 4 and 5).

1. HISTORICAL SEMANTICS: ANTEDILUVIAN

The first point and fundamental element of a literary definition of utopia is that any utopia is a *verbal construction*. This might seem self-evident, but it is in fact just beginning to be more widely recognized in the vanguard of "utopology." The *Oxford English Dictionary*, for example, defines utopia in the following ways:

> 1. An imaginary island, depicted by Sir Thomas More as enjoying a perfect social, legal and political system.
>
> . . . .
>
> b. *transf.* Any imaginary, indefinitely remote region, country, or locality.
>
> . . . .
>
> 2. A place, state, or condition ideally perfect in respect of politics, laws, customs, and conditions.
>
> . . . .
>
> b. An impossibly ideal scheme, esp. for social improvement.
>
> . . . .

Obviously, the *OED*—whose latest examples come in this case from the turn of the century—has not yet caught up to the necessity and practice of defining utopia as a literary genre.[3] If we nonetheless look for clues in the above four definitions, we shall see that the first one pertains to More's "depiction" of a locus which is, for the *OED*, defined by two aspects: (1) "imaginary" removal from the author's (and presumably the reader's) empirical environment; (2) sociopolitical perfection. The first aspect is then isolated in the semantic practice leading to definition 1b, and the second in the practice leading to 2, which is further treated derisively by hardheaded pragmatists or ideologists of the status quo in 2b. From all this a definition of utopia as a

---

3. See the stimulating discussion, with more lexicographic material, in Herbrüggen (Bibliography II); also further French, German, and Spanish material in Rita Falke, "Utopie—logische Konstruktion und chimère," in Villgradter and Krey, eds. (Bibliography II).

literary form should retain the crucial element of an *alternative location radically different in respect of sociopolitical conditions* from the author's historical environment. However, this element must be valorized in the context of a literary-theoretical approach.

Only in *OED* 1 is there even a discreet mumble about the utopia being an artistic artifact, hidden in the ambiguous "depicted" (about which more later). All the other definitions refer to its qualities of perfection, remoteness, or impossibility. This ontological equating of utopia to England, Germany, or any other empirical country was an accepted nineteenth- and early twentieth-century way of defining it. I shall adduce only a few definitions from some better-known and more helpful works pertaining to such a way of thinking, which might well— regardless of their actual year—be called antediluvian:

> (1) Utopias . . . are ideal pictures of other worlds, the existence or possibility of which cannot be scientifically demonstrated, and in which we only believe. [Voigt, 1906]
> (2) More depicted a perfect, and perhaps unrealizable, society, located in some nowhere, purged of the shortcomings, the wastes, and the confusion of our own time and living in perfect adjustment, full of happiness and contentment. [Hertzler, 1923]
> (3) an ideal commonwealth whose inhabitants exist under perfect conditions. [*Encyclopedia Britannica*, accepted by Berneri, 1950][4]

All of the above definitions or delimitations consider utopia simply as a Platonic idea and proceed to examine its believability and realizability. Hertzler (2) is the most effusive and prolix among them: the definition of utopias in general on which her whole book is predicated, is effected by a definition of More's work prefaced with the statement that this definition isolates the distinctive characteristic applicable to all "imaginary ideal societies." The vagueness ("perhaps," "some nowhere") and non-sequiturs

---

4. These definitions can be found in the following books (whenever in my quotes the subject and predicate are missing, "utopia is" is implied): Voigt, p. 1; Hertzler, pp. 1–2; Berneri, p. 320 (all in Bibliography II). A number of very useful approaches to utopia are not referred to here, as they were not found cognate to a primarily literary-theoretical viewing; a still greater number were found of little use except for a history of "utopologic thought."

(More depicted a society purged of "the confusion of our own time") make Hertzler a very good example—though greater offenders could be found in the antediluvian age—of the uselessness to our endeavors of most surveys of "Utopian Thought" as being idealistic and ideological. All the above definitions, moreover, do not (except by vague suggestions inherent in "commonwealth" or "society") distinguish between various religious "ideal pictures of other worlds" and utopias. This echoes the (once?) widely-held unexamined premise that utopias are really lay variants of paradise. Now if this is true, it is so only in the sense which would make a counterproject out of a variant. Whereas it remains very important to pursue the historical underground continuation of absolutistic religious and mythological structures (especially those drawn from the Islands of the Blessed and Terrestrial Paradises) in Plato, More, or a number of other utopian writers, it should seem clear that there is little point in discussing utopias as a separate entity, if their basic humanistic, this-worldly, *historically alternative* aspect is not stressed and adopted as one of their *differentiae genericae*. "A wishful construct has been explicated, a rational one, that does not possess chiliastic certainties of hope any more, but postulates the possibility of being constructed by its own forces, without transcendental support or intervention," observes Bloch even about More's Utopia.[5] What is literally even more important, such a construct is *located in this world*. Utopia is an Other World immanent in the world of human endeavor, dominion, and hypothetic possibility—and not transcendental in a religious sense. It is a nonexistent country on the map of *this* globe, a "this-worldly other world." No doubt, there is the pragmatic, Macaulayan sense of utopia being anything intangible and impossibly far-off, as opposed to immovable property in one's own property-owning environment ("An acre in Middlesex is better than a principality in Utopia")[6]; this sense would also englobe all Heavenly and Earthly Paradises. But from any point of view except that of a property-owner and pragmatist, religion is, as Ruyer notes, counterutopian. It is directed either towards Heaven (tran-

5. Bloch, p. 607.
6. Quoted in the *OED*; see Thomas Babington Macaulay, "Lord Bacon," in his *Critical, Historical and Miscellaneous Essays and Poems* (Albany, 1887), 2:229.

scendence) or towards Middlesex (bounded empirical environment): in either case it is incompatible with a non-transcendental overstepping of empirical boundaries.[7] The *telos* of religion is, finally, eternity or timelessness, not history. On the contrary, just as the satire is an impossible possible—what is empirically possible is felt as axiologically impossible; it should not be possible—utopia is a possible impossible. Subversion and rhetoric embrace in a paradoxical socio-political revaluation of the Petrarchan "icy fire" *impossibilia*—a "positive *adynaton*" in Barthes's term.[8]

Thus, *chemin faisant*, we have found that the (still not too precise) element of historical alternative enters any definition which would leave utopia intact as a literary genre and object of exploration. We have still to pursue the metaphors adopted as a first try at untying the embarrassing knot of utopia's being a concept and belief and yet, at the same time, obviously a (literary) artifact—a "picture" (2 and 4) or a "description" (4 and 5):

(4) A. Nom donné par Thomas Morus au pays imaginaire qu'il décrit dans son ouvrage: *De optimo reipublicae statu, deque nova insula Utopia* (1516), et dans lequel il place un peuple parfaitement sage, puissant et heureux, grâce aux institutions idéales dont il jouit.

B. Se dit par extension de tous les tableaux représentant, sous la forme d'une description concrète et détaillée (et souvent même comme un roman), l'organisation idéale d'une sociéte humaine. [Lalande, ed. of 1968, but text goes back at least to 1928]

[A. Name given by Thomas More to the imaginary country which he describes in his work *De optimo reipublicae statu, deque nova insula Utopia* (1516), and into which he collocates a people that is perfectly wise, powerful, and happy, thanks to the ideal institutions with which it is provided.

B. Said by extension of all pictures representing, by means of a detailed and concrete description (often even as a novel), the ideal organization of a human society.]

(5) la description d'un monde imaginaire, en dehors . . . de l'espace et du temps historiques et géographiques. C'est la

---

7. Ruyer (Bibliography II), p. 31; see also Schwonke (Bibliography II), pp. 1–3, in whose book this is a basic theme, and Gerber (Bibliography I), pp. 6–7.
8. Barthes (Bibliography II), p. 122.

description d'un monde constitué sur des principes différ-
ents de ceux qui sont à l'oeuvre dans le monde réel.[9] [Ruyer,
1950]

    [the description of an imaginary world, outside . . . of
historical and geographic space and time. This is a description of a world based on principles that differ from those
underlying the real world.]

"Description" is derived etymologically from "writing," but in an
archaic and ambiguous sense which, as it were, echoes the deri-
vation of writing from drawing. Above it is clearly employed
within the semantics pertaining to painting: "il décrit . . . il place"
(in 4a. placing pertains to the way a landscape painter would
arrange his figures); and "tableaux représentant, sous la forme
d'une description" is a classic witness for my thesis (4b.). Even (5),
which is more abstract than the previous definitions, continues its
discussion in the immediately following line by contrasting such
descriptions to those of a nonutopian novelist, who "lui, *place* des
personnages et des aventures imaginaires dans notre monde."[10]
Utopia, as well as "our world," is a scene for *dramatis personae* and
actions; the metaphor of author as puppeteer (stage manager),
never far beneath the metaphor of author as painter (scenog-
rapher), has here come nearer to the surface.

    Such a dramatic metaphor, linked as it is to the "all the world's
a stage" topos, is potentially much more fruitful—since drama
fuses painting and literature, temporal and spatial arts—and
very appropriate for this dialogic form. Unfortunately, it has
not, to my knowledge, been taken seriously in defining utopias.
Thus such attempts at acknowledging the artificial character of
utopia have remained half-hearted. They have failed because
they did not acknowledge that it is a *literary* artifact. This is
crucial because the problems of "depicting" a radically different
(5) because perfect (4) imaginary world are in a literary artifact
quite distinct from the problems of a "tableau," which exists in
an arrested moment of time and in a synoptic space. A picture

---

9.   These definitions can be found in Lalande (Bibliography II), p. 1179—and see the
whole discussion on pp. 1178–81—and Ruyer, p. 3. See also the definition of Dupont
(Bibliography III C), p. 14, which is transitional between the first group of definitions and
this one. All the translations in this book, unless otherwise indicated, are mine.

10.   Ruyer, p. 3; italics added.

may perhaps approximate the status of a mirror of external reality (though even the mirror reverses). In literature, a concrete and detailed "description" or, better, *verbal construction* is not, in any precise sense, a "re-presentation" of a preexisting idea which would be the content of that representation or description (where would such an idea preexist? with the *Zeitgeist*?). Literary texts cannot be divided into body and soul, only into interlocking levels of a multifunctional body, which is a human construct out of verbal denotations and connotations. Only within such a context can the definition of its *thematic field*—practically identical from (2) to (5)—become a valid part of a literary definition. The *imaginary community* (the term seems preferable to the ambiguous "world") *in which human relations are organized more perfectly than in the author's community* can be accepted as a first approximation to identifying the thematic nucleus of the utopian genre.

One further point should account for my substitution of "more perfectly" in place of the "perfect" in (2) to (4). Though historically most of the older utopias tried to imagine a certain perfection, after Bacon's *New Atlantis* and Fénelon's *Télémaque* (not to forget Plato's *Laws*) a suspicion ought to have arisen that this is not inherent in the genre. That suspicion should have grown into a certainty after Saint-Simon and Morris. By the time Wells wrote his celebrated first page of *A Modern Utopia* distinguishing between static and kinetic utopias, the laggard academic and literary critics of the genre found their work done for them. Since then we have had no further excuse for insisting on absolute perfection, but only on a state radically better or based on a more perfect principle than that prevailing in the author's community, as a hallmark of the utopian genre.[11] As for the "au-

---

11. See the analogous argument in Walsh (for the titles in this note see Bibliography II), p. 25. The position of utopia midway between the corruptible world of class history and ideal perfection is quite analogous—as will be discussed in section 4 of this chapter—to the position of Earthly Paradise in religious thought; see for example the definition of Athanasius of Alexandria:

> The Terrestrial Paradise we expound as not subject to corruption in the way in which our plants and our fruits get corrupted by putrefaction and worms. Nor is it, on the other hand, wholly incorruptible, so that it would not in future centuries decay by growing old. But if it is compared with our fruits and our gardens, it is superior to all corruption; while if it is compared to the glory of the coming Good, which eye hath not seen nor ear heard nor the heart of man comprehended, it is and is reputed to be vastly inferior.

thor's community," this phrase can be left conveniently plastic to embrace whatever the author and his ideal readers would have felt to be their community—from city to nation to planet.

2. HISTORICAL SEMANTICS: POSTDILUVIAN

In the last twenty years, at least in literary criticism and theory, the premise has become acceptable that utopia is first of all a literary genre or fiction. The Cold War "end of ideology" climate might have contributed to this (it can be felt, for example, in the disclaimers in the Negley-Patrick book discussed below), but more importantly, it has been part of a deeper epistemological shift in literary shcolarship—a belated recognition that, as Frye wrote, the literary critic "should be able to construct and dwell in a conceptual universe of his own."[12] I shall again adduce only a few definitions as characteristic examples for works of this period, after the deluge of two world wars and two cycles of worldwide revolutions:

> (6) There are three characteristics which distinguish the utopia from other forms of literature or speculation:
>   1. It is fictional.
>   2. It describes a particular state or community.
>   3. Its theme is the political structure of that fictional state or community. . . .
>
> Utopias are expressions of political philosophy and theory, to be sure, but they are descriptions of fictional states in which the philosophy and theory are already implemented in the institutions and procedures of the social structure. [Negley and Patrick, 1952]
> (7) . . . the literary ideal image of an imaginary social system (*Staatsordnung*). [Herbrüggen, 1960]
> (8) the utopian novel is the literary manifestation of a playful synopsis of man, society, and history in a variable, image-like (*bildhaft*) thought model possessing spatio-temporal autonomy, which model permits the exploration of possibilities

---

Athanasii archiep. Alexandrini, *Opera omnia quae extant* . . . (Paris, 1698) 2:279, quoted in Coli, p. 39. The insistence on utopia as wholly "ideal" can still be found in Herbrüggen—see note 13.

12.   Northrop Frye, *Anatomy of Criticism*, p. 12.

detached from social reality yet relating to it. [Krysmanski, 1963]

(9) la description littéraire individualisée d'une société imaginaire, organisée sur des bases qui impliquent une critique sous-jacente de la société réelle.[13] [Cioranescu, 1972]

[the individualized literary description of an imaginary society, organized on bases which imply an underlying critique of the real society.]

Negley and Patrick (6) seem to have been the first expressly to enunciate a differentiation between the utopia of political scientists and *Geisteswissenschaftler* ("expressions of political philosophy and theory") and that of the literary critics and theorists ("fictional states," theme and ideas "implemented"). Their pioneering status is evident in certain uneasy compromise with the older conception which they are abandoning.[14] But as well as their use of the by-now dead metaphor of describing (which in a proper context it would perhaps be pedantic to fault), their failure to elaborate what exactly fictional implementation entails and their de facto concentration in the book on sociopolitical ideas and structure unrelated to the literary structure leave their definition somewhat isolated and without consequences. But their useful and influential book at least indicated the horizons of studying what they called in their preface, in a mixture of conceptual styles, both "utopian thought in Western civilization" (old style) and also, somewhat shamefacedly, "the literary genre of the utopists" (new style).

On the other hand, Herbrüggen (7) starts boldly and happily by identifying utopia as literary, but then leaves it dangling in intense vagueness by calling it not only "imaginary" but also the "ideal image." Later in this work, he has many just and stimulating things to say about its delimitation from other genres. In particular, he has been a pioneer in drawing some structural consequences from defining utopia as possessing a literary mode of existence. However, a number of his parameters, including his

---

13. These definitions can be found in the books by Negley and Patrick, pp. 3–4; Herbrüggen, p. 7; Krysmanski, p. 19; and Cioranescu, p. 22—all in Bibliography II.

14. No doubt, there were earlier implicit or incidental suggestions that fictional utopia was primarily a literary genre, e.g. in Dupont—in spite of his definition and title—and in Frye, *Anatomy*. But the voices of these, and possibly of other, precursors fell on deaf ears.

definition, seem to fit More (his particular paradigm), or indeed a utopian program, better than they would an ideal-typical utopia.

Krysmanski's (8) sociological exploration of German "utopian novels" of the twentieth century (which ought rather to be called science fiction, as I shall argue in section 5) set itself the laudable aim of discovering and fully defining "the specific nature of the utopian novel": his definition is the conclusion of a chapter with that title. Unfortunately, for an analysis of a "literary manifestation" (*Erscheinungsform*) it is far too little conversant with fundaments of literary theory and criticism. One's sympathy and tolerance lie with his Aristotelian basic approach, striving for a definition which must be precise and comprehensive, in which case technical jargon is almost impossible to avoid. Nonetheless, it is not only the Teutonic and Mannheimian "sociology of knowledge" nature of the jargon which makes one pause, it is primarily the arbitrariness and vagueness of the elements of the definition, which seem to prove that modern definitions can be every bit as prolix-cum-insufficient as the antediluvian ones. It may be useful to draw our attention to the elements of playfulness, of simultaneous viewing or synopsis (*Zusammenschau*) of man, society, and history, or of an exploration of possibilities. But why "manifestation of a synopsis" (the German is still worse: "Erscheinungsform der . . . Zusammenschau")? Why "variable," "image-like," and "spatio-temporal autonomy"—is not every *Denkmodell* such? And the final clause evidently pertains to science fiction in general, being too wide for utopia, which is bound up with the (here missing) "more perfect community" concept.

As for Cioranescu's book devoted to "utopia and literature," a work full of stimulating and provocative statements, I shall return to later. At this point, it might suffice to point out with relief how neat and with unease how overgeneralized his definition is (9). Are not Paradise, an Island of the Blessed, or satirical SF covered by it as well? And, not to boggle at minor maters, just what is "the real society"?

3. A PROPOSED DEFINITION:
UTOPIA AS VERBAL CONSTRUCTION

The historico-semantical discussion of the preceding two sections has come up with the following elements for defining utopia: a radically different and historically alternative sociopolitical condition; an alternative locus; an imaginary community in which relations are organized more perfectly than in the author's community; the fictional or, more clearly, "verbal construction" character of any such condition, location, or community; the particular or individualized character of any such construct as opposed to general and abstract utopian projects and programs. I shall now commit the utopian imprudence of proposing after the above critique a construct or definition of my own:

> Utopia is the verbal construction of a particular quasi-human community where sociopolitical institutions, norms, and individual relationships are organized according to a more perfect principle than in the author's community, this construction being based on estrangement arising out of an alternative historical hypothesis.

I have indicated earlier in general outline the importance to be alloted to the element of *verbal construction*. This can be fully demonstrated only in particular analyses of utopian works. But its relevance can be seen even in a general answer to the question: what type of verbal construction? As Frye has pointed out, utopia belongs to a narrative form and tradition which he calls anatomy (or Menippean satire) rather than to the novel. The anatomy deals less with illusionistic "people as such than with mental attitudes" and at its most concentrated "presents us with a vision of the world in terms of a single intellectual pattern."[15] Our critical judgments should take this into account; in particular, there is no point in expecting from a characterization and plotting which are more allegorical than naturalistic the qualities and criteria induced from the psychological novel, from Prévost to Proust or Richardson to Henry James.[16] To take one example, the conclusions of Gerber's interesting book on twentieth-century utopias (or rather SF) are vitiated by his assumption and

15. Frye, pp. 309 and 310.
16. The famous quarrel between James and Wells—available in Leon Edel and Gordon N. Ray, eds., *Henry James and H. G. Wells* (Urbana, IL, 1958)—which resulted in a draw rather than in the vindication of the psychological novel the Jamesians saw in it, is a clear example of the collision between the "anatomic" or allegorical and the "novelistic" or individualistic orientations.

definition of utopia as a novel.[17] To take another, Elliott has aptly complained about one of the dominant interpretations of More's *Utopia*:

> We are given no sense . . . that these questions exist, not as abstract political, religious, or philosophical propositions, but as constitutive elements in a work of art. What is wanted instead of the Catholic interpretation of communism is an interpretation of *Utopia* that will show us how the question of communism is incorporated into the total structure of the work.[18]

Further, some basic structural characteristics of utopia seem to flow logically from its status as a discourse about a particular, historically alternative, and better community. Since such a discourse will necessarily present an opposition which is a formal analogy to the author's delimited environment and its way of life, any utopia must be (1) a rounded, *isolated locus* (valley, island, planet—later, temporal epoch). Since it has to show more perfectly organized relationships, the categories under which the author and his age subsume these relationships (government, economics, religion, warfare, etc.) must be in some way or other (2) *articulated* in a panoramic sweep whose sum is the inner organization of the isolated locus; as Barthes remarks about Fourier (and some other writers), the syntax or composition of elements is identified with creation in such works.[19] Since not only the elements but also their articulation and coordination have to be based on more perfect principles than the categorization in the author's civilization (for example, the federalist pyramid from bottom up of More's Utopia as opposed to the centralist pyramid from top down of More's England and Europe), (3) a formal *hierarchic system* becomes the supreme order and thus the supreme value in utopia: there are authoritarian and libertarian, class and classless utopias, but no unorganized ones. (Morris's reticence about organization and hierarchy in *News From Nowhere* places that work halfway between utopia

---

17. Gerber, final two chapters, and in particular pp. 121–22. See the critique by Elliott (Bibliography II), p. 104 and the whole chapter "Aesthetics of Utopia."

18. Elliott, pp. 28–29.

19. Barthes, p. 9; this whole discussion is indebted to Barthes's book, though I do not wholly share his horizons.

and Earthly Paradise; see chapter 8). Usually the installation of the new order must be explained—a contract theory, as Frye observes, is implied in each utopia (King Utopus, the socialist revolution, gas from a comet, etc., being the arbiters or contract-makers). The utopian contract is necessarily opposed to the dominant contract-myth in the author's society as the more reverent "contract behind the contract,"[20] a human potential which existing society has alienated and failed to realize. Lastly, utopia is bound to have (4) an implicit or explicit *dramatic strategy* in its panoramic review conflicting with the "normal" expectations of the reader. Though formally closed, significant utopia is thematically open: its pointings reflect back upon the reader's "topia." I have already hinted at that in section 1, and one critic has even conveniently found a three-act dramatic structure in More's *Utopia*.[21] Whether this is exact or not, there is no doubt that an analysis of ideational protagonists and settings in Burkean "dramatistic" terms is here appropriate.[22] For example, utopia is invariably a frame-within-a-frame, because it is a specific wondrous stage, set within the world stage; techniques of analyzing the play-within-the-play could be profitably employed when dealing with it. The varieties of the outer frame—usually some variant of the imaginary voyage[23]—have been readily noticeable and as such the object of critical attention; less so their correlation of say, the humanistic symposium of More or the socialist dream-which-might-be-a-vision of Morris with the experience in the inner frame. Even on the stylistic and not only compositional level, such a strategy should be fruitful: "l'écriture," remarks Barthes of Fourier, "doit mobiliser en même temps une image et son contraire [the writing must mobilize at the same time an image and its opposite]."[24]

Finally, "verbal construction" as a definitional element by-

20. Northrop Frye, "Varieties of Literary Utopias," in Manuel, ed., p. 38.
21. Edward Surtz, S.J., "Utopia as a Work of Literary Art," in Edward Surtz, S.J., and J.H. Hexter, eds., *The Complete Works of St. Thomas More* (New Haven, 1965), 4: cxxv–cliii, especially in the chapter "Dramatic Technique, Characterization, and Setting."
22. E.g. Kenneth Burke, *The Philosophy of Literary Form* (New York, 1957).
23. Historically this is especially significant in antiquity and Renaissance, when most utopias and imaginary voyages were combined, but it does not have to persist as an explicit combination. See the excellent survey of Gove (Bibliography III A), much in need of newer follow-ups.
24. Barthes, p. 115.

passes, I hope, the old theologizing quarrel whether a utopia can
be realized, whether in fact (according to one school) only that
which is realizable or on the contrary (according to another but
equally dogmatic school) only that which is unrealizable can be
called utopia. Neither prophecy nor escapism, utopia is, as many
critics have remarked, an "as if,"[25] an imaginative experiment or
"a methodical organ for the New."[26] Literary utopia—and every
description of utopia is literary—is a heuristic device for perfectibility, an epistemological and not an ontological entity.
"L'utopie est un jeu, mais un jeu sérieux. L'utopiste a le sens des
possibilités autres de la nature, mais il ne s'éloigne pas de la
notion de la nature [Utopia is a game, but a serious game. The
utopian author envisages the other possibilities of nature, but he
does not let go of the notion of nature]" argued Ruyer in two
chapters which remain among the best written on the "utopian
mode."[27] He referred to utopian subject matter as "les possibles
latéraux [the lateral possibilities]" and compared the utopian approach or view to the hypothetico-deductive method in experimental sciences and mathematics (for example, non-Euclidean
geometries). If utopia is, then, philosophically, a method rather
than a state, it cannot be realized or not realized—it can only be
applied. That application is, however, as important as it has been
claimed that the realization of utopia is: without it man is truly
alienated or one-dimensional. But to apply a literary text means
first of all (wherever it may later lead) to read as a dramatic dialogue with the reader.[28] Besides requiring the willingness of the

25.   See Hans Vaihinger, *Die Philosophie des Als Ob* (Leipzig, 1920) or *The Philosophy of
"As If,"* trans. C. K. Ogden (New York, 1924). The verbal mode appropriate to this is the
subjunctive: see Elliott, p. 115; Samuel R. Delany, "About Five Thousand One Hundred
and Seventy Five Words," in Clareson, ed., *SF* (Bibliography I); Michael Holquist, "How
to Play Utopia," in Jacques Ehrmann, ed., *Game, Play, Literature* (Boston, 1971), particularly illuminating in his discussion of utopias as a literature of the subjunctive in
"hypothetical or heuristic time," p. 112; and Claude-Gilbert Dubois, "Une architecture
fixionelle," *Revue des sciences humaines* 39, No. 155 (1974): 449–71.
26.   Bloch, p. 180.
27.   Ruyer, chapters 1 and 2; the first quotation is from p. 4 and the later one p. 9;
Ruyer acknowledges the stimulus of an observation by Lalande, p. 1180. Unfortunately,
the analysis of actual utopian characteristics and works in the rest of Ruyer's book is
much less felicitous.
28.   Some of my conclusions are very similar to those of Harry Berger, Jr., in his more
synoptic, seminal introductory discussion of the "other world" in "The Renaissance
World: Second World and Green World," *The Centennial Review* 9 (1965): 36–78. Regret-

reader to enter into dialogue, the application of utopia depends on the closeness and precision of his reading.

4. COMMENT: UTOPIA AS HISTORICAL ESTRANGEMENT

I have thus far worked upon certain premises, among them that scholarly inquiry is possible only when oriented towards, and by, an at least approximately delimited and defined field and that valid definitions in literary studies—as in anything—are historical and not transcendental, or "contextualist" and not "essentialist." Proceeding further, it is necessary to add that the basic diachronic way to define the context of a work of art is to insert it into the tradition and system of its genre (meaning by that a socioaesthetic entity with a specific inner life, yet in a constant osmosis with other literary genres, science, philosophy, everyday socioeconomic life, and so on). Understanding particular utopias really presupposes a definition and delimitation of their literary genre (or, as we shall see, subgenre), its inner processes, logic, and *telos*. What is, then, the distinctive set of traits of the literary genre "utopia," its *differentia generica*?

I have argued in my first two chapters for a division of prose literature into *naturalistic* and *estranged* genres. The literary mainstream of the individualistic age endeavors faithfully to reproduce empirical textures, surfaces, and relationships vouched for by human senses and common sense. Utopia, on the contrary, endeavors to illuminate men's relationships to other men and to their surroundings by the basic device of a radically different location for the postulated novel human relations of its fable; and I have proposed to call literary genres which have such a different formal framework "estranged." One should insist on the crucial concept of a radically different location, of an *alternative formal framework* functioning by explicit or implicit reference to the author's empirical environment. Without this reference, nonutopian readers, having no yardstick for comparison, could not understand the alternative novelty. Conversely, without such a return and feedback into the reader's normality there would be no function for utopias or other estranged genres: "the

---

fully I must add that I believe his particular argument about *Utopia*—that More differs radically from Hythloday—to be wholly unconvincing.

real function of estrangement is—and must be—the provision of
a shocking and distancing mirror above the all too familiar reality."[29] No-place is defined by both not being and yet being like
Place, by being the opposite and more perfect version of Place. It
is a "positive negation," a "merveilleux réel,"[30] the standing on its
head of an already topsy-turvy or alienated world, which thus
becomes dealienated or truly normal when measured not by
ephemeral historical norms of a particular civilization but by
"species-specific" human norms. Utopia is thus always predicated on a certain theory of human nature. It takes up and
refunctions the ancient *topos* of *mundus inversus*: utopia is a formal inversion of significant and salient aspects of the author's
world which has as its purpose or *telos* the recognition that the
author (and reader) truly live in an axiologically inverted world.
It follows, as has been increasingly recognized in modern investigations (and as has been mentioned in passing in section 1),
that the explicit utopian construction is the logical obverse of any
satire.[31] Utopia explicates what satire implicates, and vice versa.
Furthermore, there are strong indications that the two are in fact
phylogenetically connected in the folk-inversions and "saturas"
of the Saturnalias, whose theme was sexual, political, and
ideological reversal, in fact total existential "reversal of values, of
social roles, of social norms."[32] The best argument in favor of
that can be found in the ontogenesis of individual works, in—to
stick to utopias and cognate estranged genres—the most prominent titles of the tradition which runs from Lucian's *True Histories* and More's *Utopia* through Fourier, Bellamy, Morris, Wells,
and Zamyatin to modern SF. A guess could even be hazarded

29. Ernst Bloch, "Entfremdung, Verfremdung," *Verfremdungen*, 1 (Frankfurt, 1963),
English as *"Entfremdung, Verfremdung*: Alienation, Estrangement," trans. Anne Halley and
Darko Suvin, in Erika Munk, ed., *Brecht* (New York, 1972), p. 10. For "estrangement," see
the discussion and references in my first chapter (Shklovsky and Brecht), as well as Bloch,
Das Prinzip Hoffnung.
30. "Positive negation" is the term used in Mikhail Bakhtin's fundamental *Tvorchestvo
Fransua Rable* . . . (Moscow, 1965), English as *Rabelais and His World* (Bibliography II), p.
403; but see also this whole book for a rich and persuasive account of folk humor as the
source for inverting and negating a dominant, upper-class feeling of reality. "Merveilleux
réel" is an expression of Barthes's, p. 101.
31. See Frye, *Anatomy*, pp. 309–12; Lalande, p. 1180; Negley and Patrick, pp. 5–6;
and especially Elliott, chapter 1, "Saturnalia, Satire, and Utopia."
32. Elliott, p. 11.

that the significance and scope of writings in this tradition can be gauged by the degree of integration between its constructive-utopian and satiric aspects: the deadly earnest blueprint and the totally closed horizons of "new maps of hell" both lack aesthetic wisdom.

However, besides satire (which can be, like utopia, both a mode and a genre) the estranged literary genres comprise several which are differentiated from utopia by not situating what Aristophanes calls their *topos apragmon* in the field of an alternative *historical* hypothesis. The most relevant ones are, in ascending order, myth, fantasy, folktale, Cockayne, and Terrestrial Paradise.

I have tried to deal with *myth* in my earlier chapters, and I can only repeat that, although it is also shaped as a specific form of estrangement, myth is diametrically opposed to a historical approach.[33] Conceiving human relationships to be fixed and supernaturally determined, myth claims to explain phenomena by identifying their eternal essence; conceiving human relationships to be changeable and maternally determined, history attempts to explain phenomena by identifying their problematic context. From a historical point of view, myth itself is a historical phenomenon and problem, an illusion when not a fraud. Literature is, in fact, never truly a myth (though mythological tales are literature) but only, in certain cases, formally analogous to mythical structure or mythomorphic. Thus, for example, the myth of the Golden Age can have many formal analogies and elements in common with utopia, but utopia is its opposite:

> . . . man's effort to work out imaginatively what happens—or what might happen—when the primal longings embodied in the myth confront the principle of reality. In this effort man no longer merely dreams of a divine state in some remote time; he assumes the role of creator himself.
>
> A characteristic of the Golden Age . . . is that it exists outside history, usually before history beings: *in illo tempore*.[34]

33. See also Ruyer, pp. 4–6. For all my admiration of Professor Frye's insights, here I obviously disagree with the horizon and main terminology of his work—and in particular with his classifying Dante's *Paradiso* and *Purgatorio* as utopian, in Manuel, ed., p. 34.
34. Elliott, pp. 8–9.

Folktale and *fantasy*, being morphological and ideological descendants of fragmented mythology (in the case of fantasy privatized to boot), can be regarded in a similar way. Neither of them pretends to be historically oriented or in historical time. Both take place in a context of supernatural laws oriented towards the protagonist, whereas for humanistic historiosophy—including utopia—nature is neutral and man's destiny is man.

Somewhat closer to utopia is *Cockayne* (Cuccagna, Schlaraffenland), a widespread folk legend of a land of peace, plenty, and repose, probably refurbished by the student-poets of goliardic and "prandial" libertinism.[35] This legend is interesting here because the land where roasted fowls fly into your mouth, rivers flow with cream or wine, and sausages with a fork stuck into them run around crying "eat me, eat me!" is obviously an inverted image of the hunger, toil, and violence in the authors' everyday lives. Cockayne is already an inverted parallel world that relates, if not yet to a historical hypothetical possibility organized into institutions, then at least to everyday human needs and not to transcendental doctrines:

> La fiction paralléle, la préoccupation pour le destin de l'homme et la solution strictement matérialiste sont les trois traits fondamentaux qu'ont en commun l'utopie et la pays de Cocagne. . . .
>
> Le matérialisme ainsi entendu ignore les restrictions mentales et transcende la matière pour la transformer en divinité tutélaire et en providence.[36]
>
> [The parallel fiction, the preoccupation with human destiny and the strictly materialist solution are the three fundamental traits which utopia and Cockayne have in common. . . .
>
> Taken thus, materialism ignores mental restrictions and transcends matter in order to transform it into patron deity and providence.]

35. See Bakhtin's chapter "Banquet Imagery," especially pp. 296–98, and Morton (Bibliography II), pp. 15–27. For some further references to Cockayne see Ackermann, Bonner (both in Bibliography III B), Boas, pp. 167–68, Patch, pp. 51 and 170–71 (both in Bibliography II), Gatz, pp. 116–21, Grauss, Manuel and Manuel (all in Bibliography III B), and note 36.

36. Cioranescu, pp. 57 and 59, but see his whole passage on pp. 55–62, which pre-

Clearly, as Cioranescu notes, this does not jibe with the fundamental utopian context of a neutral nature: but utopia wishes to
achieve by cognitive means and in a context of hypothetically
inflected history what the legend of Cockayne achieved in a pure
wishdream outside the terrible field of history. While still a
folktale, Cockayne can be readily transferred to the vicinity of
utopia by allying its dream to a cognitive context, as in Rabelais.

The *Earthly Paradise* may be even nearer to utopia. Outside
official Christianity, it is as a rule not transhistoric, but can be
reached by an ordinary voyage. It is divided from other lands by
a barrier, which makes it usually an island in the sea—an Island
of the Blessed, as the Greek tradition from time immemorial has
it and as many other writings, anonymous or famous, also know
it, to wit, the Celtic blessed island or Dante's Paradiso Terrestre
in the western sea.[37] Often, especially in versions unaffected by
religious rewriting, the inhabitants are not disembodied, but are
simply more perfect people. The implied critique of the author's
environment is explicated in a whole group of "other world"
tales.[38] The magical or folktale element is clearly present in the
perfect climate, the freedom from cares and strife, and often in
the arrested time on such blessed islands (so that a return from
them entails instant aging or turning to dust). And yet, the proximity of utopia of Terrestrial Paradise in its unbowdlerized versions is impressively indicated by a tale such as that of the
Guarani Land-Without-Evil. That land, also called the House of
Our Ancestress,

> is difficult to reach, but it is located in this world. Although
> . . . it entails paradisiacal dimensions (for instance,

---

sents the best analysis of Cockayne I know of. For connections with satire see also Elliott,
pp. 16–17.

37. A general survey on ideas about the Golden Age, Eden, and Paradise is to be
found in Manuel and Manuel, who, however, fail to make the crucial distinction between
heavenly and earthly paradise. On Greek tales see Bonner, Lovejoy and Boas, the comment in Bloch, chap. 36 (all in Bibliography II), and a number of works from Bibliography III B, especially Gatz, Finley, Pöhlmann, Rohde, and Winston. For medieval tales
and beliefs about localized "other worlds" see Boas, Coli, Graf, "Il Mito del Paradiso
Terrestre," Patch (all in Bibliography II), and a number of works from Bibliography
III B, especially Curtius, Graus, Kampers, Peters, and Westropp; Coli, p. 130, and Patch,
p. 135, comment on the accessibility and material reality of Eden for medieval minds. See
also Giamatti (Bibliography II) for Renaissance echoes.

38. See Patch, p. 128, and Coli, p. 130.

immortality)—the Land-Without-Evil does not belong to the Beyond. . . . One arrives there . . . [not only] in soul or spirit, but in flesh and bones. . . . [It] is thus a world at once real and transfigured, where life continues according to the same familiar model, but . . . without misery or sickness, without sins or injustice, and without age.[39]

Is such a country outside history, as Eliade thinks? It is certainly outside empirical or known history, but it is at the same time an alternative, hypothetically possible, and supremely desirable history on Earth. All the above qualifications could be applied to utopia, not only in my proposed definition but according to most of the quoted definitions too. It lacks only More's great discovery of focusing on sociopolitical institutions and norms as a key to eliminating misery, sickness, and injustice. The usual utopian answer, communal ownership, is here preserved (the Guaranis did not need to attain it) by means of what Bloch calls a "medical utopia" (search for immortality, eternal health, and youth). If not utopia, this is a fraternal genre: an early and primitive branch of SF.

5. COMMENT: UTOPIA AS A MORE PERFECT ORGANIZED COMMUNITY

Finally, the relationships of utopia to other genres of what I have in the earlier chapters called "cognitive estrangement"— SF, pastoral, and nonfictional works—should also be discussed.

This will account for the necessity of all my definitional elements between "verbal construction" and the final clause. Just like Cockayne, the *pastoral* is akin at least to libertarian utopia in its rejection of money economy, cleavage between town and country, and state apparatus. But just like Cockayne, it is primarily a *unomia*, a land without formalized institutions, without organized superstructures of community life.[40] If Cockayne is the land for sensualists, Earthly Paradise for heroes, and pastoral for

---

39. Mircea Eliade, "Paradise and Utopia," in Manuel, ed., pp. 273–75. For paradises located on Earth see also Boas, pp. 154–74, Graf, pp. 15 and 24, and Coli, p. 91; and for the arrival in flesh at Earthly Paradise the Hellenic testimonies in Lovejoy and Boas, pp. 25–30 and 290–303, where further bibliography can also be found.

40. Cioranescu, pp. 60–61.

swains (sheperds as philosophers, poets, and lovers), utopia is the land for naturalistic human figures just slightly larger (more virtuous) than everyday nature.

The definitional element of a *particular* community is necessary, as observed in section 3, in order to differentiate utopia from general beliefs, programs, and unlocalized projects. However, as soon as the blueprints and beliefs become localized and approach a narrative (as in much of the writing of utopian socialists), there is little delimitation provided by any definition of utopia I can think of. The usual escape clause is that utopia is *belles lettres* or fiction, while Saint-Simon or Fourier are *lettres* or nonfiction. But that distinction, though sufficiently normative in the eighteenth-century to allow Swift to base the formal framework of *Gulliver's Travels* on playing with it, is historically a fugitive one. What was the Guarani legend of Land-Without-Evil or Columbus's letter on finding the Terrestrial Paradise beyond the Orinoco for the authors, fiction or nonfiction? And for us? What is, for that matter, the Bible—theology or "literature" in the sense of fiction? The term "literature" has always wavered between a populist or sociological inclusive extreme (everything published in printed form) and an elitist or aesthetical exclusive extreme (only those "belles" works worthy of entering into a normative history of "literature"). In brief, the eighteenth-nineteenth century escape clause does not seem to me to work any longer, since it deals in subjective values and intangible intentions. Suppose it were found that the *Supplement to Bougainville's Voyage* had been written by Bougainville instead of Diderot—would it cease to be utopian? And if Fourier had published his vision of anti-lions and a sea of lemonade with Jules Verne's editor, would it thereby become SF? We are beginning to move in the Borgesian world, where the same text has opposite meanings according to the intention of the author. This is good satiric fun, but any literary theory which can be built upon such premises would have to reject most that we now dignify with such a name. The same dilemma applies to ethnological reports: if literature is not defined by being right or wrong but by illuminating human relationships in certain ways and by certain means, I see no way of delimiting Lévi-Strauss's sequence on myths from fictional literature or belles lettres. Reports on the perfect

Inca empire, it has been argued, had inspired More. This is probably inexact, but such a report, especially if related at second hand, would have been generically indistinguishable from the *Utopia* (although, among other things, surely less witty). If I have argued all along in this chapter for utopia as literature, it is precisely because of such a breakdown in the philosophy of literature. The resulting inchoate mass should at least be judged by taking into account the whole text and not arbitrary essences abstracted from it: as imaginative, though not imaginary.[41]

The definitional element of *quasi-human* refers to such communities as those of Swift's Houyhnhnms, Stapledon's Eighteenth Men (*Homo sapiens* being the First Men), or the numerous aliens and cybernetic intelligences of modern SF.[42] It connotes that utopias are in a strange and not yet clarified way an allegorical genre akin to the parable and analogy. In the parable or analogy, the premises do not have to be realistic as long as the upshot is clear. Thus, utopia is always aimed at human relations, but its characters do not have to be human or even outwardly anthropomorphic. Their relationships and communities, though, will make sense only insofar as they can be judged as similar or dissimilar to human ones.

The element of *community* differentiates utopias on the one hand from "robinsonades," stories of castaways outside of an alternate community.[43] On the other hand, this terminology tries to steer a middle course in the debate which seems to have raged in *Mitteleuropa* between State worshippers and Kantian or anarchist individualists among critics, an echo of which is heard in Krysmanski's Solomonic solution of a "synopsis" of man, society, and history. The "anarchists" (for example, Berneri) stressed the moral behavior of individuals, the "archists" the normative power of institutions. Too narrow an interest in governmental apparatus leads to the deadly boredom of eighteenth-century *Staatsromane* in the narrow sense—say, certain works extolling constitutional monarchies in the South Seas. Too

---

41. Frye, "Varieties of Literary Utopias," p. 32.

42. See e.g. Robert Boguslaw's discussion of men as "operating units" in *The New Utopians* (Englewood Cliffs, NJ, 1965), passim, which effects a witty juxtaposition of utopias and "system design."

43. See Brüggeman (Bibliography II), especially pp. 187–89.

wide a sense of utopia, which with Bloch would embrace medical, biological, technological, erotic, and even philosophical wish-dreams, leads to incorporating Don Juan and Faust, the *Theses on Feuerbach* and *The Magic Flute*, into utopia: a somewhat overweening imperialism. The middle course suggested in what is, I hope, my prudent use of "community where sociopolitical institutions, norms, and individual relationships are organized according to a more perfect principle" (see section 3), focuses on the sociopolitical concern with justice and happiness, on the "radical eudemonism" of utopia's "detailed, serious discussion of political and sociological matters."[44] And if utopia is not a myth valid for all eternity but a historical genre, the acknowledgement of its context in the adjunct "than in the author's community" seems mandatory—most utopias would not be such for most of us today without that adjunct, since one man's perfection is another man's (or class's) terror.

Yet, finally, it cannot be denied that sociopolitical perfection, though I believe it historically crucial in our epoch, is logically only a part of Bloch's spectrum, which extends from alchemy through immortality to omniscience and the Supreme Good. All cognition can become the subject matter of an estranged verbal construction dealing with a particular quasi-human community treated as an alternative history. This "cognitive estrangement" is the basis of the literary genre of SF. Strictly and precisely speaking, utopia is not a genre but the *sociopolitical subgenre of science fiction*. Paradoxically, it can be seen as such only now that SF has expanded into its modern phase, "looking backward" from its englobing of utopia. Further, that expansion was in some not always direct ways a continuation of classical and nineteenth-century utopian literature. Thus, conversely, SF is at the same time wider than and at least collaterally descended from utopia; it is, if not a daughter, yet a niece of utopia—a niece usually ashamed of the family inheritance but unable to escape her genetic destiny. For all its adventure, romance, popularization, and wondrousness, SF can finally be written only between the

44. First quotation from Barthes, p. 86, second from Elliott, p. 110.

utopian and the anti-utopian horizons. All imaginable intelligent life, including ours, can be organized only more or less perfectly. In that sense, utopia (and anti-utopia) is first of all a literary genre; but finally, as Bloch notes, it is a horizon within which humanity is irrevocably collocated. My main point is that without a full, that is, literal and literary, analysis we are bound to oversimplify and miscontrue those horizons. For any sane understanding of utopia, the simple basic fact to start from remains that it is not hypostasis of the Holy Ghost, the *Zeitgeist*, or whatnot, but a literary genre induced from a set of man-made books within a man-made history.

4

SF and the Novum

0. It is often thought that the concept of a literary genre (here SF) can be found directly in the works investigated, that the scholar in such a genre has no need to turn to literary theory since he/she will find the concepts in the texts themselves. True, the concept of SF is in a way inherent in the literary objects—the scholar does not invent it out of whole cloth—but its specific nature and the limits of its use can be grasped only by employing theoretical methods. The concept of SF cannot be extracted intuitively or empirically from the work called thus. Positivistic critics often attempt to do so; unfortunately, the concept at which they arrive is then primitive, subjective, and unstable. In order to determine it more pertinently and delimit it more precisely, it is necessary to educe and formulate the *differentia specifica* of the SF narration. My axiomatic premise in this chapter is that *SF is distinguished by the narrative dominance or hegemony of a fictional "novum" (novelty, innovation) validated by cognitive logic.*

1. THE NOVUM AND COGNITION

1.1 What is the common denominator the presence of which is logically necessary and which has to be hegemonic in a narration in order that we may call it an SF narration? In other words, how can the proper domain of SF be determined, what is the theoretical axis of such a determining? The answering is clouded by the present wave of irrationalism, engendered by the deep structures of the irrational capitalist way of life which has reduced the dominant forms of rationality itself (quantification, reification, exchange value, and so on) to something narrow, dogmatic, and sterile inasmuch as they are the forms of reasoning of the dominant or of the dominated classes. Nonetheless, I do not see any tenable intrinsic determination of SF which would not hinge on the category of the *novum*, to borrow (and slightly adapt) a term from the best possible source, Ernst Bloch.[1] A novum or cognitive innovation is a totalizing phenomenon or relationship deviating from the author's and implied reader's norm of reality. Now, no doubt, each and every poetic metaphor is a novum, while modern prose fiction has made new insights into man its rallying cry. However, though valid SF has deep affinities with poetry and innovative realistic fiction, its novelty is "totalizing" in the sense that it entails a change of the whole universe of the tale, or at least of crucially important aspects thereof (and that it is therefore a means by which the whole tale can be analytically grasped). As a consequence, the essential tension of SF is one between the readers, representing a certain number of types of Man of our times, and the encompassing and at least equipollent Unknown or Other introduced by the novum. This tension in turn estranges the empirical norm of the implied reader (more about this later). Clearly the novum is a mediating category whose explicative potency springs from its rare bridging of literary and extraliterary, fictional and empirical, formal and ideological domains, in brief from its unalienable historicity. Conversely, this makes it impossible to give a static definition of it, since it is always codetermined by the unique, not to be anticipated situationality and processuality that it is supposed to designate and illuminate. But it is possible to distinguish various dimensions of the novum. Quantitatively, the postulated innovation can be of quite different degrees of magnitude, running from the minimum of one discrete new "invention" (gadget, technique, phenomenon, relationship) to the maximum of a setting (spatiotemporal locus), agent (main character or characters), and/or relations basically new and unknown in the author's environment. (Tangentially I might say that this environment is always identifiable from the text's historical semantics, always bound to a particular time, place, and sociolinguistic norm, so that what would have been utopian or technological SF in a given epoch is not necessarily such in another—except when read as a product of earlier history; in other words, the novum can help us understand just how is SF a *historical* genre.)

1.2 The novum is postulated on and validated by the post-

---

1. In particular: Ernst Bloch, *Das Prinzip Hoffnung* (Bibliography II) and *Experimentum Mundi* (Frankfurt, 1976).

Cartesian and post-Baconian scientific *method*. This does not mean that the novelty is primarily a matter of scientific facts or even hypotheses; and insofar as the opponents of the old popularizing Verne-to-Gernsback orthodoxy protest against such a narrow conception of SF they are quite right. But they go too far in denying that what differentiates SF from the "supernatural" literary genres (mythical tales, fairy tales, and so on, as well as horror and/or heroic fantasy in the narrow sense) is the presence of scientific cognition as the sign or correlative of a method (way, approach, atmosphere, sensibility) identical to that of a modern philosophy of science.[2] Science in this wider sense of methodically systematic cognition cannot be disjoined from the SF innovation, in spite of fashionable currents in SF criticism of the last 15 years—though it should conversely be clear that a proper analysis of SF cannot focus on its ostensible scientific *content* or scientific data. Indeed, a very useful distinction between "naturalistic" fiction, fantasy, and SF, drawn by Robert M. Philmus, is that naturalistic fiction does not require scientific explanation, fantasy does not allow it, and SF both requires and allows it.[3]

Thus, if the novum is the necessary condition of SF (differentiating it from naturalistic fiction),[4] the validation of the

2. Beyond the discussion in chapter 1, see also my essays " 'Utopian' and 'Scientific'," *The Minnesota Review* N.S. No. 6 (1976), and "Science and Marxism, Scientism and Marquit," ibidem No. 10 (1978).

3. The distinction is to be found in Robert M. Philmus, "Science Fiction: From its Beginning to 1870," in Barron, ed. (Bibliography I), pp. 5–6. My defining of SF is indebted to some earlier discussions. In particular, I find myself in some respects near to Kingsley Amis's definition in chapter 1 of *New Maps of Hell* (Bibliography I)—with the significant difference of trying to go beyond his evasive basing of the SF innovation "in science or technology, or pseudo-science or pseudo-technology" (p. 18).

4. Works avowedly written within a nonrealistic mode, principally allegory (but also whimsy, satire, and lying tall tale or Münchhauseniade), constitute a category for which the question of whether they possess a novum cannot even be posed, because they do not use the new worlds, agents, or relationships as coherent albeit provisional ends, but as *immediately transitive* and *narratively nonautonomous* means for *direct* and *sustained* reference to the author's empirical world and some system of belief in it. The question whether an allegory is SF, and vice versa, is, strictly speaking, meaningless, but for classifying purposes has to be answered in the negative. This means that—except for exceptions and grey areas—most of the works of Kafka or Borges cannot be claimed for SF: though I would argue that *In the Penal Colony* and "The Library of Babel" would be among the exceptions. But admittedly, much more work remains to be done toward the theory of modern allegory in order to render more precise the terms underlined in this note (see also section 2.2. of this chapter).

novelty by scientifically methodical cognition into which the reader is inexorably led is the *sufficient* condition for SF. Though such cognition obviously cannot, in a work of verbal fiction, be empirically tested either in the laboratory or by observation in nature, it *can* be methodically developed against the background of a body of already existing cognitions, or at the very least as a "mental experiment" following accepted scientific, that is, cognitive, logic. Of the two, the second alternative—the intrinsic, culturally acquired cognitive logic—seems theoretically the crucial one to me. Though I would be hard put to cite an SF tale the novelty in which is not in fact continuous with or at least analogous to existing scientific cognitions, I would be disposed to accept theoretically a faint possibility of a fictional novum that would at least seem to be based on quite new, imaginary cognitions, beyond all real possibilities known or dreamt of in the author's empirical reality. (My doubts here are not so much theoretical as psychological, for I do not see how anybody could imagine something not even dreamt of by anyone else before; but then I do not believe in individualistic originality.) But besides the "real" possibilities there exist also the much stricter—though also much wider—limits of "ideal" possibility, meaning any conceptual or thinkable possibility the premises and/or consequences of which are not internally contradictory.[5] Only in "hard" or near-future SF does the tale's thesis have to conform to a "real possibility"—to that which is possible in the author's reality and/or according to the scientific paradigm of his culture. On the contrary, the thesis of *any* SF tale has to conform to an "ideal possibility," as defined above. Any tale based on a metaphysical wish-dream—for example omnipotence—is "ideally impossible" as a coherent narration (can an omnipotent being create a stone it will not be able to lift? and so forth), according to the cognitive logic that human beings have acquired in their culture from the beginnings to the present day. It is intrinsically or by definition impossible for SF to acknowledge any metaphysical agency, in the literal sense of an agency going beyond *physis* (nature). Whenever it does so, it is not SF, but a metaphysical or (to translate the Greek into Latin) a supernatural fantasy-tale.

5.   I have been stimulated by the discussion of Ivan Foht, "Slika čovjeka i kosmosa," *Radio Beograd: Treći program* (Spring 1974): 523–60.

1.3. Thus science is the encompassing horizon of SF, its "initiating and dynamizing motivation."[6] I reemphasize that this does not mean that SF is "scientific fiction" in the literal, crass, or popularizing sense of gadgetry-cum-utopia/dystopia. Indeed, a number of important clarifications ought immediately to be attached: I shall mention three. A first clarification is that "horizon" is not identical to "ideology." Our view of reality or conceptual horizon is, willy-nilly, determined by the fact that our existence is based on the application of science(s), and I do not believe we can imaginatively go beyond such a horizon; a machineless Arcadia is today simply a microcosm with zero-degree industrialization and a lore standing in for zero-degree science. On the other hand, within a scientific paradigm and horizon, ideologies can be and are either fully supportive of this one and only imaginable state of affairs, or fully opposed to it, or anything in between. Thus, anti-scientific SF is just as much within the scientific horizon (namely a misguided reaction to repressive —capitalist or bureaucratic—abuse of science) as, say, literary utopia and anti-utopia both are within the perfectibilist horizon. The so-called speculative fiction (for example, Ballard's) clearly began as and has mostly remained an ideological inversion of "hard" SF. Though the credibility of SF does not depend on the particular scientific rationale in any tale, the significance of the entire fictive situation of a tale ultimately depends on the fact that "the reality that it displaces, and thereby interprets"[7] is interpretable only within the scientific or cognitive horizon.

A second clarification is that *sciences humaines* or historical-cultural sciences like anthropology-ethnology, sociology, or linguistics (that is, the mainly nonmathematical sciences) are equally based on such scientific methods as: the necessity and possibility of explicit, coherent, and immanent or nonsupernatural explanation of realities; Occam's razor; methodical doubt; hypothesis-construction; falsifiable physical or imaginary (thought) experi-

---

6. Jan Trzynadlowski, "Próba poetyki science fiction," in K. Budzyk, ed., *Z teorii i historii literatury* (Warsaw, 1963), p. 272; see also Stanislaw Lem (Bibliography I); Rafail Nudel'man, "Conversation in a Railway Compartment" (Bibliography VI); and Joanna Russ, "Towards an Aesthetic of Science Fiction," in R. D. Mullen and Darko Suvin, eds., *Science-Fiction Studies . . . 1973–1975* (Bibliography I), pp. 8–15.
7. Robert M. Philmus (Bibliography III A), p. 20.

ments; dialectical causality and statistical probability; progressively more embracing cognitive paradigms; *et sim.* These "soft sciences" can therefore most probably better serve as a basis for SF than the "hard" natural sciences; and they *have* in fact been the basis of all better works in SF—partly through the characteristic subterfuge of cybernetics, the science in which hard nature and soft humanities fuse. A third clarification, finally, is that science has since Marx and Einstein been an open-ended corpus of knowledge, so that all imaginable new corpuses which do not contravene the philosophical basis of the scientific method in the author's times (for example, the simulsequentialist physics in Le Guin's *The Dispossessed*) can play the role of scientific validation in SF.

1.4. It may be objected to this that a look into bookstores will show that a good proportion of what is sold as SF is constituted by tales of more or less supernatural or occult fantasy. However, this is the result of an ideological and commercial habit of lumping together SF (fiction whose novum *is* cognitively validated) and fantastic narrative. A misshapen subgenre born of such mingling is that of "science-fantasy," extending from Poe through Merritt to Bradbury, about which I can only repeat the even more pathological level—internalized in fictional creation —this has led to tales that incongruously mingle science-fictional and fantastic narrative. A misshappen subgenre born of such mingling is that of "science-fantasy," extending from Poe through Meritt to Bradbury, about which I can only repeat the strictures of the late James Blish, who noted how in it "plausibility is specifically invoked for most of the story, but may be cast aside in patches at the author's whim and according to no visible system or principle," in "a blind and grateful *abandonment* of the life of the mind."[8] In supernatural fantasy proper, the supposed novelty rejects cognitive logic and claims for itself a higher "occult" logic—whether Christian, a-Christian and indeed atheistic (as is the case of H. P. Lovecraft), or, most usually, an

8. William Atheling, Jr., *More Issues at Hand* (Bibliography I), pp. 98 and 104. A further warning in the same chapter that the hybrid of SF and detective tale leads—as I would say, because of the incompatibility between the detective tale's contract of informative closure with the reader and the manifold surprises inherent in the SF novum system—to a trivial lower common denominator of the resulting tale has so far been developed only by Rafail Nudel'man (see note 20).

opportunistic blend of both, openly shown in the more self-confident nineteenth century by something like Marie Corelli's "Electric Christianity" (the enormous popularity of which is echoed right down to C. S. Lewis). The consistent supernatural fantasy tale—one which does not employ only a single irruption of the supernatural into everyday normality, as in Gogol's *Nose* or Balzac's *Peau de Chagrin*, but develops the phenomenology of the supernatural at the expense of the tension with everyday norm—is usually (in England from Bulwer-Lytton on) a proto-Fascist revulsion against modern civilization, materialist rationalism, and such. It is organized around an ideology unchecked by any cognition, so that its narrative logic is simply overt ideology plus Freudian erotic patterns. If SF exists at all, this is not it.

One of the troubles with distinctions in genre theory is, of course, that literary history is full of "limit-cases." Let us briefly examine one of considerable importance, Stevenson's *The Strange Case of Dr. Jekyll and Mr. Hyde*. Despite my respect for Stevenson's literary craftsmanship, I would contend that he is cheating in terms of his basic narrative logic. On the one hand, his moral allegory of good and evil takes bodily form with the help of a chemical concoction. On the other, the transmogrification Jekyll-Hyde becomes not only unrepeatable because the concoction had unknown impurities, but Hyde also begins "returning" without any chemical stimulus, by force of desire and habit. This unclear oscillation between science and fantasy, where science is used for a partial justification or added alibi for those readers who would no longer be disposed to swallow a straightforward fantasy or moral allegory, is to my mind the reason for the elaborate, clever, but finally not satisfying exercise in detection from various points of view—which in naturalistic fashion masks but does not explain the fuzziness at the narrative nucleus. This marginal SF is therefore, to my mind, an early example of "science fantasy." Its force does not stem from any cognitive logic, but rather from Jekyll's anguish over his loss of control and from the impact of the hidden but clearly underlying moral allegory. The latter is particularly relevant to Victorian bourgeois repressions of the nonutilitarian or nonofficial aspects of life and it also holds forth an unsubstantiated promise that the oscillation between SF and fantasy does not matter since we are dealing with full-blown allegory anyway (see note 4).

2. Narrative Consequences of the Novum

2.1. The presence of the novum as the determining factor of
an SF narration is crucially testable in its explanatory power for
the basic narrative strategies in this genre. First of all, the dominance or hegemony of the cognitive novelty means that an SF
narration is not only a tale that includes this or that SF element
or aspect: utopian strivings or dystopian terrors of some kind, as
in the majority of world literature; moral allegories or transcendental visions of other worlds, better or worse from our
own, as in much literature down to Milton, Swedenborg, and
countless imitators; use of new technological gadgets, as in many
James Bond tales; and so on. An SF narration is a fiction in
which the SF element or aspect, the novum, is hegemonic, that is,
so central and significant that it determines the whole narrative
logic—or at least the overriding narrative logic—regardless of
any impurities that might be present.[9]

2.2. Furthermore, the novum intensifies and radicalizes that
movement across the boundary of a semantic field (defined by
the author's cultural norm) which always constitutes the fictional
event.[10] In "naturalistic" fiction this boundary is iconic and
isomorphic: the transgression of the cultural norm stands for a
transgression of the cultural norm; Mme. Bovary's adultery
stands for adultery. In SF, or at least in its determining events, it
is not iconic but allomorphic: a transgression of the cultural
norm is signified by the transgression of a more than merely

---

9. A major objection against so-called thematic studies of SF elements and aspects,
from J. O. Bailey's *Pilgrims Through Space and Time* (Bibliography I)—in 1947 no doubt a
pioneering work—to present-day atomistic and positivistic SF critics, is that these studies
ignore the determining feature of what they are studying: the narrative logic of a fictional tale. Correlatively, they tend to become boring catalogs of raisins picked out of the
narrative cake, and completely desiccated in the process. This does not mean that critical
discussions of, say, artificial satellites, biological mutations, or new sexual mores in SF (or
other fiction) cannot be, for some strictly limited purposes, found useful; and for such
purposes we should probably know where the mutations, satellites, or sex patterns first
appeared and how they spread. But we should not be lured by this very peripheral
necessity into annexing any and every tale with a new gadget or psychic procedure into
SF, as, for example, Bailey did with Wilkie Collins's *Moonstone* and Thomas Hardy's *Two
on a Tower*. SF scholarship that does this is sawing off the branch on which it is sitting: for
if these and such works are SF just like, say, Wells's *Invisible Man*, then in fact there is no
such thing as SF.

10. Jurij Lotman, *The Structure of the Artistic Text*, Michigan Slavic Contributions No.
7 (Ann Arbor, 1977), pp. 229 ff.

cultural, of an ontological, norm, by an ontic change in the character/agent's reality either because of his displacement in space and/or time or because the reality itself changes around him. I do not know a better characterization than to say that the novelty makes for the SF narration's specific *ontolytic* effect and properties. Or perhaps—since, as differentiated from fantasy tale or mythological tale, SF does not posit another superordinated and "more real" reality but an alternative on the same ontological level as the author's empirical reality—one should say that the necessary correlate of the novum is an *alternate reality*, one that possesses a *different historical time* corresponding to different human relationships and sociocultural norms actualized by the narration. This new reality overtly or tacitly presupposes the existence of the author's empirical reality, since it can be gauged and understood only as the empirical reality modified in such-and-such ways. Though I have argued that SF is not—by definition cannot be—an orthodox allegory with any one-to-one correspondence of its elements to elements in the author's reality, its specific modality of existence is a feedback oscillation that moves now from the author's and implied reader's norm of reality to the narratively actualized novum in order to understand the plot-events, and now back from those novelties to the author's reality, in order to see it afresh from the new perspective gained. This oscillation, called estrangement by Shklovsky and Brecht, is no doubt a consequence of every poetic, dramatic, scientific, in brief *semantic* novum. However, its second pole is in SF a narrative reality sufficiently autonomous and intransitive to be explored at length as to its own properties and the human relationships it implies. (For though mutants or Martians, ants or intelligent nautiloids can be used as signifiers, they can only signify human relationships, given that we cannot—at least so far—imagine other ones.)

2.3. The oscillation between the author's "zero world" and the new reality induces the narrative necessity of a means of reality displacement. As far as I can see, there are two such devices: a *voyage* to a new locus, and a *catalyzer* transforming the author's environment to a new locus; examples for the two could be Wells's *Time Machine* and *Invisible Man*. The first case seems better suited to a sudden and the second to a gradual introduction of a new reality; no doubt, all kinds of contaminations and twists on these two means are thinkable. When the *in medias res* technique is used in any particular SF tale, the means of displacement can be told in a retrospective or they can, apparently, totally disappear (more easily in a space/time displacement: our hero is simply a native of elsewhere/elsewhen). However, this semblance conceals the presence of displacement in a zero-form, usually as a convention tacitly extrapolated from earlier stories; the history of the genre is the missing link that made possible, for example, tales in another space/time without any textual reference to that of the author (as in most good SF novels of the last 20 years).

2.4.   The concept of novum illuminates also the historical vicissitudes of justifying the reality displacement. In naturalistic tales the voyage can only start in the author's space, and the account of the new reality has to arrive back into that space so that its telling may be naturalistically plausible. However, it would then be logically necessary that the account of such a sensational voyage to a new reality should in its turn become a catalyzer, inducing changes in the author's and reader's environment. Since this in fact, as the reader knows, has not happened, naturalistic SF has had to invent a number of lightning-rods to dissipate such expectations. Verne pretended not to notice its necessity, while Wells in some of his tales pretended we all knew it already—ploys which today make those narrations sound as if they assumed an alternate time-stream in which Nemo or the Invisible Man had in fact (as different from the reader's time-stream) been the scourge of the seas or of southern England. Many earlier writers went through other extraordinary contortions to satisfy naturalistic plausibility, usually a contamination of the "manuscript in a bottle" device (the news of a voyage to the Moon just having arrived by volcanic eruption from it and just being served piping hot to you, dear reader) and the "lost invention" device (a one-shot novelty confined to the experience of a few people and unable to extend beyond them because of the loss of the invention), as in *The First Men in the Moon*. But the most plausible variable for manipulation was *time*, inasmuch as setting the tale in the future immediately dispensed with any need for empirical plausibility. The shift of SF from space into future time is not simply due to an exhaustion of white spots on the *mappa mundi*. Rather, it is due to an interaction of two factors: on the one hand, such a narrative convenience, stunted within strict positivist ideology; on the other, the strong tendency toward temporal extrapolation inherent in life based on a capitalist economy, with its salaries, profits, and progressive ideals always expected in a future clock-time.

Thus space was a fully plausible locus for SF only before the capitalist way of life, from very early tales about the happy or unhappy valley or island—known to almost all tribal and ancient societies—to More and Swift. An Earthly Paradise or Cockayne tale, a humanist dialogue and satire, all happen in a literary or imaginative space not subject to positivistic plausibility. But a triumphant bourgeoisie introduces an epoch-making epistemological break into human imagination, by which linear or clock-time becomes the space of human development because it is the space of capitalist industrial production. The spatial dominions of even the largest feudal landowner are finite; capital, the new historical form of property—that shaper of human existences and relationships—has in principle no limits in extrapolated time. Through a powerful system of mediations infusing the whole human existence, time becomes finally the equivalent of money and thus of all things. The positivist ideology followed capitalist practice in eventually perfecting an image of time rigidified "into an exactly delimited, quantifiable continuum filled with quantifiable 'things' . . . : in short, [time] becomes space."[11] Imaginative times and spaces are now resolved into "positive," quantified ones. All existential alternatives, for better or worse, shift into such a spatialized future, which now becomes the vast ocean on whose other shore the alternative island is to be situated. Positivism shunts SF into anticipation, a form more activistic than the spatial *exemplum* because achievable in the implied reader's own space. When the industrial revolution becomes divorced from the democratic one—a divorce which is the

---

11.   Georg Lukács, *History and Class Consciousness* (London, 1971), p. 90. The whole seminal essay "Reification and the Consciousness of the Proletariat," developing insights from Marx's *Capital*, is to be consulted; also Georg Simmel, *Philosophie des Geldes* (Munich, 1930), Werner Sombart, *Der Moderne Kapitalismus*, I–II/1 (Munich, 1917), and Lewis Mumford (Bibliography IV A). I have tried to apply Lukács's ideas on quantification and reification in my essays "On Individualist World View in Drama," *Zagadnienia rodzajów literackih* 9, No. 1 (1966), and "Beckett's Purgatory of the Individual," *Tulane Drama Review* 2, No. 4 (1967), and in the historical part of this book, especially in the essay on Verne as the bard of movement in such a quantified space.

fundamental political event of the bourgeois epoch—activism becomes exasperated and leads to the demands for another epistemological and practical break, signalled by Blake's Jerusalem in
England's green and pleasant land and the cosmic "passionate
attraction" of Fourier's phalansteries. Such imaginative energies
converge in Marx, the great prefigurator of the imaginative shift
still being consummated in our times. Rather than identify it as
"postindustrial" (a fairly reified and vague term), I would tend to
call the new *episteme*—since it is in our century marked by names
such as Einstein, Picasso, Eisenstein, and Brecht—one of spatiotemporal covariance, simulsequentialism, or humanist relativism and estrangement: in brief, one of alternate historical
realities. I would argue that in such a historical perspective, all
significant SF from Zamyatin, Čapek, and Lem to Le Guin,
Disch, and Delany is neither simply spatial, as in Lucian or More,
nor simply temporal, as in all the followers of *The Time Machine*
and *When the Sleeper Wakes*, but spatiotemporal in a number of
very interesting ways, all of which approximate a reinvention
and putting to new uses of the precapitalist and preindividualis-
tic analogic times and spaces of the human imagination.

The main difference with such medieval and premedieval con-
ceptions could perhaps be expressed in terms of destiny. As
Lotman remarks, literary functions can be divided into two
groups, the active forces and the obstacles.[12] Right down to Swift
(in SF and in literature in general), the obstacles are inhuman
and superhuman forces, at best to be ethically questioned by the
tragic poet and hero but not to be materially influenced.
Whether they are called gods, God, Destiny, Nature, or even
History is relatively less important than the fact that they are
transcendental, empirically unchangeable. The great enlighten-
ing deed of the bourgeoisie was to reduce the universe to individuals, which also meant identifying the obstacles with men,
who are reachable and perhaps removable by other individual
men. I would imagine that a truly modern literature (and SF),
corresponding to our epoch, its *praxis* and *episteme*, would correspond to the third dialectical term to follow on such fatalistic
collectivism and humanistic individualism. We have learned that
the institutional and imaginative products of men—states, corpo-

12.   Lotman, p. 239.

rations, religions, wars, and the like—can very well become a destiny for each of us: tragedy is again possible in the twentieth century (as the October Revolution and Second World War, Dubček and Allende can teach us), though it is the tragedy of blindness—of failed historical possibilities—rather than of lucidity. The obstacles are superindividual but not inhuman; they have the grandeur of the ancient Destiny but they can be overcome by other men banding together for the purpose. Men are the historical destiny of man; the synthesis in this historical triad is a *humanistic collectivism*.

2.5. The alternate reality logically necessitated by and proceeding from the narrative kernel of the novum can only function in the oscillating feedback with the author's reality suggested in 2.2 because it is as a whole—or because some of its focal relationships are—an *analogy* to that empirical reality. However fantastic (in the sense of empirically unverifiable) the characters or worlds described, always *de nobis fabula narratur*. Though SF is not orthodox allegory, it transmits aesthetic information in direct proportion to its relevance and aesthetic quality. The alternative is for it to operate in semantic emptiness spiced with melodramatic sensationalism as a compensatory satisfaction, in a runaway feedback system with corrupt audience taste instead of with cognition of tendencies in the social practice of human relationships.[13] The clear dominance of that kitsch alternative in the present historical period should not, however, prevent us from discussing the significant models of SF, its horizons and yardsticks.

In my second chapter I considered heuristic models of SF under the headings of (1) extrapolation, which starts from a cognitive hypothesis incarnated in the nucleus of the tale and directly extrapolates it into the future, and (2) analogy, in which

13. "The information gained, concerning a hypothesis, may perhaps be thought of as the ratio of the a posteriori to the a priori probabilities (strictly the logarithm of this ratio)"—Colin Cherry, *On Human Communication* (Cambridge, MA, 1966), p. 63. Thus, the information gained from a work of literature is a logarithmic (that is, alas, much diminished) ratio of the existential possibilities imaginable and understandable by an ideal reader after reading, to those imaginable and understandable before the reading. The information is a function of the rearrangement of the reader's understanding of human relationships. "In general, where we speak of information, we should use the word form," argues René Thom in his impressive *Stabilité structurelle et morphogénèse* (Reading, MA, 1972), p. 133.

cognition derives only from the final import or message of the
tale, and may perhaps be only indirectly applicable to pressing
problems in the author's environment. This analysis is, so far as
it goes, useful in challenging the defining of all SF as extrapolation (to which the title of a critical journal devoted to SF still
witnesses); but it does not go far enough. In that chapter I also
noted that any futurological function SF might have was strictly
secondary, and that stressing it was dangerous since it tended to
press upon SF the role of a popularizer of the reigning ideology
of the day (technocratic, psionic, utopian, dystopian, hip, or
whatever). Thus, although extrapolation was historically a convention of much SF (as analyzed at length in the second section of
this book), pure extrapolation is flat, and the pretense at it masks
in all significant cases the employment of other methods.
Theoretical defining of any SF as extrapolation should therefore
be decently and deeply buried.[14] It seems clear that SF is material for futurology (if at all) only in the very restricted sense of
reflecting on the author's own historical period and the possibilities inherent in it: Bellamy's and Morris's different socialist
twenty-first centuries use the anticipation device so effectively
because they are about incipient collective human relationships
in the 1880s as they (differently) saw them, while *1984* or *2001*
are about incipient collective human relationships in 1948 or
1967 as certain aspects of or elements within Orwell's or Ku-
brick's mind saw them.

Any significant SF text is thus always to be read as an analogy,
somewhere between a vague symbol and a precisely aimed parable, while extrapolative SF in any futurological sense was (and is)
only a delusion of technocratic ideology—no doubt extremely
important for the historical understanding of a given period of
SF, but theoretically untenable. For extrapolation itself as a scientific procedure (and not pure arithmetic formalization) is predicated upon a strict (or, if you wish, crude) analogy between
the points from and to which the extrapolating is carried out:
extrapolation is a one-dimensional, scientific limit-case of analogy. As
Peirce put it, a scientific "effect" (or "phenomenon") "consists in

14. Wells knew this already in 1906, see note 19 in my chapter 10 and the self-
criticism it refers to. On the discussion of extrapolative, analogical, and other models for
SF see also Philmus, note 3, and Fredric Jameson, "Generic Discontinuities in SF" and
"World Reduction in Le Guin," both in Mullen and Suvin, eds., pp. 28–39 and 251–60.

the fact that when an experimentalist shall come to *act* ACCORD-
ING TO A CERTAIN SCHEME THAT HE HAS IN MIND [caps but not
italics mine], then will something else happen, and shatter the
doubts of sceptics, like the celestial fire upon the altar of
Elijah."[15] Specifically, the SF "future-story" has been well identified by Raymond Williams as

> the finding and materialization of a *formula* about society. A
> particular pattern is abstracted, from the sum of social ex-
> perience, and a society is created from this pattern . . . the
> "future" device (usually only a device, for nearly always it is
> obviously contemporary society that is being written about
> . . .) removes the ordinary tension between the selected
> pattern and normal observation.[16]

Clearly, neither is the future a quantitatively measurable space
nor will the ensemble of human relationships stand still for
one or more generations in order for a single element (or a
very few elements) to be extrapolated against an unchanging
background—which is the common invalidating premise of
futurological as well as of openly fictional extrapolation. The
future is always constituted both by a multiple crisscrossing of
developments and—in human affairs—by intentions, desires,
and beliefs rather than only by quantifiable facts. It is Peirce's
scheme or Williams's pattern rather than the end-point of a line.

Furthermore, anticipating the future of human societies and
relationships is a pursuit that shows up the impossibility of using
the orthodox—absolute or scientistic—philosophy of natural science as the model for human sciences. It is a pursuit which
shows, first, that all science (including natural sciences) is and
always has been a historical category, and second, that natural or
"objective" and human (cultural) or "subjective" sciences are ultimately to be thought of as a unity: "Natural science will in time
include the science of man as the science of man will include
natural science. There will be *one* science"—remarked an acute
observer already in the first part of the nineteenth century.[17] As

15. Charles Sanders Peirce, "What Pragmatism Is," *Collected Papers*, ed. Charles
Hartshorne and Paul Weiss (Cambridge, MA, 1934), para. 425, p. 284.

16. Raymond Williams, *The Long Revolution* (Harmondsworth, 1971), p. 307.

17. Karl Marx, "Private Property and Communism," *Writings of the Young Marx on
Philosophy and Society*, ed. Loyd D. Easton and Kurt H. Guddat (Garden City, NY, 1967),
p. 312.

a corollary, the valid SF form or subgenre of *anticipation*—tales located in the historical future of the author's society—should be strictly differentiated from the technocratic ideology of extrapolation on the one hand and the literary device of extrapolation on the other. Extrapolating one feature or possibility of the author's environment may be a legitimate literary device of hyperbolization equally in anticipation-tales, other SF (for example, that located in space and not in the future), or indeed in a number of other genres such as satire. However, the cognitive value of all SF, including anticipation-tales, is to be found in its analogical reference to the author's present rather than in predictions, discrete or global. Science-fictional cognition is based on an aesthetic hypothesis akin to the proceedings of satire or pastoral rather than those of futurology or political programs.

The problem in constructing useful models for SF is, then, one of differentiating *within* analogy. If every SF tale is some kind of analogy—and I think that *The Time Machine* or *The Iron Heel*, Heinlein's *Future History* or Pohl-Kornbluth's *Space Merchants*, even Stapledon's *Last and First Men* or Yefremov's *Andromeda*, are primarily fairly clear analogies to processes incubating in their author's epoch—then just what is in each case the degree and the kind of its anamorphic distortion, its "version" of reality? How is their implied reader supposed to respond to and deal with a narrative reality that is an inverted, reverted, converted, everted, averted, subverted Other to his certainties of Self and Norm—certainties which, as Hegel says, are clouded by their very illusion of evidence and proximity, *bekannt* but not *erkannt*?[18] A partially illuminating answer to this group of questions would also clear up why some of these versions pretend—sometimes with conviction, most often by pure convention—to be situated in an extrapolated future.

2.6. A final narrative consequence of the novum is that it shapes the SF "chronotope" (or chronotopes?). A chronotope is "the essential connection of temporal and spatial relationships, as shaped in literary art." In it, "the characteristics of time are unfolded in space, while space is given meaning and measured by

---

18. Georg Wilhelm Friedrich Hegel, *Phänomenologie des Geistes. Sämtliche Werke* (Leipzig, 1949), 2:28.

time"[19]—and both are blended into a particular plot structure. Now the novelty in SF can be either a new locus, or an agent (character) with new powers transforming the old locus, or a blend of both. The connection between the active forces (the protagonist[s]) and the obstacles to be reduced (the locus) determines the homogeneity of a tale. If the protagonists and the loci necessarily imply and richly reinforce each other—as do Wells's Time Traveller and the sequence of his devolutionary visions of the future, or Le Guin's Shevek, his physics, and the binary planetary sociopolitics and psychology of *The Dispossessed*—then we have a tale of a higher quality than the wish-dreams of, say, a Van Vogt, where all the obstacles are fake since the protagonist is a superman enforcing his will both on enemies and supposed allies.

As for plot structures, if SF is organized around an irreversible and significant change in its world and agents, then a simple addition of adventures, where *plus ça change plus c'est la même chose*, is an abuse of SF for purposes of trivial sensationalism, which degrades the genre to a simpler and less organized plot structure. Nudelman has to my mind brilliantly demonstrated the incompatibility of the plot structure of the cyclical detective tale, the conclusion of which returns the universe "to its equilibrium and order," the linear structures of the additive adventure tale, and the spiral structures of valid SF, the plot of which alters the universe of the tale.[20] On the contrary, the easiest narrative way of driving a significant change home is to have the hero or heroine grow into it (or better, to have the hero or heroine define it for the reader by growing with it), and much valid SF uses the plot structure of the "education novel," with its initially naive protagonist who by degrees arrives at some understanding of the novum for her/himself and for the readers.

As these two examples and other discussions in this chapter may indicate, it should be possible to engage in analytic evaluations of SF that would be neither purely ideological nor purely formalistic, by starting with the necessities of literary structure brought about by some variant of a novum.

19. M. Bakhtin, *Voprosy literatury i èstetiki* (Moscow, 1975), pp. 234–35.
20. Rafail Nudel'man, "An Approach to the Structure of Le Guin's SF," in Mullen and Suvin, eds., pp. 240–50.

3. The Novum and History

3.1   The novum as a creative, and especially as an aesthetic, category is not be fully or even centrally explained by such formal aspects as innovation, surprise, reshaping, or estrangement, important and indispensable though these aspects or factors are.[21] The new is always a *historical* category since it is always determined by historical forces which both bring it about in social practice (including art) and make for new semantic meanings that crystallize the novum in human consciousnesses (see 1.1 and 2.2) An analysis of SF is necessarily faced with the question of why and how was the newness recognizable as newness at the moment it appeared, what ways of understanding, horizons, and interests were implicit in the novum and required for it. The novelty is sometimes directly but sometimes in very complex ways (for example, not merely as reflection but also as prefiguration or negation) related to such new historical forces and patterns—in the final instance, to possibilities of qualitative discontinuity in the development of human relationships. An aesthetic novum is either a translation of historical cognition and ethics *into* form, or (in our age perhaps more often) a creation of historical cognition and ethics *as* form.

3.2.   Probably the most important consequence of an understanding of SF as a symbolic system centered on a novum which is to be cognitively validated within the narrative reality of the tale and its interaction with reader expectations is that the novelty has to be convincingly explained in concrete, even if imaginary, terms, that is, in terms of the *specific* time, place, agents, and cosmic and social totality of each tale. This means that, in principle, SF has to be judged, like most naturalistic or "realistic" fiction and quite unlike horror fantasy, by the density and richness of objects and agents described in the microcosm of the text. Another way of interpreting the Philmus distinction from 1.2. would be to set up a further Hegelian triad, where the thesis would be naturalistic fiction, which has an empirically validated effect of reality, the antithesis would be supernatural

---

21. See, for development of estrangement and similar notions after the Formalists and Brecht, Hans Robert Jauss, *Literaturgeschichte als Provokation* (Frankfurt, 1970), as well as critiques of and improvements on Jauss handily asembled in Peter Uwe Hohendahl, ed., *Sozialgeschichte und Wirkungsästhetik* (Frankfurt, 1974).

genres, which lack such an effect, and the synthesis would be SF, in which the effect or reality is validated by a cognitive innovation. Obversely, the particular essential novum of any SF tale must in its turn be judged by how much new insight into imaginary but coherent and this-worldly, that is, *historical*, relationships it affords and could afford.

3.3 In view of this doubly historical character of the SF novum—born in history and judged in history—this novum has to be differentiated not only according to its degree of magnitude and of cognitive validation (see 1.1. and 1.2.), but also according to its *degree of relevance*. What is *possible* should be differentiated not only from what is already real but also from what is equally empirically unreal but *necessary*. Not all possible novelties will be equally relevant, or of equally lasting relevance, from the point of view of, first, human development, and second, a positive human development. Obviously, this categorization implies, first, that there are some lawlike tendencies in men's social and cosmic history, and second, that we can today (if we are intelligent and lucky enough) judge these tendencies as parts of a spectrum that runs from positive to negative. I subscribe to both these propositions and will not argue them here—partly for rhetorical convenience, but mainly because I cannot think of any halfway significant SF narration that does not in some way subscribe to them in its narrative practice (whatever the author's private theories may be).

Thus a novum can be both superficially sweeping and cognitively validated as not impossible, and yet of very limited or brief relevance. Its relationship to a relevant novelty will be the same as the relationship of the yearly pseudo-novum of "new and improved" (when not "revolutionary") car models or clothing fashions to a really radical novelty such as a social revolution and change of scientific paradigm making, say, for life-enhancing transport or dressing. The pseudo-novum will not have the vitality of a tree, an animal species, or a belief but, to quote Bergson, the explosive, spurting *élan* of a howitzer shell exploding into successively smaller fragments, or "of an immense fireworks, which continually emits further firesparks from its midst."[22] In brief, a novum is fake unless it in some way partici-

22. Henri Bergson, *L'évolution créatrice* (Paris, 1907), pp. 99 and 270; see also Bloch's

pates in and partakes of what Bloch called the "front-line of historical process"—which for him (and for me) as a Marxist means a process intimately concerned with strivings for a dealienation of men and their social life. Capricious contingencies, consequent upon market competition and tied to copyright or patent law, have a built-in limit and taboo defined precisely by the untouchable sanctity of competition (a palpable ideology in much SF). Of brief and narrow relevance, particular rather than general (*kath'hekaston* rather than *kath'holon*, as Aristotle puts it in *Poetics*), they make for a superficial change rather than for a true novelty that deals with or makes for human relationships so qualitatively different from those dominant in the author's reality that they cannot be translated back to them merely by a change of costume. All space operas can be translated back into the Social Darwinism of the Westerns and similar adventure-tales by substituting colts for ray-guns and Indians for the slimy monsters of Betelgeuse. Most novels by Asimov can be returned to their detective-story model by a slightly more complex system of substitutions, by which, for example, Second Foundation came from Poe's Purloined Letter.

3.4. Since freedom is the possibility of something new and truly different coming about, "the possibility of making it different,"[23] the distinction between a true and fake novum is, interestingly enough, not only a key to aesthetic quality in SF but also to its ethico-political liberating qualities. As always in art, ethical pathos and effect or communal (political) relevance are the obverse of aesthetic consistency. They fuse in the realization that, finally, the only consistent novelty is one that constitutes an open-ended system "which possesses its novum continually both in itself and before itself; as befits the unfinished state of the world, nowhere determined by any transcendental supraworldly formula."[24] This connects with my argument in 1.3. about valida-

---

comment on him in *Das Prinzip Hoffnung*, p. 231—my whole argument in 3.1.–3.4. is fundamentally indebted to Bloch. See on originality within a capitalist market also Bertolt Brecht, *Gesammelte Werke* (Frankfurt, 1973), 1–20, passim—for example, 15:199–200— and Theodor W. Adorno, *Aesthetische Theorie* (Frankfurt, 1970), pp. 257 ff.

23. Bloch, *Experimentum*, p. 139; see also Antonio Gramsci, *Il Materialismo storico e la filosofia di Benedetto Croce* (Torino, 1948), quoted from *Selections from the Prison Notebooks*, ed. Quintin Hoare and Geoffrey Nowell Smith (New York, 1971), p. 360, to whom I am also much indebted.

24. Bloch, *Experimentum*, p. 143.

tion for SF being based on science as an open-ended corpus of knowledge, which argument can now be seen to be ultimately and solidly anchored to the bedrock fact that there is no end to history, and in particular that we and our ideologies are not the end-product history has been laboring for from the time of the first saber-toothed tigers and Mesopotamian city-states. It follows that SF will be the more significant and truly relevant the more clearly it eschews final solutions, be they the static utopia of the Plato-More model, the more fashionable static dystopia of the Huxley-Orwell model, or any similar metamorphosis of the *Apocalypse* (let us remember that the end of time in the *Apocalypse* encompasses not only the ultimate chaos but also the ultimate divine order).[25]

3.5. An imaginary history each time to be reimagined afresh in its human significance and values may perhaps borrow some narrative patterns from mythological tales, but the "novelty" of gods validated by unexplained supersciences at the beck of the Cambridge School's or von Däniken's supermortals is a pseudo-novelty, old meat rehashed with a new sauce. SF's analogical historicity may or may not be mythomorphic, but—as I have argued in chapter 2—it cannot be mythopoetic in any sense except the most trivial one of possessing "a vast sweep" or "a sense of wonder": another superannuated slogan of much SF criticism due for a deserved retirement into the same limbo as extrapolation. For myth is reenactment, eternal return, and the opposite of a creative human freedom.

True, even after one subtracts the more or less supernatural tales (science-fantasy, sword-and-sorcery, and the like,) 90 percent of SF will have plot structures escaping from history into Westerns, additive sensationalist adventures, or rehashes of mythography. However, as Kant said, a thousand years of any given state of affairs do not make that state necessarily right. Rather, reasons for the wrongness should be sought.

3.6 Thus this analysis has finally arrived at the point where history, in the guise of analogical historicity, is found to be the

25. I have attempted to expand on this in my "The Open-Ended Parables of Stanislaw Lem and *Solaris*," afterword to Stanislaw Lem, *Solaris* (New York, 1976); it is incorporated into a parallel to the orthodox Soviet and American SF models in my "Stanislaw Lem und das mitteleuropäische soziale Bewusstsein der Science Fiction," in Werner Berthel, ed., *Insel Almanach auf das Jahr 1976: Stanislaw Lem* (Frankfurt, 1976).

next and crucial step in the understanding of SF: story is always also history, and SF is always also a certain type of imaginative historical tale (which could be usefully compared and contrasted to the historical novel). All the epistemological, ideological, and narrative implications and correlatives of the novum lead to the conclusion that significant SF is in fact a specifically roundabout way of commenting on the author's collective context—often resulting in a surprisingly concrete and sharp-sighted comment at that. Even where SF suggests—sometimes strongly—a flight from that context, this is an optical illusion and epistemological trick. The escape is, in all such significant SF, one to a better vantage point from which to comprehend the human relations around the author. It is an escape from constrictive old norms into a different and alternative timestream, a device for historical estrangement, and an at least initial readiness for new norms of reality, for the novum of dealienating human history. I believe that the critic, in order to understand it properly, will have to integrate sociohistorical into formal knowledge, diachrony into synchrony. History has not ended with the "post-industrial" society: as Bloch said, Judgment Day is also Genesis, and Genesis is every day.

II

HISTORY

Introduction to Older SF History

Let's be realistic—let's demand the impossible.
Anonymus Sorbonensis (May 1968)

The history of science fiction, as the genre is defined in the first part of this book, gives rise to a number of significant and fascinating problems, which can in the present state of our knowledge be rather identified than resolved. One problem is the appearance of what seem to be temporal groupings or clusters—periods with a noticeably higher frequency of SF texts, separated from each other by gaps with a statistically significant lower frequency of SF texts. I am, alas, incompetent to even enter into tribal and extra-European narrative traditions (such as the Chinese one) and their independent but rich histories.[1] But the Euro-Mediterranean tradition alone, of which this second part wishes to give a partial and abbreviated overview, consists—so far as we can now tell—most probably of six clusters: the Hellenic one (from folk myths and legends reactualized in Aeschylus and Aristophanes to Plato, Theopompus, Euhemerus, Hecataeus, and Iambulus), the Hellenistic-cum-Roman one (from Virgil to Antonius Diogenes and Lucian), the Renaissance-Baroque or Columbus-to-Louis-XIV one (ca. 1500–1660), the cluster of the democratic revolution (mainly 1770–1820), the fin-de-siècle cluster (ca. 1870–1910), and the modern SF cluster in the last 50 years or so. In the meantime, in periods of absolutist practice and world view—be they Ptolemaic or Newtonian—the subversive tradition of SF was driven underground (for example, the oral literature, apocrypha, and heretical writings of the Middle Ages) or into exile (French SF between the Fronde and the Encyclopedists; or the "lowbrow" and juvenile magazines and novels of the century after Frankenstein, *from which Verne, the utopias grouped around Bellamy, and Wells emerge as volcanic archipelagos from an ocean). Not all of this is quite clear, because SF (if one agrees to this name for the genre grouping alternative historical worlds) has been a suppressed and neglected, often materially and most always ideologically persecuted tradition: it is hardly an accident that except for conservatives such as Aeschylus, Aristophanes, and Plato its first two clusters survive*

---

1.   See Simon in Bibliography III A, and Bauer, Chesneaux, and Nuita in Bibliography III B.

only in fragments and references, or that from Kepler, Francis Godwin, and Cyrano to Mark Twain its texts often had to be published posthumously.

Thus both modern and older SF are only now beginning to be identified in scholarly bibliographies, and it is possible we will find out that its historical frequency is perceptibly higher. Nonetheless, I do not believe that new data will substantially affect the basic cultural hypothesis of a coherent literary tradition of SF as part of a popular literature that (like many forms of humor and "obscenity") spread through centuries by word of mouth and other unofficial channels, and penetrated into officially accepted, normative, or "high" Literature and Culture only at favorable historical moments. (For example, evidence is emerging about the possibly high incidence of utopias and marvelous voyages in the period 1660–1770, but when these works were not rendered more or less harmless by the author's timidity, as in the cases of Paltock or Fénelon, they were forbidden by the authorities, as in the cases of Foigny or Vairasse.) However, those works which did break through the surface of officially recorded and recordable "higher" culture almost by definition had to be significant; their resonance and echoes were certainly sufficient to establish an apparently tenuous yet potent and lucidly self-conscious intellectual and formal tradition. Plato, Lucian, More, Rabelais, Swift, Diderot, Verne—writers who succeeded in breaking through because of superior personal talent, or cunning and luck in finding an interstitial political time and social space in which to go public, or (usually) a combination of both factors—are therefore not merely among the fountainheads and transmitters of that tradition. Even more importantly, in view of the largely suppressed SF tradition, the achievement of each such major writer not only has to but also legitimately can indicate and stand for the possibilities of a largely mute inglorious epoch. (In this book, the first two European clusters will be dealt with only obliquely, through their effect on the Renaissance.) No doubt this perverts somewhat what "really happened" in cultural and literary history, but no more so than any historical investigation, dealing, as it must always, with a choice from whatever data have survived rather than wie es eigentlich gewesen (how it really was). An ideal history—especially a history of culture—would have to be a geology, interested perhaps as much in the hollows produced by absence of data as in the fullnesses produced by their presence, or a geography of the ocean depths as much as of the visible islands. I confess that this book is not such an ideal, although I propose to suggest how SF, sustained by subordinate social groups with which it achieves and loses cultural legitimacy, is like an iceberg showing only a fraction above the silent surface of officially recorded culture, and how the islands limn not only themselves but also the oceans from which they grow.

It could be argued that SF always fuses the old rhetorical trope of "the impossibilities" (impossibilia) with the equally venerable notion of the wished-for country into a new and fertile form in which autonomous worlds are opposed to the author's empirical environment and its norms; and that, historically, at least the initial impulse for SF comes always from the yearnings of a repressed social group and testifies to radically other possibilities of life. Nonetheless, the different historical functions and purposes in the various clusters have molded the SF tradition into different subgenres. Its central watershed is around 1800, when space loses its monopoly upon the location of estrangement and the alternative horizons shift from space to time (however this shift might be curbed by ideological hesitations about a truly different future). Some reasons for the shift to anticipation have been brought forward in chapter 4, and its meaning will be further discussed from the beginning of chapter 6 on.

5

The Alternative Island

The really philosophical writers invent the true, by analogy. . . .
Honoré de Balzac

1. The Sociopolitics of Happiness: More's *Utopia* and its SF Context

1.1. In the first part of Thomas More's *Utopia* (1516) a long discussion of England's social ills culminates in Hythloday's famous passage on the destruction of the medieval peasantry:

> "Your sheep," I answered, "which are usually so tame and so cheaply fed, begin now, according to report, to be so greedy and wild that they devour human beings themselves and devastate and depopulate fields, houses, and towns. . . . there are noblemen, gentlemen, and even some abbots, though otherwise holy men, who . . . leave no ground to be tilled; they enclose every bit of land for pasture; they pull down houses and destroy towns, leaving only the church to pen the sheep in. . . . [trans. G.C. Richards, ed. Edward Surtz]

This description, embedded in so acute an analysis of what nascent capitalism means to the people that Marx quoted it in *Capital*, is a masterpiece of indignant humanist sarcasm. The noblemen who rage like earthquakes razing entire districts, the holy men who are brutally indifferent to their spiritual flock and leave churches standing only as profitable sheep-pens, the land which is no longer communal tilling ground for a stable yeomanry but a private enclosure for rich landlords who throw tenants out onto the roads to beg and rob, and finally the erstwhile meek sheep which have now turned into man-devouring beasts—all this, couched in the careful verisimilitude of a traveler's report from exotic countries, amounts to a picture of *a world upside down* being born in the shambles of the natural one. Rejecting all partial and reformist solutions to such radical evils, the second part of *Utopia* will therefore present a radically different model of sociopolitical life: a country that governs itself as a classless extended family. That country—whose punning name means a good place which is (as of now) nowhere—is an England recreated in a more perfect shape. It is an island of the same size and subdivision as England, but round instead of triangular; it has the same natural resources, pegged to an economy based on agriculture, but it is a just and happy country because it has abolished private property in land and other means of production. Instead of the monarchic pyramid in which power flows from the top down, it is, at least in principle, a democratic centralism that acknowledges no political elite, with a power pyramid established from the bottom up. Where Europe slavishly worships obscene war and gold, Utopia despises both; while it sometimes has to fight wars, it uses gold for chamber pots and slaves' fetters. It lives a distributive, egalitarian, preindustrial communism; much like tribal societies, or medieval villages, monasteries, and guilds, it is federalist and patriarchal. Its organization is of a piece with its way of life, the best example being the network of mutually equidistant halls where daily meals are an occasion for pleasurable communion in both physical and spiritual nourishment. Hythloday's review of such "laws and customs" in Utopia is a model of clarity and forcefulness, which answers the objections of his dialogue partners (including a "More" manipulated for self-protective irony) simply by taking to its logical end the gesture of pointing. It finds this "best state of society" based upon the pursuit of an ultimately ethical pleasure attainable only in a social order with a truly collective economy and culture. Happiness for each reached by economic justice for all is the final goal of a possible social organization—a startingly subversive idea.

Utopia is thus the reaffirmation of a world consonant with human nature. This "new island" at the antipodes puts the upside-down monstrosity of European class society back on its feet: the estrangement is a dealienation. Yet a static human nature working itself out in a family model—both concepts taken from medieval Christianity—makes for a certain clogging rigidity of relationships in Utopia, in contradiction to its fundamental ideal of a higher Epicureanism. The Utopians possess slaves (criminals and war prisoners), an official religion (albeit mostly deistic and tolerant of all creeds but not—unforgivably—of atheists), and barbarous provisions against adultery. Also, the representative democracy is tempered by a permanent rule of the Elders, the family fathers, and of the learned. Together with a proper subsistence-economy concern for husbanding resources, this subordinates freedom to an egalitarian balance, enforced where necessary by stringent measures (for example, travel restrictions). For all its dry wit, there is an air of schematic blueprint, of groundplan without adornments, about More's picture of Utopia. But finally, it is an open-ended narrative (the Utopians accept Greek learning and show interest in Christ's collectivism), the first picture of an egalitarian communism with a relatively well-defined tolerance.

1.2. More's *Utopia* subsumes all the SF forms of its epoch (and consequently fulfills the same function as Wells does for recent SF history). It fuses the permanent though sometimes primitive folk longings for a life of abundance and peace with a high-minded intellectual constructs of perfect—that is, communist—human relations known from antiquity on: it translates the Land of Cockayne and the Earthly Paradise into the language of the philosophical dialogue on the ideal state and of Renaissance discovery-literature as reinterpreted by More's unique blend of medieval collectivism and Christian humanism. These forms have been discussed in chapter 3, but a brief recapitulation will point out the specificity of More's synthesis.

Cockayne, the land of peace, sloth, and plentiful food—motifs well known already in antiquity, and constituted into a special country and topos in the Middle Ages—is already an inverted world which relates to earthly human needs, and like utopia proposes a strictly materialist solution. It can therefore be transformed into utopia by relying on human intervention instead of on a magical parallel world, and all utopias, beginning with More, will retain their abhorrence of human degradation by war, toil, and hunger. Next in the family of wondrous lands are the Islands of the Blessed at the limits of the ocean. Found already in tribal tales, Chinese and Mesopotamian legends, and Homer, such an Elysium was originally a place of magical fertility and contentment to which the blessed heroes were admitted in the flesh. In the Middle Ages such locations in far-off mountains (like the Himalayan Uttara Kuru, the echoes of which spread from China to Europe) or seas (for example, the Celtic legendary islands of sensual beauty) came to be conflated with the Earthly Paradise. It is situated in this world, and before rewritings for religious purposes its inhabitants were simply more perfect humans, endowed with happiness, health, youth, and immortality. Echoes of such folk legends are heard in Dante's account of Ulysses's final heroic voyage toward the Paradise Terrestrial, on which he is drowned by a jealous God intent on preserving his monopoly over the right of passage. In fact, Dante's *Comedy* incorporates in its astrophysical and metaphysical universe almost all the SF elements transmitted to More through the Middle Ages, when—after Augustine of Hippo's *Civitas Dei*—"the utopia is transplanted to the sky, and called the Kingdom of Heaven."[1] The *Comedy* subsumes discussions of several ideal political states, traditions of damned and blessed places, the search for the perfect kingdom, and Dante's own superb vision of the perfectly just City of God.

More was well aware of such subgenres as the Earthly Paradise, but he rejected their location outside history and took at least the first major step toward instituting in the alternative island a historical rather than a magically arrested time. Bidding also "a curt farewell" to the mythical conservatism of a Golden Age of happy forefathers, he resolutely located Utopia in an alternative but humanly attainable present, momentous exactly because nonexistent among Europeans. As in Plato's *Republic* (which looms large in the background of More's work), human destiny consists of men and their institutions; but, in direct opposition to Plato, the just place can result from a heroic deed like King Utopus's cutting off the "new island" from the tainted continent. Men's norms and institutions are not the province of religion and magic but of sociopolitics, and time is measured in terms of creative work. That is why *Utopia* differs radically from Plato's curious combination of caste society and ruling-caste communism. Plato's dialogue develops an argument for a timelessly ideal (today quite anti-utopian) blueprint, set up in order to escape popular, monarchic, or imperfectly oligarchic government. More's dialogue dramatically unfolds an actually present state of classless self-government. More lacks all sym-

1. Lewis Mumford (Bibliography III A), p. 59.

pathy for both Plato's erotic communism and his caste system. As
for the notion that a just state depends on a community of
goods, More was much closer to the early Christian Fathers and
peasant insurgents—like John Ball—who extolled communism
than he was to Plato. Besides, this notion was so widespread in
Hellenic literature before and after Plato that Aristophanes
could mock in *Ecclesiazusae* (*The Assemblywomen*) a female attempt
at instituting egalitarian communism without money and toil,
and in *The Birds* a Cloudcuckooland where "everything is everybody's" and things illegal in Athens or on Olympus are deemed
beautiful and virtuous. All such references—characteristically
surviving only in fragments or rebuttals—speak of a setup
where:

> . . . all shall be equal, and equally share
> All wealth and enjoyments, nor longer endure
> That one should be rich, and another be poor.
> [*Ecclesiazusae*, ll.590–91, trans. Rogers]

Such an *omnia sint communia* is from that time forth the constant
principle differentiating consistent utopian literature from the
established society.

When Hythloday is introduced to "More" he is compared to
Plato, but also secondarily to Ulysses, the hero of wondrous voyages to the island of Circe, that of the Phaeacians, and so on.
The genre of *imaginary voyage*, as old as fiction, was the natural
vehicle of the Earthly Paradise and utopian tales, though it often
led simply to entertaining worlds whose topsy-turviness was only
playful and not also didactic. But it could also lead to just
peoples in happy lands at the limits of the world, from Hyper-
boreans to Ethiopians, from Plato's Atlanteans to Euhemerus's
Panchaeans (and in the Middle Ages from Mandeville's Suma-
trans to the subjects of Prester John). The most significant and
nearest in spirit to More is a fragment by Iambulus (ca. 100
B.C.) about the equatorial Islands of the Sun where the usual
magically fertile nature enables men to live without private
property and state apparatus, in a loose association of communities. In such joyous work as picking fruit each in turn serves
his neighbor. They practice erotic communism, eugenics, and
euthanasia (at the age of 150); the sciences, especially astronomy,
are well developed but the liberal arts are more valued as leading

to spiritual perfection. Writing at the time of the great Mediterranean slave and proletarian revolts, Iambulus presents a
plebeian Hellenic negation of the warring empires, the privatiza-
tion of man, and the division of labor. His happy islanders live in
the fields, under the open southern sun; and his account of their
radical collectivism (found by a voyager-narrator later expelled
for his harmful old habits) is the best that has even fragmentarily
survived from the host of similar tales.

Such tales were renewed by the great geographic discoveries:
Hythloday is also introduced as a participant in the voyages of
that Vespucci who had lent his name to America and set Europe
abuzz by describing the "perfect liberty" of the natives' tribal
communism and epicureanism. Thomas More transformed all
such strange new horizons, with their potent dissolving effects
on class society, into a systematic verbal construction of a par-
ticularized community where sociopolitical institutions, norms,
and personal relations are organized according to a more perfect
principle than that prevalent in the author's community (as I
argue in chapter 3 that literary utopias should be defined). This
estranged place is presented as an *alternative history*: whoever its
author, however he twists utopian cognition, it always flows from
the hope of repressed and exploited social classes, expressing
their longing for a different but this-worldly other world. Sudden whirlpools in history which both further and permit its appearance in literature—the times of Iambulus, More, Fourier,
Morris, or indeed our own—have therefore the makings of
great ages of SF. For utopias, being social-science-fiction, the
sociopolitical variant of the radically different peoples and locations of SF, are the *sociopolitical subgenre of SF*.

More's greatness resides thus not only in ethics or prose style.
Utopia supplied the name because it supplied the logically inescapable *Ur*-model for later literary utopias: a rounded and isolated location articulated in a panoramic sweep showing its inner
organization as a formal, ordered countersystem which is at the
same time utopia's supreme value. The coming about of the new
order is explained by a new social contract; in More's age, the
contract-maker is usually a founding hero, but later it will increasingly be a democratic subversion—openly, as in Morris's
socialist revolution, or transposed into cosmic analogs as tenuous as Wells's gas from a comet. Finally, though topographically

closed, utopias are presented by a dramatic strategy which counts on the surprise effects of its presentations upon the reader: significant utopian writings are in permanent dialogue with the readers, they are open-ended—as in More.

2. THE DISSOCIATION OF PLAY AND TRUTH: RABELAIS TO BACON

2.0. More conveyed "full sooth in game." François Rabelais's imaginative voyage through a sequence of wonderful places boisterously perfected such a fusion of urgent truth and witty play to deal with the full compass of earthly preoccupations and possibilities. But by the last books of his pentalogy on the giants Gargantua and Pantagruel (1532-64) the joke had become grimmer and thinner. By the time of Campanella and Bacon, the formal exercise of utopia had dissociated intellectual gravity from plebeian play; in the process, "truth" itself grew increasingly ideological.

2.1. Gargantua's and Pantagruel's sallying out of Utopia to Paris and the ends of the world, and their insistence on the drink and food of the body as well as of the spirit, are emblematic of Rabelais's integration of sensual with philosophic materialism, of folk chronicles about the deeds of enormous and valiant giants with an uproarious intellectual critique of the sum total of contemporary life. This critique is inescapable because it reaches from rational argument and farce to the colossal deployment of synonyms and neologisms, idioms taken literally and fields encompassed encyclopedically. Language itself is no longer godgiven but a medium of human labor, enjoyment, and folly; it is formally presented as such in the SF parable of the congealed words in *The Fourth Book*. The sequence of events, too, bodies forth a gay and dynamic process of imbibing knowledge from the various provinces of reality passed in critical review—from war and education in the first two books, through marriage and sex in the third, to the wondrous and horrible islands of religion, law, and finance in the fourth and fifth books. The basic attitude of this work is "a gaiety of spirit" equated with the wine of the grape as well as the wine of learning and freedom, of friendliness and life itself. Such a draught is a blasphemous transubstantiation in which matter becomes its own conscious and cognitive enjoyment, substituting for service of the divine (*divin*) that of the vine (*du vin*). The folk enjoyment in gigantism is not separated from goodness and wisdom. Rather, matter is treated as not only the sole reality but also the supreme good, of which there can never be too much. Rabelais's whole work is one huge navigation toward liberated matter and unalienated man. This cognitive "imaginary voyage" is the exploration of a dangerous freedom: "You must be the interpreters of your own enterprise" is the final conclusion.

Thus "pantagruelism" is the liberation of a human quintessence from the impure actuality, an unbridled creation of a new human nature scorning contemporary unnatural Europe—as when Pantagruel transforms the bad, aggressive king Anarch into a good though henpecked hawker of green sauce. It oscillates between sheer fantasy and simple inversion. The latter is seen in the anti-abbey or "free university" of Thélème, set against the old educational and monastic institutions. Formally, this is the most clearly utopian passage in Rabelais, though it is not his boldest creation but an elite assembly of young people noble enough to follow the inner-directed commandment "DO WHAT YOU WILL". More importantly, "pantagruelizing" entails assimilating the whole reality of that age and regurgitating it transmuted by his laughing philosophy, just as Gargantua comprehended whole countries in his throat and regurgitated the narrator who visited them. To that end, Rabelais employs with a serene greediness all available SF traditions and all forms of delighted estrangement—Greek satire and medieval legends, marvelous voyages such as *Navigatio Sancti Brendani*, Plato and Villon, More and Lucian. Almost incidentally, he produced some episodes of SF that will stand as its constant yardstick.

2.2.   Rabelais adapted the episode in Gargantua's throat and the whole marvelous voyage in the second half of his opus from the classical tradition subsumed in Lucian of Samosata. In *True Histories* (ca. 160) Lucian laughingly settled the score with the whole tradition of vegetative myths, from the mythological tales themselves, through Homer's voyages, to popular Hellenistic adventure romances. His narrator's journey to various wondrous islands, flight to the Moon, Morning Star, and Sun, life inside a huge whale, in Cloudcuckooland, on the Island of the Blessed, and so forth is a string of model parodies, each translating a whole literary form into a critical, that is, cognitive, context. The island of vine-women is a parody of Circe's and other islands of

erotic bliss, the war of the Selenites against the Heliotes introduces aliens and combats more grotesque than in any romance
or myth; but both are also models for later SF meetings and
warfare with aliens. Lucian uses the mythical scheme of journeys
based on the cycle of death and rebirth, darkness and day, closing and opening, for ironic subversion. Its spectrum ranges
from ironic events, situations, and characters, through parodic
allusions and wordplay, to direct sarcasm. For example, his
tongue-in-cheek extrapolation of colonial warfare into interplanetary space is rendered utterly ridiculous by a farcically
pedantic and scabrous description of the semi-human Selenites.
Lucian's whole arsenal of demystification amounts to a value system in which vitality is equated with freedom. Being confined to
the country within the whale, with its oppressive fish-people, is
Lucian's equivalent of an infernal descent, after his flight
through imperialist heavens. "Lucian the Blasphemer" presented
the nonexistent "quite lightly, quite easily, as if he were an inhab-
itant of the Fortunate Isles themselves."[2] His humanistic irony
embodied in aesthetic delight became the paradigm for the
whole "prehistory" of SF, from More and Rabelais to Cyrano and
Swift.

2.3.   In More and Rabelais this tradition led to the "alchemical" procedure of creating a new homeland by a transmutation
of the baser elements in the old country (England or the Tou-
raine), so that Rabelais's fictive narrator could call himself "ab-
stractor of the Quintessence." Actuality proved different: the
marvelous countries became colonies, More died beheaded,
Rabelais barely escaped the stake, knowledge and sense were
again viciously sundered by religious wars and monarchist absolutism. In the profound crisis of the age, the first wave of the
revolutionary middle class had separated itself from the people,
and had been destroyed or absorbed by church and state. At
the beginning of the seventeenth century this was clearly spelled
out by the burning at the stake of Giordano Bruno, the heroic
philosopher who had proclaimed an infinite universe with an infinite number of autonomous and equivalent worlds.

The new power cast a spell even over utopographers. Shakespeare allotted a conservative function to the wondrous place in

2.   Ernst Bloch (Bibliography II), 1:507.

the western seas by placing the educational island of *The Tempest*
under the rule of monarchist magic; by dividing its servant-aliens
into one representative airy, angelic if repining, goody and one
earthy, sexually and politically libertine, subversive, in a word
demonic, baddy; and by using it for a laboratory demonstration
of the supreme necessity for vertical political order. To round
things properly off, he also included in Gonzalo's speech an Aris-
tophanically unfair sideswipe at the older "contrary" utopianism
of freedom: the new "commonwealth" is in a propagandistically
disingenuous way made to fuse utopian, primitivistic, and down-
right silly traits, so that it could be only too flippantly refuted.
When that speech does touch upon the central Morean contradiction of a vertically ordered, patriarchal freedom, the matter is not explored but used as a sleight-of-hand substitution for
the virtuous simplicity of Montaigne's cannibals; therefore, their
happy primitive communism leaves a sour aftertaste in Shakespeare's reversion of Caliban. Beyond this, *The Tempest* is an anthology of elements of and views on a new locus—with the exception of any sympathetic to egalitarian community, which is
ruled a priori out of court in the travesty of the plebeians' attempt at a bestial takeover. Hierarchy, the aptly named Chain of
Being as sternly benevolent salvation from dystopian chaos,
clearly prevails. Yet the Shakespearean tension of Christian
humanism—and beyond that, of the poet in class society—
produced also, in Miranda, a naively pure glance at the (if only
potentially) "beauteous mankind" and "brave new world," and in
Prospero's "revels" speech a melancholy adieu to even the grandest verticals of human society and life as "insubstantial," transient stuff of space and time. True, the official ideology of
Elizabethan morals and politics—indeed of politics as personal
morals—colors all the supple and masterly estrangements occurring within the "sea-change" that affects in different ways all the
dramatis personae on this new island with the only too familiar
absolutist relationships. Nonetheless, and most importantly, the
other pole of the Shakespearean tension created Ariel, the
emblematic cosmic representative of the tempestuous and
metamorphic island; the yearnings for self-governing freedom,
to be repressed in a colonial island or civil society, were judged
allowable at least for a pure spirit. The rich Renaissance lyricism
hides a syllogism that already prefigures Swift's dry Houyhn-

hnms: if only intelligent beings (psychozoa) were not men but possessed another nature, a radically different common-wealth "by contraries"—or the perfect anarchism of a fusion with nature—might be possible: and beautiful beyond our ken.

2.4. Disbelieving in a changeable human nature, utopographers had to cast about instead for better powers over it. Among a host of less consistent attempts, the nearest to More was Doni's sarcastic "World of the Fools" (in *I Mondi*, 1552), but even his plebeian egalitarianism succumbed to the pessimistic and static view of the age. Most memorably, in southern, Catholic Europe Tommaso Campanella reinstated astrology, that fantastic pseudo-science of absolutism, as the guiding principle of his *City of the Sun* (bp. 1623);[3] and in northern, Protestant Europe Francis Bacon, in *New Atlantis* (bp. 1627), perspicaciously discerned a natural science acting as esoteric religion to be the wave of the future. Campanella, though formally prolonging Iambulus's and More' line, describes a perfect theocracy somewhere behind India, in the seas of the old caste empires and on an island so large it is almost a continent. The traditional utopian abolition of private ownership, along with stimulating ideas on dignifying labor and on education, is mystifyingly incorporated into a monastic bureaucratism with an impersonal, militaristic order that regulates all relations, from times for sexual intercourse to the placement of buttons, in strict and grotesque detail fixed by astrology. For the explosive horizontal of the Renaissance, Campanella substituted a dogmatic vertical that descends from the Sun of Power to men. More's urbane talk between friendly humanists has in Campanella rigidified into a one-track exposition from one top oligarch to another.

Bacon's "great instauration," based on the rising force of capitalist manufacture and its technological horizons, was in the following three centuries to prove more virulent than Campanella's monastic nostalgia. For Bacon the social system is an open question no longer; rather, the key for transforming the world is a power over nature exercised by, and largely for, a politically

---

3. Since in this unseemly and subversive genre it is not too rare that books get published much later than the normal few years after the known date of composition—as in the cases of Campanella, Bacon, Kepler, Godwin, and Cyrano—such book publication is in this work indicated by its date being preceded by "bp."

quite conservative, quasi-Christian priestly hierarchy. The organized application of technology in New Atlantis is not a breakthrough to new domains of human creativity or even (except for some agricultural and biological techniques) of natural sciences; the only use mentioned for "stronger and more violent" engines is in artillery, for the old destructive purposes. Conversely, science becomes a patriarchal, genteel, and highly ceremonial religion, one that could be characterized—much as its later offshoot, Saint-Simonism, would be—as Catholicism minus Christianity. Scientists are a self-sufficient aristocracy of experts manipulating or "vexing" nature and other men; as against Plato, More, and Rabelais, their "science does not so much exude from wisdom as wisdom exudes from science,"[4] and gold is not a sign of baseness but of permanent abundance in possessions and power. The very name of Bacon's country aims to improve Plato both by correcting his account of Old Atlantis and by presenting a New Atlantis the old perfection of which has withstood not only political but even geological contingencies (the narration ends with an indication that its science can prevent earthquakes, floods, comets, and similar phenomena).

The major positive claim of New Atlantis is that it delivers the goods—abundance of things and years, and social stability—by employing the lay miracles of science. In Bacon's historical epoch, even such a filling in of extant technical possibilities, without a radical change in human relationships, constituted a huge and euphoric program; the goal of the "research foundation" of Salomon's House is formulated as "the knowledge of causes, and secret motions of things; and the enlarging of the bounds of human empire, to the effecting of all things possible." But though this science is guarded by experts who can, interestingly enough, refuse to divulge dangerous discoveries, it is by its own definition ethically indifferent: nuclear bombs and gas ovens in concentration camps will be some of the "things" possible to effect. New Atlantis is starry-eyed over inquiring into the "secret motions and causes" of fruits, winds, sounds, and clocks, yet it does not think of inquiring into motions and results with respect to the mother of the family, who is condemned to ritual

4. Howard B. White (Bibliography III C), p. 106; see also passim, especially pp. 223–25 and 171–72.

seclusion, or to the population sundered from Salomon's House. The work thus gives a foretaste of that combination of technology and autocracy which in fact became the basis of European empires at home and abroad. At this point in history, the utopian tradition fell under the sway of an upper-class ideology which staves off human problems by technocratic extrapolation, by quantitative expansion promising abundance within a fundamentally unchanged system of social domination. Bacon's "science" thus turns out to be as mythical as Campanella's astrology, though more efficient. As a verbal vision, New Atlantis, with its heavy-handed, propagandist insistence on a power hierarchy, on opulence, and on resplendent signs of public status, and with its stifling world which becomes interesting only when grandiose projects are enumerated, is in fact much inferior to the fanatic splendor of *The City of the Sun*. It is symptomatic of the quality of imagination in the ensuing age that this work (one of Bacon's poorest) should have become the master of its thought. The "outrageous piece of 'miraculous evangelism' " which founded New Atlantis, its stuffy ceremonials and barbarous human relations, completes the picture of this "curious alliance of God, Mammon and Science."[5]

Thus the developing utopian tradition dragged into the open the latent contradictions in More's crypto-religious constructing of Utopia. After the Rabelaisian flowering, Campanella and Bacon mark a reaction against Renaissance libertarian humanism; the logical next step was the end of utopia as an independent cognitive form. Official repression would have worked toward this in any case; but it would not have succeeded so swiftly and well had not the utopian camp been betrayed from within. Having lost a fertile connection with popular longings, utopia—with a few partial exceptions in the eighteenth century—disappears from the vanguard of European culture until Fourier and Chernyshevsky. Ironically, Bacon fought medieval scholasticism but inaugurated a new dogmatism of technocracy, and Campanella rotted for decades in papal prisons but announced a return to the closed, mythic world-model of Plato. History is cruel to "final solutions."

5.   First quotation from R. W. Chambers (Bibliography III C), p. 362; second quotation from V. Dupont (Bibliography III C), p. 146.

3. MONSTERS AND SATELLITES: THE SATIRICAL DEFENCE OF MAN

3.0. Expelled once again from official culture, significant SF shifted from utopian seas to the planets, which were the forefront of attention after Copernicus and Galileo. This detour led to Swift and reclaimed the wondrous islands for an oblique, satirical defense of basically utopian values by way of a sharp critique of the authors' anti-utopian actuality.

3.1. The "planet romance" (*roman planétaire*) presented a critical mirror to corrupted sublunary Earth by means of Lucianic islands in the sea of ether, mainly by means of the Moon. "Am I doing anything more monstrous [than Campanella, More and Erasmus] if, in a vivid description of the monstrous habits of our age, I transpose the scene from Earth to Moon for the sake of caution?" asked Kepler plaintively after his *Dream* (bp. 1634). In it, scientific speculation about other inhabited worlds turns into a vivid description of Selenite biology and civilization determined by such cosmographic factors as the search for water. Wells's Cavor was to remember this first attempt at a scientific exobiology and cosmo-ethnology. Similarly, the hero of Francis Godwin's *The Man in the Moon* (bp. 1638) finds giant Selenites whose social class depends on height and resistance to light, and who live in a kind of Earthly Paradise (at the time often located on the Moon) kept pure by deporting unsuitable babies to Earth. This subgenre produced in Savinien Cyrano's two novels constituting *The Other World* (bp. 1657-62) a masterpiece of embattled wit.

Cyrano's first narrative, *The States and Empires of the Moon*, plays on the opposition of "moon" and "world":

> . . . they [the Moon authorities] dressed me with great splendour as a mark of shame; they made me ride on the platform of a magnificent chariot, drawn by four princes who were yoked to it, and here is what they made me announce at every crossroads in the town:
>
> "People, I declare unto you that this moon here is not a moon, but a world; and that that world down there is not a world but a moon. Such is what *the Priests* deem it good for you to believe!" [trans. Geoffrey Strachan]

A supple alliance of simple inversion (the dress and chariot) and sophisticated satire on the ideological use of language (the proclamation) is here used for a burlesque debunking of such earthly authoritarianism as the Inquisition's against Galileo. The Moon is literally an upside-down world: in it, youth—the time when vitality is at its height—is revered instead of age, and noblemen wear bronze reproductions of genitalia in honor of creation instead of the sword, an instrument of destruction. This inclination to make love, not war, is of a piece with universal sexual rights of each to each and condemnation of warfare as dishonorable whenever one side has any advantage over the other. But Earth-bound criteria of truth are also demolished when confronted with the revolutionary vision that other planets of our Sun (and, by implication, of an infinite number of other stars) are inhabited by conscious beings: the universe has no privileged center. Sometimes Cyrano uses this cosmological, personal, and political declaration of autonomy for seriocomic exaggeration, as in the episode of the "thinking cabbage"; yet his high-minded vision of interdependent independences lends itself to witty association with a thoroughgoing materialist atomism in physics, amounting to a total rejection of the religious and absolutist world view. Even the extinction of individuality in death is only one phase in the omnipresent metamorphoses of creative matter, and it is therefore met with joy instead of grief. This deep and intimate concern for natural sciences is integrated into a sequence of satirical intellectual adventures, into a quest for knowledge as freedom—poles apart from Bacon. To cite one example, the argument of an interlocutor on the Moon that all matter is pervaded by emptiness and has thus the freedom of movement permitting "all things to meet in every thing" is not only a brilliant "experimental though imaginary verification" of philosophico-scientific value,[6] it also grounds Cyrano's libertarianism in the very structure of the universe. To cite another, the Bible is satirized when the prophet Elijah arrives into Lunar Paradise by throwing a condensed magnet repeatedly upward from his iron chariot; but his flight also sketches some technical problems, such as braking during groundfall. Cyrano's apparently whimsical yet profoundly consistent and dialectical use of innovating imagination, in both the boldness of its atheist philosophy of science and cosmology and its poetical wit, would remain unsurpassed until the nineteenth century.

6.   H. Weber (Bibliography III D), p. 28.

As Cyrano rises from Earth he encounters beings with progressively more refined senses and therefore greater intelligence: the "demons" from the Sun, for example, can sensually comprehend magnetism and tides (gravity). Conversely, when he first encounters the quadrupedal Lunarians he believes them to be beasts, and for them his bipedal stance is monstrous. Monstrosity leads to rejection; rejection by the powerful leads to expulsion or imprisonment. Cyrano's opus is built on an alternation of prisons—into which the unlucky narrator is continually clapped by various superstitious or power-hungry authorities— and escapes: ideologically and physically closed systems down here ruled by priests of all stripes are transcended by fantastic means in the direction of another world up there. The means range from light-heartedly or irreverently burlesque to technical: from dew, beef-marrow, and sacrificial odors (tending respectively toward the Sun, the Moon, and God) to the first SF use of multistage rockets. The flight from one world or existential situation to another is as a rule accompanied by some approximation to death (unconsciousness, for example) and results in what might be called debrutalization (rebirth, rejuvenation). Cyrano's characters are often interchangeable; like his protean matter, they can split and recombine. The narrator himself changes roles and situations. His situations are "metaphors realised by true metamorphoses",[7] and his roles are manipulated with great skill to expose all the possible nuances of false and true monstrosity, as seen from both his side and that of the other races. This satirical technique hits its goal—the oppressive relations prevailing on Earth—both by direct invective and by sarcastic praise, and it will be systematized to overwhelming effect by Swift. The alternation of microscopic and telescopic vision (which will be further developed in *Gulliver's Travels*) is introduced by Cyrano in his discussion of the two infinites of greatness and smallness:

> . . . there are infinite worlds within an infinite world. Picture the universe, therefore, as a vast organism. Within this vast organism the stars, which are worlds, are like a further series of vast organisms, each serving inversely as the worlds of lesser populations such as ourselves, our horses, etc. We,

7. Maurice Blanchot (Bibliography III D), p. 560.

in our turn, are also worlds from the point of view of certain organisms incomparably smaller than ourselves, like certain worms, lice, and mites. They are the Earths of others, yet more imperceptible. . . . [trans. Geoffrey Strachan]

And Cyrano continues this humorous yet implicitly serious vision (it led Pascal to panic vertigo) by ironically imagining a louse circumnavigating the world of a human head, among the tides of hair combed forward and backward.

Cyrano learned much from Rabelais, and the passage quoted above stems from that of the peoples in Gargantua's throat. But repression weighed much more heavily on him, a member of the small and isolated, if highly talented, circle of libertines, freethinkers, and burlesque poets permanently threatened by sword and stake. In *The States and Empires of the Sun* his satire grows more caustic with greater elevation from Earth, but also much more allegorical and recondite. The Moon narrative kept the mannered sensibility under uneasy but effective control. But the murderously unsettled times made impossible the sovereign enjoyment signified by Rabelais's giants; Cyrano himself died young of a mysterious accident, probably a political murder by clerical enemies. Even his charmingly whimsical yoking together of elements from disparate fields (ranging from the Apocrypha and folktales to the new philosophy understood as delight) and his characteristic paradoxes and sallies of wit show the tenuousness of his sociopolitical position between a browbeaten people and a triumphant obscurantism. His narrative moves through rapier flicks of ironic conceits or "points"; it is on a constant offensive defense, in permanent acute denial. Innocently sensual pleasure is forced to define itself as heresy, stressing what it is against rather than—as in Rabelais—what it is for. Cyrano's great Epicurean tale, encompassing both sarcasm and tenderness, accommodating the fantastic and the comical along with the ironically cognitive, was the culmination and swan-song of libertinism. A monument of European mannerism and French prose, it is also a forgotten masterpiece of SF.[8]

---

8. The thesis could be defended that only systematic repression has prevented Cyrano's historical influence from being comparable to More's or Wells's. What happened to his writing is representative of the fate of a whole tradition: the posthumous

3.2. Jonathan Swift drew on the tradition of the imaginary voyage—camouflaged into the newly popular form of real travel accounts from the South Seas—to the point of making it the basic form of *Gulliver's Travels* (1726). After Lucian, More, Rabelais, and Cyrano, the satirical-cum-utopian tradition also had an offshoot in numerous contemporary pretended travels— such as Foigny's *A New Discovery of Terra Incognita Australis* or Vairasse's *History of the Sevarambi*, both dating from the 1670s and of lasting fame though often officially persecuted—which put political satire and reforms into the mouth of virtuous and expository natives. Swift ironically manipulates many elements found in this range of sober and tall-tale journeys, from isolated borrowings to the matter-of-fact tone and a protagonist constantly claiming travelog exactness. Into this framework he drew the folktale wonders of giants and dwarfs, floating and magnetic islands, monstrous or rational beasts, transforming them into precisely observed, scientifically justified, Rationalist possible islands; but simultaneously he used these islands for radical subversion of Rationalism, for direct and indirect ethicopolitical satire of the English and European civilization. This makes *Gulliver's Travels* "at once science fiction and a witty parody of science fiction."[9] Its basic concern is with the most radical anthropological question: What is Man? In order to suggest an answer it destructively recapitulates the development of SF.

In Lilliput, it is the tradition of enchanted *islands of human dominion* that is refuted. Where Gulliver—the average "gullible worm" of his civilization—is physically superior, he does not know how to control himself, his base vanity, and political snobbery, but grows as petty as his environment (which stands for the English court and politics). In Brobdingnag Swift employs the

---

publication of *The States and Dominions of the Moon* in 1657 was heavily censored and altered. An original MS was discovered only in 1861, another in 1908, and the first critical edition published in 1910. The MS of *The States and Dominions of the Sun* was stolen on his deathbed and never found: the published version is incomplete. The third part of this trilogy, *The Spark*, has never been found. The first complete edition of the two novels comprising *The Other World*, then, was published in 1921, the first popular edition only in 1959. In the meantime, Cyrano entered popular consciousness in Rostand's crude bourgeois falsification of a long-nosed Gascon sentimentalist.

9. Samuel Holt Monk, "The Pride of Lemuel Gulliver," in Frank Brady, ed. (Bibliography III E), p. 70.

same basic device of materializing ethical qualities in order to refute the tradition of enchanted *islands of lusty and benevolent nature*. Where Gulliver tries to live up to lofty models, he is prevented both by his prejudices and by crushingly superior outside forces. Swift's satire functions by always having it both ways: whether Gulliver be subject or object of satire, Swift's spokesman or butt, the immoral European civilization is always subjected to many-sided ridicule. As we share the narrator's terror when faced with the colossal Brobdingnagian life-forms, we feel helplessly delivered into their power; as we side with the magnanimous Giant King (especially in the overwhelming gunpowder discussion), we feel the preposterous, bloodthirsty vanity of this bourgeois Everyman, representative of "the most pernicious race of little odious vermin that Nature ever suffered to crawl upon the surface of the Earth." Further, the Lilliputians and Brobdingnagians are men viewed through the two ends of that "pockets perspective" which turns up so often in Dr. Gulliver's pockets. Vision too is both literal and cognitive: in the First Voyage, Gulliver is myopic, in the second he possesses microscopic sight and shrinks appalled from the craters in the breasts of giant court-ladies. Swift inverts the cheerful relativism of Cyrano's infinite series of mites (not only the techniques of shifting satirical vision but also a number of situations in the *Travels*, including Gulliver in his cage, owe much to Cyrano); he has us look with disgust upon the corruption of the body politic in Lilliput, the land of man as paltry political animal, and of the body physical in Brobdingnag, the land of monstrous animals and dangerous bodies. By what Gulliver discovers in them and what they reveal in him, these terrifying islands function as a magnifying lens, a spyglass for Man's moral and material pettiness.

The post-Baconian descriptive precision is inscribed and yet mocked in Gulliver's very style. Right from the beginning it is "peppered with citations of numbers, figures, dimensions . . . [and] approximates an ideal of 17th Century scientists: . . . 'so many *things*, almost in an equal number of words'."[10] The style is itself a cognitive instrument turned against its Baconian originators—the middle class in alliance with the despots, the optimistic Rationalists, the projectors, the Royal Society scientists.

10.   Robert C. Elliott (Bibliography III E), p. 199.

Their irrationality is sarcastically revealed by reducing it to the absurd in the most meticulously and pedantically rational manner.

In the Third Voyage Swift shows directly this dehumanized science, its lifestyle and consequences. Working against life, it sterilizes man's relations to man and to nature. The Laputans—the first "mad scientists" in SF—have one eye turned "up to the zenith" of mathematical abstraction, and the other inward, as befits a subjective Individualism. They know neither man's place in the world nor direct, sensual as well as cerebral, relations between people: they have no poetry, their food and clothes are shaped geometrically, women assiduously cuckold their husbands with strangers, and their science is useless or—still worse—useful to political tyranny (the marvelous flying island of Laputa is used for bombing rebels, a maneuver which, however, proves powerless against a united colonial people). To Swift, Rationalism had—by accepting the quantified world view, the bourgeois emphasis on counting, weighing, and measuring, and the resultant cosmology of mechanical balance, of bodies and motions in a "value-free" space—betrayed the true, communal, and value-imbued possibilities of human reason. The most comical examples in the Third Voyage, the Word Engine and the Thing Language, are taken from the fundament of Newtonian "natural philosophy," mathematics, and from the social science most intimately impinging on human consciousness, linguistics. But the comedy is black; Swift's critique is not simply moralistic but also epistemological. The Newtonian model's absolutist pretension that its linguistic and mathematic formalizations have finally revealed reality and are therefore ends unto themselves, regardless of science's practical incidence on human lives, is treated by Swift as a logical tool or whore (*la puta*) of political oppression. Indeed, the grotesque misery of Lagado—of a piece with and in fact the final consequence of the capitalist mercantilism directly stigmatized in book 4—shows that this science is a road to ruin for the whole society. Such alienated knowledge is sterile and obscene; it is symbolized by the project of extracting food from human excrement as well as by the smooth, opaque, and crushing "adamant" bottom of the flying island. Man as the scientific master over (instead of partner with) nature is refuted in these distorted *islands of new knowledge*; they are a retraction of Bacon's New Atlantis, together with which they founded the tradition of modern SF as companion of modern science.

The frequent critical harpings on the incoherence of Swift's Third Voyage overlook such an ideological consistency and gradation. The tour of the Academy of Lagado, for example, progresses from practical projectors through "advancers of speculative learning" to "political projectors," who include experts in taxing and finding out conspiracies. Beyond Lagado, the probing into history and philosophy in Glubbdubdrib shows up modern knowledge as mere fashion and modern politics as decadent when compared to the ancient times, especially to the heroes of freedom from Brutus to More. The dialectics of this Voyage culminate in the nightmarish Immortals of Luggnagg: Swift's supreme value, human life, turns into an obscene malediction when delivered to quantity (empty duration) without the qualities of youth and health. In a sarcastic eversion of the Baconian clerical elite assumed to constitute "a living treasury of knowledge and wisdom," the reader is shown how infinite quantity becomes infinite disgust. The quantitative vision of nature, like all knowledge that is not applied to the happiness of people—all the science and politics that do not "make two ears of corn, or two blades of grass grow upon a spot of ground where only one grew before"—is thus a counsel of death, of the obscene death-in-life of the Struldbrugs.

The satire of Man's politics, his body, and his intellect in the first three voyages leads to the great opposition of the disgusting Yahoos and the rational Houyhnhnms in the Fourth Voyage. The good old times of early Lilliput and the moderation of the Brobdingnag King culminate in the Noble Horses; equally, the abuse of reason for immoral ends in politics and science is offset in their reasonable and virtuous country. But here the question "What is Man?" becomes quite inescapable. The fashionable answer for Swift's time was "the rational animal." Accordingly, the European Everyman is placed between creatures who are not just optically and ethically different humans: the Houyhnhnms are rationality without humanity, and the Yahoos humanity without a prideful pretense to reason. Gulliver (and his reader) cannot in this voyage hold apart from the aliens encountered, he is coinvolved in the confrontation of reasonable and animal species in Houyhnhnmland; shockingly, it is the horses who are nobly reasonable and the Yahoo-men who are disgustingly ignoble and brutal. No doubt such a confrontation was known from Ovid through the sixteenth-century vogue of conversations with temperate beasts that culminated in Cyrano's quadrupeds and Sun birds. But all those writers condemned an unnatural human civilization; Swift takes to task human nature itself, the generic pride of man as such. The Houyhnhnms, living without knowledge of such abominations as money, government, war, laws, or lies, are an (at times faintly comic) ideal within a moral fable rather than a direct and perfect model. Indeed, being biologically different they can *not* be physically imitated by humans, as Gulliver's ludicrous attempts make plain. Yet at the same time they possess a definite ethical superiority over a world where one is exposed to "the sight of a lawyer, a pick-pocket, a colonel, a fool, a lord, a gamester, a whore-monger, a physician, an evidence [police informer], a suborner, an attorney, a traitor." Gulliver is consequently at the end, notwithstanding all his pitiful Rationalist literalness, much like Plato's escapee from the cave of shadows: he has seen the truth but cannot communicate it to the purblind. Overridingly, the Noble Horses are the measure of what the Yahoos and men—worshipping power, gold, and excrements—are not.

Rejecting the constitution-mongering of so many middle-class "State novels" from Harrington to Fénelon, Swift—who was in a way the last of Renaissance humanists—looks back to More's radical hostility against the encroaching capitalist and Individualist civilization. But in a much more corrupted age Swift's is an integral monitory view which illuminates not only politics but also science and ideology. His narrator is "More's Hythloday [dressed up] to look like Defoe's Robinson Crusoe,"[11] whose fantastic findings recoil back on everyday English life like More's— only more savagely. True, when he finally finds utopia, it is the inimitable life of another species. But the fact of *Gulliver's Travels* being published and thus reinserted into social practice turns its extreme anti-utopian despair into a critique of the anti-utopian world which it mirros. The more passionate and precise Swift's negation, the more clearly the necessity for new worlds of humaneness appears before the reader. Swift was living in the

11. John Traugott, "A Voyage to Nowhere with Thomas More and Jonathan Swift," in Ernest Tuveson, ed. (Bibliography III E), p. 161.

heyday of bourgeois ethics, of political arithmetics treating people as computable economic atoms (see his *Modest Proposal*, that unsurpassed masterpiece of fantastic essay as a radical pamphlet). At a time when capitalist empires begin to span the globe, when "all that is holy is profaned, and man is at last compelled to face with sober senses his real conditions of life and his relations with his kind,"[12] he defeated this totalitarianism by means of a sarcasm just as total. He might have detested man as a species, but parallel to such an ideology he also provided evidence for his indictment springing from a civilization where "the rich enjoyed the fruit of the poor man's labour, and the latter were a thousand to one in proportion to the former." What is seen through both ends of Swift's spyglass in the first two voyages, in the distorted mirror of the third, and the inverted world of ethicobiological absolutes of the Fourth Voyage, is our own civilization, revealed as monstrous and inhuman, simultaneously comic and pridefully bestial. The resulting horrifying comedy is rendered in an apparently icily emotionless style of empirical realism which, turning the age's basic vision against itself, gives Swift's lucid bitterness its quite exceptional corrosive power. Using the parallelism of material and moral, Swift channels the tremendous energies of idioms and metaphors to his purpose. The rope-walking or crawling of politicians in Lilliput resurrects a dead cliché into visual and connotative concreteness, so that the inherent absurdity is imaginatively liberated to produce once more an estranging shock of recognition. The ideological and linguistic norms of European practice had glossed over, killed these metaphors, but by an uncompromising insistence on their plebeian sign-value Swift rediscovers their deep—political and philosophical—truth.

Thus, if Swift is—quite literally—reactionary, his is a radically conservative or "Tory anarchist"[13] reaction against the shameless perversions of knowledge, optimism, and dominion brought about by Individualism. If he is the opposite of a didactic utopian, he is a bitter ally of utopia. Though the reader leaves

12. Karl Marx and Friedrich Engels, *Manifesto of the Communist Party*, in their *Selected Works in One Volume* (London, 1968), p. 38.

13. George Orwell, "Politics vs. Literature," in Denis Donoghue, ed. (Bibliography III E), p. 354.

Gulliver alienated in his stable within the larger alienation of England, the values implicit in his travels remain. In such a thorough review of the human condition, it is significant that Swift's sarcasm stopped short of the Giant King's pacifism and the fighting solidarity of Lindalino, of the women and illiterates who prevented the introduction of "thing language" in Balnibarbi—in brief, of the ethics and politics associated with Brutus and More. One should not give to these glimpses of a common body politic a significance which the *Travels* themselves will not sustain; but historically that unscathed hope is a signpost for subsequent SF. It will have to deal with Swift's discovery that man's body, this battlefield of vitality and putrefaction, is his truth. After *Gulliver's Travels*, it is impossible to believe in a merely institutional, static utopia which does not face the nature of man. The new Heavens and new Earth demand a new Man, and the following age, from Blake and the Shelleys to Morris, will explore this dialectical feedback. Swift himself remains the great and desperate champion of an integral Man against the terrible pressures of Individualist monstrosity. Only somebody who deeply cared about man's potentials could have been so outraged at his Yahoodom. By this utopian outrage, in his imaginary voyages and marvelous islands, Swift created the great model for all subsequent SF. It is a wise interweaving of utopias taking on anti-utopian functions and anti-utopias as allies of utopianism; of satire using scientific language and technological extrapolation as a grotesque; of adventures in SF countries, artificial satellites and aliens, immortals and monsters, all signifying England and the gentle reader. All the later protagonists of SF, gradually piecing together their strange locales, are sons of Gulliver, and all their more or less cognitive adventures the continuation of his *Travels*.

3.3. Swift (and Defoe's *Robinson Crusoe*) stimulated an outburst of fantastic voyages in England and France. The Moon had already been used for crude political and economic satire in Defoe's *Consolidator* and the pseudonymous *Voyage to Cacklogallinia*. For the first time since the Renaissance, muted utopian themes appear on the stage, culminating in Marivaux's plays *The New Colony* (bp. as late as 1878), *The Island of Slaves* (1723), and *The Island of Reason* (1727). The playful imagination of these pieces, for all the compromises inherent in public harlequinades, at times touched the most sensitive nerve of the period between Molière and Beaumarchais—the striving for class and sexual equality. Holberg's *Niels Klim* (1741) laicized the subterranean voyage for satirical purposes. The voyages to planets culminated in Voltaire's civilized irony of *Micromégas* (bp. 1752), which brought the gigantic planetary visitors to Earth in order to explode yet again, after Cyrano and Swift, more directly and obviously than they did, the Rationalist notion of the great heights mankind was supposed to have finally scaled. But the writings of almost all the major French *philosophes* of the eighteenth century—Montesquieu's *Persian Letters* and Voltaire's Eldorado in *Candide*, Diderot's *Supplement to Bougainville's Voyage* (1772) and Sade's island of Tamoé in *Aline and Valcour*— incorporate some utopian passages for mental experiment, contrast, and satire; more than 1000 editions of such writings were published before the French Revolution. The imaginary voyage had become so popular that it could be parodied by "lying voyages" such as Münchhausen's. A recurrent figure was, from Montaigne's Cannibals to Rousseau's primeval communists, the savage whose natural nobility confounded the hypocrisy of Christian Europeans; Denis Diderot's Tahiti may be seen as only the most consistent, complex, and charming indictment of the bad European life seen against the sexually, ideologically, and economically free island life far away. One of the most interesting alliances of lower-class literature and such libertarian ideology was Nicolas Restif's *Flying Man* (*La Découverte australe*, 1781), in which the Rousseauist hero invents wings in order to fly away with his upper-class beloved to some yet unspoiled Earthly Paradise, there to enjoy a new social and natural deal. He later flies with her and their children to the Antipodes and settles down as king of one of the marvelous countries (of giants, beast-men, and the like) they visit. This naive, often crude blend of imaginary voyage, technology, and utopianism, cosmic eroticism and folk evolutionism, escapism and plebeian revolt, indicates the vast possibilities of a popular romanticism. But its development was unfortunately cut short by the collapse of the democratic revolution in the nineteenth century.

6

The Shift to Anticipation: Radical Rhapsody and Romantic Recoil

> In futurity
> I prophetic see. . . .
> William Blake

0.1. If SF is historically part of a submerged or plebeian "lower literature" expressing the yearnings of previously repressed or at any rate nonhegemonic social groups, it is understandable that its major breakthroughs to the cultural surface should come about in the periods of sudden social convulsion. Such was the age of the bourgeois-democratic and the industrial revolutions, incubating in western Europe from the time of More and Bacon, breaking out at the end of the eighteenth and in the nineteenth century. The high price of industrial revolution as a result of the repeated failures of the political ones caused in SF too a shift from the radical blueprints and rhapsodics of the revolutionary utopians in the epoch of the French Revolution to the Romantic internalization of suffering. The inflection is visible in Blake and Percy Bysshe Shelley, while Mary Wollstonecraft Shelley and the US Romantics are already on the other side of this ideological shift. The irresistible march of palaeotechnic steam and iron machinery at the middle of the nineteenth century, along with the concomitant growth of the proletariat, prompted SF to examine more directly the machine's potentialities for human good and evil. At last, at the Victorian peak of bourgeois exploitation of man and nature, SF turned, more or less sanguinely, toward the horizons of a new revolutionary dawn.

0.2. However, this age was not simply a major social convulsion comparable, say, to the Reformation. The instauration of capitalist production as the dominant and finally all-pervasive way of life engendered a fundamental reorientation of human practice and imagination: a wished-for or feared future becomes the new space of the cognitive (and increasingly of the everyday)

115

imagination, no doubt in intimate connection with and depen-
dence from the shift from the social power of land to the power
of capital (see chapter 4, 2.4.). In SF the horizon within which
the novum is developed was originally a space existing alongside
the author's empirical environment, which is thrown into question by the radical otherness and/or debunking parody conveyed
by the alternative location. As we saw in in chapter 5, the space
was an as yet unknown island beyond the fabulous seas; or
(probably an even earlier paradigm) a valley beyond the
mountain ranges, if not indeed a subterranean enclosure; or
finally an extrapolated planetary island in the ocean of ether
(Moon and Sun from mythological tales and Lucian to Cyrano
and Verne, other planets from the eighteenth century on). In its
Renaissance heyday, this ideal alternative was informed by the
wish that the "normal" space might, by a homeopathic magical
infection, begin metamorphosizing into a configuration of more
humane or humanized actuality, into—as More's title said—the
best state of the commonwealth and the new island of Utopia.
The alternative space was aesthetically structured by a central
but static philosophical (rather than natural-science) cognition.

By the eighteenth century, in the increasingly activistic
dynamics of hope and fear, SF begins turning (first in the
technologically and ideologically most advanced bourgeois nations, England and France) to a *time* into which the author's age
might evolve. This turning, that cuts decisively across all other
national, political, and formal traditions in culture, has so far not
been adequately explained. The frequently articulated thesis that
it occurred *faute de mieux*, because the white patches on the map
of the globe which might validate a different microcosm were
fast disappearing, is unconvincing. Not only did many white
patches remain right up to the development of a viable aviation
(and they were abundantly used by SF as late as Wells and E.R.
Burroughs), but there was at hand the whole tradition of planetary novels and subterranean descents. Clearly, the deeper reasons have to do with the quantification of everyday, economically
based practice—the enthronement of commodity fetishism and
money as the universal yardstick for life values—as well as of the
"natural" sciences. For the first time, capitalist technology had
united the globe, though in a discordant unity undreamt of by
the reasonable cosmopolitanism of the Stoics or Renaissance

humanists, and pregnant with the most destructive collisions of nations and classes. The same technology had made mass social change in one lifetime the rule rather than the exception. This turning point in history is thus the one at which each succeeding generation becomes itself a turning point. In SF as well, after an interlude of revolutionary anticipation that was, from Condorcet to Percy Shelley, focused on prophetic visions of immediately attainable human possibilities and validated by a dynamic philosophy of humanity, the alternative time came to be situated in an anticipated future, and SF finally grew to be aesthetically structured by a "positive" scientific cognition. It is against this norm that we must understand all subsequent nineteenth-century SF, which gradually spread through more nations as capitalism, technology, and the reacting expectations of a radically better or at any rate different future themselves spread through the contracting world, and as "world literature" in Goethe's sense loomed on the cultural horizon. This holds true even when the anticipatory norm seems to be—but is in fact not wholly—transgressed, as in Mary Shelley and Jules Verne.

1. RADICAL RHAPSODY

[The poet] beholds the future in the present, and his thoughts are the germs of the flower and the fruit of latest time.

P. B. Shelley

1.0.   When Time is the ocean on whose farther shore the alternative life is situated, Jerusalem can be latent in England:

> I will not cease from mental fight,
> Nor shall my sword sleep in my hand
> Till we have built Jerusalem
> In England's green and pleasant land.

Blake's preface to *Milton* fuses the stronger collective activism and the Biblical tradition of such future horizons: "Jerusalem is called Liberty among the children of Albion" (*Jerusalem*). In the Bible, old Hebraic communism—the desert tradition of prizing men above possessions—intermittently gave rise to expectations of a time when everyone shall "buy wine and milk without money and without price" (Isaiah) and when "nation shall not life up sword against nation . . . but they shall sit every man under his vine and under fig tree; and none shall make them

afraid" (Micah), even to "a new Heavens and a new Earth: and
the former shall not be remembered, nor come into mind"
(Isaiah). Christ's communism of love was resolutely turned toward such a millennium. Throughout the intervening centuries
heretic sects and plebeian revolts kept this longing alive. Joachim
Di Fiore announced a new age without church, state, or possessions, when the flesh should again be sinless and Christ dissolved
in the community of friends. By way of the seventeenth-century
religious revolutionaries this tradition led to Blake. His age witnesses a new, lay prophetic line from Babeuf and Shelley to
Marx, fusing poetry and politics and inveighing against the great
Babylon of class-state, "the merchants of the earth" and "the
kings of the earth who have committed fornication with her"
(Revelation). As of Blake's time the future is a new existential
horizon corroding what he calls the "apparent surfaces" of the
present, etching it in as unsatisfactory. As in Virgil's Fourth Ec-
logue, "the great succession of the ages begins anew."

   1.1.   Except for some insignificant precursors, SF anticipation
began as an integral part of the French Enlightenment's confidence in cognitive and social progress. Its "drawing-room communists" Mably and Morelly drew up blueprints transferring
Plato's argument against private property from heavenly ideas
into nature's moral laws. At the conservative end of the opposi-
tional political spectrum, Sébastien Mercier's hero, who wakes up
in *Year 2440* (1770 and 1786), dwelt in the first full-fledged utopian anticipation: in it, progress had led to constitutional government, moral and technical advances (to wit: a phonograph playing recorded cries of wounded is used to educate princes), and a
substitution of science for religion. The noblest expression of
such a horizon was Condorcet's *Esquisse d'un tableau historique des
progrès de l'esprit humain (Sketch . . . of the Progress of Human Mind,*
written in 1793), which envisaged a turning point in human
history—the advent of a new man arising out of the "limitless
perfectibility of the human faculties and the social order." Perfected institutions and scientific research would eradicate inhumanity, conquer nature and chance, extend human senses, and
lead in an infinite progression to an Elysium created by reason
and love for humanity. Condorcet tried to work toward such a
state within the Revolution, just as did François "Gracchus"
Babeuf, in whom culminates the century of utopian activism be-

fore Marx. Equality, claimed Babeuf, was a lie along with Liberty and Fraternity so long as property (including education) is not wholly equalized through gaining power for the starved against the starvers. An *association* of men in a planned production and distribution without money is the only way of "chaining destiny," of appeasing the "perpetual disquiet of each of us about our tomorrows." For a great hope was spreading among the lower classes that the just City was only a resolute hand's grasp away, that—as Babeuf's fellow conspirators wrote in *The Manifesto of the Equals*—"the French Revolution is merely the forerunner of another Revolution, much greater and more solemn, that will be the last." Even when Babeuf as well as Condorcet were permanently silenced and the revolution was taken over by Napoleon, even when anticipatory SF turned to blueprints of all-embracing ideal systems eschewing politics, it remained wedded to the concept of humanity as association. This may be seen in Blake as well as in Saint-Simon and Fourier.

1.2.   The latter two great system-builders of utopian anticipation can here be mentioned only insofar as their approaches are found in and analogous to much SF. In a way, the whole subsequent history of change within and against capitalism has oscillated between Saint-Simon's radical social engineering and Fourier's radical quest for harmonious happiness, which flank Marxism on either side. Henri de Saint-Simon anticipated that only industry, "the industrial class" (from wage-earners to industrialists), and its organizational method are pertinent in the new age. The "monde renversé" where this "second nation" is scorned must be righted by standing that world on its feet again. This full reversal means in terms of temporal orientation "the great moral, poetic, and scientific operation which will shift the Earthly Paradise and transport it from the past into the future" (*Opinions littéraires, philosophiques et industrielles*), constituting a welfare state of increasing production and technological command of a whole globe by a united White civilization. This "Golden Age of the human species" is to be attained by "a positive Science of Man" permitting predictive extrapolation. Saint-Simon is the prophet of engineers and industrial productivity, applicable equally to a regulated capitalism or an autocratic socialism. The Suez Canal as well as Stalin, and all SF writings in which the hero is the "ideologically neutral" engineering organizer—from Verne to Asimov or from Bellamy to the feebler, utopian Wells—are saintsimonian.

For all his rational organizing, Saint-Simon had forsaken eighteenth-century Rationalism by answering the great Swiftian question "What is Man?" in terms of economic life rather than of "nature" and "natural rights"—even if he then retreated to positing three separate human natures or psychophysiological classes (rational, administrative, and emotive) whose representatives will form the ruling "Council of Newton," the college of cardinals of his "New Christianity." Charles Fourier went much further, basing a radically humanized economy entirely upon a complex series of desires. Civilization "thwarted and falsified" them whereas it could and should have increased gratification of all passions—sensual, collective (desires for respect, friendship, love, and a reconstituted family), or "serial" (desire for faction, variety, and unity). It is a world turned inside out (*monde à rebours*) in which the physician has to hope for "good fevers," the builder for "good fires," and the priest for "the good dead;" where family means adultery (and Fourier enumerates with witty glee 49 types of cuckolds), riches mean bankruptcy, work is constraint, property ruins the proprietor, abundance leads to unemployment, and the machine to hunger. Against this Fourier elaborated a method of "absolute deviation" which was to lead to a world where both work and human relations would be a matter of "passionate attraction." Men and their passions are not equal but immensely varied, like notes in the harmonic scale, colors in the spectrum, or dishes at a gastronomic banquet, and have to be skilfully composed in a "calculus of the Destinies." Corresponding to the potential harmony of the "social movement" are series of animal, vegetable, geometric, and cosmic relationships. There will accordingly be 18 different creations on Earth in this passional cosmology; ours is the first and worst, having to traverse five horrible stages from Savagery down to Civilization before ascending through "Guarantism" (the economicosexual welfare state of federated productive associations or *phalanstères*) to Harmony. At that point humanity will have cleansed the Earth of sexual and economic repression, illnesses, nations, a production sundered from consumption, and the struggle for existence; and the Earth—itself a living being in love with another bisexual planet—will respond by melting the polar ice, turning the oceans into something like lemonade (all of this elaborately justified by physics), and producing useful "anti-beasts," such as the anti-lion, as well as new senses for men. The blessed life of Harmony and the succeeding 16 creations (the last one sees the end of the globe) will turn inside out the procedures of class power: courts and priests will be Courts of Love and priesthoods of sex, armies will clean, plant, and reconstruct, work will become play and art, and "abnormality" the mainspring of society. Fourier's shattering interplay of maniacal poetry and ironical dialectics, rooted in the deep longings of the classes crushed by commerce and industry, in a genuine folk imagination with its immense strengths and foibles, will reappear in garden cities and kibbutzim, communes and "retribalization." In his exemplary scenes and characters—witness Nero becoming a respected butcher in Harmony, much like Rabelais's King Anarch—he is himself writing warm SF. In spite of the important modifications, this will be reproduced by the rare but precious visions fusing relativist sociopolitics, erotics, and cosmology in SF, from Blake and Shelley through Defontenay and Stapledon to Le Guin and Delany.

1.3.   Blake and Shelley too rejected the orthodox division of man into body versus soul and of society into classes, as well as the merely given "human form." Blake. championed Man's individual and collective "imaginative body" rising as a Brobdingnagian giant into a projected free fulfillment simultaneously economic, sexual, and creative. The hypocritical and cruel civilization of Church, Army, Palace, and Merchant, with its principle of selfhood, brings about jealous possessiveness with regard to children and women, shame in sexual love, and slavery to hunger and toil. Money, the cement of this fallen society, murders the poor by stunting and the rich by corrupting their imaginative needs, thus engendering sterility: the prophetic revolutionary or "Reprobate" is the creative counterauthority to the official "Elect," and his followers constitute the "Redeemed." Therefore, Blake sang the giant American and French Revolutions in his Promethean "Orc cycle" of the 1790s—from *The French Revolution, The Marriage of Heaven and Hell, America*, and *Europe* to *The Four Zoas*—which announced the end of post-Genesis history and the advent of a new divine Man in a realm of freedom (a term Marx too would use). Revolution is identical with imagination and life, and absolutely unavoidable; but if its

beginning is in politics, its end is in a joyous Joachimite
Jerusalem where the body personal and the body politic will have
been redeemed. The world as historical process is experienced
and indeed co-created by poetic vision. However, as the American and French experiences turned to bourgeois rule and aggressive conquests, and as English repression grew virulent,
Blake's earlier work remained unpublished and unfinished. Orc
aged into his Rationalist sky-god antagonist Urizen; Blake came
to stress timeless religious apocalypse and compensation through
art instead of the imminent passage through the Earthly
Paradise of sexuality and benevolent nature to the Eden of
creativity. His fantasies of cosmogonic history read like a gigantic
inventory of later "far-out" SF, from Stapledon and E.E. Smith
to Clarke and Van Vogt. But unlike their impoverished strain-
ings into cosmic sensations, his estranging of Newton's world
model converts it into a richly (if confusingly) metamorphic creation. Even the most opaque pseudomythology in the later Blake
retains the estranging principle of multiple vision which sees the
unfallen world within the fallen one, and the cognitive orientation of an "Innocence [that] dwells with Wisdom." In his last
year, in a time of bread riots, he persisted in his biblical communism: "Give us the bread that is our due and right, by taking
away money or a price, or tax upon what is Common to all in thy
Kingdom."

1.4. Percy Bysshe Shelley was separated from Blake by the
crucial impact of the French Revolution—visible in utopian literature, for example, in the vigorous political and agrarian democracy of several works by Thomas Spence (*Description of Spensonia*,
1795)—and by an upper-class education. Both these factors set
him irrevocably against Christianity, which he identified as
tyranny; his poetry marks the gradual reorienting of the revolutionary imagination toward political parable and historical vision
rather than religious myth, toward Hellenic, Gnostic, and scientific rather than biblical and Miltonic traditions. From his youth
he had apparently constructed a cosmic, scientific, and political
anticipation for himself in which chemical philosophy would syn-
thesize food as well as dot oceans with and transmute deserts into
gardens, electricity would unlock the secrets of nature, and bal-
loons ensure the abolition of slavery in Africa (all themes that
were to pass into SF through the adventure popularizations of

Verne). His first major work, *Queen Mab* (1813), is an embattled vision of humanity's past, present, and future that draws on contemporary natural sciences as well as *philosophes* like Condorcet and their English systematizer William Godwin for the future ideally perfectible society. Godwin's *Political Justice*—invoking Plato, More, Mably, and Swift's Houyhnhnms—pleaded for property to be equalized so that men could change their character, abandon war and the monogamous family, and finally become immortal by control of mind over matter. Shelley fleshes out such a Rationalist anarchism in his anticipation of a harmonious Earth rejoicing in the perpetual Spring of a fertile and gentle Nature, where "All things are recreated, and the flame / Of consentaneous love inspires all life." In the notes to *Queen Mab*, Shelley develops his views on labor (reducible to two hours daily) as the sole source of wealth, as well as on the inexorable change of the Earth's axis in "a perfect identity between the moral and the physical improvement of the human species" and the speeding up of the mind's perception to vanquish time by "an infinite number of ideas in a minute." Such horizons, along with the poem's forceful attacks on the ruling political tyranny, capitalist selfishness and corruption, church and religion, made of it, despite legal persecution, the bible of English working-class radicalism from the Owenites to the Chartists and beyond.

Queen Mab is the concluding chord in the great sequence of societal and cosmic anticipations accompanying the democratic revolutions in America and France. From Diderot and Condorcet to Blake and almost all the European Romantics, two generations, shared the expectation of an imminent millennium of peace, freedom, and brotherhood:

> Not in Utopia—subterranean fields—
> Or some secreted island, Heaven knows where!
> But in the very world, which is the world
> Of all of us—the place where, in the end,
> We find our happiness, or not at all!
>
> [Wordsworth, *The Prelude*]

But the revulsion from the results of revolution "was terrible," observed Shelley in the preface to his *Revolt of Islam* (1818):

> Thus, many of the most ardent and tender-hearted . . . have
> been morally ruined by what a partial glimpse of the events

they deplored appeared to show as the melancholy desolation of all their cherished hopes. Hence gloom and misanthropy have become the characteristics of the age in which
we live, the solace of a disappointment that unconsciously
finds relief only in the wilful exaggeration of its own despair.

The shift of SF location from space to the present or immediate
future—that is, to a radically alternative historical turning, fusing
the present with the future—was (we can now see) arrested by a
politically caused "moral ruin," and rechanneled either back into
mythical timelessness or into the staking out of anticipation in
distant futures. These alternatives develop at that historical moment into different—twin but opposed—genres and atmos-
pheres. A *fantasy* more tenuous, internalized, and horrific than
the later Blake emerges as a new shudder and genre in Romantic
melodrama, tale, and narrative poem. In particular, Coleridge's
Ancient Mariner, using scientific observations and the polar voyage as metaphor for the breakdown of human relationships in an
alienating society, had a profound effect on Mary Shelley and
Poe, and through them on much subsequent SF. On the other
hand, Percy Shelley is (together with Fourier) the great poetic
forerunner of the SF anticipation saved from arid Victorian
political or natural-science didacticism by also being a *parabolic
analogy*. In the hands of poets, whether in verse or prose, such
analogy, simultaneously collective and intimate, has cosmic pre-
tensions over and beyond sociopolitical (later also technological)
anticipation; rather than extrapolation, it is an alternative.

The Revolt of Islam itself is a not quite focused "alternative
history" about a loving pacifist-revolutionary couple who are defeated politically but not ruined morally because they keep faith
with their personal love as well as with the future vision of
"divine Equality." Laon and Cythna must die in this "Winter of
the world," but "Spring comes, though we must pass, who
made / The promise of its birth." Parallel to the satirical comedy
Swellfoot the Tyrant, a sarcastic political travesty of *Oedipus Rex* as
beast fable, Shelley's culminating statement comes in *Prometheus
Unbound* (1820). This "lyrical drama" is a delicately tough parable or dialectical allegory in which the notions (whether lyrical
images or dramatic *personae*) flow into each other in iridescent
and eddying metamorphoses, aesthetically and philosophically

no less breathtakingly novel and daring than consistent. The characters are therefore subversive, self-renewing processes rather than fixed correspondences. Subject to this caveat, Prometheus may be said to stand for the Humanity that created evil in the shape of its oppressor Jupiter, and also for intellect and intellectuals as champions of the oppressed. In order to escape the fate of the French Revolution or of Blake's Orc, he renounces hate, in spite of torments by Furies, who stand for the forces of court, church, war, commerce, and law and also for ethical anguish and despondency: outer political and inner psychological tenor are convertible in this multiply woven "fable." Jupiter is thereupon toppled by Demogorgon (the subterranean and plebeian titanic Necessity of nature and society, and also subversive imagination, associated with volcanic and earthquake imagery), who has been contacted by Prometheus's bride Asia (Love or overriding human sympathy). Imagination, Love, and Hercules (Force both as strength and as armed insurrection) liberate Prometheus and bring about a renewed peaceable life on "Fortunate isles," where evil and ugly masks have been stripped off all nature and man remains

> Sceptreless, free, uncircumscribed,—but man:
> Equal, unclassed, tribeless, and nationless,
> Exempt from awe, worship, degree; the king
> Over himself; just, gentle, wise;—but man:
> Passionless? no: . . .
>
> . . . .
> Nor yet exempt, tho' ruling them like slaves,
> From chance, and death, and mutability. . . .
>   [3.194–201]

In the final act even this Earthly Paradise is after "an hundred ages" superseded by Time stopping in a full unfolding of human psychic and cosmic potentiality. The universe too grows Promethean, and the newly warmed and habitable Moon sings a paean of loving praise to redeemed Earth in a lyrical finale of surpassing power, imbued with the peculiar Shelleian "liquid splendor," often in images of vivifying electricity. The cosmic drama ends in such a libertarian, gravityless, "uncircumscribed" counterpart and counterproject to Dante's mystic rose of light and musical harmony at the end of *Paradiso*.

Shelley's expressionist lyricism, using poetic abstraction as an "intelligible and beautiful analogy" with the most precise apprehensions of mind and nature and their most sensitive historical oscillations, gives poetry the power to comprehend all knowledge. Politics, cosmology, and natural sciences such as chemistry, electricity, and astronomy are potential liberators of humanity. They are equally based on labor and Promethean thought:

> Our toil from thought all glorious forms shall cull,
> To make this Earth, our home, more beautiful,
> And Science, and her sister, Poesy,
> Shall clothe in light the fields and cities of the free!
>
> [*The Revolt of Islam*, canto 5]

And humanity cannot be made whole again (he resolutely agreed with Mary Wollstonecraft) as long as "Woman as the bond-slave dwells / Of man, a slave; and life is poisoned in its wells." Loving women are equal, if not indeed privileged, bearers of human redemption in all of Shelley's major poems.

Parallel to such poetry of cognition, Shelley's estrangement is the most delicate yet vigorous personal emotion at the sight of life enslaved, approaching it always "with a fresh wonder and an insatiable indignation"[1]—a line such as "Hell is a city much like London" (*Peter Bell the Third*) being quite Swiftian. Often at the limits of the expressible, "With thoughts too swift and strong for one lone human breast," his insight into scientific and political thought as strife and sympathy between men, cosmic nature, and time makes of *Prometheus Unbound* "one of the few great philosophical poems in English."[2] In it, outwardly exploding love overwhelms gravity, setting humanity off on its cosmic voyage, world without end. This anti-gravity is "[in terms of space] the pull of the void itself, in terms of time it is the future, which is also an absolute emptiness, waiting for man to 'invent' it."[3] With it culminate the tensions and resolutions of the cosmico-political revolutionary utopianism in Shelley's opus, strongly imbued with political alternative, Lucretian cosmic and anthropological speculation, humanized science, and indeed utopian romance from

---

1. H. N. Brailsford (Bibliography IV A), p. 158.
2. Carl H. Grabo (Bibliography IV A), p. 198.
3. Christopher Small (Bibliography IV A), p. 239.

works such as Paltock's *Peter Wilkins* (1750) and J. H. Lawrence's matriarchal *Empire of the Nairs* (1801). In their texture and structure, Shelley's significant poems "are microcosmic revolutions which help 'quicken' the unborn worlds whose outlines they reflect and describe."[4] Though the integral revolutionary and utopian optimism of Shelley's is a lone, soon-quenched blaze halfway between the cosmic voyages of Rabelais or Cyrano and those of the Leninist "storm and stress" of 1915–25 (Mayakovsky's or Krleža's, for example),[5] it is a proof that SF can be supreme poetry: and vice versa.

2. Romantic Recoil

Forward, forward, ay and backward, downward too into the abysm. . . .
—Alfred Tennyson

2.1 Mary Shelley was the daughter of two prominent radical writers, William Godwin and Mary Wollstonecraft, and wrote *Frankenstein, or The Modern Prometheus* (1818) as her husband was preparing to write *Prometheus Unbound*. Yet in this revealingly flawed hybrid of horror tale and philosophical SF she indicated with considerable force the widespread recoil from Promethean utopianism, that "disappointment that unconsciously finds relief only in the wilful exaggeration of its own despair" which was to become a dominant tendency in subsequent English-language SF. The novel's theme is twofold: the unfolding of Frankenstein's hybris in creating artificial life is intertwined with a parable on the fate of an alienated representative individual—his Creature (called "monster" only twice, I think, in the text). A series of paralogisms and contradictions emerges from the opposition of these two themes and characters.

A comparison of Mary Shelley's stance to the radical Romanticism of her husband can best identify the main contradictions. Both Victor Frankenstein's resolve to "pioneer a new way, explore unknown powers, and unfold to the world the deepest mysteries of creation" (chapter 3), and Walton's parallel resolve to discover (for the Romantics practically a synonym of "invent" and "create") the unfrozen, warm geographic and magnetic pole,

---

4. Gerald McNiece (Bibliography IV A), p. 135.
5. See on Mayakovsky chapter 11, and on Krleža my essay "Voyage to the Stars and Pannonian Mire," *Mosaic* 6 (Summer 1973).

the hyperborean utopia of "a country of eternal light" and "a land surpassing in wonders and beauty every region hitherto discovered on the habitable globe" (Letter 1), represent favorite, permanent, and passionately held ideals of Percy Shelley. True, in such a philosophical romance, the discoverer-inventor's desire to learn "the secrets of heaven and earth . . . the outward substance of things, or the inner spirit of nature and the mysterious soul of man" (chap. 2) might be punished by the Powers That Be. But a suffering Prometheus would remain as unbowed as Lucifer in *Paradise Lost*, romantically reinterpreted after the image of all the subversive poets, *philosophes*, and scientists, all the utopian enthusiasts in the spectrum that runs from Rousseau through the "philanthropic" revolutionists (notably the Illuminati who hailed from the same university of Ingolstadt where Frankenstein studies and fashions his creature)[6] and through Condorcet to Byron. No doubt: the central grandiose event of the age, the French Revolution—the awful course, consequences, and lessons of which shaped both Shelleys and guided all the other influences on them—was a burning disappointment. But for Percy Shelley it had at the same time "created and nourished hopes that could never die," and his programmatic passion became to discover the causes of and remedies to the corruption within men and society that had led to its failure.[7] Obversely, though sharing his anguish at that failure and his belief that one major cause for it was hateful violence on both sides, Mary Shelley was nearer to her father in stressing the supreme necessity for civil order, and therefore the unacceptability of sudden radical change and the proneness of the lower classes and fanatic intellectuals to bloodshed. The Promethean inventor was for her possible and impressive, but his invention was from the outset doomed to failure. Such a "fit of enthusiastic madness" (chap. 24), transferred from the ideal realm of artistic shaping and marvelous voyage of discovery to actual philosophico-scientific intervention in everyday social life, grew for her into a blasphemous horror tale, one related to Walton as an awful warning not to pursue discovery by solitary imagina-

6. On the Illuminati and their importance for the Shelleys' understanding of the French Revolution see the persuasive indications of McNiece, pp. 22–23 and 96–99.
7. McNiece, p. 41.

tion, which will inevitably sunder him from warm fellow-feeling. As he was rendered friendless by Romantic poetry, science, and utopian travel dreams, so too had Frankenstein spurned languages and politics, recapitulating in his personal history the exclusion of human values from the "objective" post-Baconian science. Just as Walton is ruthlessly prepared to sacrifice his crew and his own life for the advancement of knowledge, which he equates with dominion over nature in the name of an abstract mankind, so had Frankenstein quite scientifically concluded that "to examine the causes of life, we must first have recourse to death" (chap. 4) and proudly gone about creating a quasi-human being with the aid of a merely analytical science. Of the two traditional Promethean pursuits of animating and shaping man, he had succeeded in the first but failed in the second: Prometheus *pyrphoros*, the subversive thief of the "divine spark," had unaccountably become divorced from Prometheus *plasticator*, the artist-molder of human clay. As in some horror tales of blasphemous alchemists and their elixir of life (Godwin's *St. Leon*, for example), the resulting creation is sterile and indeed demonically destructive of all values. When the Promethean overreacher finally acknowledges the rightness of Jovian power and its values, he turns into a rightly punishable Faust. What Orwell would expose as brainwashing, Mary Shelley shows as just expiation.

However, if Frankenstein's Creature is sterile, it is living; if botched, it is suffering. For Percy Shelley, electricity was vital energy imbued with natural human sympathy, while the "calculating faculty" or principle (*Defence of Poetry*)—the calculation of mechanical and social power—informed both unimaginative technology and the ideology of private profit. Mary's Frankenstein, on the contrary, used electricity precisely with mathematics and charnel-house dissection, as a quantifying rather than qualitative tool. His theme is in the tradition of the Gothic story, in which the universal horror and disgust at his creature would simply prefigure its behavior and its hideous looks testify to its corrupt essence. Yet the Creature's pathetic story of awakening to sentience and consciousness of his untenable position as a subject (for whom "he" is used right from the moment of animation) provides an almost diametrically opposed point of view. His theme is both the compositional core and the real SF novum that lifts *Frankenstein* above the level of a grippingly mindless Gothic

thriller. The objective eye looking at empirical surfaces, that orthodox organ of things as they are, is balanced by the inward
sympathy with the Creature's subjective feelings. Far from being
foul within, he sets out as an ideal "noble savage," benevolent
and good, loving and yearning for love. His is not the Individualistic quest of superior discoverer-geniuses like Frankenstein and Walton, but a humbler and more basic search for
human solidarity and communion. His terrible disappointment
and alienation is that of the typical Romantic hero—as he himself
points out, of Goethe's Werther or the Romantic Lucifer—
wandering outcast through the icy landscape. Mary Shelley's very
important contribution was to find an objective correlative for
her characteristic ideological oscillation between Shelleyan rebellion and Godwinian protesting quietism by transferring this outcast status into the strategic halfway house between orthodox
theology and radical politics: into biological necessity. The Creature is caught between his vital spark of freedom and the iron
grip of scorn and persecution that arises from his racial or
species alienness.

The aspect in which the Creature is a representative of suffering Mankind oppressed by a hidden and at least indifferent (if
not evil) Creator is still astoundingly alive as well as directly on
the axis of the main, heretic SF tradition that links Swift to Wells.
We are back on the shores of Houyhnhnmland as seen by Godwin: a "sensitive and rational animal" (chap. 24), less guilty than
man, is again demystifying human history, politics, psychology,
and metaphysics, as, for example, in the Creature's bizarre education by proxy that recapitulates in brief the Romantic world
view:

> The strange system of human society was explained to me.
> . . . I learned that the possessions most esteemed by your
> fellow-creatures were, high and unsullied descent united
> with riches. A man might be respected with only one of
> those advantages; but without either, he was considered . . .
> as a vagabond and a slave, doomed to waste his powers for
> the profits of the chosen few! And what was I? I knew that I
> possessed no money, no friends, no kind of property. I was,
> besides, endued with a figure hideously deformed and
> loathsome; I was not even of the same nature as man. . . .
> Was I then a monster . . . ? [chap. 13]

However, the More-to-Diderot tradition of "contrary" SF is not only continued by the Romantics but also undergoes a metamorphosis at their hands. The addition of "sensitive" to the definition of man as a rational animal that (as is discussed in the preceding chapter) dominated Swift's whole epoch points to a great shift across the watershed of the failed democratic and costly industrial revolutions. Humanity is now being shown up not only as irrational but also as cruel, in impassioned rather than satirical accents, by a suffering and wronged creature who wants to belong rather than by an enlightened and wondering observer. This shift corresponds exactly to the shift from far-off spaces to the present that should be radically transformed, from More's or Swift's static juxtaposition of islands and cities to the dynamic mutual pursuit of Frankenstein and his Creature across the extreme landscapes of lifeless cold and desolation, from behavioral to sentimental psychology, from universal human nature to mutual relationships of men and women in society. Life, the central category of the Romantics, "is opposed to being in the same way as movement to immobility, as time to space, as the secret wish to the visible expression."[8]

This hallowed status of sentient life and its genesis was threatened by a capitalist social practice—including ever more prominently a use of physical sciences—that substituted "mechanical or two-way time for history, the dissected corpse for the living body, dismantled units called 'individuals' for men-in-groups, or in general the mechanically measurable or reproducible for the inaccessible and the complicated and the organically whole."[9] Among other consequences, this led to a growing preoccupation and fascination with *automata* as puzzling "doubles" of man. Before Mary Shelley, such a semi-alien twin had either been treated as a wondrously ingenious toy (in the eighteenth century) or as an unclean demonic manifestation (in most German Romantics). In the first case it belonged to "naturalistic" literature, in the second to horror fantasy. The nearest approximation to an artificial creature seen as perfect human loveliness but later revealed to be a horrible mechanical construct was provided by E.T.A. Hoffmann in *The Sandman*

8.   Michel Foucault, *The Order of Things* (London, 1970), p. 278.
9.   Lewis Mumford (Bibliography IV A), p. 50.

(1816). But even he oscillated between fiends and physics, and his Olimpia is seen solely through the perceptions of a dazzled observer. Mary Shelley's Creature is not only undoubtedly alive though alien, fashioned out of human material instead of the inorganic wires of puppetry, and unmistakably this-worldly, he is also allowed to gain our sympathy by being shown from the inside, as a subject degradingly treated like an object. However, because of the "exaggerated despair" which Percy Shelley accurately diagnosed, it is not only human society that is monstrous in its dealing with the Creature, but he too is "objectively" a Monster: sentient and intelligent though inhuman, animated creature without animating harmony, starting out like a newborn baby yet from no woman born—the intolerable paradox, in brief, of living *and* unnatural.

In a book pervaded by the pathetic if again paradoxical sympathy between man and inorganic nature, both the thermodynamic metaphors and the compositional metonymies meet in the body and its psychophysiology (that is to say, again in biology). The devastation of feeling has a correlative in the icy landscape and isolated characters; the ever narrowing imaginative vortex plunges through the three narrations from the North Pole into the inner warmth of the Creature and his observation of the family sentiments, at whose center lies the feminine and Mediterranean warmth of the Safie story,[10] only to reascend back into the killings, masculine loneliness, and final coldness of death at the top of the world. The hidden marvelous voyage of (not merely in) the text is a double inversion of Dante's or Milton's descent in that, first, the chthonic warmth of the Earth's center is positive and vivifying, a deep and consoling "maternal nature" (chap. 9), and second, the protagonists are barred and driven away from this Earthly Paradise into the outer darkness of

10. I am indebted to Marc A. Rubenstein's stimulating insights (Bibliography IV A) into the "maternal" metaphoric system hidden in the novel and opposed to its "masculine creation," even where I largely disagree with the uses he puts them to. See also James Rieger (Bibliography IV A), pp. 79–81, 156, et passim, who rightly refers to Symmes, Poe, and the Hollow Earth theory. In fact, *Frankenstein* is structured as a Maelstrom the vivifying center of whose spiral can only be tantalizingly approached before the reader-voyager is symmetrically spewed out. Jules Verne's *Journey to the Center of the Earth* (see chapter 7) is an optimistic counterproject belonging to the same morphological family, and explicating (probably by way of Poe) a number of *Frankenstein*'s structural implications.

mutual pursuit, misery, and commiseration, into the Coleridgean hell of dazzling icefields: "For Mary Shelley, there are only lost paradises."[11]

Frankenstein's relationship to his Creature remains thus unclear: their two themes and viewpoints contradict each other. If there is a moral focus to this parable outside of vaguely Christian melodramatics, then the Creature is that focus, so that the reader cannot treat him as a Gothic Monster, merely validated by science rather than by demonology. But conversely, if one is to look at this novel as SF, a whole cluster of fundamental but unresolved cognitive questions appears: and centrally, why did the Creature have to be hideous or the Creation botched? Frankenstein's unmotivated creative haste might conceivably (though I do not think so) be put down to Mary Shelley's technical clumsiness: even then, why should alienness have to be equated with hideousness? The tenor and the vehicle are startlingly discrepant—a signal that strong psychic censorship is at work. Yet the vitality of the parable shows that Mary Shelley's personal history and imagination fused here with the passions and nightmares of a whole social class—the intelligentsia in capitalism, oscillating between radical titanism and conservative recuperation. Both of these positions are viewed in the wavering light of Mary Shelley's central ambiguity: the interfusion of an understanding sympathy with a guilty horror at the subversive novelty, the radical Other. As in Percy Shelley, "new chemistry is but old alchemy writ legibly; both are ciphers for politics."[12] Victor Frankenstein and his startling creation are a scientific cipher for an overhasty radical intellectual at the time of the French Revolution animating (like the Ingolstadt Illuminati, so well known to the Shelleys) the "[hardly adequate] materials" (chap. 4) of the broad popular forces. The *philosophe*-scientist who awakens and animates these victimized masses with "no kind of property" in the hope of a new and glorious creation finds that persecution and injustice exacerbate them to the point of indiscriminate slaughtering. Such a hypothesis, in which the novel is the emblematic self-awareness of a wavering and guilt-ridden rebellious intelligentsia looking at the implications of the French Revolution, can solve

11.   Jean de Palacio (Bibliography IV A), p. 41.
12.   Rieger, p. 29.

the unexplained (and as far as I can see otherwise unexplainable) cruces of the Creature's unsuccessful fashioning and the universal revulsion felt for it. Mary Shelley's reservations about the effects of revolutionary animation went much further than her husband's and amounted almost to a guilty retraction. The frozen whiteness, for example, which is for Percy Shelley the element of a tyrannical Jupiter (as with Blake's Urizen or Nobodaddy), is in Mary returned to the scene where the overreachers who attempted to break through the "ideal bounds" of natural and divine order "and pour a torrent of light into our dark world" (chap. 4) get their pathetic but finally appropriate deserts. The perversion of their utopian dreams results in a gloom and misanthropy that, as Percy suggested in the preface to *The Revolt of Islam*, was rooted in the moral ruin and revulsion from the French Revolution, as a consequence of which "misery has come home, and men appear . . . as monsters thirsting for each other's blood" (chap. 9).

This also explains why both Frankenstein and the Creature decline from great expectations and naive optimism to self-devouring, mutually obsessed, and community-destroying loneliness. If there is little logic of events in the plot, there is a logic of feelings, which can alone unify the not quite compatible aspects of the Frankenstein-Creature relationship. This relationship is, incongruously, one of creator and creature, of two biological aliens, and finally of a soon repentant intellectual animator and a soon exasperated plebeian force. Frankenstein and the Creature may also be in some ways comparable to Freud's Ego and Id, but they are not reducible to such a Jekyll-and-Hyde constellation. Just as in Blake and Percy Shelley—or in *The Tempest*—the relationships in *Frankenstein* body forth a collective rather than private psychology. The Creature is warmer and finally more intelligent than his creator, like Milton's Adam turned Satan; nor can Freudianism explain why the lower class of Id, that plebs of the psyche, must always be deemed destructive and lawless. Indeed, a more revealing parallel is (with all due reservations) to be found in the Creature's exchanging an admiring, Miranda-like naive and benevolent wonder at humanity for a Calibanic rampage of slaughter: the ideal Godwinian anarchist finds he can become a social being only by perpetuating society's most cruel norms. H.G. Wells was to describe *his* novel of the indifferent creator painfully fashioning monstrous creatures, *The Island of Dr. Moreau*, as a theological grotesque (see chapter 9). *Frankenstein*'s peculiar historical position and advantage is that on the one hand its biology partakes of a political as well as a theological grotesque, while on the other its pioneering scientific horizons proved more potent than Blake's or even Percy Shelley's heretic but archaic abstractions. Biology, the Romantics' central science in a spread that runs from Shelley's electric fluid to Goethe's *Ur*-plant, can in its "objective" version disjoin ethical ideals, such as compassion for the Creature, from living reality, such as that of his crucial ugliness: "I compassioned him, and sometimes felt a wish to console him; but when I looked upon him, when I saw the filthy mass that moved and talked, my heart sickened, and my feelings were altered to those of horror and hatred" (chap. 17). Biology is thus the privileged form of pseudo-scientific critique of revolutionary utopianism: "if Prometheus, in the romantic tradition, is identified with human revolt, is the monster what that revolt looks like from the other side?"[13]

Not that Mary Shelley was a Social Darwinist *avant la lettre* (although once outside Percy's magnetic field she soon reverted to a staunch upholder of bourgeois law and order). In fact, the paradoxes of a novel based on the principle of human sympathy yet also guilty of a racism which betokens total failure of sympathy[14] could find a resolution only in the peace of universal

13. M. K. Joseph (Bibliography IV A), p. xiv.

14. A very curious feedback system between fiction and social history, that confirms the position of Frankenstein's Creature within what one might call the Caliban Complex of bourgeois imagination, with particular reference to England's tropical colonies and its darker races, can be found in the fact (which I take from McNiece, pp. 29 ff.) that Percy Shelley read very carefully Bryan Edwards's *History of the West Indies* and its lengthy account of the savage Black and mulatto revolt in San Domingo in 1791, attributed by the author to incitement to "subversion and innovation" by visionary intellectuals and politicians from Paris, and replete with strongly imagined scenes of mass murder and cruel butchery as the inevitable result of "the monstrous folly of suddenly emancipating barbarous men" (both quotes from Edwards). Mary must have either read or at least known of it, since Percy's reading is recorded in her journal for 1814–15. Reinforced by absorption into Frankenstein's Creature as seen by right-wing simplification, the same ideology reappeared in Canning's 1824 speech in the House of Commons against freeing Black slaves in the Antilles (which I take from Palacio, pp. 649–50). In spite of its length, the pertinent fragment must be quoted: "In dealing with the negro, Sir, we must remember that we are dealing with a being possessing the form and strength of a man, but the intellect only of a child. To turn him loose in the manhood of his physical strength, in the maturity of his physical passions, but in the infancy of his uninstructed reason, would be

death. The Creature's fiery self-immolation on the ice can finally
reconcile action and suffering, warmth and coldness, revolt and
consolation, and return the uncouth product of masculine creation into the womb of maternal nature, to the entropic rest of the
ultimate generic anti-utopia of Death. This final horizon will
recur in Wells's *Time Machine* and, as I argue in chapter 10, a
whole wing of subsequent SF. In it, as in Mary Shelley's revoca-
tion of the radical rhapsodies, it is possible to initiate a revolutionary novum but not to curb its destructiveness. The pursuit of
life, liberty, and happiness ends in misery, bondage, and death as
the novum, in a supposedly inevitable Faustian hybris, oversteps
the familiar, "natural" bondaries of order. Mary Shelley's faithful
transcription of this central antinomy of bourgeois practice is
much superior to any orthodox demonology, as well as to any
Panglossian optimism that (in SF, say, from Godwin to Asimov)
blandly denies the existence of such antinomic evil. But it is also
cognitively inferior to a dialectic which she herself adumbrates at
the end of the novel, when Frankenstein can acknowledge that
his Promethean creation of life has, in the best demonic tradition, boomeranged into death for all his dear ones, and yet can
still exclaim: "I have myself been blasted in these hopes, yet
another may succeed." In this view he was an improper Prometheus or bearer of the novum—a truly new one, with more
patience, love, and success, was to be presented in Percy Shelley's
Prometheus Unbound.

Mary Shelley's other SF novel, *The Last Man* (1826), is a renewed reversal of the perspectives in *Prometheus Unbound*. It first
fashions a somewhat rosewatery romance out of the political liberation of Percy's poem, and then reverses its cosmic optimism
by sending upon mankind a plague that leaves the sole survivor
finally even more isolated, but also more privatized, than Frankenstein or his Creature. The shift of the locale into the historical

---

to raise up a creature resembling the splendid fiction of a recent romance [i.e. *Frankenstein*]; the hero of which constructs a human form, with all the corporeal capabilities of
man, and with the thews and sinews of a giant; but being unable to impart to the work of
his hands a perception of right and wrong, he finds too late that he has only created a
more than mortal power of doing mischief, and himself recoils from the monster which
he has made."

For Mary Shelley's political slide after the 1820s, see Palacio pp. 194 ff., 218 ff., 230 ff.,
et passim, and on *Frankenstein*'s conservative aspects Christian Kreutz (Bibliography
IV A), pp. 144–52.

future (the "tale of the future" becomes six times more frequent after 1800)[15] both enlarges the loneliness of the desert island tale to inescapable planetary proportions and translates the apocalyptic or simply melodramatic fantasy tale into a *black SF anticipation*. Mary Shelley's novel canonizes a tradition adumbrated in several works which followed the debacle of eighteenth-century hopes and often posited a new ice age (Cousin de Grainville's prose epic *Le Dernier homme* translated as the "romance in futurity" *Last Men*, Byron's poem "Darkness," and others) by imparting a realistic believability to their topoi of lone landscapes and ghostly cities. This makes *The Last Man* a precursor of the SF biophysics of alienation which extends from Poe and Flammarion to *The Time Machine* and beyond. But the more complex *Frankenstein* remains her permanent contribution, claiming for SF the concern for a personalized working out of overriding sociopolitical and scientific dilemmas. It compromised with horror fantasy by treating them largely in terms of a humorless if not hysterical biology, thus announcing the legions of menacing aliens and androids from Melville, Wells, and Čapek on. Yet even the inconsistent sympathy and responsibility for the Creature which are established in the novel transcend the contrived coincidences, sensational murders, and purple patches of the novel and indeed of most SF writing on this theme (not to speak of Hollywood movies, which as a rule revert to one-dimensional Gothic Monsters). The sense of urgency in *Frankenstein*, situated in an exotic present, interweaves the characters' intimate reactions with their social destiny, an understanding for Promethean science with a feeling for its human results, and marries the exploratory SF parable with the (still somewhat shaky) tradition of the novel. This indicated the way SF would go in meeting the challenge of the cruel times and of Swift's great question what was human nature—to be answered in terms of the human body and of social history.

2.2.   However, the way proved long and thorny. A number of scattered SF writings in Europe appeared in the second third of the nineteenth century with the revival of utopian expectations and Romantic dreams on both slopes of the watershed constituted by the failed 1848 revolutions. In Russia Odoevsky wrote a

15.   My calculation, based on data to be found in Ian Clarke (Bibliography I).

mild anticipation, *The Year 4338* (discussed in chapter 11). In France Louis Geoffroy's *Napoléon apocryphe, 1812-1832* (1836) and Charles Renouvier's aptly titled *Uchronie* (1857 and 1876) introduced into the novel the "alternative history" that was to reach a bittersweet consummation in the twentieth century with and after Anatole France's *Penguin Island* and *On the White Stone*. Emile Souvestre disguised a sermon on the immorality of mechanical progress, which had destroyed the old pieties and would therefore be destroyed by God, as possibly the first systematic anti-utopian anticipation in *Le Monde tel qu'il sera* (*The World as It Shall Be*, 1845); and Etienne Cabet set a treatise expounding authoritarian collectivism and thinly disguised as fiction in the fittingly regressive spatial location of *Voyage en Icarie* (1840); both were only less insipid than Lamartine's dream of a petty-bourgeois European confederation translated as *France and England* (1848). The most significant echo of warm, Fourierist utopian enthusiasms was C.I. Defontenay's *Star* (1854), which used a revived interest in the planetary novel—marked already by Restif's *Les Posthumes* (1802)—for a vivid description, in prose mixed with verse, of a whole solar system with different humanoid species, their physics, politics, and ethics. A utopian humanism and sensibility, which even supplied samples of Starian literature, vivifies Defontenay's narration of their history, which includes a cosmic exodus and return. This work is a lone masterpiece not to be equaled before Stapledon and C. S. Lewis, if not the 1960s. The publication dates of two books written in the same period by exiled workers testify in mute eloquence to the repressive reasons for Defontenay's loneness and such cosmic flights: the Chartist John Francis Bray's *A Voyage from Utopia* (bp. 1957) attempted to merge Swiftian techniques with radical socialist propaganda; and the Fourierist anarchist Joseph Déjacque's *L'Humanisphère* (partial bp. 1899, full 1971) gives a vituperative and rhapsodic vent to his visions of sexual, religious, and sociopolitical libertarianism in 2858. Charles Henningsen's voluminous romance *Sixty Years Hence* (1846), echoing Byron and the Shelleys in its avenger-hero and critique of an extreme plutocracy, though in prudence published anonymously, had a somewhat better fate, probably because of the sentimental and scientific melodrama it deftly fused with politics and economics.

2.3. In the United States, too, utopian writings—popular

since the secularization of the first colonizing impulse—showed some signs of reviving. But such attempts at utopian colonies as Cabet's Icaria or the Brook Farm venture failed, and the detachment from—indeed hostility toward—the everyday world increased among North American writers of the mid-nineteenth century. Living in the country in which the bourgeois way of life progressed most rapidly, these writers recoiled from its optimism most thoroughly. Instead of treating the wondrous novelty in terms of Prometheus, the revolutionary, they came to treat it in terms of Faust, the overreacher who sold his soul to the Devil. Already Goethe had adopted Faust as symbol of the permanent dynamism borne by the bourgeois, and Mary Shelley had substituted him for the Greek Titan midway through *Frankenstein*. The most prominent of the SF recoilers who followed them were Hawthorne, Melville, and Poe. The first often used allegorical fantasy, the second a more or less imaginary voyage, and the third both. In some cases, admittedly marginal to the ensemble of their work, such narratives bordered on or passed into SF.

One of the strong American literary traditions was that of the world supplying moral symbols for the writer, and in particular of the adventurous voyage as an inner quest. It flowed from various updatings of *Pilgrim's Progress*, beginning with Joseph Morgan's Puritan allegory *The History of the Kingdom of Basaruah* (1715), and into the Enlightenment world vision explicated in Joel Barlow's *Columbiad* (1787), a not quite felicitous precursor of *Queen Mab*. This tradition approached SF in the degree in which it adopted a consistently this-worldly novum, as in Brockden Brown and Washington Irving (whose *History of New York* contains a satirical SF sketch, midway between Voltaire and Wells, of Lunarians dealing with Earthmen as Whites did with Indians). Fenimore Cooper also wrote two crotchety and rather perfunctory novels satirizing upstart politics, the better of which, *The Monikins* (1835), at times rises to bitter socioeconomic lucidity. The tradition culminated in Nathaniel Hawthorne's writings as the working out of hypotheses with a symbolically collective rather than individualist character. In short, "there was no major 19th-century American writer of fiction, and indeed few of the second rank, who did not write some SF or at least one utopian romance."[16]

16.   H. Bruce Franklin, *Future Perfect* (Bibliography IV A), p. x.

Hawthorne usually equivocates between the natural and the supernatural, so that the hypnotism and other controlling influences are never cognitively dominant in his major romances. Even in the stories that hinge on the scientist-artist, the somewhat melodramatic allegory suggests that his Faustian urge is unnatural—at worst criminal, as in "The Birthmark," and at best useless except for his inner satisfaction, as in "The Artist of the Beautiful." Only in "Rappaccini's Daughter" (1846) is Hawthorne momentarily prepared to envisage an alternative world and person on their own merits. Though Beatrice is not given as spirited a defense as Frankenstein's Creature, she is at least an innocent and wronged Alien and exercizes considerable passionate attraction (analogous to and probably as a parable for the Fourierist ideas which Hawthorne was to renounce as senseless and wicked after his Brook Farm experience, itself comparable to a poisoned Eden). But finally, her father's revolutionary countercreation is dismissed in an ending more akin to exorcism than to SF.

2.4. On the contrary Edgar Allan Poe took to an exemplary extreme both the autonomy of his imaginary worlds and the isolation of the individual who does not relate to a coherent community but to some metaphysical principle. Poe was economically more exposed to a consistently capitalist society that was finding the artist unnecessary except as a leisure-time entertainer for marginal social strata. History and community meant to him merely a rapidly expanding "dollar-manufacture," a hateful democracy or mob rule, so that his typical protagonist—raising the stakes in comparison with the revolts of the first Romantic generation—ignores almost all human interactions, not only in politics and work but also in sex and knowledge. Science, technology, and all knowledge have become Mephistophelean instead of Promethean powers, fascinating but leading only to dead-ends and destruction; "Poe confronts and represents, as few authors before him, the alienated and alienating quality of the technological environment."[17] Therefore he constructed a compensatory fantasy world connecting an exacerbated inner reality directly to the universe. But this fantasy is a kind of photographic negative of his environment. Feeling is dissociated from

17. David Halliburton (Bibliography IV A), p. 247.

the intelligence and will that had normally acted upon a socially recognizable reality, and a subjective timelessness (indeed a dream time or nightmare time) or instant apprehension of horror efface any objectively measurable or progressing duration: personality and consciousness are here disintegrating. In the actuality "time-keeping had merged with record-keeping in the art of communication."[18] Poe was with Mary Shelley the first significant figure in this tradition to make a living by writing for periodicals (both of them even wrote stories to fit an illustration in a yearbook or magazine, as did many authors of later SF); accordingly, he concentrated on the obstacles to communication. Communication is for Poe a maze of masks, hoaxes, and cryptograms, typified in the manuscript put into a bottle, falsely sent or mysteriously received, revealing truth ambiguously if at all.

Most of Poe's tales exist within the horizons of terror, of flight "out of space—out of time" ("Dream-land"); they are horror-fantasies pretending to a private supernatural reality that is in fact based upon prescientific lore. In this light, Poe is the originator of what is least mature in the writing commercially peddled as SF—an adolescent combination of hysterical sensibility and sensational violence, a dissociation of symbol from imaginative consistency of any (however imaginary) world, a vague intensity of style used for creepy incantation. His protagonist is often "the perpetual American boy-man" with a somewhat hysterical urge "to express himself . . . above, or away from, or beyond our commoner range of experience"; T.S. Eliot, acknowledging his "very exceptional mind and sensibility," has even suggested that Poe's intellect was that "of a highly gifted young person before puberty."[19] Though this may not be fair to Poe, who at his best knew how to present his limitations with ironic distancing, it accurately pinpoints the emotional age of his imitators in the no-man's-land of fantasy passed off as SF, from the work of Haggard and Lovecraft to Bradbury and Beyond.

Three groups of Poe's works have a more direct claim to attention in this overview: those marginally using some SF conven-

18. Mumford, p. 136.
19. First quotation Edward H. Davidson (Bibliography IV A), p. 214; second quotation T.S. Eliot, "From Poe to Valéry," in Eric W. Carlson, ed. (Bibliography IV A), pp. 212–13.

tions, those using SF for comic comment or ideological revelation, and those dealing with cosmological speculations. The first
group comprises the poem "Al Aaraaf," the dialogues "Eiros and
Charmion" (which mentions for the first time the destruction of
Earth in a conflagration caused by a comet) and "The Power
of Words," and the tales of oceanic descent culminating in *The
Narrative of Arthur Gordon Pym* (1838). *Pym* appropriates the
extraordinary-voyage tradition for a metaphysical (and, in the
Tsalal episode, passably racist) quest for purity in the unknown,
presents an interesting use of correspondences between the
world and the protagonist, and possibly ends with the Pole being
an entrance to the hollow Earth popularized in the pseudonymous *Symzonia* (1820). The second group used contemporary
popular SF interests for anticipations like balloon flights across
the Atlantic or—in the wake of George Tucker's *A Voyage to the
Moon* and Richard Locke Adams's celebrated "Moon Hoax"—
to the Moon, and suspended animation (in "The Unparallelled
Adventure of One Hans Pfaall," "The Balloon Hoax," "Some
Words With a Mummy," "Mellonta Tauta," "Von Kempelen and
His Discovery"); but again, it transmuted them into hoaxes and
satires of present-day certainties of progress. "The Man That
Was Used Up" (1840) in this group is the first tale about a man
almost totally composed of artificial organs. The most substantial
among these stories, "Pfaall" (1840) and "Mellonta Tauta" (bp.
1850), are most strongly science-fictional. The interplanetary
flight prepared by an amateur inventor in his backyard, the
verisimilar flight perils and observations, and the glimpses of
grotesque yet kindred Aliens in "Pfaall" gave the cue to much
later space-travel SF. More subtly, so did the future inventions,
political satire, and barriers to understanding of the reader's
times in "Mellonta Tauta" (as also, retrospectively, in "The Thousand and Second Tale of Scheherazade") to later time-travel
SF. The three "mesmeric tales" culminating in the scientifically
motivated horrors of "The Facts in the Case of M. Valdemar"
(bp. 1850), whether used for revelation of Poe's cosmology or
tongue-in-cheek sensationalism, are ancillary to his fantastic
system of correspondences. This third group is subsumed under
Eureka (1848), Poe's crowning piece of essayistic SF, which explicates the highly heretical, complex web of analogies and con-
versions by which, in Poe, life does not end with death, sen-

tience is not confined to organic matter, cosmogony is analogous to individual sensibility and creativity (as in "The Power of Words"), and the universe is God's coded monologue. Such mechanistic metaphysics leads finally to solipsism: whatever the writer can imagine is as good as created, and conversely all that is created is imagined. No wonder Poe appealed to later lonely writers.

In fact, Poe's influence has been immense in both Anglo-American and French SF (the latter has yet to recover from it). Though his ideology and time-horizon tend to horror-fantasy, the pioneering incompleteness of his work provided SF too with a wealth of hints for fusing the rational with the symbolical, such as his techniques of gradual domestication of the extraordinary and of the "half-closed eye" estrangement just glimpsing the extraordinary. With Poe, the tradition of the moral quest became urbanized, escapist, and unorthodox. His influence encompasses on the one hand the mechanical marvels of Verne and the dime-novels, and on the other the escapist strain in some of the "hardest" U.S. SF, for example, Robert A. Heinlein's time-traveling solipsism. Both are blended in the Wellsian grotesque tradition, from some of Wells's cumulations of believable terrors to, say, the symbolical tales of James Blish or Damon Knight. Poe's notes stressing verisimilitude, analogy, and probability for the wondrous story made him also the first theoretician of SF.

2.5. Herman Melville's whole opus is "a major contribution to the literature of created societies,"[20] for he took the Faustian quest more seriously than Hawthorne and less necrophilically than Mary Shelley and Poe. *Mardi* (1849), though somewhat formless, is an iconoclastic "extraordinary voyage" among islands of unsatisfactory mythologies, politics, and philosophies that blends memories of Polynesia with elements from Rabelais. "The Tartarus of Maids," a revulsion against sexual physiology masked as a burlesque alternative, is on the margins of SF by virtue of its sustained parallel between organic creation and paper production (just as Frankenstein's uncouth creation is in some ways analogous to the novel, *Frankenstein*). Most interestingly, in "The Bell-Tower" (1856), the "practical materialist" merchant-mechanician protagonist "enriched through commerce

---

20.   Franklin, p. 135; see also his stimulating discussion of "The Bell-Tower," ibidem.

with the Levant," rising as a new force in a feudal society, and raising his tower with the clock and the "state-bell", is a potent symbol for rising capitalism and the emblematic U.S. Liberty Bell. But his bell has been cast with an admixture of workman's blood, and the automaton created by him to be the bell's ringer, the "iron slave" who represents the servitude of Negroes and all workers, finally slays his master. The complex—even if not always congruous—religious, sexual, and political symbolism makes this the nearest that mid-nineteenth-century narrative prose SF came to a Blakean approach. The American SF story continued to be well represented into the second half of the century, especially by some of Fitz-James O'Brien's tales, which culminated in the somber story of microscopic fatality and elective affinity "The Diamond Lens" (bp. 1881). But he was killed in the Civil War, and the ensuing Gilded Age was not propitious to sustained SF, which revived only with Bellamy.

3.   And so the period that opened with universal anticipations of liberation, with Blake's and Percy Shelley's rhapsodies, found its central expression in the anguished immediacy of Frankenstein's costly failure and ended in the symbolic gloom of representative writers from what began as liberty's first and last frontier but turned out to be a Liberty Bell fracturing because it was cast with an admixture of toilers' blood. As Wordsworth precisely noted: "We Poets in our youth begin in gladness; / But thereof comes despondency and madness" ("Resolution and Independence"). These words can be seen as a characterization of the age more than of the poets it molded, turning them from Shelley's unacknowledged legislating to Melville's passionate witnessing.

7

Liberalism Mutes the Anticipation:
The Space-Binding Machines

Bring out number, weight and measure
in a year of dearth.
William Blake

0. After experiencing the first railroad from Liverpool to
Manchester, and either thinking that the train ran in grooves or
being dazzled by the seemingly absolute stability and preor-
dained course of wheels on rails, Alfred Tennyson incorporated
this new industrial imagery into some significant contrasts in
Locksley Hall:

> . . . Summer isles of Eden lying in dark-purple spheres of
>   sea.
> There methinks would be enjoyment more than in this
>   march of mind,
> In the steamship, in the railway, in the thoughts that shake
>   mankind.
> . . . .
> Fool, again the dream, the fancy! but I *know* my words are
>   wild,
> . . . .
> Not in vain the distance beacons. Forward, forward let us
>   range,
> Let the great world spin for ever down the ringing grooves
>   of change.
>
> [164–82]

These lines embody and explicate a very interesting intimate
debate between, on the one hand, the personal, painful, escapist,
and timeless dream of Edenic, half-Greek and half-Oriental
islands—Tennyson's recurring temptation of the Lotos Eaters—
in a Homeric wine-dark sea; and on the other hand, the public
and official beliefs of the "great world" of Victorian industrial

capitalism exporting not only the products of Manchester, Pittsburgh, and the Ruhr but also the concomitant ideology of linear liberal progress. Tennyson's references to the "march of mind," to the spacious ranging "forward, forward" (or "excelsior," as Longfellow said), to the thoughts that truly shook mankind (we have not stopped shaking since) are a pregnant formulation of the orthodox liberal optimism of progress radiating by way of the steamship and the railway. His earlier lines, "Saw the heavens fill with commerce, argosies of magic sails / Pilots of the purple twilight, dropping down with the costly bales," could have been taken from the leading missionary of free trade, Richard Cobden:

> Commerce is the grand panacea, which like a beneficent medical discovery, will serve to inoculate with the healthy and saving taste for civilization all the nations of the world. Not a bale of merchandise leaves our shores, but it bears the seeds of intelligence and fruitful thought to the members of some less enlightened community; not a merchant visits our seats of manufacturing industry, but he returns to his own country the missionary of freedom, peace and good government—while our steam boats, that now visit every port of Europe, and our miraculous railroads, that are the talk of all nations, are the advertisements and vouchers for the value of our enlightened institutions.[1]

Yet Tennyson's concluding image of a linear, forward-going progress spinning down the grooves of change is ultimately ambiguous. Spinning is, after all, a cyclical motion, either round and round (as a top) or to and fro (as a distaff), which always returns to the initial situation and point. Tennyson was in all probability, as witness the whole poem and his reference to "the great world," thinking here of Earth's motion simultaneously around its axis and "forward"—but since even this "forward" is a seasonal motion around the Sun, the ambiguity is only shelved, not resolved. We shall perhaps find the proper clue if we remember that Earth's spinning round the Sun is a measure of time—the true space of liberal progress.

---

1. Richard Cobden, quoted in David Thomson, *England in the Nineteenth Century (1815–1914)* (London, 1964), p. 29.

Tennyson's lines are thus an especially compressed and apt introduction to the *convertibility of quantified space and time* for the Victorian liberal mind. However, a prolific novelist will naturally be able to show the implications of these ambiguous and antinomic historical horizons more fully. In the case of an SF novelist, who operates by definition at the "outer limits of desire,"[2] these implications can be shown in a magnified and explicated form, seen in a parabolic mirror—as happened for the culmination of palaeotechnic liberalism in the work of Jules Verne.

1. COMMUNICATION IN QUANTIFIED SPACE: VERNE'S *roman scientifique*

It would be instructive to compare two excellent reports on Vernean studies, written 13 years apart by Mark R. Hillegas and Marc Angenot, to see the extraordinary, qualitative jump in Verne's reputation as a writer not only symptomatic but—for all his drawbacks—aesthetically worthwhile as well.[3] The major names and currents of French criticism—Michel Butor and Roland Barthes, structuralists and neo-Marxists, psychoanalysts and archetype hunters—all discovered him more or less simultaneously, independently, and with equal enthusiasm after 1960. He was of course always known as one of the founding fathers of SF. He created a specific early and basic variant of it, the *roman scientifique* (novel of science), and gained a permanent popularity for the genre among a mass readership, mainly but not exclusively juvenile. As the overall title of his shelf-ful of novels—*Extraordinary Voyages: Known and Unknown Worlds*—indicates, he refurbished the oldest tradition of SF, that of the marvelous voyages of tribal legends, antiquity, and the Middle Ages, for new purposes in the age of industrial adventure. However, precisely because the French Second Empire, in its increasingly desperate attempts at adventure in Italy, the Crimea, and Mexico, collapsed much sooner than its British (and in our days the US) parallel, a sensitive French writer like Verne can be discussed in

2. Northrop Frye, *Anatomy of Criticism*, p. 136.
3. Mark R. Hillegas, "A Bibliography of Secondary Materials on Jules Verne," *Extrapolation* 2 (December 1960):5–16; Marc Angenot, "Jules Verne and French Literary Criticism," *Science-Fiction Studies* 1 (Spring 1973): 33–37, supplemented by his second survey of the same title, *Science-Fiction Studies* 3 (March 1976): 46–49.

terms of a changing cognition of historical horizons for such industrialized promenades around the map—in terms of the paradoxically unstable yet appealing mirage that I propose to call "utopian liberalism."

The utopian aspect of Verne is an echo and deformation of several strong French traditions, mainly the saintsimonian one. Saint-Simon's crucial place in the development of "forward-going" horizons has been indicated in the preceding chapter.[4] Rather than adopting his orientation toward "[shifting] the Earthly Paradise from the past into the future," however, Verne in his exemplary microcosms developed the saintsimonian universal communication involving large human collectives that is the obverse and complement of the quantified convertibility between time and space:

> The symbols and instruments of the saintsimonians' collective will to power will be that which physically breaks down the barriers between the peoples . . . and permits their quicker linking. . . . The "utopia" of physical communication bringing about the internationalization of ideas will take a most tangible form: ships, vehicles, locomotives.[5]

Indeed, in spite of saintsimonian ascendencies, it is significant that Verne, often referred to as the prophet of future gadgetry, did not in fact write any anticipations (except for a very few late stories to which I shall return). His works are not extrapolations in time but ostensibly factual, newspaper-style reports about parallel universes or alternate time-tracks in which Professor Lidenbrock had just a few months earlier journeyed under the Earth, Nemo under the sea, and the Columbiad trio around the Moon. These reports are neither a Swiftian open satirical conspiracy calculated to estrange the reader from his environment, nor a Poean hoax playing upon his gullibility toward a magically omnipotent science. Verne transferred Walter Scott's, Dumas *père*'s, and particularly Fenimore Cooper's exotic otherwhen into

4.   For Saint-Simon, see Ernst Bloch (Bibliography II), Max Beer (Bibliography III A), and works by Ansart, Cole, Desanti, Durkheim, Engels, Leroy, Manuel, and Volgin in Bibliography IV A. For the parallels between Saint-Simon and Verne all students are indebted to the pioneering hints of Kirill Andreev and the study by Jean Chesneaux (Bibliography IV B).

5.   Dominique Desanti (Bibliography IV A), p. 56.

an alternative and extraordinary but strictly natural "other-where"—the voyage, equally as believable as but more glamorous than the everyday Europe or North America where it begins and ends. Its time is exactly measured and wholly filled by the traversing and mapping of space. "The whole history of the Carboniferous period was inscribed on these walls" (chap. 20), comments the narrator of his first SF novel *Journey to the Center of the Earth* (1864), which is also a descent into the depths of geological past. Later, the subterranean travelers encounter an immense "plain of bones" constituted by 20 centuries of animal generations: "There, on three square miles perhaps, the whole history of animal life was gathered, scarcely written on the too recent grounds of the inhabited world" (chap. 37). *Quantified time translated into quantified space* constitutes the book of Nature, which is decoded and claimed for knowledge by the act of motion through it that permits the reading of its hidden information. The key for decoding, the instrument through which human imagination seizes upon Nature, is pre-Darwinian measuring and classificatory natural science: geology, geography, astronomy, or zoology. That is why "novels of science" can be written, but also why they do not contain any new principles or theories. Only that can be discovered which is already known to be there—as for example the trail to the center of the Earth or the poles—and has now to be verified by physical proximity and scanning, conducive to imaginative absorption by the reader. Only the possession of a sure compass and guide permits the basic Vernean pursuit of orientation and mapmaking, so that his enduring fascination with the magnetic pole reactualizes Sinbad's magnetic island in terms of a nineteenth-century metaphor for human cognition. Two of the major plot entanglements of the subterranean voyage are caused by the loss of the guiding thread (the Hans-Brook) in the granite labyrinth and by the reversal of the compass in one of Verne's recurrent electromagnetic storms. But all the numerous scientific dilemmas (that, for instance, about Earth's inner heat), red herrings, puzzles, and cryptograms are—as in Poe's ratiocinative tales but not as in *Pym*—finally clarified and solved. The voyage is in fact a spatial equivalent of the process of reasoning necessary for solving the initial riddle. In that sense, Verne's SF draws its excitement from the prestige of the mid-nineteenth-century scientific method by which Cuvier reconstituted a mastodon from one bone, and in turn popularizes it.

The world of Verne's early books is, accordingly, more *interpolated* into than extrapolated from the imaginative space of textbooks of exotic geography, zoology, mineralogy and similar, which he quotes at great (and by now wearisome) length. Yet the voyagers are not only verifying the plenitude and solidity of this "positive" material universe—which is in Verne identical with what pertains to the Earth. They are also voyaging toward one of its privileged points—the center of the Earth, the poles, the Moon—or on the privileged circular line of Fogg's civilized and Nemo's subversive circuit. Verne's SF is in a way the triumph of imaginative cartography, of the great measuring adventure of mankind which succeeded in quantifying the planisphere, the flow of time, and human relationships. All his heroes, from Nemo through Cyrus Smith to Kaw Djer, assume at moments of crucial conflict the characteristic Napoleonic (perhaps one should say Byronic) stance of surveying the battlefield with folded arms and fixed gaze.

This geometric imagination has clear limitations. Verne's voyages fill in the white spots of already sketched space. In *From the Earth to the Moon* (1865) and *All Around the Moon* (1870) the Moon is never reached; the same is true, with one exception, of all the privileged cartographic points in other novels. Verne's innovations (the subterranean Mediteranean and "lava lift," the Moon projectile and the Nautilus, the human time-binding machine Phileas Fogg, Robur's airplane and all-purpose vehicle, Servadac's comet) may be stimulating technical dreams but they are infirm scientific extrapolation, on the one hand just one step beyond existing blueprints and on the other tending toward the inexact or even the grossly unscientific (humans could survive neither the lava lift nor the firing of the Columbiad). But all these innovations are vehicles of an *epic of communication* for the age of industrial liberalism. In the two Moon novels, the four logical stages of such a new epic—the conceiving and the creating of technical means for the extraordinary locomotion, its vicissitudes, and the delirious discussions fostered by it—are systematically orchestrated to culminate each in one strong set scene: Barbican's speech, the casting of the Columbiad, the space and time point of zero gravity, and the oxygen intoxication (al-

ready used in Verne's story "Dr. Ox" to symbolize the acceleration of life by scientific progress). Though technology is used to
verify the Moon map, its main function is to induce enthusiasm
for the extraordinary locomotive adventure which vanquishes
measurable space and time. The movement at a breathless pace
is the soul, the exhilaration of covering ground the supreme
passion, and the various vehicles practically the heroes of Verne's
plots.

However, all his plots describe the neutralized trajectory of the
Moon "double novel": they are a momentary escape from and
final return to bourgeois normality. The whirl around the globe
is the obverse of a longing for the still point of repose; even the
limited novum of the wondrous means of locomotion is destroyed or otherwise repudiated at the end of each story. Verne's
voyages and plots approximate a circle, the figure which recon-
ciles dynamics and statics, the geometrical locus of a movement
that never violates a preestablished track. Hythloday, Gulliver,
Frankenstein, or the Time Traveller are profoundly changed by
what they learn during their travels. For Verne, space does not
harbor a hierarchy of values but a quantified grid convertible to
quantified time through speed (see *Around the World in 80 Days*).
His voyagers are swept up in a movement where, as in Cartesian
analytic geometry and kinetics, only bodies, forces, and obstacles
to motion (which also serve for narrative retardation) exist. Conversely, his world is a sum of discrete points or objects the only
possible relationship of which is distance or a collision course.
People too have become equivalent to physical molecules and
energies, able to communicate only by movement through space
and time. As in *Robinson Crusoe,* Verne's great model, his characters are constantly menaced by the doom of dehumanizing sol-
itude on their individual psychic islands, as it were. "Only con-
nect" could have been Verne's slogan—for example in the
emblematic episode of Axel's losing his way in *Journey to the
Center of the Earth*. In this individualistic world it is impossible to
find the unexpected, the fundamentally different—say a new
mode of life—even under the globe, on the Moon, or in time.
The estrangement of Verne's early voyages is limited to a transient pleasure in adventure, and the cognition to adding one
technical innovation or bit of locomotive know-how (as the Moon
projectile) to an unchanged world. His "novel of science" can be

compared to a pool after a stone has been thrown into it: there is a ripple of excitement on the surface, the waves go to the periphery and back to their point of origin, and everything settles down as it was, with the addition of one discrete fact—the stone at the bottom of the pool. Both the pleasure in adventure as such and the pedagogic addition of one new bit of information at a time are suitable for—and were aimed at—a childish or juvenile audience of pre-teens. As an introduction to SF in an industrial age, Verne's best stories work very well at that boy-scout level of a group of male friends in an exciting mapping venture.

And yet there is more to Verne than a closed world validating its own certainties: there is also a longing to escape from it. The distant spaces, and especially the sea, allow his characters to manifest their individualities far from the regulated dullness of bourgeois respectability. Verne's vivid eccentrics are individualists escaping the Individualistic metropolis. In utopian and indeed folktale fashion he wants the privileges of industrial productivity without the relationships of production and the political institutions in which it came about. He accepts the tenet of the steam, iron, and coal "palaeotechnic" age, that value lies in movement; but instead of its orientation toward a future of infinitely expanding Manchesters, Pittsburghs, and Ruhrs, he inclines toward clean electricity and movement in an ultimately circular space, toward traveling rather than arriving. He wants the power of marvelous machines but only for a kind of ship with a crew of friends, or at least loyal followers, which leaves the sooty factory and its class divisions behind—exactly as the Moon projectile, escaping social as well as physical gravity, leaves the explosive Columbiad on Earth. Verne's furthest venture into such waters, where escapism blends with subversion, is *20,000 Leagues Under the Sea* (1870):

> The world, so to speak, began with the sea, and who knows but that it will also end in the sea! There lies supreme tranquillity. The sea does not belong to tyrants. On its surface, they can still exercise their iniquitous rights, fighting, destroying one another, indulging in all other earthly horrors. But thirty feet below its surface their power ceases, their influence dies out, their domination disappears! Ah, Monsieur, one must live—live within the ocean! Only there can

one be independent! There I acknowledge no master!
There I am free! [chap. 10; trans. A. Bonner]

The frequent Romantic identification of sea with freedom is not
only explicitly recalled in this outburst of Captain Nemo's but
incarnated in him. This "Nobody," a disdainful Byronic political
pirate, scientist, and visionary hoists a black flag with a capital N:
he is a Napoleon turned heroic Unknown Avenger from popular
literature, alone as Prometheus against the whole civilized order.
He lives sheltered and supplied by the sea, a shepherd of its
flocks and guardian of its treasures, the tutelary genius of a fully
furnished world which is simultaneously on Earth and as foreign
to terrestrial life as a different planet would be. In Nemo's—and
in Lidenbrock's—travels Verne comes much nearer to outer-
space SF than in the two Moon novels. In both cases the exciting
and yet almost dreamlike ease of travel is allied to electricity,
which is for Verne a Shelleyan, libidinous "soul of the industrial
world" (*The Clipper of the Clouds,* chap. 6). Nemo and his electrical
submarine Nautilus are perfectly adapted to the sea, "mobile in
the mobile." Within it, this great anarchoindividualist's violent desire has for the nonce produced a parallel and rival microcosm—
a potent weapon against the oppressors but also museum, gal-
lery, concert-hall, and library stocked with the spacious works of
freedom: "poetry, fiction, and science from Homer to Hugo, from
Xenophon to Michelet, from Rabelais to George Sand." Civilization is the Frankenstein of the Nemo/Nautilus "monster," that
ally and avenger of the Third World, of the national liberation
movements in the wake of the French Revolution, against the
imperial powers. The strong Romantic leanings of Verne, a lover
of caverns, tempests, volcanoes, polar zones, and old castles,
come in this novel very close to a revolutionary liberalism. Within
his politically ambiguous opus, Nemo is an exceptionally sympathetic and lucid achievement, an Odysseus with both superior
technology and liberating aims, redeeming the novel's boring
ichthyological passages. Nemo the "superman" is Verne's only
hero to plant his flag on the pole, though even he comes peril-
ously close to immobilization and asphyxiation (the contrary of
oxygen inebriation) as punishment for this encroachment on the
still point of the whirling globe, the Faustian moment of blissful
arrest. Verne's major voyages are either directed toward a
privileged point, or they approximate a girdle around the Earth

as in *The Children of Captain Grant* and *Around the World in 80 Days* (which became his most popular book because it presented a safe encyclopedia of means and adventures of speeding locomotion). Only Nemo—even if he is at the end sucked into the Maelström—manages to combine this great circle with the attainment of Earth's axis and navel, for which the heroes of *Journey to the Center of the Earth* and *The Adventures of Captain Hatteras*—like those of *Frankenstein*—had striven in vain.

Nemo's rich character also combines the traveler, rescuer, scientist, and explorer monomaniacs of Verne's above four novels. In each of Verne's tales, his protagonist is a passionate incarnation of the theme. Lidenbrock, the energetic German professor of transcendent crystallography, is a Hoffmannesque incarnation of geology; Barbican, Nicholl, and Ardan are embodiments, we are told, of Science, Industry, and Art, but (one would have to add) also of projectile-making, iron plate, and aerial voyaging in high spirits, and of Yankee, Scotsman, and Frenchman; Fogg of Anglo-Saxon coolness and chronometric precision in traversing time and space. Verne's "humours" characterization and his alternation of thrill and exposition is straight out of the operas or boulevard vaudevilles of Second Empire Paris, and so is his scenery, be it the outdoors of electric tempests or the indoors of the upholstered Moon projectile or the Nautilus. The trio of main characters, Verne's "three musketeers," usually takes the roles of resolute explorer, loyal companion, and more or less comic servant (Lidenbrock, Axel, and Hans; Nemo, the not wholly loyal Arronax, and Conseil with Land for added tension; Barbican, Ardan, who becomes a second protagonist, and Nicholl usurping the place of Marston). But as important as any persons are the machine-vehicles that often steal the limelight as objectivizations of the theme and of its protagonist. The protagonist and the SF concept (the machine-vehicle or some other islandlike microcosm) are therefore linked by the strongest secret sympathies within a cluster of correspondences at the center of which is the story's theme or "element."[6] The Moon projectile, the elevation out of gravity, and the ejected trio; Nautilus, the sea, and Nemo; Fogg, chronometry, and the spectrum of means for swift locomotion; Robur, the air, and *The Albatross*; Schulze, the as-

6. Michel Butor (Bibliography IV B), pp. 48 ff.

phyxiating cold, and the supercannon factory—they all form
homogeneous symbolic systems. Around them are distributed
the supernumeraries: crew, wayside acquaintances, dastardly
enemies (usually dark-skinned, but this too is reversed in Nemo's
system). Finally, there is the "sublime father," the representative
of providence (Nemo in *The Mysterious Island,* Antekirtt in
Mathias Sandorf).

TABLE 1

Book	Theme, "Element," or Semantic Field	SF Concept = Microcosmic Novum	Protagonist
Journey to Center of the Earth	Geology	Underground world	Lidenbrock
Moon Novels	Sublation of gravity	Moon projectile	Trio
20,000 Leagues	Sea = freedom	*Nautilus*	Nemo
Around the World in 80 Days	Chronometry	Ensemble of palaeotechnic means of locomotion	Fogg
Mysterious Island	Colonization of nature	Emblematic island	Cyrus Smith
500 Million of the Begum	Asphyxiating cold	Superfactory for supercannons	Schulze
Clipper of the Clouds	Flight as scientific power	Airship	Robur

With unimportant exceptions, the cast is an all-male one. The
whole libido in Verne's ultimately sterile world is invested in
machines instead of in women. The phallic connotations of
Nautilus or the Columbiad ejection are unmistakable, but so is
their fruitlessness. Finally, in *The Carpathian Castle* (1892), the
opticoelectrical machine resurrects or replaces the image of the
woman. The lively machine integrates man into space, it allows
him to be in harmony with nature, to move his individual microcosm through it and closer to other people, and thus to communicate with them. These "clean" machines or mechanisms *"do
not produce surplus value"*[7] nor consume human labor, since they
tap the miraculous electricity. Along with women, the working

7. Chesneaux, p. 43 (his italics).

class is also absent from Verne's world of boyish innocence. Discoverers and dastards face each other like noble and ignoble savages, translated from Cooper's forests into a space validated by science.

A clean technology, worldwide communications, science and art ruling the world—the whole outlook represented by Barbican plus Ardan or by Nemo has a strong kinship with saintsimonist utopianism. In his most optimistic parable, *The Mysterious Island* (1875), Verne presents the rise of a fraternal community fertilizing nature by applying scientific knowledge. The voyage has been reduced to a rudimentary framework, the favored microcosm is an island instead of a ship (but the two are in Verne, as in SF generally, largely interchangeable, both being analogs to the author's world), the SF concept is resolutely sociological as well as technological, and the all-embracing theme is man's scientific colonization of Nature, including but superseding simple communication. This novel is Verne's "recapitulation of race history"[8] and a culmination of his opus. Its mysterious island is privileged because, like Crusoe's, it is a figure of our globe, to the point of possessing mutually incompatible geographic zones. Cyrus Smith, Verne's supreme "knower" and source of energy, is that saintsimonian ideal: an engineer, communicator, and organizer who is "man of action at the same time as man of thought" (part 1, chap. 1), in fact "a microcosm, a composite of all human knowledge and intelligence!" (part 1, chap. 9). He is flanked by two loyal seconds, a hunter-cum-artist and a teenage heir gifted for recognizing the classes of Nature, and by two comic servants, one white and one black. To complete this vertical chain of being, there is also a dog and a tamed orangoutan (loyal companion and comic servant in the animal realm); and at its demonic and angelic ends a repented criminal and the dying Nemo are eventually discovered. This island crew starts out with its know-how, two watches (which Cyrus uses for the Promethean gift of fire by means of their curved glasses, and for surveying space), a single sliver of steel, and a single grain of wheat. It progresses through gathering and hunting to pottery, metallurgy, and a series of increasingly sophisticated tools and techniques. With the help of a hidden and providential Nemo, and in

8. Kenneth Allott (Bibliography IV B), p. 77.

a cooperative, though strictly graded, exploitation of Nature, they increase and multiply their possessions, eventually attaining a wholly cultivated island home, truly civilized since it can boast roads, bridges, a lift, boat, and electric telegraph line.

But this program of—as the saintsimonists said—all by steam and electricity, "[substituting] for the exploitation of man by man . . . the harmonious action of man on nature,"[9] has problematic blind spots and ambiguities for a parable on history. First of all, it is a colonization unhampered by aborigines, which allows it to progress, in Vernean ease, as a cross between a holiday and a utopian colony. Yet the colonists' ambition (like Ardan's more lighthearted reason for traveling to the Moon) is to valorize and then annex the island to the USA. The building of the Columbiad had proceeded on territory recently "cleared" of Indians in the Seminole wars; equally, after the volcanic earthquake which destroys the island, Cyrus Smith (the Yankee Everyman as imperial conqueror of space) and his companions use Nemo's saved treasure to found a vague utopian colony in Iowa (equally cleared of the Sioux). Sympathy with enslaved peoples is, in Verne as in Saint-Simon, limited to Whites—from the Québecois and the Irish to the Greeks; the colored races are either bloodthirsty beasts or natural inferiors, so that Nab in *The Mysterious Island* is even given an instinctive affinity to the orangoutan! Nemo, Verne's sympathetic rebel, is in this novel retracted: he dies alone and mellowed, and Smith's judgment on him is that for all his heroic qualities he was wrong in "fighting the necessary progress" (part 3, chap. 16). Second, this is a human history without the lower class: of the two manual workers in the novel, the White is a seaman and the Black devotion personified. Third—even more strictly than usual—not a single woman appears in the novel. This history has no future, and Verne had to employ a whole series of somewhat weary plot tricks to destroy the colony without destroying the sense of the colonists' work.

For this thematic culmination is also the point at which Verne's enthusiasm flags and his writing starts to slip badly. The adventurous Second Empire had ended in ignominious defeat; the ensuing Third Republic had begun with the bloody suppression

9. *The Doctrine of Saint-Simon* (New York, 1972), p. 29; the quote is considered to be by B. P. Enfantin.

of the Paris Commune and continued in a welter of corrupt factions; free competition in the major bourgeois countries was giving way to trusts and monopolies; the boom in colonial annexations dividing the globe among imperial powers was on: the precariousness of liberal enthusiasm was becoming quite manifest. At this very time finance capital was fast ascending to power at the expense of Saint-Simon's privileged industry and industrial capital, and was inaugurating the full panoply of imperialism as "the highest stage of capitalism."[10] With startlingly close parallelism, Verne's horizon grows more and more gloomy after the mid-1870s, and his marvelous inventions—both vehicles and communities—more and more malignant and destructive, prisons instead of harmonies. The menacing potential of science—seen already in Dr. Ox, the mutilated artillerists of the Gun Club, or Nemo—is no longer neutralized by, respectively, farce, peaceful international cooperation in exploring the universe, or political justice. Instead, the irascible but selfless eccentrics and explorers change into power-mad inventors or—historically more farsighted—into willing scientific tools of mad militarists. The petty feuds of Barbican and Nicholl or Florida and Texas, once soothed by the dreams of communication and peaceful colonization, explode into nightmares of world dominion and a total war of faction against faction, each against each. In *The Begum's Fortune* (1879) the asphyxiating Teutonic hell of Steel-City with its ballistic MIRVs is still vaguely balanced by a roseate, hygienic France-Ville. But the formerly exemplary America of freedom and progress is now seen as a plutocratic microcosm tearing itself apart (Milliard-City in *Propeller Island*, 1895). Equally, Robur, the conqueror of the air, instead of founding an "aerial Icaria" has to recognize that "science should not overtake the morals" in a civilization of selfish and opposed interests (*The Clipper of the Clouds*, 1886); and when he reappears in the still shriller and feebler *Master of the World* (1904) he has changed from "the science of the future" to a madman, whose Promethean vehicle for all elements is—as all other novelties in the later Verne—destroyed by Providence. Verne's racism narrows to French chauvinism, and his confident alliance of science with commerce and finance changes to a condemnation of the

10.   See V. I. Lenin's 1917 booklet of that optimistic title.

sterility of gold and money. Both fuse in the cosmic flight of *Hector Servadac*, in which Anglophobia and anti-Semitism have to figure as substitutes for the euphoria of the Moon voyage. The fraternal exploitation of nature by men has turned to a discord which amounts to the end of Verne's world. In three interesting posthumous works, *The Survivors of the "Jonathan"* (bp. 1909), *The Eternal Adam* (bp. 1910), and *The Barsac Mission* (bp. 1919), he retracts the saintsimonian optimism of *The Mysterious Island. The Survivors of the "Jonathan"* (translated in two books as *The Masterless Man* and *The Unwilling Dictator*) is Verne's most explicit political parable, and it is situated symbolically on the furthest shore of the world, an island halfway between the lost freedom and progress of the Americas and the privileged but dangerous point of the South Pole. There, a cargo of suffering and ill-adjusted humanity from a wrecked ship all officers of which have been swept overboard is subjected to the equally pernicious enticements of state socialism, egalitarian communism (both professed by failed intellectuals), and usurious capitalism. The childlike workers would have gone under but for the intervention of a mysterious and noble anarchoindividualist, the Kaw-djer, who ultimately discovers that political leadership demands violence and retires embittered to a lighthouse at the end of the inhabited world. Though full of clichés, this novel at least manifests an interest in different political horizons together with a disbelief in their success. *The Eternal Adam*, Verne's only significant anticipation, opts therefore for a cycle of eternal return. The leading scientist of a future civilization discovers to his horror a receding vista of lost civilizations, including an account of the end of ours in cataclysm and savagery. The story conveys the realization that, as Valéry will put it, "we civilizations, we also know now that we are mortal"—quite a feat for the erstwhile bard of technologically conquered space. Finally, Blackland in *Mission Barsac* (also translated as *City in the Sahara*) is Verne's most developed anti-utopian city (though the text might have been rewritten by Verne's son), astoundingly similar to a Nazi concentration camp plus war factory, with its segregated quarters, slavery, super-weapons, and megalomania, even to a rival SA and SS. As in Steel-City, there is a rare appearance of the cowed industrial proletariat, which here even participates in an uprising, and a strong stress on the scientist's social responsibility. All three

works look thus into a threatening future rather than a cheery
present—a fitting final chord to Verne's SF at the beginning of
the twentieth century.

Thus Verne's initial dream of space can be seen as a flight
from uncertain time, and his fascination with filling in the in-
terstices of geography and science as leading to a subtle reification. Time and Nature have to be strictly mastered, for they
threaten to run down to the cold immobility of those poles and
interplanetary spaces which attract and imperil Verne's voyagers.
But the obsessive control over time, which enabled Fogg to vanquish space as well as the aptly named threat of Fix and to gain
the warmth of Aouda, has in Schulze (in *500 Million . . .*) become
a bearer of thermodynamic death. In Verne's first phase the
energetic hero always taps a saving electric or volcanic energy; in
the second, Prometheus turns into Luciferian blasphemer and
energy into destruction. Verne's world is not quite mechanical, it
is thermodynamic. Both communication and colonization mean
civilized conquest of space, which is a decrease of entropy. On
the contrary, the destruction or perversion to destructive ends of
the vehicles and embodiments of civilization, from means of
locomotion to cities and colonies, is in his post-1875 writing the
mark of entropy, of insidious Time, culminating in Time's deadly reign in *The Eternal Adam*. From *Journey to the Center of the
Earth* to *The Mysterious Island*, decoding or understanding space
led to a happy end; understanding time leads to a dead end.
Though Verne is not a writer of anticipations, he lived in the age
of anticipation and could turn his back on it only for a brief
historical moment and at the price of seeing time as the deadly
enemy. In that he was a representative writer of the positivist
epoch. Rejecting the radical rhapsodists and the introverted
Romantics, the Victorians thought of themselves as realists. The
great scenes of Verne's SF—Axel's dream or the vision of prehistoric man in *Journey to the Center of the Earth*, the saintsimonian
poetry of rapid motion (as in the Moon novels and the Nautilus),
of creative labor (as in the casting of the Columbiad), or of discovery (as in Nemo's underwater forest or in the congealing of
the supercooled sea even in the second-rate *Servadac*)—all fuse
science or nature with the mysterious liberating excitement
brought by a "real" novelty. Yet his work is pervaded first by a
rhapsodic Romanticism channeled toward exotic space, and later

by a dread of time that breaks out from beneath the positive certainty. Verne accepts from the enthusiasts of "utopian socialism" what can be accepted by a Christian liberal—a common denominator of individual affirmation within social engineering that one must paradoxically call "utopian liberalism." The fact that this contains something for everybody who shares the dreams and fears of an industrial society explains Verne's wide popularity. But it also situates his "novel of science" halfway between the science-oriented middle class's[11] saintsimonian utopianism at the beginning and anti-utopian gloom at the end of the nineteenth century. Creatively, this precarious balance lasted only a dozen years, so long as that class could still conceive of science and liberal capitalism as wholly concordant. After Verne, in his imitators all around the world that balance disintegrated into its components of subliterary adventure, gadget popularization, and pretentious ideology. But while it lasted Verne's work itself, in spite of its long slack stretches, gave shape to some of the most persistent because most threatened mirages of his age: the joy of human contact by way of mastery over nature, its mapping, and intimate penetration; the binding of time and its translation into energetic motion and civilized expansion by means of wondrous machines. In the second phase, he substituted for spatial wonder some sensitive prefigurations of the dark forces menacing the liberal society. Verne's steady vision made him the Balzac of space-machines, as his vehicles and colonies can be called. With his twenty-odd SF books, he is the first systematic novelist initiating dynamic plotting and the overview of a fully furnished world in SF—"what a style; nothing but nouns," remarked Apollinaire admiringly of him.[12] Verne revived the subterranean and interplanetary journey and introduced technology into the heart of utopianism. He turned SF toward a juvenile audience, but drew into this audience readers of serious periodicals interested in scientific puzzles, thus setting up the basic equation for SF consumption in the ensuing 100 years (including fan mail and fan visitors). Perhaps most impor-

11. A homologous analysis for twentieth-century Anglo-American SF by Gérard Klein, "Discontent in American Science Fiction," *Science-Fiction Studies* 4 (March 1977): 3–13, offers interesting parallels to Verne's trajectory as well as the best sociological hypothesis for its causes so far to be found in SF criticism.

12. Quoted in Marguerite Allotte de la Fuÿe (Bibliography IV B), p. 66.

tantly, he presented this specialized reading public with the joy of free movement outside the compartments of Victorian society. The bard of palaeotechnics was ambiguously—as every significant writer—also the bard of its alternatives: electricity, wide-open spaces, peace, fraternal utopian colonies.

In all these respects Verne is one of the shapers of modern SF, and an important link in as well as modifier of the chain of its development. He was himself acutely aware of that chain and how he was continuing it. Apart from his wide though superficial scientific gleanings, the allusions or outright lectures in many of his novels show that he knew practically the whole tradition of significant SF before him, his taste in books being similar to Nemo's. In the two Moon novels, for example, he details the entire tradition of both beliefs and romances about the Moon, from Thales through Cyrano to Poe, in whose honor the scene is set in Baltimore. Poe, of whom he wrote a study, was an omnipresent though superficial influence on his puzzles and their solutions, his polar voyages, and his characterization (compare the Gun Club members and Poe's Man Who Was Used Up). Another major influence was Cooper—not only his Leatherstocking Tales but also the sea stories and the utopian romances with their black pattern of discovery and retraction. Biblical associations are common. Swift can be felt in the conflict of the Starbordians and the Larbordians of *Propeller Island*, and Verne seems to have known not only German Romantics but also Hawthorne. He followed attentively his contemporaries, even those who were learning from him, and appears to have used E. E. Hale's *Brick Moon* (1872) satellite story for *Servadac*, Villiers and Robida for *The Carpathian Castle*, and Wells's *Invisible Man* for a later attempt on the same theme. As for his direct influence, a whole school of Verneans lasted well into the twentieth-century—from his collaborators Laurie-Grousset and Michel Verne to writers like D'Ivoi, Graffigny, Le Rouge, or the ingenious writer-designer Robida (*La Guerre au 20e siècle*, 1883, and *La Vie électrique*, 1893) in France, Kraft and Dominik in Germany, Jókai in Hungary, Salgari in Italy, and countless other imitators as far away as Russia and Japan. Also evident are the debts to Verne of many inferior English-language works of adventure SF, from the early 1870s through E. D. Fawcett, Max Pemberton, George Griffith, Conan Doyle, and the dime novels to E. R. Burroughs and the

Gernsbackians. Perhaps most curious is the case of Wells, who fought so furiously against being "the English Verne" that in some cases he apparently undertook to go Verne one better—so, for example, in the underground life of Cavor's Moon and in the Time Traveller's depths of time as compared to the descents in *Journey to the Center of the Earth* or *Les Indes Noires*, but also in his whole program of meeting a different life as opposed to Verne's shying away from it. Directly and through Wells, Verne is thus behind all modern SF dealing with the conquest of space and social engineering.

2. COMMUNICATION BREAKS DOWN

2.0. Verne's popularity stands in startling contrast to the conspicuous lack of popularity of other SF between *Frankenstein* and the 1870s, despite the quality of some texts. Powerful social pressures on writers, running the full gamut from exile through lack of social recognition and finances to internalization of despair and resignation, "impeded any success for forms with an intense speculative drift or a strong utopian and social-satire element." Verne's genius made a virtue of the resulting very limited "narrative recipe," with its elements of verisimilitude, positivistic popularization, closed world with circular plots, and taboos on such radical novums as extraterrestrials, mutations, and different sexual practices. But such limitations were in effect an interdict by the bourgeois aesthetic practice of the times against a simultaneously far-reaching and hopeful imagination, against "dreams of expanding universes . . . or of the happiness of metamorphoses."[13] As the lines from Tennyson quoted at the beginning of this chapter imply, only fools were supposed to believe in the "dream" or the "fancy" of a change that would not be identical with the "ringing grooves" of railways carrying Victorian gentlemen and the products of capitalist industry into the world.

2.1. It is understandable, then, that the main body of SF published in the age of Verne shows an equal uneasiness about strange novelties which might imply a radically different horizon

---

13. For the quotes and the general argument in this paragraph I am indebted to Marc Angenot's allowing me to read in manuscript his pioneering essay "Science Fiction in France Before Verne," now in *Science-Fiction Studies* 5 (March 1978): 58–66—all quotes in this paragraph are from ibidem, 64–65.

of human relationships in the future, or indeed a radical alternative in the present. On the outskirts of capitalism, in Russia, two
seeming exceptions (which will be discussed more fully in chapter 11) confirm the rule. Reacting against the overt pressures of
blatant police repression, Chernyshevsky's *What Is To Be Done*
(bp. 1905, 42 years after magazine publication) was a prefiguration set in an alternative present but issuing into a utopian, classless future that is its fulfillment. This imaginative but not escapist
attempt of bridging time-horizons or diverting the flow of time is
a revealing contrast to Verne's only momentarily diverging present, bereft of any such future and reduced to finding its pathos
in the actual adventures of momentary deviation, validated by
"positive" knowledge, while they were happening and so far as
they went. A confirmation of the correspondence between the
location of an SF tale and its historical horizon is to be found in
Dostoevsky's "The Dream of a Ridiculous Man" (1877), which
acts out a fruitful tension between his skepticism about the feasibility of, and his heartfelt longing after, a salvation within history. The dream of this tale is a framework for what is clearly
spelled out as a parallel universe standing for ours. The ensuing
complex balance permits Dostoevsky for the nonce to use simultaneously a twin, parallel history and an orientation toward the
future recovery of lost innocence.

2.2.   Edward Bulwer-Lytton's *The Coming Race* (1871) opts for
a subterranean location. Yet the Romantic system of correspondences between depths, warmth, energy, and femininity is
in this apostate from radicalism and admirer of *Frankenstein* presented with mingled fascination and horror. Sympathy and will
came for Bulwer, because of their associations with revolution
and communism, to represent a power for evil as well as for
good. The addition of a banalized version of the occult, quasi-
magnetic fluid permeating men and all nature—the vril—
completes the basic givens of and explains his ambiguous attitude toward the incompatibly different mode of life in the
novel. While the novel contains incidental sallies into sub-
Swiftian satire on Darwinism and American democracy, Bulwer
is mainly preoccupied with and uneasily indecisive about the scientific power, the collective social organization using technics instead of a "separate working class" (chap. 26), and the sexual
emancipation of the Vril-ya. His device of a menaced protagonist

was adopted by Wells and has since become the staple of anti-utopian SF. However, the subterranean place is neither the classical Hell, nor Holberg's excuse for satire, nor Verne's exhilarating Mediterranean, but an omnium gatherum of demonic menace, neutral device, and matriarchal womb—or Owen (and even Fourier), Paltock, and Tory occultism in mindless admixture. Wanting to touch all bases, such demagoguery ends finally with no score. But obversely, at the time of publication it had a great success with the mid-Victorian reading public and—together with Verne, *Erewhon*, and the "future war" vogue—ushered in a revival of publishing interest in an SF suggesting but also warning against the significant novum and presenting an individualistic—usually sentimental and horrific—melodrama alongside new gadgetry. One of the most interesting variants of a Bulwerian ambiguity toward the horrible but fascinating topsy-turvy country is James De Mille's *A Strange Manuscript Found in a Copper Cylinder* (bp. 1888), which self-consciously fused it with the marvelous-voyage tradition from More to Poe's *Pym*. A positive evaluation of the radical break implicit in a reasonable country of female parthenogenesis is allied to an equal indecisiveness about relating to and communicating with it in Mary Bradley Lane's *Mizora* (bp. 1890), located in a warm, hyperborean "Symmesian hole." The same location is used in William Bradshaw's *The Goddess of Atvatabar* (1891) more in the vein of Haggard (and of some Bellamy) than of Bulwer. The "lost race" tale is here turned into a semioccultist yoking together of supergadgetry, feverish sentimentality, and spiritual "magnicity." The baroque exuberance of this fine piece of eccentric Americana, with its holy locomotives, zoophytes, mass eroticism, and mass slaughter, teeters between the naive and the ridiculous, and reveals more frankly than Bulwer some of the central libidinal wishdreams impelling these writings.

2.3.   Samuel Butler's *Erewhon* (1872) is a somewhat more lasting text because it at least approaches a sketch of the country where ulterior motives of Victorian society are explicitly unveiled. However, Butler too uses a Vernean yet undiscovered country "over the range," on the traditionally upside-down antipodes. The diverse cognitive discussions in the text—the interchanging of illness and crime, Unreason and Reason, or religion and banking—are not only mutually incompatible expositions, they also hesitate between Swiftian bite and middle-class propriety, mildly diverting paradox and cynical justification. The fable of the Unborn has a certain Platonic charm, but what survives today is the application of Darwinist evolution to machines that could enslave man (beginning with the time-machine of the watch), prefiguring as it does the discussion of reification and of machine consciousness in cybernetics. A generation later, Butler's sequel *Erewhon Revisited* retracted even such partial estrangement, as well as his own satire on the rise of religion, by its final horizon of a saving annexation to England. It is as if the anxious limitations of Trollope's intervening venture into SF, *The Fixed Period*, had mediated between Butler's two novels.

2.4. Finally, under the immediate stimulus of 1871, the momentous year of the German victory over France and the Paris Commune, the "future war" tale blossomed forth. Though precursors can be found as far back as the anonymous *The Reign of George VI 1900–1925* (1763), Mary Shelley's *Last Man*, Louis Geoffroy, and the pseudonymous "Herrmann Lang" 's *The Air Battle* (1859) in which the southern hemisphere and dark races rule Europe, it was immediate political anxiety that prompted George T. Chesney's *The Battle of Dorking* (1871). The sensational echo, the imitations, rejoinders, and alternatives it provoked, first from other military and political gentlemen and then from popular writers jumping on a rolling bandwagon, resulted in the publication of hundreds of books before 1914, ringing changes upon political lineups, the ruthlessness of the enemy, and the unpreparedness but speedy victory of one's own gullible country.[14] Their hallmark was crass Anglo-Saxon, Gallic, or Teutonic chauvinism, escalating to the "yellow danger" racism, and location in a shockingly imminent future well within the implied middle-aged reader's life expectancy. Though decisive super-weapons were often resorted to, these tales evidence a general inability to imagine the real economic, technological, and psychological aspects of the coming world war.[15] The rise of the "fu-

14. The fundamental but certainly incomplete bibliography appended to I. F. Clarke's *Voices Prophesying War, 1763–1984* (Bibliography IV B) lists about 300 book titles in English, French, and German. Including titles from the United States, and with fuller data on European titles, the number, I would guess, would easily surpass 500. This does not even attempt to take into account the numerous serials in boys' magazines, etc.

15. Clarke, p. 90, notes that the only writers who came anywhere near seeing the

ture war" tale demonstrates how politics can directly bring about a new literary form, how SF can be effectively used as a factor in international and domestic politics, and how bourgeois expertise could imagine a genuine future location only as awful warning —here (as different from Verne's *Eternal Adam*) meretriciously combined with uplifting finale. The only justification of the subgenre is that Wells transmuted it in *The War of the Worlds*—by fusing it with the "fall of civilization" subgenre—into a reflection on the whole historical epoch of liberalism and thus into significant SF.

2.5.   As we saw in considering Verne, any significant novum, in space as well as in time, grew untenable within liberal horizons. The hesitant groping toward new horizons that ensued will be discussed in the next two chapters. What remained was mostly subliterature, popularizing past writing paradigms a generation or two after they were exhausted; examples include the US post-Civil-War dime-novel series of the "Frank Reade Jr." or the "Tom Swift" variety, set mostly in a Never-never Far West and destined to have a strong influence on modern SF. There also remained a few eccentrics swimming against the current. Among those who are the true progenitors of significant modern SF is Edwin A. Abbott. In his tale *Flatland* (1884) the location in other geometrical dimensions is the bearer of analogies to human class perception, conceiving, and behavior; its brief sketches show how strictly scientific cognition and even popularization can ascend to philosophical parable. Some other writers of the time—among them Edward Page Mitchell in the United States, whose stories touched upon a menacing android, a future of racial equality, visiting the past, invisibility, and a gracious plant intelligence— dealt with themes which were to flower in Wells and after him.[16] The most interesting of such marginal people was Auguste Villiers de l'Isle Adam, a symbolist whose *Cruel Tales* had already

---

possible scientific changes in a future war were Robida, Doyle, and Wells (who foresaw not only the tank but also poison gas and the atom bomb). The latter is the only one who, to my knowledge, identified the psychological correlative of total warfare, and nobody saw the economic ones.

16.   Though two of Mitchell's SF stories were published in an anthology in 1884, their first book collection seems to be the one by Sam Moskowitz as *The Crystal Man* (Garden City, NY, 1973), who also supplied a pioneering but hyperbolic introduction on the man and the themes of his work.

sometimes hovered close to SF. His *L'Ève future* (1886) grafts onto
a defiant Romanticism of the Hoffmann and Poe kind a concern
with wondrous possibilities of modern science, personified in
Edison and the "electrohuman" or "android" woman he fashions
for a disenchanted Byronic or Baudelairean Lord. The Shelleys'
and Verne's electricity has here literally become the soul or
Promethean spark animating an artificial, metal and plastic creation. But for all its intelligent guesses about radiant matter in
vacuum, "photosculpture," color movies, and human electro-
magnetism, the interest of Villiers's novel lies in its twofold
theme: how to find a non-philistine Beauty in the world and how
to determine the difference between a "real" but insensitive
woman and an "illusion" whose behavior is more intelligent and
generically more human than that of the original "bourgeois
goddess." The possibility of androids is suggested by the
stereotyped behavior and ideas of people in the world of propriety and self-interest. "Chimaera for chimaera," why should not
an openly and purely artificial being, incarnating the best of
human knowledge and genius, constant, sexless, and immortal,
be preferable and indeed more real than such people are? And
could not an ideal love be felt for such a humanized being, a
"machine for manufacturing the Ideal," rather than for the false
humans?

In a divergence from Verne, this alternative present of pessimistic idealism does not evade but passionately hates the future
in which the steam-boiler and egotistical aridity have suppressed
the old values. Hadaly, the "future Eve," is both the logical end-
product of bourgeois reification or standardization (satirized also
in some of the "cruel stories," for example, "The Heavenly Ads")
and a rich countercreation named after the Ideal. A strong dose
of misogyny, amounting at times to a kind of sexual racism, leads
paradoxically to the concept of a Platonic, superhuman yet
woman-shaped, soul-sister as the worthy companion of man in
his terrestrial exile. The novel teeters between the sublime and
the ridiculous, with many a passage of exclamative sentimentality
and shrill preaching, and ends with the usual twist into timeless—
supernatural and even occult—fantasy and the destruction of the
novum. Yet it not only contains splendid scenes of a Decadent,
Salammbô-like otherwhere, like Edison's underground realm of
electricity with its artificial birds and flowers, it also uncovers the

psychological source of many seemingly erotic but in fact asexual robot tales; and at its nucleus there is an incipient modern discussion of free will, creations with different types of logic, the burden of consciousness, and mass production of "ideals." Puzzles of identity, role playing, and semantics appear in Villiers amid long stretches of philosophical and technical monologues. Thus, for all its impurities, *The Future Eve* carries the discussions of *Frankenstein* or "Rappaccini's Daughter" into the age of Verne and Butler, envisaging their fascination with machines and final anti-utopian distrust of bourgeois progress as an existential problem of human sensitivity and intelligence. More than the Nemo/Nautilus centaur, or even Frankenstein's Creature, the melancholy Hadaly, a union of spirit and scientific hardware, is the liveliest space-machine of the century.

3. Muted and transferred from time to space, the novum turned malevolent there too. Verne's spinning world of progress spun finally into a cheerless cycle of eternal return. Communication was turning into a nightmare of Butler's grinning statues and rigidifying orthodoxies, Bulwer's collective superwomen, or the exchange of high explosives in future wars. In "Locksley Hall Sixty Years After" the hesitant Tennyson swung toward the disenchanting result of the century's original if ambiguous promise:

> Gone the cry of "Forward, Forward," lost within a growing
>   gloom;
> Lost, or only heard in silence from the silence of a tomb.
> Half the marvels of my morning, triumphs over time and
>   space,
> "Forward" rang the voices then, and of the many mine was
>   one.
> Let us hush this cry of "Forward" till ten thousand years
>   have gone.
>
>   [73–78]

But the denial of the future led to such stifling closed worlds and so acute menaces that it eventually provided the basis for rehabilitating the possibility of a brighter anticipation in the dawning of socialist hope with Bellamy and Morris.

8

Anticipating the Sunburst:
Dream, Vision—or Nightmare?

The great cry that rises from all our manufacturing cities, louder than the furnace blast, is all in very deed for this,—that we manufacture there everything except men; we blanch cotton, and strengthen steel, and refine sugar, and shape pottery; but to brighten, to strengthen, to refine, or to form a single living spirit, never enters into our estimate of advantages.

> John Ruskin

Is the Earth so?
Let her change then.
Let the Earth quicken.
Search until you know.

> Bertolt Brecht

Was it a vision, or a waking dream?
Fled is that music:—do I wake or sleep?

> John Keats

0.   The gloom and recantation of SF—including utopian or social-science-fiction—writers from Mary Shelley and Herman Melville to Jules Verne and Villiers de l'Isle Adam was part of the increasing closure of liberal bourgeois horizons. Yet at the same time the thirst for anticipations—fictional pictures of an excitingly different future—rose sharply (one assessment puts their frequency from 1871 to 1916 at 35 times the pre-1870 rate of publication).[1] SF is as a genre potentially and even intrinsically oriented toward humanity's furthest horizons, and therefore in quite aesthetic terms (that are, of course, inseparable from ethical and cognitive ones) not fully developed in the timeless, cyclical, or merely catastrophic realizations discussed in the last two chapters. Consequently, the radical alternative of a socialist dawn found an even more congenial soil and erupted

---

1. Calculated by me from Ian Clarke (Bibliography I).

even more strongly in it than in the contemporary political surge in Germany, Britain, the United States, and elsewhere. In addition to its thematic and ideological appeal this alternative had the merit of solving the racking dilemmas brought into existence by the time of the radical Romantics—of movement forward versus the closed circle, wish versus realization, freedom versus brotherhood, skepticism versus belief, individual versus society. A whole century had dealt with these dilemmas by ingenious or feeble evasions within a spatial symbolism, and had in plot-endings washed its hands of the cognitive reason for the story's existence. Therefore the SF narrations from *Frankenstein* to Villiers and most of Verne culminated in destructions and murders as the logical end and outcome of the quantitative, individually anguished Faustian quest—as opposed to the qualitative, collectively subversive Promethean quest of earlier utopian and SF writers, from More and Cyrano to Percy Shelley. Even Goethe felt he could avoid such an outcome only by tacking on to his *Faust* a religious happy-ending incompatible with the initial wager that validates the plot. The socialist vision of a classless millennium on Earth was thus a solution to both the ideational and the formal problems of nineteenth-century SF. It flourished for a brief time in Bellamy and Morris, the absence of its open horizon explains Mark Twain's impatience and despairing failure in *A Connecticut Yankee*, and at the end of the century it provided one of the basic ingredients for Wells's ambiguous synthesis.

1.1. In *Looking Backward 2000-1887* (1888) Edward Bellamy started not only from the widespread Victorian observation that, as Disraeli put it, the rich and the poor were "two nations," but also from the observation that "[the] working classes had quite suddenly and very generally become infected with a profound discontent with their condition, and an idea that it could be greatly bettered if they only knew how to go about it." Bellamy was willing to show them how, for it was "[not] only the toilers of the world who are engaged in something like a world-wide insurrection, but true and humane men and women, of every degree, are in a mood of exasperation, verging on absolute revolt, against social conditions that reduce life to a brutal struggle for existence . . ." (chap. 1). In *Equality* (1897), a sequel which set out to plug the gaps left by the first novel, he added to these

sources of discontent the ruin of prairie farmers by capitalist
mortgages, the degradation of women fostered by economic exploitation, the recurrent economic crises of the last third of the
nineteenth century, and the concentration of three-quarters of
all national wealth into the hands of 10 percent of the population. Bellamy's utopianism was the point at which all these deep
discontents (which in the decade of the Chicago Haymarket trial
ran the whole gamut between bankrupt smaller businessmen and
the industrial workers who participated in the almost 6,000
strikes per year) intersected with the earlier utopian-socialist tradition of American religious and lay associationism and with the
experiences of the nineteenth-century socialist movement. As a
spokesman of the American "immense average of villagers, of
small-town-dwellers," Bellamy believed in "modern inventions,
modern conveniences, modern facilities"[2]—in Yankee gadgetry
as a white magic for overcoming drudgery. This perspective differed from the Populist revolt, which inveighed in the name of
the smallholder against the financial trusts of Wall Street enslav-
ing the countryside by means of railways. Bellamy accepted
the trusts as more efficient and—following their own logic—
condemned only their private character as economically too
wasteful and politically too dangerous to tolerate. Instead of this
corporate tyranny, his practical streak of "Yankee communism,
or, to be more precise, 'Associationism' "[3] led him to envisage
"the nation . . . organized as the one great corporation . . . , the
sole employer, the final monopoly . . . in the profits and
economies of which all citizens shared" (chap. 5). Bellamy's new
frontier, replacing the West traversed by the irreversible rails, is
the future. It offers not only better railways, motor carriages,
air-cars, telephones, and TV, but also a classless social brotherhood of affluence which will make these means of communication generally accessible and will socialize all other upper-class
privileges such as culture. Comfort and security are the ends of
Bellamy's utopia, and economic reorganization the means. In
this pragmatic socialism, unhappiness is ethical waste: *Looking
Backward* shows forth "the economy of happiness."[4] That is

2. W. D. Howells (Bibliography IV C), p. ix and vii.
3. Daniel Aaron (Bibliography IV C), p. 95.
4. Unlocated quotation, apparently from Bellamy's diary, in Aaron, p. 97.

brought about by universal high education, universal industrial service from the twenty-first to the forty-fifth year, equal and guaranteed income (in nontransferable yearly credits) for every citizen including the old, children, and the sick, a flexible planning adjusting workloads and production according to demand, and a highly developed system of public bestowal of honors. Government is reduced to the operations of the Great Trust or—since the economy is run on the lines of universal civic service analogous to the military service—the Industrial Army. In it, every citizen rises through the ranks as far as his capacity will carry him. The generals of each guild or industrial branch are, however, not appointed from above but chosen by all the retired members or alumni of the guild, and so on up to the head of the army who is president of the United States. Doctors and teachers have their own guilds and regents outside this army, and a writer, artist, journal editor, or inventor can be exempted from it if a sufficient number of buyers sign over a part of their credit to support him. The sequel in *Equality* clarifies that economic equality gives free play to the greatest possible expansion of individuality, that there is a reservation for Thoreau-like objectors to "work out a better solution of the problem of existence than our society offers" (chap. 5—possibly the first use of this recurring escape hatch of later utopias), that the population of the cities has drastically shrunk, that all tools are electrically powered and garments made from disposable paper, and so on.

Bellamy's economic blueprint is integrated into the story of Julian West, who wakes from a mesmeric sleep begun in 1887 into the year 2000, is given information about the new order by Dr. Leete, and falls in love with Leete's daughter Edith. Further, all this is a "romantic narrative" (Preface) by an anonymous historian writing in the festive year 2000 to instruct his readers in the contrasts of past and present, by looking backward. This system of mirrors and receding vistas in time is memorably reactualized in the nightmarish ending when Julian dreams of awakening back in the capitalist society of 1887. He meets its folly and moral repulsiveness with an anguished eye which supplies to each spectral place and person a counterpossibility. This utopian estrangement culminates in the hallucination about "the possible face that would have been actual if mind and soul had lived" which he sees superimposed upon the living dead of the poor quarter; the lesson is that living in this nightmare and "pleading for crucified humanity" might yet be better than reawakening into the golden twenty-first century—as, in a final twist, Julian does (chap. 28). *Looking Backward*—intimately informed by Bellamy's constant preoccupation with human plasticity, with memory and identity (concerns of his *Dr. Heidenhoff's Process* [1880] and *Miss Ludington's Sister* as well as a number of his short stories), with brute reality and ideal possibility—reposes on a symbolic balance of time horizons. Its plot is, in fact, Julian's change of identity. In two of Bellamy's later SF stories, "The Blindman's World" and "To Whom This May Come" (1898), the improvident Earthmen, sundered from their neighbors and self-knowledge, are contrasted to worlds of brotherhood and transparency where men are "lords of themselves." Julian West, the idealistic and insomniac rich idler with a revealing name, becomes an apostate from such a life in the West of 1887 through his education into a citizen of 2000, which is effected through a healer's reasonable lectures and his daughter's healing sympathy and intercession. *The construction of a social system for the reader is also the reconstruction of the hero.* This innovation in the utopian and SF tradition uses the radical-democratic paradigm which (as was noted in chapter 6) began with the American Revolution, for a positive answer to Shakespeare's and Swift's challenge that changing the world entails changing the "nature" of men. On the other extreme from *Frankenstein*, such a dialectical malleability is also an epoch-making pointer to future SF.

On the other hand, Bellamy immediately retreated from this discovery. Just as Julian is the mediator between two social systems for the reader, so Edith Leete—the descendant and, as it were, reincarnation of Julian's fiancée from 1887—is the steadying emotional mediator in his passage to a new world, a personal female Christ of earthly love and brotherhood. Bellamy's is an ethical socialism, abhorring violence and hatred. The "sunburst" of a new order, "when heroes burst the barred gate of the future" (chap. 20), is validated equally by economics, ethical evolution, and Christian love; unethical economics was for him unworkable. Such a millenary horizon makes for a fundamental, qualitative change: the future brings a different, purified space and man. The friendly house of Dr. Leete stands on the burnt-down remnants of Julian's house and on top of his underground shelter, which have to be excavated as a feat of archeology for the twenty-first century. For Julian, the Leete household is the hearth of spacious, reasonable, clean, classless Boston of the year 2000, and Edith is not too far from an image of his favorite writer Dickens, the cricket on the hearth. The hard-headed civic pragmatism is only the obverse of a soft-hearted petty-bourgeois romance or "fairy tale of social felicity."[5]

This fairytale character is most evident in Bellamy's sanguine expectation of a nonviolent, imminent, and instantaneous abandonment of private capitalism by universal recognition of its folly. With telling effect he extrapolated bourgeois rationality, ethics, and institutions to a logical end-product of universal public ownership. But this consistent pedagogic starting from the known signifies a sanitizing of capitalism to ensure the freedom, equality, brotherhood, and abundance of the Rationalist or Jeffersonian dreams. Bellamy remained limited by such ideals, which form an important part but by no means the final horizon of a socialist future. It is perhaps unfair to judge his fascination with the army as a model of rational organization by the normative ethical reaction toward armies today, since he acquired it in Lincoln's days and translated it into peaceful and constructive terms, just as Fourier did. Further, any self-respecting utopia before automation had to ensure its working by a certain harshness for recalcitrants (and Bellamy—possibly learning from Morris—clearly evolved toward greater openness and participatory democracy in *Equality*, where all officials are subject to recall). Nonetheless, even there he continued to stress a hybrid of state mobilization and "public capitalism" (chap. 22); neither did he modify his patronizing dismissal from *Looking Backward* of "the more backward races" (chap. 13) and political efforts by narrow-minded workingmen, nor, above all, his faith in technocratic regimentation *within* economic production as opposed to ideal classless relations outside them, all of which strike an alienating note in the tradition of Saint-Simon and Cabet rather than that of Fourier or Marx. That note is out of harmony with his basic libertarian preoccupations, and introduces into his romance a cold and static element.

5. Edward Bellamy, "How I Came to Write *Looking Backward*," *The Nationalist* (May 1889): 1; reprinted in *Science-Fiction Studies* 4 (July 1977): 194.

But if Bellamy is a pragmatist who is not comfortable when depicting sweeping processes of change, he is at his strongest in the shrewd treatment of the economics of everyday life—of dressing and love, the distribution of goods, the cultural activities— and in the brilliant passages on making democratic supply and demand work outside a capitalist framework, for example, in organizing a journal or in solving brain-drain between countries. On such occasions, Bellamy is quite free from a State Socialism regulating everything from above. When contrasting such warm possibilities with the irrationality and dead-end character of private competition, his clear and attractive, though sometimes pedestrian, style rises to little parabolic inserts of great force, as the initial allegory of the Coach, the parables of the Collective Umbrella and of the Rosebush, or (in *Equality*) the parables of the Water-Tank and of the Masters of the Bread. All such apologues, exempla, and parables come from a laicized and radical pulpit style, openly displayed in the sermon on the sunburst from *Looking Backward*. It is within this New England oral and public tradition, from the Bible and the Platonic dialogues and not from the genteel literature of Gilded Age mandarins, that Bellamy's rhetoric arises as an imposing and sometimes splendid accomplishment of its kind. Such addresses were primarily meant for middle-class women, and Julian's sentimental intrigue as well as the whole ethical tone of *Looking Backward* addressed itself to them, and generally to that part of the educated classes which felt insecure and unfree in bourgeois society. Thus Bellamy's homely lucidity made his romance, with all its limitations, the first authentically American socialist anticipation tale.

Bellamy's success can—as always in significant SF—be expressed in terms of a creative fusion of various strands and traditions. These were not only literary, but reached back to the hundreds of religious or lay utopian communities which had been tried in the young United States. Though all of them finally collapsed as utopian communities under the violent pressures of an inimical environment, their legacy to American horizons from Hawthorne to our day has been larger than commonly assumed. An attenuated lay vision of the glorious City had now and then crossed from the oral and hortatory into the written fictional tradition, in works such as Mary Griffith's feminist, abolitionist, and technological anticipation "Three Hundred Years Hence"

(1836), Edward Kent's and Jane S. Appleton's future city of Bangor in *Voices from the Kenduskeag* (1848), and several descriptions by Edward Everett Hale culminating in "My Visit to Sybaris" (1869) and *How They Lived in Hampton* (1888). Though Howells exaggerated when he claimed for Bellamy "a romantic imagination surpassed only by that of Hawthorne,"[6] Bellamy did interfuse such narratively helpless precursors—to whom one should add Fénelon, Cabet, and contemporary British anticipations by E. Maitland (*By and By*, 1873), H.C.M. Watson (*Erchomenon*, 1879), W.D. Hay (*Three Hundred Years Hence*, 1881), or C. Wise (*Darkness and Dawn*, 1884)—with an effective Romantic system of correspondences. In particular, he seems to have drawn on a number of important elements from John Macnie's *The Diothas* (1883), such as a utopia with an industrial army, love with a descendant of the nineteenth-century sweetheart named Edith like her ancestress, or the use of radio.[7] But, most importantly, Bellamy was the first to go all the way with such a lay millenarianism. Therefore, his ending, which refuses the easy alibi of it all being a dream—a norm from Mercier and Griffith to Macnie—marks the historical moment when this tradition came of age and changed from defensive to self-confident. The new vision achieves, within the text, a reality equal to that of the author's empirical actuality. This claim translates into historical cognition Hawthorne's psychological fantasy and, especially, the long sleep of Irving's Rip van Winkle, itself cognate to folktales such as the Sleeping Beauty or the Seven Sleepers (Hawthorne and Irving are the only U.S. authors in Dr. Leete's library). Bellamy links thus two strong American traditions: the fantastic one of unknown worlds and potentialities, and the practical one of organizing a new world—both of which avail themselves of powerful biblical parallels while translating them from religion to economics. His materialist view of history as a coherent succession of changing human relationships and social structures was continued by Morris and Wells, and thence was

6. Howells, p. xiii.
7. Arthur E. Morgan's refutation, in his *Plagiarism in Utopia* (Yellow Springs, OH, 1944), of Bellamy's supposed plagiarism from *The Diothas* seems both unconvincing and unnecessarily fond of the shibboleth of "originality," exactly as pertinent to literary value as bourgeois copyright law, and particularly inapplicable to SF, including utopian fiction.

built into the fundaments of subsequent SF. The same holds
for the plot that educates the reader into acceptance of the
strange locus and its values by following the puzzled education
of a representative protagonist. Modern SF, though it has forgotten this one among its ancestors, builds on *Looking Backward*
much as Dr. Leete's house was built on Julian's ruins and on top
of the hermetically sealed sleeping chamber under its foundations.

Particular traits from Bellamy's other works also drew from
and returned into the SF tradition. The Flammarion-like cosmi-
cally exceptional blindness of C.S. Lewis's Earthmen and E.R.
Burroughs's transferral by spirit to Mars are also found in "The
Blindman's World," and the despotic oligarchy as the alternative
to revolution in Wells and London has a direct precursor in
Equality. Most immediately, the immense ideologico-political echo
of *Looking Backward* reverberated around the globe through
numerous writers of sequels, rebuttals, and parallels. Bellamy
had hit exactly the right note at a time of widespread search for
alternatives to ruthless plutocracy, and between 100 and 200
utopian tales expounding or satirizing social democracy, state
regulation of economy, a Populist capitalism, or various uncouth
combinations thereof were published in the United States from
1888 to the first World War. Though none of them approached
Bellamy's coherence, the most notable were Ignatius Donnelly's
melodramatic *Caesar's Column* (1890) and Howells's politely satirical discussions in *A Traveller From Altruria* (1894). In Britain the
echo was to be felt down to Wells, and in Germany it resulted in at least three dozen utopian and anti-utopian tales. But
the perfect complement to *Looking Backward* was written by William Morris.

1.2. As so many other utopias, Morris's *News From Nowhere*
(1890) was a direct reply to *Looking Backward*. Reviewing it, he
had denounced Bellamy's "unhistoric and unartistic" tempera-
ment which "makes its owner (if a socialist) perfectly satisfied
with modern civilization, if only the injustice, misery and waste
of class society could be got rid of" and whose ideal of life "is
that of the industrious *professional* middle-class man of today,
purified from [the] crime of complicity with the monopolist
class"; whence it follows "that he conceives of the change to
socialism as taking place without any breakdown of that life, or

indeed disturbance of it." Morris especially objected to Bellamy's stress on both technological and social machinery that leaves the impression "of a huge standing army, tightly drilled," to the corresponding "State Communism" as opposed to direct participatory democracy, and to the reduction of labor instead of its change to work as pleasure, work blended with an art which "is not a mere adjunct of life . . . but the necessary and indispensable instrument of human happiness."[8]

Accordingly, it is direct, sensual relationships of men to each other and to nature, a different civilization where useful work is pleasure, that provide the fundament of *News From Nowhere*. It adopts the frame of *Looking Backward*, which begins with the narrator falling asleep and waking up in the future house built on the place of his own, and ends with his terrible return to his own time. But from the very beginning, Morris's story is a counterproject to Bellamy's. It is presented neither as a safe retrospective from the year 2000 nor as the voice of a lone member of the upper class, but as one privileged voice and vision of the future among several others possible and held within the socialist party of which Morris was a member, and in whose periodical *News From Nowhere* was published serially. The whole story is informed by the tone of a man displaying his personal vision for consent to potential comrades in bringing it about, and yet very aware of its distance in the future. This approach blends collective validity and personal heartbreak. It is much richer than the easy Christian Socialist resolution of Julian West's private anguish by means of a resurrected bride, for it takes into full consideration both the collective difficulty of arriving at and the personal impossibility of setting up an abode in the promised classless land: the narrator William Guest—Morris's *persona*—is in the position of Moses walking through a vision of Canaan. Therefore, the story does not, as does that of West, progress through sallies from a safe individual hearth. It retains the obligatory outlining of the future in the Mercier-to-Bellamy tradition—here a ride from Hammersmith to the British Museum, that repository of collective memory; but it adds two further

8. William Morris, *"Looking Backward," The Commonweal*, 22 June 1889; reprinted in *Science-Fiction Studies* 3 (November 1976): 287–90, together with Morris's also pertinent introduction to his Kelmscott Press edition of More's *Utopia*.

and historically new elements. First, it introduces an account
of the revolution that brought the future about; though today
this account may seem still too naive and optimistic, it is of a different order of credibility than the sudden wholesale social con-
versions depicted by previous writers up to and including Bellamy. Second, the bittersweet rowing up the Thames shows
what the future might have meant to the author-narrator personally. Together with the ubiquitous guide Dick, the average
Nowherean, Guest's main partner in the first part of the story is
Old Hammond, the custodian of history, and in the second part
Ellen, the incarnation of the "pleasure of life" of the future
present.

The narrator's vision is also a dream. Not only can it naturalistically be considered a dream in his nineteenth-century Hammersmith bed, it is also a wish-dream. Reacting against the
capitalist use of machinery that polluted the life of man and the
Earth and created ugliness and misery, Morris began with the
Pre-Raphaelite tradition of art as daydreaming. However, in its
refusal to look deeper into the basic problems of reality such an
art became nonetheless the complement of reality, as green
complements red, and thus directly dependent upon it—pretty
where actuality is ugly, sweet where it is bitter, brightly shaped
where it is amorphous and sooty, a pastoral where it is an ulcer
of slums:

> Forget six counties overhung with smoke,
> Forget the snorting steam and piston stroke,
> Forget the spreading of the hideous town;
> Think rather of the pack-horse on the down,
> And dream of London, small, and white, and clean,
> The clear Thames bordered by its gardens green. . . .
>
> [Morris, *The Earthly Paradise*]

Steam-age capitalism was ruthlessly transforming towns into "an
extension of the coal mine"[9] and the countryside into the spoils
for the railway that already Thoreau complained about, and developing the war of each against each into global imperialisms.
In a technique similar to More's, *News From Nowhere* is primarily
a counterproject to that life:

---

9. Lewis Mumford (Bibliography IV A), p. 159—but see his whole chapter 4.

> The hope of the past times was gone. . . . Was it all to
> end in a counting-house on the top of a cinder-heap,
> with Podsnap's drawing-room in the offing, an a Whig
> committee dealing champagne to the rich and mar-
> garine to the poor in such convenient proportions as
> would make all men contended together, though the plea-
> sure of the eyes was gone from the world . . . ?
>
> [Morris, "How I Became a Socialist"[10]]

At this high point of the paleotechnic world, any sensitive artist
might have wished with Guest "for days of peace and rest, and
cleanness and smiling goodwill" (chap. 1). For its "realities were
money, price, capital, shares: the environment itself, like most of
human existence, was treated as an abstraction. Air and sunlight,
because of their deplorable lack of value in exchange, had no
reality at all."[11] On the contrary, *News From Nowhere* presents an
airy and sunny environment, where only direct interhuman relations are clearly envisaged. In contrast to the capitalist gospel of
toil, work as playful human necessity stands at the novel's moral
center. In contrast to the Victorian starvation of the mind and
the senses, the novel's figures are perhaps the fullest and least
self-conscious Epicureans in modern English literature. And in
contrast to the terrible anxieties of blood-and-iron progress, the
novel's subtitle is "An Epoch of Rest."

There is accordingly a strong element of mere escape in *News
From Nowhere*. With disturbing implications for a utopian romance, Morris overreacted into a total refusal to envisage any
machinery, technological or societal. This amounts to leaving his
future society without any economic or organizational basis. As
to the economy, a "force-barge" with an undisclosed new energy
is the only exception to a turning away from and indeed dis-
mantling of technology in Nowhere. People who are so minded
can collect together to draw on the universally available "power"
(energy) in workshops, but this is used only for handicrafts; for
the rest, England is now a garden. Morris makes some telling

---

10. All of Morris's essays cited in this chapter in parenthesis by title are to be found in
Political Writings of William Morris, ed. A. L. Morton (New York, 1973), an indispensable
companion to his novel; in particular, the essay "The Society of the Future" (1887) is the
nearest thing to an ideological nucleus of *News From Nowhere*.

11. Mumford, p. 168.

points about the "never-ending series [of] sham or artificial
necessaries" (chap. 15) imposed by the capitalist world market
that necessarily enslaved colonial countries as a counterpart to
the corruption of consumer taste. But to reject resolutely not
only useless forms of technology and industrial organization but
technical productivity and inventiveness in general while keeping
the population stable and affluent, as *News From Nowhere* does, is
self-defeating. Any utopographer has the right to fashion his
Land of Heart's Desire; but he has a corresponding obligation to
make it an at least arguable alternative possibility.

It could be argued that the gap left by Morris's disgust with
modern economics might today be filled in by an imaginative
reader supplying his own economics, based on the possibilities
of automation and other ways of "post-industrial" productivity
which Morris could not know about—though his vision assumed
that humanity would somehow evolve "immensely improved
machinery" (chap. 15) for irksome tasks if only basic problems of
social organization were solved. Unfortunately, the absence of
sociopolitical organization in Nowhere is a gap that cannot be
argued away and denies it the status of a utopia. True, there is a
classical Marxist glimpse of "communes and colleges" (chap. 5)
run by participatory democracy. However, overcompensating for
Bellamy's state apparatus and clear lines of power, *News From
Nowhere* omits all machinery for determining priorities between
communes or any other basic units. Yet all production, including very much an automated one, requires—as long as it is not
simply magical—coordination and a (however truly participatory) system of vertical decision making. As Bellamy astutely
countered in his review of Morris, "[no] degree of moral improvement [will] lessen the necessity of a strictly economic ad-
ministration for the directing of the productive and distributive
machinery."[12] *News From Nowhere* sacrifices human productivity
in order to get rid of Statism and technocracy.

But if it is not a utopia, and much less prophetic anticipation,
News From Nowhere is the finest specimen of Earthly Paradise
story in modern literature. As I argued in chapters 3 and 5, the
Terrestrial Paradise—a place of this-worldly fleshly contentment,

---

12. [Edward Bellamy,] "News from Nowhere," *New Nation*, 14 February 1891, p. 47,
quoted in Sylvia E. Bowman et al. (Bibliography IV C), p. 94.

magical fertility, happiness, health, and youth—is a wish-dream
that does not focus on economic and sociopolitical organization;
it is a magical parallel world akin to folktale and pastoral yet of
collective import as an alternative community to be striven for.
Morris's tale has almost all of these elements. The weather and
the people are (perhaps a shade monotonously) perpetually
summery, the salmon are back in the Thames, and Shelleyan
consentaneous love inspires all breasts (though there is just
enough exception to keep it from being too saccharine). Liberated from grim capitalism, the world has entered upon its "second childhood" (chap. 19), very similar to an idealized version
of the fourteenth century and characterized by a childishly unspoiled enjoyment in artful work not sundered from play: all its
people look younger than they would in our civilization. Above
all, the dryness of the usual utopian panoramic sweep is avoided
by Morris's fashioning the second part of the story as a personal
working out of the new country, as a glimpse of the narrator's
alternative—happy and wholesome—life. His journey up the
magical waters of the fertile Thames, signposted with references
to a range of legends from the Grimm Brothers tales "from the
childhood of the world" (chap. 16) to Tennyson's Lotos Eaters,
shows Morris's rich and contrapuntal use of the Romantic fairy
tale. The newly fertile land and happy relationships in the future
England are the result of a metamorphosis from the ugly
Victorian past—still inscribed in Guest's clothes, looks, and
memories—to the clear and colorful beauty of the Nowherean
present, a metamorphosis analogous to Andersen's ugly duckling
reborn as a beautiful swan. Under the spell of his rejuvenating
journey toward the sources, the narrator also moves toward the
happiness felt in his childhood.

Nonetheless, "shades of the prison-house" are inescapably
upon the narrator-protagonist: he personally can only testify to,
not accomplish for himself, the metamorphosis that brings happiness. The tension between the report about collective happiness and the personal melancholy of the guest-reporter in that
Earthly Paradise—for him truly a Nowhere—refuses a Bellamy-
type sentimental happy ending. The crucially more mature resolution is not one of ethical salvation, as in *Looking Backward*, but
one of political strife. We are back at Blake's great oath not to let
"the sword sleep in my hand" until Jerusalem is built "in Eng-

land's green and pleasant land." But here such a strife is translated from Blake's arena of a single mind to public political
struggle, as personal compensation for and collective justification
of Guest's visit and departure;

> . . . Ellen's last mournful look seemed to say, "No, it will not
> do; you cannot be of us; you belong so entirely to the un-
> happiness of the past that our happiness even would weary
> you. . . . Go back and be the happier for having seen us, for
> having added a little hope to your struggle. Go on living
> while you may, striving, with whatsoever pain and labour
> needs must be, to build up little by little the new day of
> fellowship, and rest, and happiness."
>
> Yes, surely! and if others can see it as I have seen it, then
> it may be called a vision rather than a dream. [chap. 32]

For this dream is, finally, to be understood in the tradition of
the medieval genre of the same name, in which the convention,
as in Langland or Chaucer, is that the author relates the dream
as a non-naturalistic analogy—often using the fable or other allegorical means—to public problems of great personal import.
Morris had already used this convention in his SF story about the
peasant revolt in the Middle Ages, *A Dream of John Ball* (1888). Its
narrator, double horizon of defeat and yet victory, historical assumptions, and time scheme combined with color imagery (night
and moon opposed to "the east crimson with sunrise") prefigure
the fuller use in *News From Nowhere*. But just as *A Dream of John
Ball* was not an Individualistic historical novel, so the later work
is not to be taken for positivistic prophecy but for the figure or
type of a fulfilment that could or should come. In that roundabout, dialectical way *News From Nowhere* and its "ideal of the old
pastoral poets" can, through its nucleus of frank and beautiful
human relationships to other humans and to nature, be reinte-
grated into anticipatory utopianism. Its Earthly Paradise is an
analogy to the classless socialist day. Its collective dream, "if
others can see it," will finally also be a vision reinserted into
history. Staying within the bourgeois—or indeed WASP—
existential horizons, Bellamy had pursued the everyday need for
security to its logical conclusion and ended up with the socialist
dawn as an order of things, a *societas rerum*. Reneging on the
bourgeois existential horizons but opposing to them unrealisti-

cally idealized preindustrial—indeed bohemian—horizons, Morris pursued the arrested timeless moment, the visionary dream (in all the above senses) of Earthly Paradise to its logical conclusion and ended up with another aspect of that same dawn: creative and therefore beautiful human relations, a *societas hominum*. Between them, they covered the technical premises and sensual horizons of that dawn: each lacks what the other has. For a brief but still significant historical moment—which extended to Wells, London, and Zamyatin—the discussion about darkness and dawn became one inside the international socialist movement.

Dawn or sunburst, a favorite image of that whole movement, is here particularly appropriate because of close correspondences among people, vegetation, and the seasons of day and year. Morris's narrator went to sleep in a wintry night, when the young moon portended renewal; he wakes up, "by witness of the riverside trees," in a bright morning of spring or summer. The sunlight denotes happiness, as the moonlight throughout the story reminds the narrator of the past times. Colors too are connected with the opposed tempers and historical epochs, "the sombre greyness, or rather brownness, of the nineteenth century" versus "the gaiety and brightness" of the twenty-first (chap. 19). Mankind has again become a part of nature, "men and women [are] worthy of the sweet abundance of midsummer" (chap. 21), and the river-side trees are emblems as much as witnesses to it. The representative denizen of the future, Ellen, sums it up in her cry: "O me! O me! How I love the earth, and the seasons, and weather, and all things that deal with it, and all that grows out of it . . ." (chap. 31). She is the ideal partner or *anima* of Morris, who characterized himself in "How I Became a Socialist" as a man "careless of metaphysics and religion, as well as of scientific analysis, but with a deep love of the earth and the life on it, and a passion for the history of the past of mankind."

The arrested moment of Earthly Paradise is conveyed by a series of pictures, one of Morris's basic stylistic devices. The vision in *News From Nowhere* sharply etches in colors and shades, time and place—especially the topography of London and the Thames valley—but it is most attentive to the sensual nuances of behavior and movement of humans through a nature produced by their hands' work. The beautiful bridges, the gardenlike

banks of the Thames, the haysels, and the old house that grows
out of the earth are of the same stuff as the nut-brown maids
"born out of the summer day itself" (chap. 21), flowers in the
green countryside. Yet this pictorial, at times somewhat pictur-
esque vision is ever and again clouded by the dreamlike melancholy and alienation of the beholder. The bemused and never
quite sunny narrator does not fully fit into the bright day of the
pictorial narration. He comes from the wrong, moony or night
side of the dawn, and he finally has to step outside the picture
frame and fade from the Earthly Paradise. Yet, in their turn,
the translucent characters, scenery, and style all harmonize with
the yearning of the narrator in an "identity of situation and
feeling."[13] Nowhere and William Guest are two polar aspects
of Morris the author—the healing, achieved hope and the
wounded, hoping subject. Both the subject and his hope are in
some ways marked by Pre-Raphaelite narcissism and thus very
much at odds with modern taste. But the sensual immediacy and
clarity of their interaction render with great fidelity and
economy a genuine poetry of human beauty and transience. The
characters are ranged along a graduated spectrum which extends from the clouded narrator to Ellen, the personification of
sunshine loveliness. Nearest to Guest are Old Hammond with his
knowledge of, and the "grumbler" with his eccentric penchant
for, the old-time unhappiness, while the fulcrum of the narration is occupied by Dick and Clara. Since this is "a land of fellowship rather than authority, there are no fathers: a generation is always skipped."[14] But all characters are mirror-images
of the narrator (Old Hammond) or of the landscape, and all
elements of the story a system of stylistic mirrors which would
easily become tedious were it not for the fundamental existential
estrangement and opposition between Nowhere and England,
the twenty-first and the nineteenth century, light and soot, summer and winter. The narration glides in a leisurely manner
among these clarifying mirrors, progressing from Guest's first
immersions into the Thames of the future and the deurbanized
London to the explanation of history, the beauty of the river
journey, and—since he cannot be in at the fruition—his final

13.   Raymond Williams, *Culture and Society 1780–1950* (Bibliography IV C), p. 234.
14.   Tom Middlebro' (Bibliography IV C), p. 10.

expulsion from the harvest celebration.

The horizons of *News From Nowhere* are a variant of Marxism, with a bias toward Fourier's passionate attraction for work and pleasure but without his systematization. Human history is seen as a dialectical development from tribal communism, or from Morris's beloved Middle Ages, through capitalism to classless society, "from the older imperfect communal period, through the time of the confused struggle and tyranny of the rights of property, into the present rest and happiness of complete Communism" (chap. 27). The chapter "How the Change Came" extrapolates from the experience of French revolutions and English working-class agitation, such as the Bloody Sunday demonstration of 1887, a first approximation to realistic revolution in SF. There are also shrewd hints about the transitional period after the revolution. True, the resulting life, in which mathematics is an eccentric foible on a par with antiquarian novels and education is left to haphazard communion with the society of people and things, is in many important aspects a multiplication ad infinitum of ideals from Morris's arts and crafts circle. However, if he sees life somewhat too exclusively as a Pre-Raphaelite work of art, at least Morris went to the logical end of his generation's demand that life should become a work of art. He took it seriously, that is, literally and collectively, and tried to depict its realization. If the attempt was not wholly successful because of Morris's well-founded but one-sided distrust of science, still the further horizons of such life are open-ended. Like any Golden Age or Eden in or after Morris's favorites Homer, Hesiod, and the Bible, this is a static society. But in Morris's scheme of history it is explicitly an epoch of cleansing rest, which might well evolve further.

1.3. News From Nowhere is an alternative not only to what Morris felt as mawkish bourgeois novels and as the technocracy of *Looking Backward*. In the spectrum of SF it is also an alternative to both of the contemporary basic variants of the "post-catastrophe tale"—W. H. Hudson's merely escapist and idiosyncratic pastoral and Richard Jefferies's embracing of "hard" barbarism and primitivism. Jefferies's *After London* (1885) introduced a fall of civilization patterned after that of the Roman Empire, which results in a return to the barbarian—part feudal and part slave-owning—social order. In his novel the reasons for the catastrophe are unclear—possibly economic, perhaps cosmic—but in such works reasons are as a rule secondary to the middle classes' sense of impending doom and wish-dream of a new start. The reassertion of wild life which Jefferies renders with peculiar intensity, the legends about "the ancients" and their knowledge, the poisonous site of the old metropolis, and the new geopolitics superimposed on old maps subsequently became the staple of a whole range of SF. Hudson's mellifluous *A Crystal Age* (1887) introduced the other timeless simplification of pastoral, here recomplicated by changed sexual behavior in a beehive-type matriarchal family. In a reversal of Bulwer, the fever of sexual passion is equated with the individualist civilization, but it is again both a sign of sickness and indispensably sweet to the protagonist. Both of these works have some elements similar to Morris's, since they totally reject the present and the city. Morris read *After London* before he wrote his book and was stimulated to "absurd hopes"[15] by its picture of deurbanization. But his romance is a third way, transcending the opposition between Bellamy's ethicoreligious pacification and Jefferies's politicogeological devolution, as well as that between escapism à la Hudson and naturalistic sentimentality. Guest and his hosts are obscurely conscious of meeting "as if I were a being from another planet" (chap. 9); but he is also the link between the universes of darkness and sunlight, and Morris overcomes the one-sidedness of these various traditions by a blend of verisimilitude and Earthly Paradise, by a future sunlight constantly contrasting with our darkness—as befits a dawn.

Finally, Morris's underlying view of world and man is simply and beautifully but inexorably materialistic. Though there is no immortality in Nowhere—the only feature of Earthly Paradise not incorporated—death and sorrow, as in the episode of the jealousy killing, do not destroy but confirm the paradise. For in this view the individual is bound up with his fellows and nature in an existence that has wholly eradicated the social and cosmic alienation of man. Morris "seems to retire far from the real world and to build a world out of his wishes; but when he has finished the result stands out as a picture of experience inelucta-

---

15. Quoted (from Morris's letter to Mrs. Burne-Jones of 28 April 1885) in A. L. Morton (Bibliography II), p. 204.

bly true."[16] In Bellamy's romance the new vision evolved systematically out of facets of the old; his "colder" political stance is accompanied by a closed and often oppressive narrative structure. In Morris's romance the new vision as a whole is incompatible with the old; its open and airier structure is homologous to his warmer, nonregimenting politics. As we have seen, Bellamy's vision achieved therefore within his book a reality *equal* to that of the author's empirical environment; but Morris's achieved an "ineluctable" reality *superior* to that of the old civilization. That is why his narrator, tragically marked by the old, must in the end be extruded from the vision.

Let us compare one representative feature: Dr. Leete's private room in the communal dining house stands for Bellamy's general treatment of the public whole as a sum of rationalized and sanitized private elements, no doubt spatially transposed and regrouped but qualitatively unchanged. It is a dining room for a monogamous family and its private guests, just as the speech, furniture, dress, maidenly blushes, and the like—in short, the whole lifestyle of the future Bostonians—is for all practical purposes simply extrapolated from the style of "their cultured ancestors of the nineteenth [century]" (chap. 4). On the contrary, Morris's dining rooms harbor truly communal feasts, open to the abundant fertility of nature, and with a large cast of erotically sympathetic and open "neighbours" who transmit information to the narrator by asking him curious questions rather than simply lecturing him, and us, as affable but omniscient teachers. The Hammersmith Guest House, likewise erected on the site of the narrator's nineteenth-century dwelling, is its temporal extension not into a safer private home, as in Bellamy, but into a collective entity that has done away with the pernicious sundering of private and public, indoors and outdoors, beauty and utility. Morris's dining place is a fusion of an idealized fourteenth century and classical antiquity, open to the garden and river glimpsed beyond: but the improved architecture, food, and flowers have a counterpart in men and women who age at less than half the Victorian rate. For all the borrowings from the past, such a sweeping biological improvement is the measure of the qualita-

16. C. S. Lewis (Bibliography IV A), p. 54.

tive difference between Nowhere and any, however "cultured," nineteenth-century lifestyle.

Furthermore, the whole narrative of *Looking Backward* progresses as a retrospective series of West's topographical and ideological sallies into the new Boston from the individual, monogamous hearth of the Leetes and under their reassuring guidance. Any unaccompanied personal venture from this safe cocoon immediately provokes in West a "horror of strangeness" (chap. 5), an existential or indeed existentialist nausea that is— most revealingly—quite as violent in the supposedly safe new Boston of the future as in the nightmare of returning to the competitive old Boston of the past. This microcosm, consisting of a very restricted number of spaces and characters, imparts a strong agoraphobic aura to Bellamy's millennium: it harbors a panic fear, for which only the closure of space, of ideas (State Socialism), and of the narration itself can provide a remedy. The underlying metaphoric cluster of his book is one of static healing, whereas in Morris's book it is one of dynamic observation during a journey. That is why, though Bellamy came within an ace of returning his narrator to the nineteenth century to work in his own epoch for his new vision, and furthermore made it clear that this would have been the ethically proper course to follow, it was left for the libertarian communist Morris, with his less hidebound readership, to actually effect this large step. The supreme sacrament of acceptance into Bellamy's society is a mystically subromantic marriage into which the narrator once and for all escapes, in a sentimental happy ending of ethical—rather than political—salvation. Quite homologously, Bellamy's fear of existential openness unshielded by a personal savior or vertical hierarchy is also the motivation for his ideological stance, for example, that in favor of strict industrial organization and against a forcible political revolution: in utopian writings, politics are based on the author's simultaneously deeply personal and deeply classbound psychology. Thus Morris's novel not only more than doubles the number of characters (two main women and two main guides instead of one each in Bellamy—plus a great number of subsidiary characters instead of the lone Mrs. Leete and some disembodied voices and faces); it also enriches the times, spaces, and overall complexity of their relationships. In brief, Morris transcends Bellamy's model of fraternity under the "fatherhood of God" (chap. 26) and of lay elders (the alumni, the father-figure of Dr. Leete) in favor of the youthful, self-governing, and as it were parthenogenetic model of potential lovers. Where Bellamy opts for a psychological repression of self-determination, equally of the workers at their working place and of sexual relationships (demurely identical to those in the contemporary sentimental novel), Morris opts for an extension of sympathy or libido to the whole of the gardenlike nature, a sinless Earthly Paradise. The supreme sacrament of acceptance into his society is, therefore, not sentimentality but the actual journeying and working together, as far as is realistically feasible.

This is not to belittle the achievements of Bellamy or to ignore the gaps in Morris. Both writers are deeply committed to an anguished distancing from nineteenth-century capitalism and to a different life. However, following the main US tradition, Bellamy's "scheme was arithmetic and comfort,"[17] and it resulted mainly in a sentimental dream and a tight and earnest embracing of *security*, where anguish is discharged upon a series of personal mediators, whereas Morris's journeying results mainly in a painterly vision and an attempt at direct *creativity*, which, being open-ended, is inseparable from a possible anguish to be resolved only in self-determined practice or praxis. Yet, in other ways, the dreams or visions of Bellamy and Morris can also be treated as complementary: there is, finally, no need to make an exclusive choice between them. The paradox of *Looking Backward* being both more limited than and yet complementary to *News From Nowhere* is finally the paradox of Christian Socialism itself, simultaneously committed to the patriarchal vertical of the "fatherhood of God" and to the libertarian horizontal of the "brotherhood of Man." Such conflicting Protestant and middle-class abstractions are resolved by Morris: radically careless of the fatherhood, he explores the meaning and price of brotherhood in terms of an intimate neighborliness.

Accordingly, it is not discrete scenes of estrangement and parables that stand out in *News From Nowhere*, as they do in Bellamy. Learning from him, Morris also provides a few such scenes: the phantasmagoric vision of Bloody Sunday superimposed upon

17. Emerson's note (in *Journals* 5: 473–74, quoted in Vernon Louis Parrington [Bibliography IV A], 2:349) on the Brook Farm project.

the sight of the orchard leading to "the Parliament House, or Dung Market" (chap. 7); the shocking final recognition of the dark cloud and the servile men of the nineteenth century. But it is the tone of the whole vision-dream—the book-length parable of new human relations in a society of "wealthy freemen" (chap. 14), beauty, and "free exercise of the senses and passions of a healthy human animal, so far as this [does] not injure the other individuals of the community" (Morris, "The Society of the Future")—that remains with the reader. It is the historical horizon, the spectacle of people who "pass [their] lives in a reasonable strife with nature, exercising not one side of [themselves] only, but all sides, taking the keenest pleasure in all the life of the world" (chap. 9), in counterpoint with a Marxist "optimistic tragedy" borne by the narrator bereft of such a life, that gives *News From Nowhere* its bittersweet, tensile strength. Within a well-defined, deep but narrow sensibility, its dialectics of consciousness and unconsciousness establishes an Earthly Paradise more real and more human than the reader's tawdry actuality. If Morris's romance harkens back to almost animistic elements, it does so as the crown of a plebeian tradition of legends and folktales. Morris could have claimed for himself, in Fourier's phrase, that unlike the best political economists who wanted to throw light on the chaos, he wanted to lead out of it. Though *News From Nowhere* only partly escapes the weakness of utopias— their abstractness—it fully shares their strength, which lies *"in the ineluctable and the absolute."*[18] And even the abstractness is overcome in Morris's late essays, his crowning and truly utopian works such as "How We Live and How We Might Live," "The Society of the Future," "How I Became a Socialist," and "Communism." In them he even accepted the cognitive necessity of (as he wrote in "Communism") "time [teaching] us what new machinery may be necessary to the new life." This is Morris's final marriage of art with history.

Morris bequeathed to SF several key elements. He endowed Bellamy's suffering narrator in the new country with philosophical and poetic value. He transferred a believable revolution from political tracts into fiction, fathering a line that stretches from

18. Ernst Bloch (Bibliography II), 1:679; from here, 1:677, is also the paraphrase of Fourier's dictum.

Wells's *The Sleeper Wakes* through Jack London, Alexei Tolstoy, G. B. Shaw and Robert A. Heinlein to the flood of SF revolts in the last 40 years. His utopian pastoral or Earthly Paradise has had less success than Jefferies's neobarbarism or Hudson's titillating escapism, though it can be felt as the endangered alternative from Wells's Eloi to C. S. Lewis's Venus or Le Guin's New Tahiti (in *The Word for World Is Forest*). But his dialectical, tragic, and victorious Epicurean socialism remains the mature horizon of all SF drawing upon hopes of an open future for human beings and for the Earth. No one has yet surpassed Morris in his intimate understanding that "times of change, disruption, and revolution are naturally times of hope also" ("The Hopes of Civilization"). No one in nineteenth-century SF, and few outside it, conveyed this understanding in such lucid and warm prose.

   2.1. Mark Twain's *A Connecticut Yankee in King Arthur's Court* (1889) can be compared in very revealing ways with *Looking Backward* (and *News From Nowhere*) responding as it does to the same acute social dilemma which powered the anticipation stories. It too is "a philosophical fable which sets forth a theory of capitalism and an interpretation of the historical process that has brought it into being."[19] Twain too confronts two historical epochs by means of a narrator-commentator from the author's epoch, a stranger to the epoch he is strangely projected into and which finally ejects him (in Bellamy this ejection is then reversed, proving to be a dream, as it is in a way in "Twain's" postscript). But instead of finding himself in a bright future, Twain's Hank Morgan arrives in the darkest Middle Ages. Bellamy's story was presented as a new type of hortative historical romance written in and in praise of an estranged utopian future; Twain's is presented as a donated manuscript, but it uses the old historical and exotic novel for subversive SF purposes, which include a bitter debunking of Scott's, Cooper's, and Tennyson's sentimentality toward feudalism and savagery. Shifting the standpoint from Bellamy's utopian future to a common-sense Yankee present, this new type of epoch-collision looks backward at the author's past instead of at his present. But the backward glance discovers in both cases a dark dystopia: "In Bellamy's analysis contemporary America, a Yankee phenomenon, was as benighted and

19. Henry Nash Smith, *Mark Twain's Fable of Progress* (Bibliography IV C), p. 39.

brutalized as Athur's England. The American labourer was
scarcely better off than the chained slaves, in *A Connecticut Yankee*, driven to market in London."[20] However, Twain's Hank has
to live in the midst of that brutalized epoch, not merely to judge
it at leisure. Unlike Bellamy's hero, who is accepted into the
security of a changed and better world, or Morris's hero, who
finds in the new, future world enough tragic optimism to return
fortified for his struggle inside and against the old, past world,
Hank sets about changing his adoptive bad old world. An outsider activist, he intervenes in the affairs of the sixth century in
the name of the nineteenth.

However, the nineteenth-century values in the name of which
he intervenes are deeply contradictory and finally frustrating.
On the one hand Hank is an engineering foreman, a convinced
democratic ideologue, radical to the point of Jacobin terror:
"When he snatched up the banners under which the middleclass
was forcing the nobility to disgorge, he was eloquently sincere;
his flaming calls to revolt against self-appointed masters are great
statements of that right . . . [to] self-respecting manliness and
political equality."[21] On the other, he is a thoroughgoing bourgeois Individualist and businessman—as he says, "just another
Robinson Crusoe cast away on an uninhabited island, with no
society but some more or less tame animals, and if I wanted to
make life bearable I must do as he did—invent, contrive, create
. . ." (chap. 7). Hank starts his reforms as "the Baconian utilitarian
and progressive, the Whig bourgeois"[22]—by opening a patent
office; his idea of creation is patterned after his patron saints
"Gutenberg, Watt, Arkwright, Whitney, Morse, Stephenson,
Bell," the patent-office giants of the capitalist industrial and
communicational revolution (chap. 33). His next enterprises are
special schools, somewhat chillingly called Man-Factories, and
frontier-type sensational newspapers accepting and dispensing
political and economic patronage; then come factories, "iron and
steel missionaries of my future civilization" (chap. 10). Hank
Morgan reenacts thus the historical ascent of the bourgeois class
both politically and paleotechnically, and he memorably typifies

    20.   Justin Kaplan (Bibliography IV C), p. 16.
    21.   Louis Budd (Bibliography IV C), p. 144.
    22.   Roger B. Salomon (Bibliography IV C), pp. 30–31.

its Yankee variant—a blend of political radicalism, go-getting commercialism, profitable showmanship, and technological gadgetry, issuing finally in ruinous stock market speculation. But he also shares the historical fate of the Yankee bourgeoisie as felt by Mark Twain in the Gilded Age: a separation from the laboring people.

The first part of *A Connecticut Yankee* is taken up with Hank's orientation at the court of Camelot. It concentrates on hearty lampooning of Malory's and Tennyson's Arthurian styles and ideologies and on Hank's use of scientific knowledge as a burlesque magic superior to that of his rival Merlin. Having become on the strength of that magic "Sir Boss," a reformist prime minister to Arthur, Hank travels through the country on an obligatory knightly mission. In this second part there is added to the burlesque of knight-errantry and miraculous religion and to technical spoofs a democratic indignation at the oppressive laws of feudalism. In the third part the Yankee and the king travel incognito in the style of Harun-al-Rashid, plumbing the depths of slavery and demoralization in the country. This is the crucial juncture for a supposedly radical and a quasi-historical novel. Wanting to overthrow the Dark Ages, the Yankee has to find out whether the people would follow him. This hegemony had in fact been the historical achievement of the bourgeoisie up to "the ever-memorable and blessed [French] Revolution." But Hank cannot achieve this alliance, because Twain quite realistically does not believe in it any more: "I knew that the Jack Cade or Wat Tyler who tries [a revolution] without first educating his materials up to revolution-grade is almost absolutely certain to get left" (chap. 13). It is difficult to see how Hank could proceed with this education since he is continually envisaging the people as commodities or animals, a view endorsed by the author as he focuses on the snobbery, pusillanimity, and finally mob lynchings of an environment reminiscent of the antebellum South with its chain gangs and poor whites. The Yankee had fulminated against a class training that blinds the people. Yet he comes to act as a manufacturer, tamer-trainer, or indeed a being of superior race among "human muck" (chap. 43). These are hardly becoming roles for a democrat setting the stage for freemen. Faithfully the author shows us that, in spite of all his sententiousness, the Yankee in the end "gets left" high and dry by a receding tide of history. Not seeing beyond the ebb of bourgeois democracy and revolutionism, it is Mark Twain as much as Hank Morgan who concludes that "there are times when one would like to hang the whole human race and finish the farce" (chap. 31).

The indignation of the first half of *A Connecticut Yankee* against feudal and church oppression was closer to Swift than to the lukewarm iconoclasm of *Erewhon*. But Swift's satire had been so savagely efficient because he kept the authorial distance from Gulliver subtly flexible and yet precisely controlled, correlative to a radical pessimism about what Twain himself was to call the damned human race. In this second half of the novel, Twain's attempt to do the same in relation to Hank fails. This narrative cannot sustain Swift's singleminded control over a comicosatirical narrator, who travels within a didactic, estranged country, because *A Connecticut Yankee* oscillates between commitment to a historical ideal and horror at its workings in history. Early on the novel affirms the progressive theory of history that emerged from the heyday of bourgeois revolutions and a positive hero upholding it. But this came to clash with Twain's increasing alienation from the effects of the industrial revolution as appropriated by the bourgeoisie and his consequent pessimistic theory of human nature, and the book was left without a moral and political core—which is fatal equally for satire and utopia. Sundered from the people, all the Yankee can do is train a small band of elite technocratic enthusiasts, whose program is opposed to the Arthurian Age as the Yankee Gilded Age exploitation of the frontier, or of any new market, is to Southern slavery: "Look at the opportunities here for a man of knowledge, brains, pluck, and enterprise to sail in and grow with the country. The grandest field that ever was; and all my own; not a competitor . . ." (chap. 8). Their main trump—historically exact again—is science and technology.

Twain's attitude to technological progress oscillates into confusion and despair in strict parallel to his attitudes toward its historical bearer, the middle class, and especially the technics-committed Yankee bourgeoisie. Hank's superior know-how is shown first as spoofs, ambiguously magical tricks used as a joyous means to power. The degradation of science and technology to the role of magic, a fundamentally different attempt at controlling nature, leads to their becoming a juggernaut and, finally,

means which turn into their own end—the end being mass carnage. The Yankee's societal counterconstruction ends in an Armageddon, prefigured in the book's volcanic and explosive imagery.

Though Twain's stance as outsider does not do justice to the
liberating possibilities of science, it enables him to pass a shrewd
judgment on its historical sociopolitical uses. Sundered from the
artisans and peasants, "Jack Cade or Wat Tyler," Baconian science is able only to destroy impartially the upper classes and its
wielders. Finally, even this potent means is only a theatrical "effect" of Barnumian proportions, effecting no social change. The
new Crusoe-type, Individualistic civilization collapses under the
interdict of an omnipotent Catholic Church that we have never
really seen in *A Connecticut Yankee*, yet that pops up as a *diabolus
ex machina*, a fit antagonist for the lone Protestant Great Man or
Whig Robinson Crusoe. As Twain's superficial treatment of
Arthur's court—culminating in the faceless knights of the final
battle—testifies, feudalism was not a believable antagonist in the
American 1880s. Nor was—at a time when Twain was defend-
ing the young trade unions and Howells was agonizing over the
judicial murder of the Chicago anarchists—a robber-baron
bourgeoisie a believable protagonist. Indeed, as Howells noted,
"there are passages in which we see that the noble of Arthur's
day, who battened on the blood and sweat of his bondsmen,
is one in essence with the capitalist of [1889] who grows rich
on the labor of his underpaid wagemen,"[23] and Hank's progress through England ends in an almost Dickensian, or indeed
Blakean, horrible London. Thus the book collapses in a rather
perfunctory mixture of shadow-boxing and savage despair,
pronouncing "a curse on both parts."[24]

This devolution of the story's hopes for a plebeian progres-
sivism is also embodied in its language. In the comical, confident
beginning of the novel, Hank's "machine-shop lingo collides with
the Malory-ese of the Age of Chivalry." By the end, it has become clear that the Yankee's "language [is grounded] in clichés
and conventional syntax, [and] its character emerges by means of

    23. W. D. Howells, review in *Harper's* (January 1890), p. 320, quoted in Henry Nash
Smith, *Mark Twain: The Development of a Writer* (Bibliography IV C), p. 146.
    24. Kaplan, p. 19.

exaggeration and calculated vulgarity," that it is an artificial ver-
nacular of an artificial democrat, only "masquerading as burly,
rough talk." This means that it attains neither consistently precise satire nor consistently wholehearted burlesque, but that in
final analysis it remains "a *show*, an act . . . not necessary to the
action, but simply decoration . . . [nothing] more than one of
Hank Morgan's *effects*."[25]

Twain's liberal utopianism seems to have followed a course
quite parallel to Jules Verne's—a writer whose interest in mapping and clean communications he shares in this book with its
providential telephone wires and industries without a working
class. Twain's fabulation relies, as does Verne, on the bedrock of
popular melodrama and farce, or on travelers' tales (such as
balloon travel in *Tom Sawyer Abroad*, 1894). As it did with Verne,
the dimming of liberal horizons turned Twain toward a cyclical
theory of history (compare his *Papers of the Adam Family* [bp.
1962] and Verne's *Eternal Adam*) and superdestructive weaponry,
which together account for the breakdown of a class society rent
by antagonisms in *A Connecticut Yankee* as in Verne's *Propeller
Island*. On the other hand, Twain was quite alien to any idea of a
new social system going beyond the bourgeois-democratic one.
Though he privately much admired Bellamy's sunburst of a
wholly different state of affairs, he could creatively envisage it
only as the glare of Armageddon, of the "fifty electric suns" by
whose light the final Battle of the Sand-Belt is fought, with its
ominous hint of our atomic bomb brighter than a thousand suns.
In Twain, as in the Mary Shelley-to-Verne tradition, the only
novelties are destructive ones; in opposition to the socialist tradition, culminating in Morris, the imagery of moon and sun,
eclipse and displacement, leads to catastrophe instead of millennium, to violent nightmare instead of vision and dream of restful
dawn.

However, Twain is much more profoundly distressed than
Verne by the closure of progressive horizons. This distress issues
in a deep ambivalence toward not only the values but the reality
itself of the opposed epochs. The dreamy Arthurian Britain may
be the antebellum South of slavery, but it has likewise a pastoral,
childhood freshness. Obversely, the energetic Yankee represents

25. James M. Cox (Bibliography IV C), pp. 203, 215, 213, and 219.

the capitalist North of the nineteenth century both as political liberator and industrial destroyer. In the end, Twain's hero therefore sheds his representative, allegorical class traits and takes a double refuge: first from the sixth century—where the original "white Indians" have turned into sophisticated stock exchange scalpers—into the ultimate reality of private life and family, and then from the nineteenth century into dreams of such a privatized sixth century. Finally, in the "plague on both your houses" situation, when annihilation has disposed of both sides, Hank becomes adrift in time and withdraws into a dreaming wholly outside the catastrophic history. Indeed, there is a hint that he is not quite certain which is a dream, the sixth or the nineteenth century. For all his genuine radical leanings, Mark Twain is to be ranged on the other side from Bellamy and Morris across the watershed of hope. This historical position led even so powerful a writer to a formal dead end.

Thus, while there are richly burlesque or satirical as well as generously indignant passages in *A Connecticut Yankee*, its final horizon of havoc and sterility is what makes it both memorable and indicative for a long-lasting historical moment. The activist-hero battling against the age will recur in SF, from the pages of Wells and London to innumerable later time travelers and political plotters. But Twain was the first in SF to face directly, without theological or biological myths, how "in bourgeois society . . . the past dominates the present,"[26] and the first to analyze rather than merely present the obscure forces of history that rise from the past not only to overwhelm the Promethean progressive hero from the outside, but also to hollow him out from the inside. Hank's career could be called "Prometheus Re-Bound" or "the making of Victor Frankenstein," for it shows how the bearer of Promethean progress turns into the absurd causer of historical catastrophe. Twain thus revived for the modern novel the central ideological dilemmas of the age of anticipation, which would be developed in twentieth-century SF because they would remain the most sensitive historical problems. For example, the motif of outside intervention or exporting of revolution into an "underdeveloped" country will recur up to the Strugatskys and Le

26. Karl Marx and Friedrich Engels, "Manifesto of the Communist Party," in *Selected Works in One Volume* (New York, 1968), p. 48.

Guin, and the concomitant or obverse motif of the lone hero
becoming adrift in time will accompany the devolution of history
from Wells to Vonnegut and Sheckley.

A Connecticut Yankee does not handle such seminal motifs and
types in a fully satisfactory way. Its "juvenile fantasy" treatment
of the "collision between superstition and modern technology"[27]
and of politics reduced to a duel between the lone protagonist
and the world crops up, increasingly, as a cliché of space-opera
and other "degree zero" SF. Perhaps the causally and formally
central failing of A Connecticut Yankee, the one that made its
structure analogous to juvenile fantasy, was the absence of what
one might call a political economics of existence from Hank's
social changes. It remains completely unclear whether and how
the laboring people that the Yankee meets on his peregrinations
have benefited or will benefit from his despotic industrialism or
State capitalism. The ads displayed on knights imply a market
economy, other passages imply unpaid distribution; but the
technical problems of political economy are not so important as
the fact that nobody in the novel even poses the question how
people would receive their sustenance in a post-Arthurian industrialized system, or who would determine its amount and distribution channels. This is one of the sorriest blind spots in the
center of the imaginative picture that Twain has bequeathed to
practically the whole of subsequent English language SF, born of
the selfsame "New Deal" hope which took its name from a
phrase in this text. But finally, by the same token, this novel
shows the necessary collapse of Twain's own and all such private
fantasies, and provides the means by which to identify them as a
flight from history. A Connecticut Yankee's function as yardstick
for the tradition it set in motion is also an indication of the
novel's importance.

Many other SF fragments show Mark Twain's concern with the
grimness of the coming times in which America's uniqueness
would fall prey to the general fate of imperialist power—a suspicion that grew into certainty after the 1898 Spanish-American
War for the "open door" to Latin America and East Asia. Twain
returned frequently in his fragmentary sketches to the image of
a future dictatorship—monarchist, technological, or theologi-

27. Smith, Mark Twain: Development, p. 166.

cal—in the United States, establishing in this way too a central theme for SF. Had these fragments been completed and published, he would have beyond a doubt stood instead of Wells as the major turning point in the tradition leading to modern SF, and instead of Stapledon as the inventor of fictional historiography. But even without these fragments there is sufficient evidence that strange places and states fascinated him, as witness "The Curious Republic of Gondour," "The Comedy of Those Extraordinary Twins" (progenitors of the mutant twins that recur from Heinlein to Dick), or "From the *London Times* of 1904" (where even extraordinary technology cannot prevail against bourgeois law). The gloomy historical horizons were transferred to the theme of other dimensions of life that might perhaps be as real as ours in a number of SF stories culminating in the fragmentary masterpieces of "The Great Dark" (bp. 1962) and "Three Thousand Years Among the Microbes" (bp. 1966). In the former, Edgar Allan Poe's eerie exotic voyage combines with Fitz-James O'Brien's life in a drop under the microscope as the setting for a multiple inversion of normal parameters such as size, duration, and memory; the story would have constituted a haunting parable of man's insecurity in the itinerary of life. In the latter, the microbic microcosm becomes the scene of what approaches a consistent satirical epic. More importantly, in this late, testamentary text the satire often leaves behind the hesitations caused both by Twain's earlier illusions and by his self-censorship in order to respect the propriety his bourgeois readership demanded, and rises to truly Swiftian bitterness and relevance. It is the mark of Twain's stature that he was the first SF writer able to respond to the cruel times by exploring Swift's implicit query "What is Man?" in fully explicit, destructive terms. Nonetheless, the completed *Connecticut Yankee*, which joins life's cruel and insecure itinerary to the movement of history, remains Twain's major contribution to SF. The deep existential distress and even epistemological puzzles of the individual in high capitalism were already acknowledged in—were indeed the motive force of—Bellamy's and Morris's utopias, but they were there superseded by the security or the beauty of human relations in the new community. By disjoining the individual hero from the bright communal novum while continuing to uphold the absolute necessity and value of the utopian supersession, Twain situated his novel at the wellspring of the preoccupation that was to dominate the next century of significant SF, from Wells and Zamyatin to Lem and Dick.

2.2. Another way out of such an existential distress was to transfer utopian yearning out of material history, into an incongruous physico-religious heaven, as did Camille Flammarion. In the last third of the nineteenth century he tirelessly ground out a great number of nonfictional books ranging from astronomical and geographic popularizations to arguments for a scientifically proved psychic life after death. Some of his other works—*Lumen*, *Rêves étoilés*, or *Uranie*—were an indigested mixture of reincarnation on planets of our solar system or of distant galaxies and supposed validation of the spiritual forces entailed by the marvels of modern cosmology and electricity, in which regard they were not unlike writings of the contemporary occultist wave in Britain and the USA, from Bulwer to Mrs. Blavatsky and thence to bestsellers like the novels of Marie Corelli. Flammarion's rather frenzied anti-materialism vented itself in pet peeves against such indignities as material food-taking and in insufferable passages detailing (literally) ethereal love encounters. Having written the first modern survey of literature on imaginary worlds, *Les Mondes imaginaires et les mondes réels* (1865), he blithely pillaged that whole tradition from Cyrano through Grainville and Fourier to Defontenay for bizarre figures and incidents of life on other planets which he inserted into his long lectures and tirades. The life forms were either anthropomorphic or only slightly changed—by being flying creatures, or androgynes, or by having 17 heavenly senses (including, of course, electric, ultraviolet, and psychic ones)—or they could be quite different: asexual, phosphorescent, telepathic, vegetable, or mineral. This was heady brew for Victorians and had an immense influence throughout the world by the 1880s. For late nineteenth-century fantasy and SF it functioned as a repository of ideas and topoi—much as Stapledon was to function for the SF after 1930, but without his intelligence and tragic humanism. Flammarion's variations on Kant's idea that the physical and moral perfection of psychozoa is proportional to the planet's distance from the Sun contributed to a spate of spiritualist or utopian ideals being reached by interplanetary voyages to Mars, Jupiter, or Saturn as brainless as his were but more straightforwardly fictional, as in

Robert Cromie's *A Plunge Into Space* (1890) or John Jacob Astor's *A Journey in Other Worlds* (1894). When an at least partially consistent picture of new social institutions was accompanied by satire of Earth customs, the result was slightly better, as in the anonymous presentation of cooperative and progressive *Politics and Life in Mars* (1883) or Robert D. Braine's attempt at mixing Flammarion with Plato in *Messages From Mars* (1892?). The nearest Flammarion himself got to coherent books of fiction— which was not very near—was in his *La Fin du Monde* (1893, translated as *Omega*), which included again an anthologic review of possible endings of the world and anticipations of a slightly technocratic future ending after ten million years in an ice-death of the human race, whose souls, however, flit on to better things on Jupiter. The book is a good example of the strange feedback between Flammarion and Verne, in which the former stressed "far out" psychic phenomena and the latter a near time and space but, by the last quarter of the century, both shared a similar pessimism toward the horizons of mundane history.

2.3.   Some writers in the 1880s and 90s paralleled or echoed Bellamy's and Morris's concern with a better political social future; the intelligent anti-revolutionary account of the collapse of an oppressive State Communism in W. A. Watlock's *The Next 'Ninety Three* (1886) or the pleas for women's equality in George Noyes Miller's *The Strike of a Sex* (1883?) and in the rather melodramatic *Gloriana* of Lady Florence Dixie (1890) can be adduced as examples with a certain interest. But in the dramatically expanding production of SF—which, for example, doubled in Britain each decade, from approximately 45 book publications in the 1870s to some 90 in the 1880s and 170 in the 1890s—the great majority of works up to Wells remained immature. To take an example from the United States, the two poles that Mark Twain attempted to fuse in *Connecticut Yankee* can be seen sundered and impoverished in the shallow optimism of Stockton and the monotonous horrors of Bierce. Frank Stockton wrote several Vernean technological adventure tales. *The Great War Syndicate* (1889) transferred the future war subgenre to the United States. A capitalist syndicate, hired by the American government, wins a war by means of superweapons, including a tremendous rocket missile, whereupon the vanquished Britons join in an Anglo-American domination of the world—a revealing story by a popular writer. Ambrose Bierce is a weightier writer in the psychofantastic tradition of Poe, on the borders of SF and fantasy. Some of his stories, such as "The Damned Thing," motivate invisible beasts and similar horrors rationally, while "Moxon's Master" (both 1893) returns the Frankenstein theme to mechanical automata, paving the way for the countless bloodthirsty robots of Gernsbackian SF. Stockton's shallow politics and jaunty plots as well as Bierce's deep ontological fears and haunting moods have one common denominator with *A Connecticut Yankee*: the omnipresent violence. Only Wells was to render justice to this increasingly menacing atmosphere, which belied the hopes for a pure classless dawn.

Introduction to Newer SF History

> I was thinking this globe enough till there sprang out so noiseless
> around me myriads of other globes.
>
> Walt Whitman

This survey stops at the threshold of contemporary SF, which can be said to arise between the World Wars, after the October Revolution and before the atomic bomb, with the modern "mass culture" of movies, radio, and specialized magazines and paperback book-lines for commercial literary "genres"—one of the most prominent of which SF has become. The period marked by E.R. Burroughs and Hugo Gernsback in the United States (and some parallel developments in Germany, cut short by Nazism) and by the influence this country has exerted, beginning in the 1930s, on the rest of the world, was to be one not only of a huge quantitative explosion of SF publication, distribution, and popularity—which alone would be sufficient reason for a separate book to describe it—but also, even more significantly, of qualitative complications in the status of "paraliterature" which have so far not been adequately dealt with in literary history and theory. What makes contemporary paraliterature, and especially SF, so complicated is the sea-change it suffered in the last couple of generations. In almost all the earlier epochs, as I have tried to point out in my introduction to the first part of this historical overview, there was a profound difference between the unofficial, popular or plebeian (largely oral), culture and the official, dominant or upper-class (usually written), culture. The cultures of these "two nations" within each linguistico-ethnic domain have, no doubt, always been connected in various ways, from antagonistic suppression to partial permeation, but as a rule they have been—except for such exceptional moments of cohesion as a portion of the Elizabethan Age—sufficiently separate to preserve distinct identities. A renewal of given official, higher, or canonic Literature and Culture came about by the ascent of earlier noncanonic forms to canonic status together with the social class or group that was the "ideal reader" of those forms or genres (for example, the psychological novel and the bourgeoisie). But the complication with twentieth-century paraliterature—and especially SF—is, to put it baldly, briefly, and without any mediation, that neither the Jacobin nor the Bolshevik revolutions have accomplished their objectives, so that radically enlarged literacy and economic welfare in the "North" of our planet (Europe, North America, Japan) have coincided with and become enmeshed in the rise of imperialism and the welfare-warfare state. The ensuing very complicated amalgam of suppression and permeation—occurring at different rates and in somewhat different forms in diverse geopolitical areas—has just begun to be identified but has not yet been properly studied.[1] *One might hazard the hypothesis that in this period the domination or hegemony of the bourgeois ideology and taste has been challenged but on the whole not overthrown: new forms and genres rise into official culture largely at the expense of their pristine plebeian horizons, from the ranks, not with the ranks, of its social originators, and at the price of containment and cooption. However this might be, it is clearly a field for different methodological approaches than the ones used in this book, though one of the major aims of this book is to reach the threshold not only of contemporary SF history but also of a methodology that would render it justice.*

It could be argued that both the proliferation and the changed status of SF begin with and at the time of H.G. Wells. I am not sure whether this is in fact so, and at any rate new cultural epochs do not begin on a given New Year's Day. What is certain is that Wells's opus could both intrinsically and in its interrelations with the popular media of his time be a promising starting point for a simultaneously extensive and intensive investigation. But this too would certainly demand a book unto itself. I have compromised with such an ideal by aiming in this section for a kind of stereoscopic effect, which might, I hope, arise from the reader's benevolent superposition of a broad overview of Wells's opus (attempted in chapter 9) on a depth probe of his model for SF as found in the paradigmatic "Time Machine" (attempted in chapter 10 in brief comparison to the Morean model of earlier SF history). Since world cultures are not synchronic, I have concluded my historical survey with two European probes, one of a national tradition and one of an important single writer, but both leading in their own context again to the historical and methodo-

1. The fundaments for such a study have been laid in the notes of Antonio Gramsci available only since the war, for example, *Il materialismo storico e la filosofia di Benedetto Croce* (Torino, 1948) or the useful compilation *Letteratura e vita nazionale* (Torino, 1966); in English partly available in *The Modern Prince and Other Writings* (New York, 1972) and *Selections From the Prison Notebooks* (New York, 1975). An excellent first systematization of theoretical achievements and problems so far can be found in the relevant chapters of Raymond Williams's *Marxism and Literature* (London, 1977). Not only for SF, see also the "Sociology of SF" issue of *Science-Fiction Studies* 4 (November 1977), with Marc Angenot's annotated bibliography of the sociology of literature and some introductory comments of mine enlarging on the problems touched upon in this introduction.

logical thresholds for understanding contemporary SF. No doubt, even within the period or periods chosen, it might have been possible to deal with some more works by prominent writers—Jack London, Rosny Aîné, or Paul Scheerbart—or with more national traditions—such as the French one from 1900 to 1940.[2] However, since this book opts for representativeness suggesting a tradition rather than for the inclusiveness of a formal literary history, I have remained consistent to this option.

2. I might perhaps be the more readily excused since I have contributed to some spadework for a better understanding of Wells and London elsewhere: Darko Suvin, with Robert M. Philmus, eds., *H. G. Wells and Modern Science Fiction* (Bibliography V); Darko Suvin and David Douglas, "Jack London and His Science Fiction: A Select Bibliography," *Science-Fiction Studies* 3 (July 1976): 181–87.

9

Wells as the Turning Point of the SF Tradition

H. G. Wells's first and most significant SF cycle (roughly to 1904) is based on the vision of a horrible novum as the evolutionary sociobiological prospect for mankind. His basic situation is that of a destructive newness encroaching upon the tranquillity of the Victorian environment. Often this is managed as a contrast between an outer framework and a story within the story. The framework is set in surroundings as staid and familiarly Dickensian as possible, such as the cozy study of *The Time Machine*, the old antiquity shop of "The Crystal Egg," or the small towns and villages of southern England in *The War of the Worlds* and *The First Men in the Moon*. With the exception of the protagonist, who also participates in the inner story, the characters in the outer frame, representing the almost invincible inertia and banality of prosperous bourgeois England, are reluctant to credit the strange newness. By contrast, the inner story details the observation of the gradual, hesitant coming to grips with an alien superindividual force that menaces such life and its certainties by behaving exactly as the bourgeois progress did in world history—as a quite ruthless but technologically superior mode of life. This Wellsian inversion exploits the uneasy conscience of an imperial civilization that did not wipe out only the bison and the dodo: "The Tasmanians, in spite of their human likeness, were entirely swept out of existence in a war of extermination waged by European immigrants. Are we such apostles of mercy as to complain if the Martians warred in the same spirit?" (*The War of the Worlds*, book 1, chap. 1).

As Wells observed, the "fantastic element" or novum is "the strange property or the strange world."[1] The strange property can be the invention that renders Griffin invisible, or, obversely, a new way of seeing—literally, as in "The Crystal Egg," "The

---

1. "Preface" to *Seven Famous Novels by H. G. Wells* (Garden City, NY, 1934), p. vii.

Remarkable Case of Davidson's Eyes," and "The New Accelerator," or indirectly, as the Time Machine or the Cavorite sphere. It is always cloaked in a pseudo-scientific explanation, the possibility of which turns out, upon closer inspection, to be no more than a conjuring trick by the deft writer, with "precision in the unessential and vagueness in the essential"[2]—the best example being the Time Machine itself. The strange world is elsewhen or elsewhere. It is reached by means of a strange invention or it irrupts directly into the Victorian world in the guise of the invading Martians or the Invisible Man. But even when Wells's own bourgeois world is not so explicitly assaulted, the strange novelty always reflects back on its illusions; an SF story by Wells is intended to be "the valid realization of some disregarded possibility in such a way as to comment on the false securities and fatuous self-satisfaction of everyday life."[3]

The strange is menacing because it looms in the future of man. Wells masterfully translates some of man's oldest terrors—the fear of darkness, monstrous beasts, giants and ogres, creepy crawly insects, and Things outside the light of his campfire, outside tamed nature—into an evolutionary perspective that is supposed to be validated by Darwinian biology, evolutionary cosmology, and the fin-de-siècle sense of a historical epoch ending. Wells, a student of T. H. Huxley, eagerly used alien and powerful biological species as a rod to chastize Victorian man, thus setting up the model for all the Bug-Eyed Monsters of later chauvinistic SF. But the most memorable of those aliens, the octopuslike Martians and the antlike Selenites, are identical to "The Man of the Year Million" in one of Wells's early articles (alluded to in *The War of the Worlds*): they are emotionless higher products of evolution judging us as we would judge insects. In the final analysis, since the aliens are a scary, alternative human future, Wellsian space travel is an optical illusion, a variation on his seminal model of *The Time Machine*. The function of his interplanetary contacts is quite different from Verne's liberal interest in the mechanics of locomotion within a safely homogeneous space. Wells is interested exclusively in the opposition

2. Unsigned review (by Basil Williams) in *Athenaeum*, 26 June 1897, reprinted in Patrick Parrinder, ed. (Bibliography V), p. 57.
3. H. G. Wells, "An Experiment in Illustration," *Strand Magazine*, February 1920, quoted in Geoffrey West (Bibliography V), p. 112.

between the bourgeois reader's expectations and the strange relationships found at the other end: that is why his men do land
on the Moon and his Martians on Earth.

Science is the true, demonic master of all the sorcerer's ap-
prentices in Wells, who have—like Frankenstein or certain
folktale characters—revealed and brought about destructive
powers and monsters. From the Time Traveller through Moreau
and Griffin to Cavor, the prime character of his SF is the
scientist-adventurer as searcher for the New, disregarding common sense and received opinion. Though powerful, since it
brings about the future, science is a hard master. Like Moreau, it
is indifferent to human suffering; like the Martians, it explodes
the nineteenth-century optimistic pretentions, liberal or socialist,
of lording it over the universe:

> Science is a match that man has just got alight. He thought
> he was in a room—in moments of devotion, a temple—and
> that his light would be reflected from and display walls in-
> scribed with wonderful secrets and pillars carved with
> philosophical systems wrought into harmony. It is a curious
> sensation, now that the preliminary splutter is over and the
> flame burns up clear, to see his hands and just a glimpse of
> himself and the patch he stands on visible, and around him,
> in place of all that human comfort and beauty he antici-
> pated—darkness still.[4]

This science is no longer, as it was for Verne, the bright noonday
certainty of Newtonian physics. Verne protested after *The First
Men in the Moon*: "I make use of physics. He invents . . . he
constructs . . . a metal which does away with the law of gravita-
tion . . . but show me this metal." For Wells human evolution is
an open question with two possible answers, bright and dark;
and in his first cycle darkness is the basic tonality. The cognitive
"match" by whose small light he determines his stance is Darwinian evolution, a flame which fitfully illumines man, his hands
(by interaction of which with the brain and the eye he evolved
from ape), and the "patch he stands on." Therefore Wells could
much later even the score by talking about "the anticipatory in-

    4. Wells, "The Rediscovery of the Unique," *The Fortnightly Review*, N.S. 50 (July
1891), reprinted in Robert Philmus and David Y. Hughes, eds. (Bibliography V), pp.
30–31.

ventions of the great Frenchman" who "told that this and that thing could be done, which was not at that time done"—in fact, by defining Verne as a short-term technological popularizer.[5] From the point of view of a votary of physics, Wells "invents" in the sense of inventing objective untruths. From the point of view of the evolutionist, who does not believe in objects but in processes—which we have only begun to elucidate—Verne is the one who "invents" in the sense of inventing banal gadgets. For the evolutionist, Nemo's submarine is in itself of no importance; what matters is whether intelligent life exists on the ocean floor (as in "In the Abyss" and "The Sea Raiders"). Accordingly, Wells's physical and technical motivations can and do remain quite superficial where not faked. Reacting against a mechanical view of the world, he is ready to approach again the imaginative, analogic veracity of Lucian's and Swift's story-telling centered on strange creatures, and to call his works "romances." Cavorite or the Invisible Man partake more of the flying carpet and the magic invisibility hood than of metallurgy or optics. The various aliens represent a vigorous refashioning of the talking and symbolic animals of folktale, bestiary, and fable lore into Swiftian grotesque mirrors to man, but with the crowning collocation within an evolutionary prospect. Since this prospect is temporal rather than spatial, it is also much more urgent and immediate than Swift's controlled disgust, and a note of fairly malicious hysteria is not absent from the ever-present violence—fires, explosions, fights, killings, and large-scale devastations—in Wells's SF.

The Time Machine (1895), Wells's programmatic and (but for the mawkish character of Weena) most consistent work, shows his way of proceeding and his ultimate horizon. The horizon of sociobiological regression leading to cosmic extinction, simplified from Darwinism into a series of vivid pictures in the Eloi, the giant crabs, and the eclipse episodes, is established by the Time Traveller's narration as a stark contrast to the Victorian after-dinner discussions in his comfortable residence. The Time Machine itself is validated by an efficient forestalling of possible objections, put into the mouth of schematic, none too bright, and reluctantly persuaded listeners, rather than by the bogus theory of the fourth dimension or any explanation of the gleaming bars glimpsed in the machine. Similarly, the sequence of narrated episodes gains much of its impact from the careful foreshortening of ever larger perspectives in an ever more breathless rhythm (discussed at length in the following chapter). Also, the narrator-observer's gradually deepening involvement in the Eloi episode is marked by cognitive hypotheses that run the whole logical gamut of sociological SF. From a parodied Morrisite model ("Communism," says the Time Traveller at first sight) through the discovery of degeneration and of persistence of class divisions, he arrives at the anti-utopian form most horrifying to the Victorians—a run-down class society ruled by a grotesque equivalent of the nineteenth-century industrial proletariat. Characteristically, the sociological perspective then blends into biology. The laboring and upper classes are envisioned as having developed into different races or indeed species, with the Morlocks raising the Eloi as cattle to be eaten. In spite of a certain contempt for their effeteness, the Time Traveller quickly identifies with the butterfly-like upper-class Eloi and so far forsakes his position as neutral observer as to engage in bloody and fiery carnage of the repugnant spider-monkey-like Morlocks, on the model of the most sensationalist exotic adventure stories. His commitment is never logically argued, and there is a strong suggestion that it flows from the social consciousness of Wells himself, who came from the lower middle class, which lives on the edge of the "proletarian abyss" and thus "looks upon the proletariat as being something disgusting and evil and dangerous."[6] Instead, the Time Traveller's attitude is powerfully supported by the prevailing imagery—both by animal parallels, and by the pervasive open-air green and bright colors of the almost Edenic garden (associated with the Eloi) opposed to the subterranean blackness and the dim reddish glow (associated with the Morlocks and the struggle against them). Later in the story these menacing, untamed colors lead to the reddish-black eclipse, symbolizing the end of the Earth and of the solar system. The bright pastoral of the Eloi is gradually submerged by the encroaching night of the Morlocks, and the Time Traveller's

6.   Christopher Caudwell (Bibliography V), pp. 76 and 93.

matches sputter out in their oppressive abyss. At the end, the unforgettable picture of the dead world is validated by the disappearance of the Time Traveller in the opaque depths of time.

Many of these devices reappear in Wells's other major works. The technique of domesticating the improbable by previews on a smaller scale, employed in the vivid vanishing of the model machine, is repeated in the introduction to the Grand Lunar through a series of other Selenites up to Phi-oo, or to Moreau's bestial people through the brutal struggles in the boat and through the ship captain, or to the Cavorite sphere's flight through the experimental explosion raising the roof. The loss of the narrator's vehicle and the ensuing panic of being a castaway under alien rule (in *The War of the Worlds* this is inverted as hiding in a trap with dwindling supplies) recurs time and again as an effective cliff-hanger. Above all, as we will see in the next chapter, Wells's whole first cycle is a reversal of the popular concept by which the lower social and biological classes were considered as "natural" prey in the struggle for survival. In their turn they become the predators: as laborers turn into Morlocks, so insects, arthropods, or colonial peoples turn into Martians, Selenites, and the like. This exalting of the humble into horrible masters supplies a subversive shock to the bourgeois believer in Social Darwinism; at the same time, Wells vividly testifies that a predatory state of affairs is the only even fantastically imaginable alternative. The world upside-down—where strange animals hunt Man, and the subterranean lower class devours the upper class—recurs in Wells, as in Thomas More. But whereas More's sheep were rendered unnatural by political economics, Wells's Morlocks, Beast People, and so forth, are the result of a "natural" evolution from the author's present. Nature has become not only malleable—it was already becoming such in More and particularly in Swift—but also a practically value-free category, as in bourgeois scientism. At the end, the bourgeois framework is shaken, but neither destroyed nor replaced by any livable alternative. What remains is a very ambiguous attack on liberalism from the position of "the petty bourgeois which will either turn towards socialism or towards fascism."[7]

The human/animal inversion comes openly to the fore in *The*

---

7. V. S. Pritchett (Bibliography V), p. 128.

Island of Dr. Moreau (1896) with admirable Swiftian stringency. Dr. Moreau's fashioning of humans out of beasts is clearly analogous to the pitiless procedures of Nature and its evolutionary creation. He is not only a latter-day Dr. Frankenstein but also a demonically inverted God of Genesis, and his surgically humanized Beast Folk are a counterpart of ourselves, semibestial humans. Wells's calling their attempts to mimic the Decalogue in the litanies of "The Saying of the Law" and their collapse back into bestiality a "theological grotesque" indicates that this view of mankind's future reversed Christian as well as socialist millennialism into the bleak vistas of an evolution liable to regression. *The Island of Dr. Moreau* turns the imperial order of Kipling's *Jungle Book* into a degenerative slaughterhouse, where the law loses out to bestiality.

Wells's next two famous SF novels, though full of vivid local color, seem today less felicitous. Both have problems of focusing. In *The Invisible Man* (1897) the delineation of Griffin hesitates between a man in advance of his time within an indifferent society and the symbol of a humanity that does not know how to use science. This makes of him almost an old-fashioned "mad scientist," and yet he is too important and too sinned against to be comic relief. The vigor of the narration, which unfolds in the form of a hunt, and the strengths of an inverted fairy tale cannot compensate for the failure of the supposedly omniscient author to explain why Griffin had got into the position of being his own Frankenstein and Monster at the same time. In this context, the dubious scientific premises (an invisible eye cannot see, and so forth) become distressing and tend to deprive the story of the needed suspension of disbelief. *The War of the Worlds* (1898), which extrapolates into xenobiology the catastrophic stories of the "future wars" subgenre discussed in chapter 7, descends in places to a gleeful sensationalism difficult to stomach, especially in its horror-fantasy portraiture of the Martians. The immediate serialization in the US yellow press, which simply suppressed the parts without action, made this portraiture the most influential model for countless later Things from Outer Space, extendable to any foreign group that the public was at that moment supposed to hate, and a prototype of mass-media use of SF for mindless scare-mongering (inaugurated by Orson Welles's famous 1938 broadcast). The novel's composition is marred by the clumsy system of two eyewitness narrators, improvised in order to reconcile the sensational immediacy and the necessary overview. Of course, *The War of the Worlds* also contains striking and indeed prophetic insights such as the picture of modern total warfare, with its panics, refugees, quislings, underground hidings, and an envisaged Resistance movement, as well as race-theory justifications, poison gas, and a "spontaneous" bacteriological weapon. (In other tales, Wells—a lifelong lover of war games—added air warfare, tanks, atom bombing of a major city, and other bellicose devices.)

Except for the superb late parable "The Country of the Blind" (bp. 1911), Wells's sociobiological and cosmological SF cycle culminated in *The First Men in the Moon* (1901). It has the merit of summarizing and explicating openly his main motifs and devices. The usual two narrators have grown into the contrasting characters of Bedford, the Social-Darwinist speculator-adventurer, and Cavor, the selfless scientist in whom Wells manages for once to fuse the cliché of absent-mindedness with open-mindedness and a final suffering rendered irremediable by the cosmic vistas involved. The sharply focused lens of spatial pinpointing and temporal acceleration through which the travelers perceive the miraculous growth of Lunar vegetation is the most striking rendering of the precise yet wondering scientific regard often associated with the observatories and observation posts of Wells's stories. The Selenites not only possess the Aesopian fable background and an endearing grotesqueness worthy of Edward Lear's creatures, they are also a profound image of sociopolitical functional overspecialization and of an absolute caste or race State, readily translatable from insect biology back into some of the most menacing tendencies of modern power concentration. Most Swiftian among Wells's aliens, they serve a double-edged satire, in the authentic tone of savage and cognitive indignation:

> . . . I came upon a number of young Selenites, confined in jars from which only the fore limbs protruded, who were being compressed to become machine-minders of a special sort. . . . these glimpses of the educational methods of these beings have affected me disagreeably. I hope, however, that may pass off and I may be able to see more of this aspect of this wonderful social order. That wretched-looking hand

sticking out of its jar seemed to appeal for lost possibilities; it haunts me still, although, of course, it is really in the end a far more humane proceeding than our earthly method of leaving children to grow into human beings, and then making machines of them. [chap. 23]

The usual final estrangement fuses biological and social disgust into Bedford's schizophrenic cosmic vision of himself "not only as an ass, but as the son of many generations of asses" (chap. 19). Parallel to that, Cavor formulates most clearly the uselessness of cosmic as well as earthly imperialism, and articulates a refusal to let science go on serving them (had this been heeded, we would have been spared the Galactic Empire politics and swashbuckling of later SF). Finally, Bedford's narration in guise of a literary manuscript with pretenses to scientific veracity, combined with Cavor's narration in guise of interplanetary telegraphic reports, exhibit openly Wells's ubiquitous mimicry of the journalistic style from that heyday of early "mass communications"—the style of "an Associated Press dispatch, describing a universal nightmare."[8]

Yet such virtuosity cannot mask the fundamental ambiguity that constitutes both the richness and the weakness of Wells. Is he horrified or grimly elated by the high price of evolution (*The Island of Dr. Moreau*)? Does he condemn class divisions or simply the existence of a menacing lower class (*The Time Machine*)? Does he condemn imperialism (*The First Men in the Moon*) or only dislike being at the receiving end of it (*The War of the Worlds*)? In brief, are his preoccupations with violence and alienation those of a diagnostician or of a fan? Both of these stances coexist in his works in a shifting and often unclear balance. For example,—to translate such alternatives into an immediate determinant of narration—Wells's central morphological dilemma in the years of his first and best SF cycle was: which is' the privileged way of understanding the world, the scientifically systematic one or the artistically vivid one? Faced with the tension between "scientific" classification and "artistic" individuation, a tension that remained constant (albeit with different outcomes) throughout his life, Wells had already in 1891 satirized the deterministic rigidity in

8. Unsigned review in *Critic*, 23 April 1898, reprinted in Parrinder, ed., p. 69.

his essay "The Universe Rigid" and gone on to find a first compromise in his "The Rediscovery of the Unique" and its successive avatars in "The Cyclic Delusion," "Scepticism of the Instrument," and *First and Last Things* (1908). These articles attempt to formulate the deep though unclear pulls which Wells at his best reconciled by opting for representativeness, for fusing individuum and species into socially *and* biologically typical figures like the Time Traveller, but which he often left unreconciled.

Wells's SF makes thus an aesthetic form of hesitations, intimations, and glimpses of an ambiguously disquieting strangeness. The strange novum is gleefully wielded as a sensational scare thrown into the bourgeois reader, but its values are finally held at arm's length. In admitting and using their possibility he went decisively beyond Verne, in identifying them as horrible he decisively opposed Morris. Wells's SF works are clearly "ideological fables,"[9] yet he is a virtuoso in having it ideologically both ways. His satisfaction at the destruction of the false bourgeois idyll is matched by his horror at the alien forces destroying it. He resolutely clung to his insight that such forces must be portrayed, but he portrayed them within a sensationalism that neutralizes most of the genuine newness. Except in his maturest moments, the conflicts in his SF are therefore transferred—following the Social-Darwinist model—from society to biology. This is a risky proceeding which can lead to some striking analogies but—as was discussed in chapter 6 à propos of *Frankenstein*—as a rule indicates a return to quasi-religious eschatology and fatal absolutes. Wells expressed this, no doubt, in sincerely Darwinist terms, but his approach is in fact marked by a contamination of echoes from a culturally sunken medieval bestiary and a Miltonic or Bunyanesque color scheme (dark and red, for example, as satanic) with the new possibilities of scientific dooms (compare the Ruskinian Angel of *The Wonderful Visit* [1895], presented as an alien from a parallel world). The annihilation of this world is the only future alternative to its present state; the present bourgeois way of life is with scientific certainty leading the Individualist *homme moyen sensuel* toward the hell of physical indignity and psychic terror, yet this *is* still the only way of life he can return to and rely on, the best of all the bad possible worlds. Thus Wells's

9. Parrinder (Bibliography V), p. 18.

central anxious question about the future in store for his
Everyman—who is, characteristically, a bright, aggressive, White,
middle-class male—cannot be resolved as posed. His early SF can
present the future only as a highly menacing yet finally inopera-
tive novum, the connection with its bearers (Time Traveller,
Moreau, Griffin, Martians, Selenites, or Cavor) being always broken off. Formally, this impasse explains his troubles with works
of novel length: his most successful form is either the short story
or the novelette, which lend themselves to ingenious balancings
on the razor's edge between shock and cognitive development.
In them he set the pace for the commercial norms of most later
SF (which adds insult to injury by calling such works novels).

Wells's later SF abandoned such fragile but rich ambiguity in
favor of short-range extrapolations. His first attempt in that direction, *When the Sleeper Wakes* (1899), was the most interesting.
Its picture of a futuristic megalopolis with mass social struggles
led by demagogic leaders was "a nightmare of Capitalism triumph-
phant" and an explicit polemic against Bellamy's complacent optimism about taming the organizing urge and the jungle of the
cities. In Wells's complex corporate capitalism "everything was
bigger, quicker and more crowded; there was more and more
flying and the wildest financial speculation."[10] Since Wells's
sketch of the future was full of brilliant and detailed insights (as,
for example, those about competing police forces and stultifying
mass media) that turned out to be close to actual developments
in the twentieth century, this novel became the model for anti-
utopian anticipation from Zamyatin and von Harbou to Heinlein
and Pohl. But Wells's imaginative energy flagged here at the crucial narrative level: the observer-hero waking after two centuries
behaves alternatively like a savior (suffering his final passion on
an airplane instead of a cross) and vacillating liberal intellectual.
The jerky plot concerns itself primarily with the adventure of a
beautiful soul in the future, and is thus coresponsible for a spate
of similar inferior SF with more rugged heroes who are given
wonderful powers and who experience sentimental entanglements. "A Story of Days To Come" (1899) and "A Dream of
Armageddon" (1903), told wholly from inside the same future,

10. Wells, first quotation from his "Author's Preface" to *The Sleeper Awakes* (London,
1921), second quotation from his *Experiment in Autobiography* (New York, 1934), p. 551.

are not much more than an exploitation of that interesting locale for sentimental tales seen from the bottom, respectively the
top, of society. Wells's later SF novels—though even at their
worst never lacking flashes of genuine insight or redeeming
provocation—do not attain the imaginative consistency of his
first cycle. In *The Food of the Gods* (1904) the fundamental equation of material and moral greatness is never worked out. His
series of programmatic utopias, from *A Modern Utopia* (1905) to
The Holy Terror (1939), has interesting moments, especially when
he is describing a new psychology of power and responsibility
such as that of the "Samurai" or the "holy terror" dictator. However, its central search for a caste of technocratic managers as
"competent receivers"[11] for a bankrupt capitalist society oscillates wildly from enlightened monarchs or dictators, through
Fabian-like artists and engineers, to airmen and Keynesians (in
The Shape of Things to Come, 1933): millennium has always been
the most colorless part of Christian apocalypse. What is worst,
Wells's fascinated sensitivity to the uncertain horizons of humanity gives only too often way to impatient discursive scolding,
often correct but rarely memorable. A visit to young Soviet Russia (where his meeting with Lenin provided an almost textbook
example of contrasts between abstract and concrete utopianism)
resulted in the perhaps most interesting work in that series, *Men
Like Gods* (1923), where Wells gave a transient and somewhat
etiolated glimpse of a Morris-like brightness. But his work after
the first World War vacillated, not illogically for an apocalyptic
writer, between equally superficial optimism and despair. His
position in the middle, wishing a plague on both the upper and
the working classes, proved singularly fruitless in creative
terms—though extremely influential and bearing strange fruit in
subsequent SF, the writers and readers of which mostly come
from precisely those "new middle classes" that Wells advanced as
the hope of the future.

   With all his strengths and weaknesses Wells remains the central writer in the tradition of SF. His ideological impasses are
fought out as memorable and rich contradictions tied to an inexorably developing future. He collected, as it were, all the main
influences of earlier writers—from Lucian and Swift to Kepler,

11. Wells, *Experiment in Autobiography*, p. 206.

Verne, and Flammarion, from Plato and Morris to Mary Shelley, Poe, Bulwer, and the subliterature of planetary and subterranean voyages, future wars, and the like—and transformed them in his own image, whence they entered the treasury of subsequent SF. He invented a new thing under the sun in the time-travel story made plausible or verisimilar by physics. He codified, for better or worse, the notions of invasion from space and cosmic catastrophe (as in his story "The Star," 1899), of social and biological degeneration, of fourth dimension, of future megalopolis, of biological plasticity. Together with Verne's *roman scientifique*, Wells's "scientific romances" and short stories became the privileged form in which SF was admitted into an official culture that rejected socialist utopianism. True, of his twenty-odd books that can be considered SF, only perhaps eight or nine are still of living interest, but those contain unforgettable visions (all in the five "romances" and the short stories of the early sociobiological-cum-cosmic cycle): the solar eclipse at the end of time, the faded flowers from the future, the invincible obtuseness of southern England and the Country of the Blind confronted with the New, the Saying of the Law on Moreau's island, the wildfire spread of the red Martian weed and invasion panic toward London, the last Martian's lugubrious ululations in Regent's Park, the frozen world of "The New Accelerator," the springing to life of the Moon vegetation, the lunar society. These summits of Wells's are a demonstration of what is possible in SF, of the cognitive shudder peculiar to it. Their poetry is based on a shocking transmutation of scientific into aesthetic cognition, and poets from Eliot to Borges have paid tribute to it. More harrowing than in the socialist utopians, more sustained than in Twain, embracing a whole dimension of radical doubt and questioning that makes Verne look bland, it is a grim caricature of bestial bondage and an explosive liberation achieved by means of knowledge. Wells was the first significant writer who started to write SF from within the world of science, and not merely facing it. Though his catastrophes are a retraction of Bellamy's and Morris's utopian optimism, even in the spatial disguises of a parallel present on Moreau's island or in southern England it is always a possible future evolving from the neglected horrors of today that is analyzed in its (as a rule) maleficent consequences, and his hero has "an epic and public . . . mission" intimately bound up with "the major cognitive challenge of the Darwinist age."[12] For all his vacillations, Wells's basic historical lesson is that the stifling bourgeois society is but a short moment in an impredictable, menacing, but at least theoretically open-ended human evolution under the stars. He endowed later SF with a basically materialist look back at human life and a rebelliousness against its entropic closure. For such reasons, all subsequent significant SF can be said to have sprung from Wells's *Time Machine*, which will be examined next.

12. Parrinder (Bibliography IV C), p. 273.

10

The Time Machine versus
Utopia as Structural Models for SF

In this chapter I shall try to show that Wells's *The Time Machine* is (to put it prudently in the absence of further evidence) at least one, and that More's *Utopia* was another, among the basic historical models for the structuring of subsequent SF. One does not need to be a structuralist in the sectarian sense of opposing synchronic analysis to cultural genetics or taking myth as synonymous with literature to use some of the methods which structuralism shares with a whole exegetic tradition extending from, say, medieval discussions to some of Lukács's analyses or Kuhn's *Structure of Scientific Revolutions*. A student of Wells is emboldened in such an approach by the fact that comparative morphology was in Wells's student days one of the first great modern breakthroughs of the structural method. As he himself noted, biology was in T. H. Huxley's days establishing the phylogenetic tree, or "family tree of life": "Our chief discipline was a rigorous analysis of vertebrate structure, vertebrate embryology, and *the succession of vertebrate forms in time. We felt our particular task was the determination of the relationships of groups by the acutest possible criticism of structure*."[1] Wells left no doubt of the indelible vistas the "sweepingly magnificent series" of zoological exercises imprinted on his eager imagination, leaving him with an urgency for "coherence and consistency": *"It was a grammar of form and a criticism of fact*. That year I spent in Huxley's class was, beyond all question, the most educational year of my life."[2]

---

1. H. G. Wells, *Experiment in Autobiography* (New York, 1934), p. 160, italics added. Students of Wells will recognize my large debts toward the critics and scholars, from Brooks and West to Bergonzi and Hillegas, Parrinder and Philmus, listed in Bibliography V, which will as a rule be acknowledged only in cases of direct mention or quote.

2. Wells, pp. 160–61, italics added. Compare also Wells's explicit preoccupation with biological "degradation" inherent in evolution under capitalism in the articles "Zoological Retrogression," *The Gentleman's Magazine*, 7 September 1891; "On Extinction," *Chambers's*

It should not, thus, be too surprising to find in *The Time Machine*—which has much to say about succession of zoological forms in time—an attempt at coherence and consistency, "a grammar of form and criticism of fact." Of course, this does not prejudice the particular grammar or criticism, the type of coherence and consistency that might be found in it.

I am proceeding on the hypothesis that the basic device of *The Time Machine* is an opposition of the Time Traveller's visions of the future to the ideal reader's norm of a complacent bourgeois class consciousness with its belief in linear progress, Spencerian "Social Darwinism," and the like. The Victorian norm is set up in the framework of *The Time Machine* and supplemented by the Time Traveller's reactions. His visions are shaped by means of two basic and interlocking symbolic systems: that of biological regression, and that of a color imagery polarized between light and darkness—both systems being allied with violence, pain, and the basic confrontation between Man and Death.

1. THE CONVERGING BIOLOGICAL SERIES

The one thing earlier drafts of *The Time Machine* have in common with the vastly different and superior final version is an opposition between the present and a different future.[3] However, the narrative organization of the final version manifestly took its cue from Darwinism as expounded by Wells's teacher Huxley from 1860 on, and applied to "Evolution and Ethics" by Huxley's homonymous Romanes Lecture and the subsequent "Prolegomena" in the year preceding Wells's writing of the final version (1893-94).

In the "Prolegomena," Huxley tried to face the implications of evolution applying not only to "progressive development" but also to "retrogressive modification," not only to "gradual change

Journal, 30 September 1893; "The Man of the Year Million," *Pall Mall Gazette*, 9 November 1893; and "The Extinction of Man," *Pall Mall Gazette*, 23 September 1894—the first two reprinted in Philmus and Hughes, ed. (Bibliography V) and the last two in H. G. Wells, *Certain Personal Matters* (London, 1898 [1897]); also Wells's comment in *'42 to '44* (London, 1944), p. 9.

3. See Bernard Bergonzi, "The Publication of *The Time Machine*, 1894–1895," *Review of English Studies*, N.S. 11 (1960): 42–51; also Bergonzi, *The Early H. G. Wells* (Bibliography V), and Philmus and Hughes, ed.

4. T. H. Huxley, "Evolution and Ethics—Prolegomena," in his *Evolution and Ethics. Collected Essays*, 9 (London, 1903), note 1 on p. 4, and p. 6.

from a condition of relative uniformity to one of relative complexity" but also to "the phenomena of retrogressive metamorphosis, that is, of progress from a condition of relative complexity to one of relative uniformity."[4] Evidently the connotations of progress in the bourgeois liberal sense were being challenged by connotations that made it synonymous with any evolutionary change, for better or for worse; progress was being expanded to encompass the antonymic possibility of "retrogressive metamorphosis." Another variation of this ambiguity is the possibility of envisaging evolution in terms of devolution. Again in the "Prolegomena," setting up his basic exemplum or parable of English vegetation that might evolve from a primitive state of nature into a garden under purposeful (that is, ethical) human intervention, Huxley mused that "if every link in the ancestry of these humble indigenous plants had been preserved and were accessible to us, the whole would present *a converging series of forms of gradually diminishing complexity*, until, at some period in the history of the earth . . . they would merge in those low groups among which the boundaries between animal and vegetable life become effaced."[5]

Huxley was, of course, only indulging in the common evolutionist device of exalting even the humblest "indigenous plants" as wonderful products of an evolutionary chain.[6] This chain is here traversed backward into the past and functioning as

5.   Huxley, p. 5, italics added.

6.   See, as outstanding examples, the final paragraph of chapter 6 and also chapter 21, in Darwin's *The Descent of Man* (London, 1874)—not to mention the famous parable of the tangled bank that concludes *The Origin of Species*. T. H. Huxley uses the same device, for example, at the end of chap. 2 ("On the Relations of Man to the Lower Animals") of *Man's Place in Nature* (London, 1863). The collocations of such passages at the climaxes of books or book sections testifies both to the rhetorical effectiveness of the parable and to the Darwinist sense of its importance as ethico-aesthetical justification of evolution. The upward, *excelsior* course of the arrow of time provided a new type of dynamic sublimity analogical to the *per aspera ad astra* (*per evolutionem ad hominem?*) rise of the Victorian "self-made man." For an approach to Darwin's aesthetics and rhetoric see Stanley Edgar Hyman, *The Tangled Bank* (New York, 1962), and Walter F. Cannon, "Darwin's Vision in *On the Origin of Species*," in George Levine and William Madden, eds., *The Art of Victorian Prose* (New York, 1968), pp. 154–76, who situate them convincingly in ideological time and place. On Darwin's concept of the sublime see Donald Fleming's "Charles Darwin, the Anaesthetic Man," in Philip Appleman, ed., *Darwin* (New York, 1970), pp. 573–89; Fleming speaks of Darwin's hidden "Carlylean self," p. 583, but for differences between them see Theodore Baird, "Darwin and the Tangled Bank," *American Scholar* 15 (Autumn 1946).

a kind of double negation—since the reader is tacitly invited to reascend the evolutionary ladder from the Protistae to the "humble" (now not so humble) indigenous plant in the direction of a diverging series of increasing complexity. But what if one were to take this formal exercise of Huxley's literally, and his sense of uneasiness about evolution and progress versus devolution and regress seriously—that is, refusing a rhetoric that descends into the deeps of the problem and of time in order to end with an upward flourish? All that would be needed is to suppress Huxley's second negation by inverting his vision from past to future, and to imagine a canonic sociobiological "converging series of forms of gradually diminishing complexity" unfolding as a *de*volution that retraverses the path of evolution backward to a *fin du globe*. That is what Huxley's heretical student did in *The Time Machine*: a slip under the time telescope, to use a Wellsian phrase.[7]

"Canonic series," of course, begs the question "according to

7. This inversion of the Darwinian time-arrow seems to have been one of Wells's basic intellectual, morphological, and visionary discoveries. His first work that transcends adolescent doodling (a student debating address in 1885) was entitled *The Past and Future of the Human Race*, the title of a key book in 1902 is *The Discovery of the Future*, and in 1936 it is (characteristically) the archaeologist in his *The Croquet Player* who speaks of the abyss of the future bringing the ancestral savage beast back (chapter 3). In *The Future in America* (London, 1906), p. 10, Wells explicitly connects monstrous science-fictional projections with such Darwinian anticipations.

Strictly speaking, Darwin's theory is neutral as far as prospects or the present state of mankind are concerned. He himself, although quite aware of biological retrogression, extinction, and such, assumed that biological groups "which are now large and triumphant . . . will for a long period continue to increase," and stressed the ennobling aspects of evolution—see note 6, and *On the Origin of Species* (Cambridge, MA, 1964), pp. 126 and 488–90. For philosophical implications of the Darwinian time-arrow see, e.g., Loren Eiseley, *Darwin's Century* (New York, 1958), pp. 330–31; for literary ones, the stimulating essay by A. Dwight Culler, "The Darwinian Revolution and Literary Form," in Levine and Madden, eds., pp. 224–46. It was the opponents of Darwin's theory who first seized upon its malevolent aspect—see chapters 12–14 of Leo J. Henkin, *Darwinism in the English Novel 1860–1910* (New York, 1940). On the other extreme, Spencer's contention that evolution through struggle for life "can end only in the establishment of the greatest perfection and the most complete happiness"—*First Principles* (New York, 1900), p. 530 —is the real villain of this ideological drama or *pièce à thèse*. The naive capitalist Spencerians or Social Darwinists (in the United States, e.g., Rockefeller or Carnegie) wholeheartedly embraced trampling the "less *fit*" multitude; John D. Rockefeller's parable of the American Beauty rose, "produced . . . only by sacrificing the early buds," deserves to be as famous as Darwin's tangled bank or Menenius Agrippa's fable of the belly and the members; see Richard Hofstadter, *Social Darwinism in American Thought* (Bibliography IV C), especially chapter 2.

what type of canon?" An answer is to be found by comparing the orthodox Darwinist and Huxleyan canon with the one actually used in *The Time Machine*. The orthodox seriation would, in simplified outline, look as follows:[8]

FIGURE 1

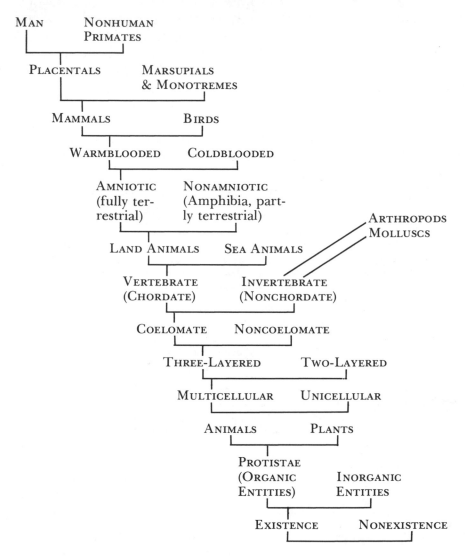

8.   Adapted from J. B. S. Haldane and Julian Huxley, *Animal Biology* (Oxford, 1927), fig. 81 on pp. 258–59.

The final two levels are an extrapolation going beyond biology but present in Lyell, Darwin, and T. H. Huxley.

As differing from this converging series, Wells not only used the symmetrically inverse time direction, changing the sign from plus to minus, but also considerably foreshortened and re-grouped the series (see figure 2). Comparing the two series, a number of significant divergencies obtrude:

(1) Even the simplified Darwinian seriation (omitting the level of chordates versus nonchordates, the distinctions between bony fish, cartilaginous fish, and cyclostomes, and so on) contains 12 levels beginning with placentals versus marsupials, whereas the corresponding Wellsian seriation contains six levels beginning with placentals versus marsupials, or five without this level, which is omitted in Wells's final version. The levels Wells retained are those that can be vividly represented by striking images. The differences between existence and eclipse, plant and animal, sea and land animal, "amphibian" crab and mammal are readily understood without the Darwinian schematism. They are based on a "self-evident" or commonsensical topical bestiary antedating Linnaeus, indeed, harking back to the dawn of human imagination. Therefore, they were eminently usable for producing in the average nonscientific but science-believing reader effects of stark opposition, such as the revulsion felt by the Time Traveller when faced with the giant crabs or with the unnamed archetypal "thing" from the sea. Though Wells's task as far as lower rungs of the phylogenetic series are concerned was facilitated by the unsettled state of invertebrate phylogeny at the time,[9] there is little reason to suppose scientific scruples carried significant weight with him. Indeed, when Wells had to choose between the ABC of Darwinian classification and a kind of folk biology, he unhesitatingly chose the latter, inventing—like the hero of his parable "The Triumphs of a Taxidermist"—new taxonomic positions: the triumph of a quasi-taxonomist, indeed.[10] This is evident in the third episode of The Time Machine where the crabs are—against all biological taxonomy—situated

9. See Wells, Experiment, p. 160.

10. See Wells, Experiment, for his references to "de-individualizing" and perceiving individuals in relation to a story and a thesis, on p. 175, p. 520, and particularly the "seriational" account of his creative imagination in the dispute with Conrad on p. 528.

FIGURE 2

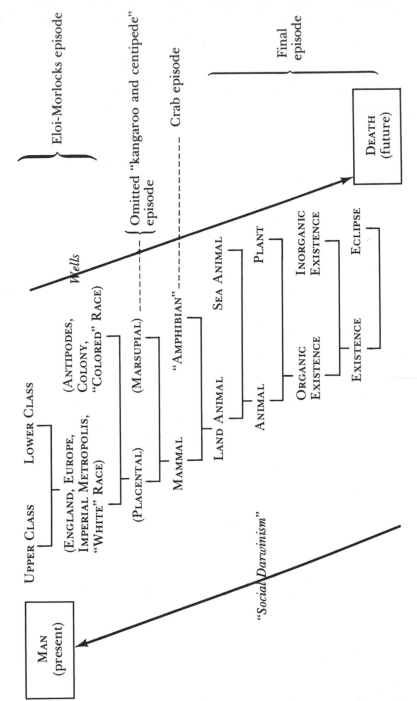

between the opposition placental versus marsupial (in the omitted "kangaroo" episode) and land animal versus sea animal, that
is, in the false, "folk taxonomic" position of amphibian creature
because of their location or ecological niche. That ecological
niche—the line where sea meets land—is easily represented and
possesses rich literary overtones; the representation of a true,
taxonomic amphibian (say Čapek's giant salamanders) would lack
the element of menace present in the insectoid antennae and
claws, the alienness of eyes wriggling on stalks, and so on. Wells
was to use this biologically collateral branch of arthropods for
similar "creepy crawly" effects in "The Empire of the Ants" and
"The Valley of Spiders," just as he was to do with the taxono-
mically isotopic molluscs in "The Sea Raiders." Incidentally,
through the octopoid Martians from *The War of the Worlds*, the
insectoid Selenites from *The First Men in the Moon*, and perhaps
the vaguely reptilian bipeds of "In the Abyss," Wells set the xeno-
biological paradigm for SF's Bug-Eyed Monsters and Menaces
from Outer Space right down to the supremely unscientific ap-
pellative "the thing."

(2) The beginning or top of Wells's devolutionary series stems
from a curious hybrid of deterministic or Malthusian pseudo-
Darwinism and bourgeois, or indeed imperialist, social theory
(and practice). That hybrid was represented not only by the "Social Darwinism" of Spencer but also, later, by Carnegie, Rockefeller, Nietzsche, and fascists of various stripes, all of whom
translated differences in socioeconomic position into a biological
terminology and stressed the "survival of the fittest." T.H. Huxley's concern with the relationships of evolution and ethics is due
precisely to an uneasiness about such uses of Darwinism. However, the usual strategy of the Social Darwinists was to use the
more convenient and mystified vocabulary of racism, preaching
social peace in the imperial metropolis and among "Whites" at
the expense of colonial peoples or "lower races."[11] Wells's personal class experiences and conversance with Plato, Blake, Shel-

11. See, e.g., Wells's explicit comment on such an attitude, which fused scientific
progress and a sense of imperial mission in fin-de-siècle Britain, in *Joan and Peter*
(London, 1918), book 1, chap. 3. In his admiration of Malthus, however, Wells himself
was not always immune from it—say in *Anticipations* (New York and London, 1902), pp.
313–14 and the last three chapters generally. Such instances could be multiplied.

ley, Morris, and Marx precluded at the moment of writing *The Time Machine* such a mystification and induced him to put the problem in its basic terms of social class rather than in pseudobiological ones. He was to be followed on that level by some of the best social criticism in SF, from Jack London's fusion of Wells and utopianism in *The Iron Heel* to the anti-utopia of Zamyatin, the political "new maps of hell" of American SF in the 1940s and 1050s, and the satirical SF from the Warsaw Pact countries (Lem, Dneprov, the Strugatskys).[12] Indeed, the sequence of the Time Traveller's hypotheses about the "Eloi episode"—(a) Communist classless society; (b) degenerated classless society; (c) degenerated class society; (d) degenerated inverted class society—comprises the whole logical gamut of sociopolitical SF, or of utopian and antiutopian fiction as the ideal poles of sociological SF, from More and Plato to the present day. Finally, with the Time Traveller's realization that the capitalists and workers have not only degenerated and inverted their power roles but have also differentiated into separate biological species, one of which is the "cattle" of the other,[13] Huxley's evolution that encompasses devolution comes true with a vengeance, even as the ideological basis of such speculations in real class fears and hopes is uncovered. The resulting "race" level of oppositions was to be used by Wells, again inverted, in *The War of the Worlds* or stories such as "Lord of the Dynamos." Reverting to crude xenophobia and losing Wells's ambiguities, this became the model for a whole group of subsequent and inferior SF narratives exporting social and national conflicts into outer space.

(3) It also becomes clear why Wells felt he had to delete the "kangaroo and centipede" episode. Not only did it completely break up the narrative rhythm by introducing at a still leisurely stage of narration two new phylogenetic levels in a single episode—marsupial and arthropod, of which, furthermore, the arthropod level is used again in the following "crab episode"—it added little to the basic opposition of the Time Traveller as mammal, land animal, and so forth, to non-mammals, sea animals, and so forth. On the contrary, it logically raised the disso-

12.   See some of their stories in (and also the preface to) D. Suvin, ed., *Other Worlds, Other Seas* (New York, 1972).

13.   See the identical and no doubt seminal metaphor in Huxley, *Evolution*, p. 17.

nant question of using a full Darwino-Huxleyan converging series, beginning with the opposition of man (Time Traveller) to primates. With commendable tact, Wells was unwilling to venture onto grounds later annexed by Tarzan of the Apes, although he subsequently compromised under Kipling's influence to the point of exploring the opposition Man versus (mammalian) Beast in *The Island of Dr. Moreau* (where Kipling's serpent is needs omitted).

(4) Finally, if one looks at the distribution of the seriation levels in the episodes of *The Time Machine*, it is possible to gain further insight about its basic narrative rhythm, also characterized by growing pace and compression as the reader is swept into the story, the motivations and justifications gradually dispensed with, and the levels cumulated in an exponential progression. *The Time Machine* consists of a framework and the three phantasmagoric evolutionary futures I have called the "Eloi," the "crab", and the "eclipse" episodes. In the first British edition, their quantitative relationships are as follows:

> Framework established, chapters 1-3, pp. 1-26
> Eloi episode, chapters 4-13, pp. 27-133
> Crab episode, first half of chapter 14, pp. 134-39
> Eclipse episode, second half of chapter 14, pp. 139-41
> Framework reestablished, chapters 15-16 and Epilogue, pp. 142-52

Or, taking into account only the inner narration of the Time Traveller's experiences:

> Eloi episode, year 802,701—one seriation level (or two), 107 pages
> (Omitted "kangaroo and centipede" episode, year?—two seriation
>   levels, ca. 4 pages)
> Crab episode, several million years hence—one seriation level, 5 pages
> Eclipse episode, 30 million years hence—four seriation levels, 3 pages

Taking the Eloi episode as two levels (first a class and then a "race" or species one[14]), there is in the above four future episodes:

---

14. Some evidence that Wells associated class and race as isomorphic antagonistic oppositions in conflicts between oppressors and oppressed, such as those that presumably led to the development of the Eloi and Morlocks, can be found in statements like the following: "the driving discontent has often appeared as a conflict between oppressors and oppressed, either as a class or as a race conflict . . ." (*Experiment*, p. 626).

1. one level per 54 pages
2. (one level per ca. 2 pages—omitted)
3. one level per 5 pages
4. one level per 0.7 pages

One could venture further into a discussion of such an exponentially regressing rhythm—which is certainly analogous on its own structural level to the whole regressive structure of *The Time Machine*—but I shall confine myself to one general observation. The rhythm starts as *lento*, with two sociobiological levels envisioned for 107 pages. It continues as *presto*, with one biological level (mammal versus "amphibian") for five pages, and ends in an abrupt *prestissimo* with four existential levels (land versus sea animal; animal versus plant—lowest plant forms at that; organic existence versus sand, snow, rocks, and sea; and existence of Earth versus eclipse) all present pell-mell, outside of their proper taxonomic order, within about three pages. This telescoping and foreshortening powerfully contributes to and indeed shapes the effect of the logical or biological series. Also, this asymptotic series makes it imperative that the Traveller finally vanish: its final and validating member can only be zero or nonexistence, extinction.[15]

Thus, Wells's *Time Machine* has in the organization of its cognitive thematic material hit upon the law—inherited, as much else was, from *Gulliver's Travels*, and apparently unshaken in subsequent significant SF—that the cognitive nucleus of narration, or theme, can become a principle of narrative organization only by fitting into the storytelling parameters of pace, sequence, symbolic systematization, and so on. Wells knew of Haeckel's law that ontogenesis (development of any species' embryo) is a foreshortened recapitulation of phylogenesis (that species' evolution); in other words, that the new environment of individual embryonic gestation inflects and modifies—though it does not change the general outline of—the evolutionary sequence. Consciously or not, he applied the same principle to the new narrative and aesthetic environment—an environment to which the cognitive evolutionary sequence of Darwinian seriation had to adapt by evolving or indeed mutating. *The principle of a Wellsian structure*

15. See Robert M. Philmus, "The Logic of 'Prophecy' in *The Time Machine*," in Bergonzi, ed. (Bibliography V), for effects of this structural device.

of science fiction is mutation of scientific into aesthetic cognition. A Wellsian narration is oriented toward cognitive horizons that it shares with any good handbook of sociology, biology, or philosophy of science. But the orientation is achieved in its own way, following the autonomy of a narrative, fictional aesthetic mode.

2. THE SYNOPTIC PARADIGM

Obviously, in order to account for Wellsian narrative strategies paradigmatic of later SF, one would have to analyze the symbolic system that is intertwined with this regressive biological seriation inflected toward "folk taxonomy." As a number of critics have noted, this symbolic system is based on violent oppositions of color, polarized between the Doomsday connotations of "eclipse black" and "fiery red" on one hand, and the green and bright colors of the utopian garden and sunlit landscaped vegetation on the other. It is not too difficult to see in these poles a coloristic translation of the opposition between tamed and untamed, safe and menacing, evolutive and devolutive nature. Huxley's parable of the cultivated garden or evolutionary Eden is thus supplied with the missing black hues.[16] Moreover, the analysis of this aspect would entail a full and lengthy exploration of Wells's particular anthropology and cosmology. Instead, I would like to further examine the temporal orientation of *The Time Machine* and the basic oppositions implicit in the annunciation of the bad, devolutionary, or black future in store for the bourgeois reader as a sociobiological entity, or for any reader as a cosmological entity, and compare this to the utopian alternative.

The Time Traveller's futures are a geometrically progressive series of devolutions, which can, by explicating the implicit opposition between (1) Social-Darwinist Britain and (2) the particular future vision, be tabulated using a Lévi-Straussian schematism. This would play upon the Social-Darwinist preconceptions of a "natural" order of power and of a safe evolutionary progress keeping each "lower" evolutionary rung in its place as prey of the "higher" predator; Wells takes these preconceptions over wholesale and simply inverts them. What results is an inverse and symmetrical structure, which can be finally reduced to a general abstract scheme or paradigm:

16.   But see *Evolution*, pp. 17 ff., for Huxley's Malthusian "serpent within the garden."

FIGURE 3

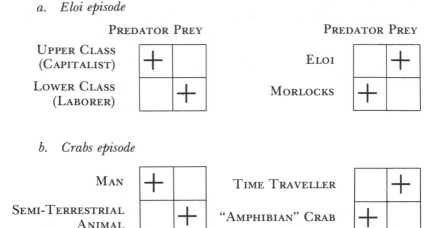

(1) Social-Darwinist Britain   (2) The Future

a. *Eloi episode*

This cumulates the logical progression of man/mammal and land animal/sea animal—compare the "kangaroo" episode left out.[17] (Clearly, the missing link in and paradigm behind *The Time Machine*, that is, the opposition between man and land animal, is to be found—as are many other aspects—in *Gulliver's Travels*.)

FIGURE 4

c. *Eclipse episode*

LAND ANIMAL	+			TIME TRAVELLER		+
SEA ANIMAL		+		"THING"	+	

17. Wells's 1894 essay "The Extinction of Man" (see note 2) discusses this inversion of power roles with man succumbing—among other possibilities, all later used in his SF—to huge land-crabs or unknown sea monsters: "In the case of every other predominant animal the world has ever seen, I repeat, the hour of its complete ascendency has been the eve of its complete overthrow," he concluded in the hyperbolic night-and-day imagery he was to use in his SF too.

In the last episode, the tentacled "thing" does not attack the Time Traveller because he flees in time, but it is clearly the master of that situation. It is reinforced by the additional presence of liverwort and lichen, the only land survivors; of the desolate inorganic landscape; and of the blood-red Sun in eclipse, which suggests the nearing end of Earth and the whole solar system. The episode, as has been explained, telescopes the taxonomic progression of land animal/sea animal, animals/plants, organic/inorganic, existence of the Earth and the solar system/destruction of same—the last being left to the by-now-conditioned extrapolative mechanism of the reader.

The progression is a "black" progression, or regression, also insofar as both parties of any preceding paradigm are subsumed as prey in the succeeding one. All classes of mammals are (symbolically, by way of the Time Traveller as Everyman) the prey of crabs in (b); all land animals, even the "amphibious" crabs, have by (c) succumbed to more vital and primitive sea animals, mosses, and lichens; and in the suggested extrapolation of a destruction of Earth and/or the solar system, all life would succumb or "become prey" to inorganic being, cosmic processes, or just entropy.

The general scheme of Wellsian SF, true of his whole early period of SF novels and stories, is thus:

FIGURE 5

(1) SOCIAL-DARWINIST BRITAIN   (2) THE FUTURE

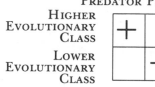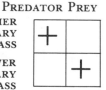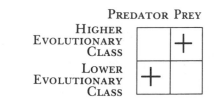

It is logically, genetically, and genologically relevant to compare this scheme to the basic opposition in More's *Utopia* and Morris's *News From Nowhere*—[18] it should be remembered the

---

18. In *News From Nowhere* the formally identical opposition is no more spatial (as with More) but temporal, an opposition between present and future but a hopeful rather than a black one (as with Wells). Morris's norm of a utopian future is historically, in fact, the

first reaction of the Time Traveller was to suppose he had found a pastoral communism. The relevant oppositions here are: England is empirically present, but axiologically empty or bad; utopia is empirically absent (*ou-topos*, nowhere) but its values are axiologically affirmed (*eu-topos*) or present. The oppositions Locus/Value and Present/Absent give rise to the following scheme, and it should be no surprise that it shows Utopia or Nowhere as (inverted) mirror images of England in Wells's here-and-now:

FIGURE 6

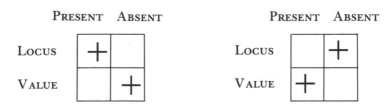

(1) BRITAIN (2) UTOPIA

Utopia as a literary genre is defined by a radically different location and a radically more perfect community, by an *alternative formal framework* functioning by reference to the author's empirical environment. As it is argued in chapter 3, No-place is defined by both not being and yet being like Place, by being the opposite and more perfect version of Place. It stands on its head an already topsy-turvy or alienated world, which thus becomes dealienated or truly normal when measured not by ephemeral historical norms of a particular civilization but by "species-specific" human norms. Utopia is thus—like *The Time Machine* but also quite unlike it—always predicated on a certain theory of human nature. It takes up and refunctions the ancient topos of *mundus inversus*: utopia is a formal inversion of significant and salient aspects of the author's world, an inversion which has as its ultimate purpose the recognition that the author (and reader) truly live in an axiologically inverted world.

---

hinge between the norms of Renaissance utopia (spatial and optimistic) and Wellsian SF. Together with the liberal optimism of, say, a Verne, Morris's norm was thus what Wells was reacting against by returning to Swift's horizon. See more about this at the end of this chapter as well as in the preceding historical chapters. However, it should already be clear that the two main influences on modern SF are sociological optimism and anthropological pessimism. Wells's career oscillates between these two.

In More's *Utopia* the analysis of space without value in book 1 (England; "here") is opposed to an axiologically "full" space presented in book 2 as Hythloday's revelation (Utopia; "out there," isomorphic with folktales of a just and abundant place beyond seven seas). This induces the logical and magical possibility of arriving at that utopia in space or time, of finding or constructing a sociopolitical Earthly Paradise. On the contrary, the general predatory paradigm of Wellsian SF is finally ambiguous. In its *inversion* of Social Darwinism, it supplies a subversive shock to the bourgeois reader; in its *use* of the parameters of Social Darwinism, however inverted—that is, of the anthropological vision dividing all life, including man, into predator and prey—it supplies a subversive shock to the humanist and socialist reader, it is anti-utopian or black. Wells's seriation converges upon absence of value and existence, a lay hell:

FIGURE 7

as opposed to the utopian terrestrial paradise of More and Morris:

FIGURE 8

3. The Proportions of Power, and
A Return Into History

One final aspect of *The Time Machine*'s structure, which is again a methodological key for much SF, is the use of *proportion* or *rule of three* (A is to B as B is to C). Wells himself admitted he used this extrapolative method—arriving at C given the known increase from A to B—to depict the megalopolis in *When the Sleeper*

Wakes, but lamented its arithmetic linearity and obviousness as "thoroughly wrong."[19] As often, he was right in the particular and wrong in the general, for proportion does not have to be used as a simple arithmetic rule of three or linear extrapolation: that is merely its more primitive variant (see chapter 4, section 2.5.). Indeed, proportion as a specific method for formalizing classification and seriation seems to be one of the basic approaches and inescapable epistemological tools of SF, if this literary genre is based upon the cognitive estrangement induced by a significantly different novum (figures and/or loci) of narration. For "significantly different" means also "belonging to another classifying category" (sociological, biological, anthropological, cosmological, and so on).

In both the Darwino-Huxleyan and the Wellsian biological series from section 1 of this chapter, each subsequent term cumulates, as was noted in section 2, the two preceding terms, thus setting up a new opposition on a more primitive evolutionary level. Thus in the Darwinian series placentals embraces both man and nonhuman primates in opposition to marsupials, warm-blooded subsumes mammals and birds in opposition to cold-blooded, and so forth. The peculiarity of this seriation, Wells saw, is that its two extremes, Man and Nonexistence, are privileged members. In both series, Man is the highest evolutionary category, and he is contained in all the left-hand members of both Huxley's and Wells's series. In the Darwino-Huxleyan series, Man is placental, mammal, warm-blooded, amniotic, land animal, vertebrate, and so on down to organic being. In the Wellsian series, Man is mammal, land animal, animal, organic being, and existing entity as against the respective negations. Any negation can come into play only when opposed to Man, that is, when the Time Traveller in the last two episodes beholds for himself, and for the human readers, the crabs, the "thing" from the sea, the lichen and liverwort, the desolate rocks and sea, and the eclipse. At those points, the Time Traveller is a generic representative of Homo sapiens, an Everyman defined in terms of biological rather than theological classification, as a species-creature and not a temporarily embodied soul. The medieval Everyman was an immortal soul in a mortal body; the

19.   Wells, *The Future in America*, pp. 11–12.

principle of individuation was saved. Symmetrically but inversely the Darwinist Everyman is a quasi-immortal species (germ-plasm) in a mortal body; the principle of individuation is lost. But quasi-immortal is not immortal:[20] even the generic principle could get lost, and biology is full of cautionary tales about dominant species or whole orders (such as the giant reptiles, significantly absent in *The Time Machine* though a staple of much SF since Jules Verne's *Journey to the Centre of the Earth*) that disappeared in the depths of geological time. The mighty are humbled indeed in such perspectives, which Wells turned against Victorian complacency with zest and relish.

In the Eloi-Morlocks episode, however, the Time Traveller cannot be simply a representative Man, since he is faced with creatures that are maybe no longer Homo sapiens, but are certainly other races or species of the genus *Homo* (say *Homo eloii* and *Homo morlockius*).[21] What he can be, as against the unifunctional Hominidae of year 802,701, is a complex Victorian gentleman-inventor who displays various fin-de-siècle attitudes when faced with shifting situations and interpretations of the Eloi and the Eloi-Morlocks relationship. Christopher Caudwell's critique implying that the Time Traveller occupies an intermediate position between the two new species, a position isotopic

---

20. See, e.g., Wells's anonymous article "Death" in 1895, reprinted in Philmus and Hughes, eds., which makes exactly this point.

21. Tangentially be it remarked that T. H. Huxley explained at length in his works—and no doubt in his lectures—the difference between physiological and morphological species, which is intricate and mainly resolvable by experimental crossbreeding. In Weena, the mawkish avatar of Dickens's Little Nell and similar Victorian girlish heroines, Wells supplied the Time Traveller with a somewhat imperfect subject for such experimentation. Wells's private and later literary efforts at sexual liberation prove, I think, that he passed up the clearly present sexual considerations only out of deference to very strong social taboos. One has to regret this, though one can blame him the less, considering that the taboo has been prudently respected in SF until the end of the 1960s in the most ludicrous ways (see for the example of the Tarzan-Jane relationship Richard D. Mullen, "E. R. Burroughs and the Fate Worse than Death," *Riverside Quarterly* 4 [June 1970]: 186–91; and in the last decade this sex taboo has often been as ludicrously and immaturely infringed. It almost goes without saying that French SF was different, from *L'Ève future* by Villiers de l'Isle Adam to Vercors's *Murder of the Missing Like* (*Les Animaux dénaturés*), which has exactly this experiment in miscegenation—performed by a Daniel Ellsberg among zoologists to force a test-trial for antigenocidal purposes—for its theme. Still, it is a loss that Wells never really fused his sexual liberation novels and his scientific romances into xenoerotics of the Rosny Aîné, Dorémieux, or Farmer type; but here, too, he provided at least an "empty" model.

with the position of the petty bourgeois Wells disdainful of a
decadent upper class but horrified and repelled by a crude lower
class, seems to me, for all the nuances and elaborations it needs,
to remain a key for interpreting the topographic and the color
symbolism of that episode.[22] In the later episodes the Time
Traveller is placed in an ever widening temporal perspective that
corresponds to the descent down the phylogenetic series.

Returning to the proportions inherent in *The Time Machine*,
it becomes clear that section 2 of this chapter is a synchronic
presentation of the devolutionary diachrony discussed in section 1. On each devolutionary level in Wells's narration there is
a symmetrically inverted situation usually mediated by the Time
Traveller, as:

(a) Victorian upper class dominates over the Victorian working class, which is the inverse of the Eloi's position in respect to
Morlocks; or $VUC : VWC = [E : M]^{-1}$.

(b) In the present geological epoch, Mammals are more powerful than "Amphibians," which is the inverse of what the Crabs
are to the Time Traveller; or $M : A = [TT : C]^{-1}$.

(c) In the present geological epoch, Land Animals prevail in
the mastery of the globe, which is the inverse of the panic flight
the "thing" from the sea puts the Time Traveller to; or $LA : SA
= [TT : Th]^{-1}$. The "normal" hierarchical relation Animals :
Plants is inverted in the survival of hardy lichen and liverwort
after animals have died out (though there is a sleight-of-hand
here since the sea "thing" has not died out, thence its first inani-
mate appearance), thus $A : P = [TT : L\&L]^{-1}$. The same holds
true for the relations Organic : Inorganic Existence, and finally
for Existence : Entropy.

---

22. See Caudwell (Bibliography V). For Wells's view of any historical "social edifice"
as divided into a basic "labouring class" and a "superior class"—a view clearly echoing *The
Communist Manifesto*, probably by way of Morris—see his *Anticipations*, pp. 75–83; that
passage leads into a discussion on pp. 83–91 of the parasitic decadence of both the
fin-de-siècle upper and lower classes, the "shareholders" and the "abyss" (the latter a
metaphor that Jack London was to pick up in *The People of the Abyss* and *The Iron Heel*).
That such a "future decadence" is the source of the Eloi-Morlocks episode is explicitly
brought out in the conversation with Theodore Roosevelt at the end of *The Future in
America*. However, the *Anticipations* passage continues with a long discussion, pp. 92 ff., of
the rise of a new middle class of educated engineers and scientific managers that holds
the only hope for the future. Wells's subsequent ideological career is, as Caudwell rightly
remarked, a search for this third social force.

The unity of this series of proportions and of *The Time Machine*'s composition hinges on the full—though somewhat unmotivated because ideologically mystified—sympathy the Time Traveller must, for all his cavils, feel for the Eloi. They occupy the same position, which is simultaneously characterized by functionally appertaining to the upper class and yet being powerless in relation to the "lower" Social-Darwinist class of Morlock, Crab, "Thing," and so further into cosmological entropy. The series of proportions can be recapitulated as:

$$\text{VUC} : \text{VWC} = [\text{E} : \text{M}]^{-1}$$
$$\text{M} \quad : \text{A} \quad = [\text{TT} : \text{C}]^{-1}$$
$$\text{LA} \quad : \text{SA} \quad = [\text{TT} : \text{Th}]^{-1}$$
$$\text{A} \quad : \text{P} \quad = [\text{TT} : \text{L\&L}]^{-1}$$
(and so on)

One notices the isotopism of the Eloi and the Time Traveller. It springs from the fact that the horror of this inversion of basic *power norms* is predicated upon the Time Traveller's being also a mammal, a land animal, an animal, an organic being, and finally an existing entity; this is a continuation and validation of the Eloi and Morlocks being descended from, apparently corresponding to, and certainly being magically associated with the Victorian upper and lower class. The different sociological, biological, and cosmological oppositions in the Wellsian series have the final common denominator of dominant existence or power. *Power is the arbiter, fate, or nemesis in SF*—and in utopias as social-science fiction.

As was suggested in section 2, the paradigm for these proportions is undoubtedly supplied by the relationships in *Gulliver's Travels*, in particular the black Swiftian variant of book 4: Horse : Houynhnhnm = Man : X. "X" is the *animal rationale* Swift believed might perhaps be found in some individuals but not in mankind as a whole. Though there might be a few noble men *rationis capax*, such as Captain Mendez or Lord Munodi, there was no rational Noble Man corresponding *sub specie humanitatis* to the Noble Horse, and the only fully consistent categorical alternative was that mankind is Yahookind, *animal implume bipes*.[23] Be-

---

23. For a first approach to the complicated categories and proportions in book 4 of *Gulliver's Travels*, see Elliott (Bibliography II), Brady, ed., Greenberg, ed., and Tuveson, ed. (all in Bibliography III E), especially the essays by R. S. Crane in the Brady volume

yond that, section 2 tried to show how Wells's paradigm leads back to More's *Utopia*. Between More's inversion from axiologically bad to good, and Wells's inversion of biologically dominant to dominated, Swift's absence of the Noble Man (synthesizing axiology and biology) provides the middle term. This section on proportion might fittingly conclude with noting the secular proportion:

Utopia : *Gulliver's Travels* = *Gulliver's Travels* : *The Time Machine*.

In terms of ideological vision—though perhaps not in terms of formal accomplishment—this is also a devolutionary series. Beside Man, Nonexistence or Death is the second privileged member of Wells's scale. Finally, as in the magnificent eclipse description, the two allegorical protagonists Everyman and Death meet again: and it is not Everyman who wins. Having adopted such horizons, modern Anglophone SF from Stapledon to Heinlein or Orwell, Pohl or Aldiss, Vonnegut or Ballard had to concentrate on filling in Wells's paradigm and varying its surface. The only other course would have been to return, on a higher bend of the spiral, to the original Morean paradigm: a turn that it has so far been either unwilling or unable to take. For better or for worse (as Russian literature is said to have sprung from Gogol's *Overcoat*), all of this SF has sprung from *The Time Machine*. Furthermore, even the temporary or final abandoning of SF in favor of futurology, popular punditry, and more prestigious literary genres is another case of Wells's paradigmatic position in relation to the sociology of SF (from Asimov and Pohl to Vonnegut and Ballard). And in Wells's concomitant utopian speculations (so much more muddled and less cognitive than his early SF) there can be found the reasons for and social roots of such unwillingness, inability, and abandonings.

---

and Joseph Horrell in the Tuveson volume. See for these categories, as well as the evident connections between Swift and More, also my chapter 5.

Aristotle points out in *Poetics* 1457b that any metaphor is either (1) a relation of species to or within genus, or (2) an analogy that always presupposes the A : B = C : D proportion. In the theoretical chapters of this book I attempted to demonstrate that significant SF operates on the analogical model. It is thus understandable that the clearest paradigm of SF is to be found in *Gulliver's Travels*, and that Wells closely followed it. He revived the paradigm by substituting Darwinist evolution for Swiftian or Christian-humanist ethics, and the classification methods of *arbor huxleiana* for those of *arbor porphyriana*—Huxley being to Darwin what Porphyrius was to Aristotle (on the Porphyrian tree see Walter J. Ong, S. J., *Ramus, Method, and the Decay of Dialogue* [Cambridge, MA, 1958], pp. 78–79 and passim).

11

Russian SF and Its Utopian Tradition

1. The tradition of SF is a time-honored one in Russia. Its strength is based on blending the rationalist Western European strain of utopianism and satire with the native folk longings for abundance and justice. These were embodied, first, in the ubiquitous dream of a land of Cockayne-like abundance, often the goal of extraordinary voyages (in the case of landlocked Russia, overland ones) toward India, Persia, or China: Marco Polo's Cathay was not more fabulous than the luxurious Kitezh-gorod of folk imagination. Justice to man regardless of the traps and trappings of his social station is the central interest of a second large segment of oral and folk literature. Perhaps it might be enough to mention here only the strong theme of the humble person who is finally exalted. From the wishful and magical folktales about Ivanushka the Fool, the youngest or third son who is poorer and apparently more stupid than his brothers but ends up more successful than the norms of class society would allow for, through a fusion with plebeian (especially heretical and sectarian) Christianity, such a theme flowed into the mainstream of modern Russian literature. From Pushkin's and Mussorgsky's mad folk prophet in *Boris Godunov*, through the memorable humble arrogants in Dostoevsky, (say, Prince Myshkin in *The Idiot*), all the way to many Tolstoian and Chekhovian characters, these figures bear utopian values into a world not yet ready for them.

In the middle of the nineteenth century this tradition fused with earlier echoes of imaginary sociopolitical set-ups. The first traces of an exemplary political tale used as vehicle for a fictional blueprint go as far back as Ivan Peresvetov's sixteenth-century *Legend of Sultan Mahomet*, a plea to Tsar Ivan the Terrible for strong state centralization, which was to be remembered approvingly and appropriately by Stalin. But a real trend in that direction developed in Russian literature following the continent-wide spread of the Rationalist *Staatsroman* in the eighteenth century. From the middle of that century on, utopian writings such as Lvov's and Levshin's extolled ideally harmonious countries of economic abundance and enlightened absolutism. Tredyakovsky adapted Fénelon's *Télémaque*; writers like Kheraskov, Dmitriev-Mamonov, and Emin supplied in their works parallels and parables on such an "enlightened absolutist prince" model, usually in a spurious classical setting. In the second half of the century, prince Mikhail Shcherbatov wrote an incomplete *Voyage to the Land of Ophir* (bp. 1896) expressing the longings of the higher aristocracy; and More's *Utopia* was translated into Russian in the year of the French Revolution. That event, as well as the ensuing wars, prompted a speedy suppression of the whole genre for a generation. Empress Catherine, who had affected friendship with Voltaire and Diderot while quenching the peasant rebellions, brutally supressed any "natural right" pleas against serfdom—such as Aleksandr Radishchev's famous *Journey from Petersburg to Moscow*, which contained passages of a democratic blueprint for the future.

2.   It was only in the 1820s that the official propagandist Thaddeus Bulgarin could publish in his magazine three mildly satirical marvelous voyage tales. The most substantial of them, his *Untrue Un-Events, or a Voyage to the Center of the Earth* (1825), is supposedly the manuscript of an anonymous narrator's voyage through three underworld countries—an idea taken from Holberg's *Niels Klim* (also translated into Russian in the eighteenth century, but having in turn for antecedents ubiquitous myths and folktales which were to be revived for SF 40 years later by Jules Verne). Bulgarin's narrator falls down a cave in an arctic island into the country of Ignorance, where grotesque inhabitants live in perpetual darkness, caring only for food, drink, gossip, and gambling, A whirlpool takes him into the dawnlight country of Beastliness, where apelike inhabitants are half-blind and have some superficial and mistaken acquaintance with arts and sciences. Finally, the narrator finds an underground passage to the nethermost country of Enlightedness perpetually lit by the fires of Earth's center, where humans live in the capital city of Utopia and outlying villages. The Enlightened are brought up to be self-disciplined, obedient to lawful authority and to a strict code of life which regulates working, writing, traveling, and even

women's fashions. Obviously, though he differentiates his countries by spiritual "enlightenment," Bulgarin's country of Ignorance is a satire on the lower orders, mainly on the Russian peasant living under what Tolstoy will—using the same metaphor—aptly call "the power of darkness." The country of Beastliness, in which people are in a way worse than the Ignorantians because they pretend to knowledge they do not possess, is in many ways a put-down of the middle class and the intellectuals just emerging in tsarist Russia. Finally, the smug patriarchal country of Enlightedness is an autocratic emasculation of More, silent on his basic insights about property and economics, propagating an idealized stance popular at the tsarist court from the times of Peter the Great. With all its obvious limitations, Bulgarin's work nonetheless testifies to a certain interest in the field and to a rather good knowledge of its stock devices, and its obscurantist depicting of social classes as separate races and nations prefigures Wells's triumphant use of this device in *The Time Machine*.

The Russian SF tradition came up to worldwide nineteenth-century standards with Prince Vladimir Odoevsky's unfinished *Year 4338*, circulated in manuscript in the 1840s and published only in Soviet times. In this epistolary tale the Enlightenment tradition—visible in the reliance on new knowledge as well as in the form, taken from Montesquieu's *Persian Letters* with a dash of Mercier's *Year 2440*—is supplemented with Romantic extrapolation by Odoevsky, a disciple of Hoffmann and Pushkin as well as of Schelling. Furthermore, although SF had—in a generally more activistic Europe affected by the French Revolution and stubborn utopian hopes—even in lagging Russia already shifted from space to time, as, for example, in Bulgarin's *True Un-Events, or Voyages in the World of the 29th Century* (1829), yet Odoevsky's tale was the first significant Russian anticipation. Not that this rich and erudite eccentric, amateur scientist, philosopher, and litterateur went any further than to envisage an enlightened aristocratic empire rewarding both birth and talent. Human nature was for him rather static, and in social relations he envisaged only more of the same: a conurbation extends from Petersburg to Moscow; having sold everything else under the sun, Americans are now auctioning off their cities and trying to loot China, this being the only armed conflict left in the world. But Russian officers and peasants returning from the Napoleonic wars had

brought a spark of novelty home, and at least once in the intervening years, in the Decembrist revolt of 1825, this spark had
threatened to set fire to the antiquated tsarist structure. For
Odoevsky, the new is to be expected from effects of scientific
development, about which he is quite sanguine. In his notes to
the fragmentary *Year 4338* often as interesting as the torso itself)
he criticizes Mary Shelley's gloomy *The Last Man* for not looking
far enough into the future. He envisages aerostatic communication radically changing the commerce, politics, and morals of the
future; expeditions for mineral exploitation of the Moon, taking
their own atmosphere along and solving the problems of global
overpopulation; renewed nomadism; machine authorship of
novels and patriotic plays, with other printing and fiction giving
way to pure information, "electrical" talking, and public lecturing; and scholars who do not publish but lecture daily in a dozen
places flying from each to each.

The novel itself is supposed to have been written with the help
of a mesmeric visionary, who had tuned into the mind of a
young Chinese writing back to a friend in Peking from the
Petersburg of 4338 or 4339, on the eve of a comet's crash onto
Earth. Odoevsky obviously never dreamed of a social upheaval
of such proportions as to change the hallowed tsarist name of the
city. But again, he interestingly discusses such matters as the use
of "elastic glass" or "elastic crystal" for clothing, odoriferous
gases instead of wines, photocopied newsletters by the important
families, teleprinters, air and underground electric traffic, electric lights, heating of northern countries by giant hot air tubes
from the Equator, and the breeding of horses down to the size
and nature of lapdogs. The main high society game is a "magnetic bath" inducing somnambulism, in which state many people
declare their secret actions and sympathies, making hypocrisy
impossible. Clearly, the society envisaged is hierarchical and
bureaucratic. In one of his notes Odoevsky—who is quite sarcastic about middle-class equality—describes a Platonic scientific
oligarchy, headed by poet-philosophers. They are flanked by his-
toriographers, linguists, physicists, and other scientists of the
second highest rank. Each historiographer heads in his turn a
group of chroniclers, philologists, geographers, archeologists,
and so forth; each physicist a group of chemists, mineralogists,
and other third-rank scientists. A mineralogist has assigned to

him fourth-rank metallurgists, and so on down to the lowest rank of copyists and laboratory assistants. Odoevsky's *Year 4338* can thus be thought of as a liberal-aristocratic answer to Bulgarin, pioneering in scientific extrapolation into the future, but failing to realize that a radically new productivity demands radically new social relations. Since even much of present-day SF is still stricken with the same blindness, Odoevsky remains one of the more interesting SF writers of the pre-Wellsian age in Europe, particularly if one also takes into account his anti-utopian and anti-bourgeois stories "The Nameless City" (bp. 1844) and "The Final Suicide" (1844), which are the obverse of his rationalist optimism.

3.   The fact that even such politically timid anticipation could not be printed under tsarism testifies to the unfavorable climate of obscurantism SF had to contend with in Russia. Thus the significant fusion of political utopianism and anthropological anticipation, which came about in Nikolai Chernyshevsky's *What Is To Be Done?* (1862), saw the light of the day from the dungeon in which it was written only because of a bureaucratic snarl-up in tsarist censorship; even so, it did not get into book form until the 1905 revolution. Nevertheless, its impact was immense, comparable only to Bellamy's in the United States (and in Russia too): every high-school girl read handwritten copies under her bench, and for half a century the populists and later the socialists used it in underground education. Much of the veneration was initially attributable to the legendary figure of the author, the leader of Russian radical intelligentsia, who was to remain in prison or strict Siberian internation for the rest of his life. A brilliant critic and pre-Marxian materialist who uncompromisingly rejected both tsarism and the capitalism toward which the regime was groping, Chernyshevsky cautiously smuggled into the novel his ideal of a cooperative and communal libertarian socialism, in which the self-enlightened interest of each would be guaranteed by the free development of all, based on the liberation of labor. But the main reason for the novel's lasting success in stagnant eastern Europe (both Lenin in Russia and Dimitrov in Bulgaria glowingly remembered its decisive influence on their personal commitment to the revolution) was Chernyshevsky's refusal to separate the public and private lives of his heroes. "Freedom now" could have been the slogan of these "new people," and

while devoting themselves to the radical cause, they prefigured in their exemplary, free, and sincere personal relationships Russia's utopian future. Despite some old-fashioned literary conventions used by Chernyshevsky, an admirer of George Sand and Thackeray, his novel remains of considerable interest. The liberation of mankind symbolized by Woman is its main theme, and in the loving happiness Vera Pavlovna pursues there is no break, although there are interesting tensions, between the erotic and the political aspects, just as there is none between the conscious and the subconscious. In fact, the utopian anticipation is formally present in a sequence of four dreams Vera Pavlovna dreams within the novel, a brilliant innovation soon to be picked up and turned against its originators by Dostoevsky's rebuttal of radicalism in Raskolnikov.

Most clearly utopian in the strict formal sense is the famous Fourth Dream. A vision in two parts, divided by a self-censored space which stands for the account of the liberating revolution, this dream shows, first, the liberation of female personality through a series of allegorical glimpses leading to the new woman born of revolutionary equality, and second, a future socialist utopia incorporating both Fourier's idea of cooperative producing collectives (*phalanstères*) which would annul the contradictions between town and rural life, and Owen's idea of a new moral world based on equality and made possible by machine productivity. These ideas were widespread in nineteenth-century Europe and America, but Chernyshevsky was, after Cabet, one of the first to use them in fiction. More importantly, he was the first largely to avoid didactic dryness by making them the supreme emotional interest of his characters. The political dream is also the deepest personal dream of a warm heroine, in a manner which would have been entirely understandable to Dante, Langland, Cervantes, or Marvell, but which had since disappeared from the European cultural mainstream. Chernyshevsky's Fourth Dream fused romantic pathos and rational belief in social change. The huge crystal palace in the midst of fertile fields where a happy association of free producers lives and works, each at variegated tasks changing every few hours, symbolizes even architecturally—by uniting under the same roof a variety of apartments, workplaces, studios, theaters, museums—the harmony of personal and public life. The dream of Vera Pavlovna is thus not unworthy of the great liberating current of "warm" utopias in western Europe, from More and Rabelais to Chernyshevsky's teachers—Rousseau and the utopian socialists, who set up the principle that the emancipation of women is the measure of social liberation. It certainly set the tradition of a whole aspect of Russian SF.

A countercurrent to radicalism, equally messianic and anti-bourgeois but with a diametrically opposed point of view, found a most powerful voice in Fyodor Dostoevsky. In his youth a member of an illegal circle which propagated utopian-socialist ideas and even tried to put them into practice, Dostoevsky's shattering prison and Siberian experience channelled his utopian concerns into a mystical deification of the tsarist system. His deepest hatreds were from that time evenly divided between the degradation of man under the impact of capitalist economics and the radical proposals for rational rehumanization; curiously, he had come to think of these opposites as two faces of the same prideful coin. The famous Crystal Palace of the mid-century London World Exhibition became for him the symbol of industrialized inhumanity, dividing brothers into the domineering rich and the gin-sodden, sectarian poor. In his *Notes from the Underground*, written immediately after the publication of *What Is To Be Done?*, he sarcastically adduced the irrationality of the individual's free will, the stupidity evidenced by unceasing mass bloodshed, and the general senselessness of world history against the rationalist builders of new economic relations and of the Crystal Palace. Although unnamed in these repressive circumstances (where even Dostoevsky was censored), there is little doubt that Chernyshevsky's novel was meant. In Raskolnikov, the hero of Dostoevsky's next novel, all radicals recognized a distorted portrait of themselves.

Though he was energetically battering away at the idea of a future Crystal Palace, the ambiguous Dostoevsky remained obsessed with its themes of innocence, brotherly love, and transcending social antagonisms. True to his religious bent, he placed them in a static, arcadian Golden Age, a motif which was to run through his whole work, breaking out explicitly in places like Versilov's speech in *A Raw Youth*, the suppressed chapter of *The Possessed*, and finally formalized into a separate work as *The Dream of a Ridiculous Man* (1877). That story is a far cry from the venomous polemics of the 1860s. Although Dostoevsky remained skeptical about the *feasibility* of man's salvation through history—witness the Grand Inquisitor passages in *The Brothers Karamazov*—*The Dream of a Ridiculous Man* is a heartfelt cry for the *necessity* of such a salvation. It depicts a distraught narrator, who has lost all touch with humanity and who decides to commit suicide, dreaming that he has died and been transported across space to a perfect twin of our Earth. There, on a Greek island, he finds an unfallen and loving people in a pastoral Golden Age; yet after a while he corrupts the happy utopians through lies, cruelty, and individualism. A complete civil society soon evolves, with crimes, science, codes of honor and law, warfare, and a full history of slaves and saints, suffering and formal religion. The horrified narrator asks to be crucified but is laughed at, and awakes. He abandons his suicidal intention and devotes the rest of his life to preaching the possibility of happiness and beauty on our planet. Dostoevsky's fulminations against the utopian abolition of suffering notwithstanding, for once the spell of an earthly happiness has managed to assert itself in this neglected gem of his: a tardy, isolated, and wistful but significant concession to the dream of Vera Pavlovna.

4.   Never absent from Russian literature, the anticipatory alternative became especially relevant at times of revolutionary resurgence, which also chipped away at censorship. Such a period were the 1900s, when the utopian flame flared up in many non-SF works, for which the future-oriented daydreams of some Chekhovian heroes, such as Vershinin in *The Three Sisters*, may be taken as representative. In circumstances that called for active intervention into the here and now, the traditional far-away utopian country, such as the one expounded by the Tolstoian folk-preacher Luka in Gorky's *Lower Depths*, was already felt as evading the issue. The major SF witness to the urgency of intervening was the prominent symbolist poet Valery Bryusov. In his play *Earth* (1904) a revolt of youth shatters the glass dome that bars people in a decadent giant city from sunshine and open space; the revolt is seen both as seeking liberation and exposing the city to the risk of annihilation. At the same time as London's more precise *The Iron Heel*, Bryusov thus saw the distant possibilities of a new culture and the immediate prospect of destroying the present one. After the defeat of the 1905 revolution, Bryusov's

horizons contracted; his Poesque story about a future city, *The Republic of the Southern Cross* (1907), is frankly dystopian: a huge capitalist metropolis on the very South Pole, capital of the greatest industrial power of the world and again enclosed by an impenetrable dome, falls prey to a mortal epidemic of *mania contradicens* which makes the afflicted do the opposite from what they wish to do. Science and society are powerless to prevent its spread, and a resolute bourgeois minority fighting for order is finally overwhelmed by the brutalized inhabitants. The story is a curious prefiguration of Camus's *The Plague*, possibly because both descend from Raskolnikov's dream at the end of *Crime and Punishment*, of a worldwide epidemic, but more significantly because they both allegorize the great social convulsions of our century. But Bryusov was readier to pay any price for the destruction of the "ugly and shameful" capitalist system. Though his apocalyptic verse, stimulated not only by other poets but also by Flammarion, Verne, Wells, and Renard, envisaged wolves baying on the banks of the Seine and happy children burning books in the London Parliament, he apostrophized "the coming Huns" (see also his story *The Last Martyrs*): "But you, who will destroy me, / I meet with an anthem of welcome!" Together with his great fellow-symbolist Alexander Blok, who had also envisaged the coming of new "Scythians," Bryusov became thus one of the few prominent non-Marxist writers who took an active part in post-revolutionary cultural life in Soviet Russia.

All these examples testify to a continued interest in and a significant tradition of Russian SF. One could add to them a few more scattered works: on the one hand, the theocratic apocalypse of Vladimir Solovyev's *Short History of the Antichrist* (1900), the confused occult interplanetary voyages of Mrs. Kryzhanovskaia, and Sharapov's Slavophile, anti-Bellamy utopia *Fifty Years Later* (1902); and on the other end of the ideological spread, Alexander Kuprin's popular stories "A Toast" (1906) and "The Liquid Sun" (1913) and some technological anticipations written with popularizing aims by engineers and scientists—like V. Chikolev's *Electrical Story (Neither True Nor Made Up*, 1895), A. Rodnykh's *Rolling Road* (1902), V. Bakhmetyev's *The Billionaire's Legacy* (1904), and N. Komarov's *Coldtown* (1917)—and culminating in the opus of Tsiolkovsky. Komarov's anticipation of a refrigerating technique on a scale to counter-

act a rise of atmospheric temperature already led into a technocratic sketch of the next two centuries' history. Concentrating on the sociopolitical aspects of such a history, Alexander
Bogdanov-Malinovsky, a prominent though ideologically unorthodox Bolshevik leader, became, alongside Bryusov and Tsiolkovsky, the most interesting SF writer of the prerevolutionary
years. His novels about an exemplary Martian society, *The Red
Star* (1908) and *Engineer Menni* (1913)—especially the first one—
renewed the tradition for left-wing Russian SF, which had been
in abeyance since Chernyshevsky's times. They fused earthly
political struggles with the interplanetary tale (Mars is a "red
star" both because of its Wellsian reddish vegetation and because
of the proletarian movement) either directly or by juxtaposition
within the same work as prefigurations, extrapolations, or alternative paths. Bogdanov's superior Martian technology (including
a foretaste of nuclear energy, automation, anti-matter, and interplanetary vessels with ionic propulsion) and social organization successfully updated the European "Martian story" of
Lasswitz and Wells in a manner unsurpassed between them and
the American 1940s, or even 1960s. The free, science-oriented
social system will be taken up 50 years later by Yefremov, the
revolutionary protagonist's illumination and love affair on
another planet by Tolstoy, and both these elements by much
Soviet SF in the 1920s and 1960s. Even Bogdanov's activistic
characters and, in places, lyrical style were to prove trend-setting.

Yet for all its vitality, the prerevolutionary SF tradition was
very tenuous, written at great cost by exceptional, heroic, and
isolated figures. The weight of industrial and scientific back-
wardness combined with the obtuse oppression of tsarism was
too great to allow a flowering of the genre. In the twenty years
before 1917, only about 25 original Russian SF books were published. Nonetheless, together with copious translations and imitations of Jules Verne (by Volokhov-Pervukhin and Semenov,
for example), as well as Wells, Flammarion, Renard, or Uminsky,
they prepared the ground for the flowering. This came about
with a vengeance in the 1920s, in the first flush of a revolutionary regime committed to industrialization and modern science as
a means for achieving utopian mastery over man's destiny.

5.   In Russia this was one of those epochs when new Heavens
touch the old Earth, when the future actively overpowers the

present, and the sluggish and disjointed flow of time is suddenly channelled into a wild waterfall, generating a rainbow on the near horizon and capable of dispensing light and warmth from scores of dynamos. Wells visited the Soviet state in the midst of the Volga famine and found Lenin confidently tracing plans for a fully electrified self-governing Russia. Quite rightly, he recognized in the author of *State and Revolution* a utopian dreamer: but Wells the utopographer had forgotten that certain utopias are realizable.

5.1. In the literature of the 1920s this atmosphere evoked a flurry of anticipations and planetary novels. The tireless Bryusov, long an enthusiast for interplanetary travel, dreamed with Pasternak and the Futurists of a scientific poetry, and wrote of billions of worlds ready to hear the call of an Earth spiralling in its "planetary revolution" (*Distances*, 1922). Two of his unpublished plays discussed the possibilities and pitfalls of interplanetary relations. The tragedy *Dictator*, probably modeled on Wells's *When the Sleeper Wakes*, portrays a militarist who wants Earth to conquer the universe, but is overthrown by the partisans of peaceful labor. *The World of 7 Generations* (1923) takes place on a Flammarion-inspired comet, symbolizing the revolved historical cycle, the inhabitants of which are called upon to sacrifice themselves in order to save Earth. Taking off from such a widespread identification of the social revolution with man's leap into the universe, a whole school of Russian versifiers called themselves the "Cosmists" and extolled a somewhat vague "planetary awareness." Much too little is known about such sociologically representative Chernyshevskian or Bogdanov-type visions of a perfect classless future as Vivian Itin's warm *Land of Gonguri* (1922), Yakov Okunev's *Tomorrow* (1924), and several other works of that kind up to V. Nikolsky's *In a Thousand Years* (1927, featuring intelligent plant life and the first nuclear explosion in 1945), E. Zelikovich's *Coming World* (1930), and the remarkable Yan Larri's *Land of the Happy* (1931), a novel which even contains a satirical portrait of Stalin. A number of noted prose writers wrote at the outset of their careers at least one largely or marginally SF work, often with a setting in the near-future and with strong elements of a political adventure or crime story, such as some stories of Nikolai Aseyev, Ilya Ehrenburg's novel *Trust D.E.* (1923), Valentin Katayev's *Ehrendorf Island* (1924), Marietta Shaginyan's "Jim

Dollar" trilogy beginning with *Mess-Mend* (1924-26), Boris Lavrenyev's *The Fall of the Ytl Republic* (1925), and Vsevolod Ivanov
and Victor Shklovsky's *Yperite* (1926).

Another and similar type was "the catastrophe novel," which
dealt with the social consequences of a new scientific invention
(often a kind of "death ray," and brought about by a solitary
scientist of the Frankenstein-Nemo type) ending invariably with
a catastrophic downfall of the capitalist system and the victory of
world revolution. One can mention, for example, the self-
explanatory titles of Katayev's novel *The Lord of Iron* (1925) or of
two works from 1927—A. Paley's *Gulf Stream*, in which a socialist
Old World is contrasted with a Taylorite and alienated United
States, and A. Shishko's *The Microbes' Appetite*, operating with
robots and chemical warfare. This type of story started from the
Vernean *roman scientifique* and broadened it into sociopolitical
anticipations of a near future. Its global dimensions latched on to
Wells's middle-period romances *The War in the Air, The World Set
Free*, and especially *When the Sleeper Wakes*, but their primary
impulse came from the general Soviet anticipation of a world
revolutionary upheaval in the first ten years after the October
Revolution. The undoubted culmination of this type was Alexei
Tolstoy's *Hyperboloid of Engineer Garin* (translated as *The Garin
Death Ray*), published in its first version in 1925-26. Tolstoy's
revisions of this political anticipation over the next dozen years
would almost suffice to provide a microhistory of shifting attitudes in and around Soviet SF in that period. Finally, the tor-
mented and ironic aspects of a Zamyatin-like skepticism were
continued by Sergei Bobrov's *Revolt of the Misanthropes* (1922),
Lev Lunts's expressionistic drama *The City of Truth* (1923), some
stories of Veniamin Kaverin, and especially by Mikhail Bulgakov
(*The Fatal Eggs*, 1924; *The Heart of a Dog*, 1925) who soon crossed
into allegorical or satirical fantasy.

Perhaps most representative of this 1920s mainstream were
certain works—even though, or perhaps because, only partly or
marginally SF—of Vladimir Mayakovsky, its most popular poet.
In poems such as "About It," "150,000,000" and "The Fifth International," in short propagandist pieces such as *Before and
Now*, in film scenarios, and most clearly in his three post-
revolutionary plays, the mainspring of Mayakovsky's creation
was the tension between anticipatory utopianism and recalcitrant

reality. A Futurist and admirer of Wells and London, Mayakovsky wrote his witty masterpiece *Mystery Buffo* to celebrate the first anniversary of the October revolution, envisaging it as a second cleansing Flood in which the working classes, inspired by a poetic vision from the future, get successively rid of their masters, devils, heaven, and (in the 1921 version) of economic chaos, and finally achieve a Terrestrial Paradise of reconciliation with Things around them. The revolution is thus both political and cosmic, it is an irreversible and eschatological, irreverent and mysterious, earthy and tender return to direct sensuous relationships of men with a no longer alien universe. No wonder that Mayakovsky's two later plays became satirical protests against the threatening separation of the classless heavens from the Earth. The future heavens of the sun-lit Commune remain the constant horizon of Mayakovsky's imaginative experiments, and it is by its values that the grotesque tendencies of petty-bourgeois restoration in *The Bedbug* (1928) or of bureaucratic degeneration in *The Bath* (1929) are savaged. Indeed, in the second part of both plays, the future—though too vaguely imagined for scenic purposes—irrupts into the play. In *The Bedbug* it absorbs and quarantines the petty "bedbugus normalis" in its bestiary. In *The Bath* the newly proclaimed Soviet Five-Year-Plan slogan of "Time forward!" materializes into the invention of a time machine that communicates with and leaps into the future, sweeping along the productive and the downtrodden characters but spewing out the bureaucrats. The victory over time was for Mayakovsky a matter of central political, cosmic, and personal importance: intrigued with Einstein's theory of relativity, he firmly expected it to make immortality possible for men. His suicide in 1930 cut him off in the middle of a fierce fight against the bureaucrats whom he envisaged as holding time back and who engineered the failure of Meyerhold's first-rate production of *The Bath*.

The seemingly divergent concerns of Evgeny Zamyatin, when looked at more closely, turn out also to deal with the relationships of the new, future heavens and the old, present earth. The difference is that Zamyatin did not believe in any eschatological end of history. An ex-Bolshevik and rebel against tsarism, a scientist-specialist in ship-building who introduced into his novel *We* (1920–21; bp. 1927) the atmosphere of the shipyards and of the illegal movement, Zamyatin too despised Western capitalism as life-crushing. Certain of the features of a novel satirizing bourgeois respectability and clerical philistinism, which he wrote in England during World War I, such as coupons for sex and a Taylorite "table of compulsory salvation" through minutely regulated daily occupations, recur in *We*. Even after he left the USSR, his major project in the 1930s was a historical novel about Attila and the fall of decadent Rome, a situation which he—with Bryusov and Blok—considered analogous to the East-West conflict of our times. Most significantly, for Zamyatin too the revolution is the undoubted sunlike principle of life and movement, while he bestowed the name of entropy on the principle of dogmatic evil and death. An anti-entropic science, society, and, of course, literature is needed, he affirmed, "as a means for struggling against hardening of arteries, rigidity, moss and peace . . . a utopian literature, absurd as Babeuf in 1797; it will be proved right after 150 years." It is evident that Zamyatin thought of himself as a utopian, paradoxically more revolutionary than the latter-day Bolsheviks, since "the truths of today are the errors of tomorrow: there is no final number" ("On Literature, Revolution and Entropy"). It is thus disingenuous to present him as a primarily anti-Soviet author—even though the increasingly dogmatic and bureaucratic high priests of Soviet letters thought of him so, never allowed his novel to be printed in the USSR, and induced him to leave his country in 1931. Extrapolating the repressive potentials of every strong state and technocratic setup, including the socialist ones, Zamyatin describes a United or Unique State 12 centuries hence having for its leader "the Benefactor" (a prototype for Orwell's Big Brother and the situation in *1984*), where art has become a public utilitarian service, and science a faultless guide for linear, undeviating happiness. Zamyatin's sarcasm against abstract utopian prescriptions (like those of the feebler Wells) takes on Dostoevskian overtones: the threat of the Crystal Palace echoes in the totally rationalized city. The only irrational element left is people, like the split (Marx would have said alienated) narrator, the mathematician and rocketship builder D-503, and the temptress from the underground movement who for a moment makes of him a deviant. But man has, as Dostoevsky's Grand Inquisitor explained to Christ, a built-in instinct for slavery, the rebellion fails, and all the citizen "Numbers" are subjected to brain surgery removing the possibility of harmful imagination.

However, Zamyatin's novel is not consistent. Of a bold general concept, it hesitates midway between Chernyshevsky and Dostoevsky—undecided as to what it thinks of science and reason. After the physician and philosopher Bogdanov and the mathematician Tsiolkovsky, Zamyatin was the first practicing scientist and engineer among significant Russian SF writers. The scientific method provided the paradigm for his thinking, and he could not seriously blame it for the deformations of life. In that case, how is it that a certain type of rationalism, claiming to be scientific, can be harmful in certain social usages? This question, which came up in SF with Butler's *Erewhon* and Wells's best works, Zamyatin was unable to answer except in mythical, Dostoevskian terms: there is "only one conceivable victory—to be crucified. . . . Christ, when factually the victor, becomes the Grand Inquisitor" (in his essay "Scythians?"). The achievement of any lofty ideal inevitably causes it to founder in philistinism. To the extent that *We* equates Leninist Communism with institutionalized Christianity and models its fable on an inevitable Fall from Eden ending in an ironical crucifixion, it has a strong anti-utopian streak. Zamyatin's evocative style shifted the focus to systematic image-building at the expense of the plot, making thus a virtue of his inability to explicate the chosen situation and to reconcile its poles of rationalism and irrationalism, science and art (including the art of love). However, this obscures the problem of whether *any* utopia—even a dynamic one that refuses More's Platonic and Christian model—must of inherent necessity become repressive and dehumanizing. Zamyatin's social ideology conflicts with his own favorite experimental approach: a meaningful exploration of this theme and situation would have to be conducted in terms of the least alienating utopia imaginable—one in which there is no misuse of natural sciences by a dogmatic science of man.

Yet when all this is said, the basic values of *We* imply a stubborn revolutionary vision of a classless new moral world free from all social alienations, a vision common to Anarchism and libertarian Marxism. Zamyatin confronts an anti-utopian, absolutistic, military-type control—extrapolated both from the bourgeois and early socialist state practices—with a utopian-socialist norm. As he wrote in the essay "Tomorrow": "We do not turn to those who reject the present in the name of a return to the past, nor to those hopelessly stupefied by the present, but to those who can see the far-off tomorrow—and in the name of tomorrow, in the name of man, we judge the present." This point of view differs from Mayakovsky's in *The Bath* principally by its ascetic concentration on the deformities, without the explicit counterbalance of a vague future. Indeed, it is significant how for Mayakovsky, too, the utopian anticipation draws further off in time: in poetry, from the twenty-first century of "The Fifth International" (1922) to the 30th century of "The Flying Proletarian" (1925); in dramaturgy, from the 25 years of the scenario *Forget the Hearth* (1927) to the 100 years of *The Bath* (1929). Simultaneously with the poetry of Mayakovsky (whom he called "a magnificent beacon"), Zamyatin brought to Russian SF the realization that the new utopian world cannot be a static changeless paradise of a new religion, albeit a religion of steel, mathematics, and interplanetary flights. Refusing all canonization, the materialist utopia must subject itself to a constant scrutiny by the light of its own principles; its values are for Zamyatin centered in an ever-developing human personality and expressed in an irreducible, life-giving, and subversive erotic passion. For all its resolute one-sidedness, the uses of Zamyatin's bitter and paradoxical warning in a dialectical utopianism seem to be obvious.

The language of the novel is an interesting Expressionist medium vouching for at least some cognitive veracity. It is manipulated for speed and economy, which Zamyatin himself defined as "a high voltage of every word":

> In one second there has to be condensed what before fitted into a whole minute; the syntax becomes elliptical and airy, the complex pyramids of the paragraph are scattered into stone blocks of independent sentences. . . . The picture is sharply focussed, synthetic, it has one basic trait only, which could be noticed from a moving car. Provincialiams, neologisms, science, mathematics, engineering have invaded a vocabulary canonized by usage. ["On Literature, Revolution, and Entropy"]

Zamyatin is a heretic; in places vague and possibly confused, he probably fails to attain a fully consistent structure because of the one-sided assumptions which underlie his writing—but he is certainly not counterrevolutionary. On the contrary, in his own way he tried to work for a future different from that of the envisioned United State. His protagonist is defeated, but the novel as a whole remains concerned with the integrity of man's knowledge (science) and practice (love and art). Even the symbol of $\sqrt{-1}$ (which has an equivalent in the retribalized, "hippie" Mephis in the Green World) is an antithesis to and appeal against a limited Rationalism (the United State) that does not simply reject the thesis—as Dostoevsky's Underground Man did—but includes it in a higher dialectical synthesis prefigured in D-503's oscillation between love and the Integral. Yet, as they are not in Wells, the guilt and possible solution are here placed squarely on man and not on mythical outsiders. Like the formal model of D-503's personalized notes, the laboratory conspectus, the structure of *We* remains open to new cognitions, restless, anti-entropic, and never finally complete. By systematically and sensitively subjecting the deformities it describes to the experimental examination and hyperbolic magnification of SF, Zamyatin's method makes it possible to identify and cope with them. In his own vocabulary, the protagonist's defeat is of the day but not necessarily of the epoch. The defeat in the novel *We* is not the defeat of the novel itself, but an exasperated shocking of the reader into thought and action. It is a document of an acute clash between the "cold" and the "warm" utopia: a judgment on Campanella or Bacon as given by Rabelais or Shelley.

5.2. The 1920s saw, parallel to predominatingly social-science-fiction, the first wave of Russian SF that organically blended sociological with natural-science fiction primarily oriented toward interplanetary adventures. The great pioneer of both Russian astronautics and Soviet SF was Konstantin Tsiolkovsky, a mathematics teacher who by the 1890s had begun his speculations on mankind's cosmic destiny in the depths of a tsarist provincial town, writing for propagandist purposes two SF booklets illustrating a possible happy weightless life on asteroids, the Moon, and on rocket colonies in space (*On the Moon*, 1887; *Daydreams of Earth and Heavens*, 1894). The Soviet regime enthusiastically took up his unheeded ideas; Tsiolkovsky wrote his best SF story, *Outside Earth*, in 1918 and proceeded to develop his scientific plans with public means, becoming the venerated teacher of

the future Sputnik and Vostok constructors as well as of SF fans
and writers such as Belyaev. I referred earlier to the general
enthusiasm for a revolutionary "storming of the heavens" in the
1920s, as expressed by Bryusov, Mayakovsky, and the "Cosmists," and skeptically reflected even in Zamyatin's *We* as well as
in his story "The Most Important Thing" (1924). Astronautic
study circles, public lectures and expositions got under way at
that time; in the midst of the civil war the tireless Lenin, having
read Percival Lowell's book about Mars and debated the Martian
novels with Bogdanov, went in 1920 to listen to a public lecture
on the project of a cosmic ship, and, talking with Wells, concluded that if mankind ever comes to other planets all our
philosophical, moral and social assumptions will have to be re-
examined. In 1925 Moscow University organized a debate on
"The Flight to Other Worlds," and in 1925–26 the first specialized adventure periodicals carrying largely SF appeared, such
as *War of the Worlds, Universal Detective, Knowledge is Strength*,
and *World of Adventure*. In the NEP heyday of private publishing
the Soviet book market was flooded by large quantities of translated European and US subliterary SF, such as E.Ṙ. Burroughs's
Martian cycle; not counting the perennially popular Verne and
Wells, more than 100 novels and stories were translated between
1923 and 1930 (as compared with 155 original Soviet Russian
novels and stories published between 1920 and 1927). In such an
atmosphere the genre was given the accolade of literary quality
and respectability by the well-known writer Alexei N. Tolstoy,
who in his novels *Aelita* and *The Garin Death-Ray* blended the
adventure of interplanetary flight and conflicts—namely, the
global struggle for a new scientific invention—with a utopian
pathos arising from revolutionary social perspectives in a way
calculated to please almost all segments of the reading public.
This blend was to remain the basic Soviet SF tradition till the end
of the 1960s.

In *Aelita* (1922), written while Tolstoy was still an emigré preparing to return to the Soviet Union, this blend is endearingly
enriched with a lyrical component, the love of Los, the inventor
of the rocketship, for the Martian princess Aelita. Los, the creative intellectual, with his vacillations and individualist concerns,
is contrasted to but also allied with Gusev, a shrewd man of the
people and fearless fighter who leads the revolt of Martian

workers (the Martians are descendants of the Atlantans) against the decadent dictatorship of the Engineers' Council. If the standard adventure and romance were taken over from Wells and the contemporary subliterary SF (Benoit's *Atlantis* and Burroughs's *A Princess of the Moon* probably—both were translated in the USSR), the politics are diametrically opposed to Lasswitz's and Bogdanov's idea of a Martian benevolent technocracy. Yet if the workers' uprising led by a Red Army man was a clear parable for the times, such as could have been shared by all Soviet SF from Mayakovsky to Zamyatin, the dejected and somewhat hasty return which has Los listening at the end to the desperate wireless calls of his beloved is as clearly of a Wellsian gloom (*The First Men on the Moon*). But this ambiguity, which sometimes strains the plot mechanics, makes also for a counterpointing richness, an encompassing of differing attitudes and levels that envisages the price as well as the necessity of an activist happiness. Since the novel's plastic characterization, rich and differentiated language, and consistent verisimilitude (once the reader accepts the underlying premise) lifted it to the level of the literary mainstream, much as Wells had done for the SF novel in Britain, it became the first universally accepted masterpiece of Soviet SF. In particular, *Aelita* raised extraterrestrial utopianism beyond pulp imitations of Verne, Wells, and Burroughs (by Mukhanov, Arelsky, Grave, Yazvitsky or Goncharov), to a height not to be reached again until Yefremov.

Tolstoy's second SF novel, *Engineer Garin's Death-Ray* (in four versions from 1926 to 1937), is a retreat to the "catastrophe" novel: Vernean adventures and Chestertonian detections and conspiracies center around an amoral scientist who beats the capitalist industry kings at their own game but comes to grief when faced with popular revolt. It moves fast if jerkily; as Tolstoy was a trained engineer, its science is believable (atomic distintegration of a transuranium element is posited as well as something resembling lasers), and it remains a prototype of the anti-imperialist and anti-fascist concern in Soviet SF. This concern has always been a vigorous strand in its skein, whether as direct political satire (as in Ehrenburg or Lavrenyev, or in later interwar works such as Turov's *Island of Gorilloids*, Zuyev-Ordynets's *Panurge's Herd*, or Shishko's *The End of Common Sense*), as the more dubious Soviet-invention-cum-foreign-spy thrillers cropping up frequently from that time on (for example, atomic energy in the play *Gold and Brains* by A. Glebov, 1929), or as the pamphleteering story popular among postwar writers like Lagin, Savchenko, Toman, Dneprov, and Varshavsky. In the 1920s numerous novels adopted the *Garin Death-Ray* combination of scientific thriller and politically virtuous anticipation (beside those already mentioned: A. Yaroslavski's *The Argonauts of Space*, V. Orlovsky's *The Horror Machine* and *The Revolt of Atoms*, N. Karpov's *Death Rays*, S. Grigoryev's *The Fall of Britain*, F. Bogdanov's *Twice Born*, I. Keller and V. Hirschhorn's *Universal Rays*, and others).

Soviet SF of the 1920s had thus established a tradition ranging sociologically from facile subliterature to some of the most interesting works of "highbrow" fiction produced in that golden age. It had embraced further and nearer anticipation, global and interplanetary tales; adventure, politics, utopianism, and technology; ethics and romance; novels, stories, poems, plays, essays, and movies (eight silent SF movies were shot in the years before 1926, beginning with Jack London's *Iron Heel* in 1919, for which the scenario was written by no less a dignitary than the comissar for education Lunacharsky; continuing with a rather bad *Aelita* in 1924, and ending with *The Sale of an Appetite* based on Paul Lafargue's story). It had sketched in most of the themes and topoi of modern SF—galactic warfare being conspicuously rare —including anti-utopianism, automation, and the social consequences of "value-free" natural science. Its common denominator was a sometimes naive but genuinely enthusiastic, thoroughgoing, and humanist critique of old Europe and America, that is to say, of the short-sighted and alienating capitalist lifestyle.

6. In about 1927 Soviet concentration on national industrial buildup at the expense of global revolutionary romanticism, with future sociological horizons jelling into a planned quantitative growth and thus decreasing in imaginative novelty, began strongly to favor linear technological and natural-science extrapolation. Within a general European movement toward a "realistic objectivity" (*Neue Sachlichkeit*), Soviet literary horizons grew less cosmic and grandiose: the SF estrangement shifted into the domain of amazing adventures and/or inventions. World revolution and far-ranging anticipations were replaced with detailed but flat descriptions of the technologically changed near

future or of SF adventures in an abstract, often foreign-sounding (a convention still strong today) or planetary setting. This constituted a return to the nineteenth-century traditions of Verne and Wells. Prerevolutionary Vernean writings had continued to exert influence, as in the geologist and geographer V. Obruchev's two novels about prehistoric environments, *Plutonia* (1924, a hollow-Earth setting) and *Sannikov-Land* (1926, North Pole oasis). As for the never-ceasing Russian fascination with Wells, it could simply turn to his ostensibly shorter-range tales like *The Island of Dr. Moreau* or *The Invisible Man*. In this tradition, the most prominent and still widely read author is Alexander Belyaev, the first Russian writing exclusively SF. In numerous stories and about 20 novels he fused breathtaking Vernean adventures of a romantically alienated hero with new and bold scientific themes: biological adaptation and transplantation, often brain surgery, as in his first novel *Professor Dowell's Head* (1925)—much superior to its French predecessor, Maurice Renard's *Le Docteur Lerne*; the impact of various, often humorous scientific inventions in the cycle of "Professor Wagner," 1926–36; and several novels in the 1930s domesticating Tsiolkovski's notions. His most interesting works focus on the resistances to and anxiety of the novum's bearer—a scientist with humanistic ideals, a biologically modified man like the flying Ariel in the novel of the same title (1941) or Ichthyander in his most popular novel *The Amphibian Man* (1928), or quite openly an artist like Presto in the two variant novels *The Man Who Lost His Face* (1929) and *The Man Who Found His Face* (1940). Such works, imbued with an aching lyricism and a vibrant humanistic vehemence, remain of significance today, as do some articles by this penetrating SF critic. But often Belyaev's hero triumphs simply thanks to an essentially fairytale metamorphosis that allows him to vanquish physical gravity and social injustice. The black-and-white opposition of his threatened hero to a grotesque capitalist environment becomes then a form of escapism into a wicked Ruritania, to which Belyaev added in the 1930s—partly because of political constraints—detective and spy-thriller elements.

In fact, the promise of the revolutionary years—when it appeared probable that the Russian school (or indeed schools) would dominate our times in SF as well as in movies, painting, or theater—was not fulfiled: the historical sense, the dimension of imaginative experimentation (both utopian and anti-utopian) was forcibly expunged from it. The sectarian RAPP critics opened in 1929–30 a strong campaign against SF as a harmful genre, and succeeded in ending almost totally its publication. From an average of about 25 new books per year in the mid-1920s (47 in the peak year 1927), the publication plummeted to 4 in 1931, and one each in 1933 and 1934. Only in 1935 was SF, properly sterilized, partly rehabilitated as a marginal,—juvenile and popularizing—genre. Anticipating possible developments became a suicidal pursuit at a time when Stalin was the only one supposed to "foresee" the future, when cosmonautics were mentioned in the same breath with bourgeois cosmopolitism, and a number of scientists and writers—including the utopographer Nikolsky and most of the Leningrad Section for Scientific Fiction, comprising the well-known SF writers and critics Perelman, Rynin, Uspensky, as well as others—were jailed or indeed executed. As a result, in the 25 years beginning with Mayakovsky's death and Zamyatin's departure and up to Yefremov's *Andromeda*, of the approximately 300 new stories or novels in Russian SF, extremely few were significant anticipations—though the appearance of anticipations by oblique incorporation into the work of major fiction and screen writers such as Yury Olesha, Aleksandr Dovzhenko, or Leonid Leonov (one layer of his three-level novel *The Journey Toward the Ocean*, 1935, with its picture of future world wars and interplanetary flight, verges on a self-contained vision worthy of Wells and *The Iron Heel*) testifies to its latent vitality. But the constitution of SF moods and elements into a significant genre in its own right was cut short by the imposed Stalinist attitude toward SF known as the "theory of limits" or, with more sophistry, the "theory of nearer aims." Its acolytes propounded that (as the Soviet critic Riurikov sums it up) literary anticipation had to solve only technological problems of the nearest future, and that it should not attempt to go beyond such limits, for only thus will it remain based on socialist realism. Thus SF was reduced to extolling technology, and its ethics turned pragmatic. Of all such novels about bigger and better oil-drills, radars, or solar energy uses, the least boring were those depicting Arctic exploration and transformation (Lissovoy, Grebnev, Adamov, Kazantsev), since this was luckily both in the Vernean semi-utopian tradition and the region of many intrepid exploits of the Soviet 1930s. But just as the few remaining anticipation novels were exclusively juvenile, so all of these mixtures of technological adventure and patriotic—sometimes even military—pride (for example, the closing sections of Pavlenko's *In the East* or Adamov's *Secret of Two Oceans*) fade more or less into subliterature. Yuriy Dolgushin's novel *The Generator of Miracles* (1940, bp. 1959), approaching some bionic ideas, was probably the most interesting among them.

Such stagnation within utilitarian horizons and stereotyped situations and characters (the heroic expedition or project-leader, the corrupted intellectual doubter, the foreign spy or saboteur) earned Soviet SF from the mid-1930s to the mid-1950s the reputation of a second-rate cross-breed, neither really artistic nor scientific. A first reaction to this was an increase, in the 1950s, of detective and adventure elements (Nemtsov, Kazantsev). This was perhaps helpful in momentarily dispelling the reigning monotony, but a meteor alarm instead of a sabotage does not much raise the cognitive or imaginative level of SF. (The technological-adventure SF—analogous to the SF in the United States in the 1930s—based on a Morality triangle of a starry-eyed beginner set between a wise elder leader and a careerist, egotistic antagonist has lived on tenaciously in the foothills of Soviet SF.)

7.   The second great age of Soviet SF accordingly came about with a specific regeneration of its utopian imaginativeness in the decade or so following on 1956. The reasons which made it possible are obvious. The twentieth congress of the Soviet Communist party in 1956 destroyed the indisputability of Stalinist myths about society and literature. They were further shaken by the sensational achievements of Soviet natural sciences, exemplified by the first Sputnik. The new SF wave, rich in tradition and individual talent, eager to deal with an increasing range of subjects, from sociological to cosmological and anthropological, from astronautic through cybernetic to anticipatory-utopian, found a wide audience among the young and the intelligentsia. We have no sure statistics on this reading public, but it was probably as large if not at times larger than its American counterpart. It was perhaps unsophisticated, but impatient of the old clichés and thirsting after knowledge and imagination. Its tastes carried the day in the great "Yefremov debate."

Indeed, in the history of Russian and Soviet SF, only

Chernyshevsky's—and probably Mayakovsky's—work had so taken by storm young people, especially the younger scientists, and earned the genre such general esteem as did Yefremov's novel *Andromeda*. Subsequent developments in Soviet SF can be understood only as growing out of its having, against violent ideological opposition, consummated in 1957–58 the victory of the new wave—which was really the victory of the pristine Soviet Russian tradition, in abeyance since the Leninist 1920s. The writers and critics of the "cold stream" rebuked the novel's heroes as being "too far from our times" and thus unintelligible to the reader, especially the juvenile reader(!). In short, they were saying that Yefremov's scope was too daring. Such pressure had for 15 years hindered the publication and development of Yefremov's SF (his first SF story, "The Hellenic Secret" from 1942, dealing with "gene memory," was thought of as mystical and published only in 1966). However, the opinion of "warm stream" critics, and of the thousands of readers who wrote to the author, newspapers, and periodicals, that this was a liberating turning-point in Soviet SF finally prevailed. The novel has since been reprinted about 30 times, not counting its probably equally numerous translations.

Yefremov's work achieved such historical significance because, in its own way, it creatively revived the classical utopian and socialist vision, the resilience of which had so flabbergasted Wells in his meeting with Lenin. This vision (Marx's, Chernyshevsky's, Morris's, or even the mellower Wells's) looks forward to a unified, affluent, humanist, classless, and stateless world. *Andromeda* is situated in the four hundred and eighth year of the Era of the Great Ring, when mankind has established informational contact with inhabitants of distant constellations who pass on such information to each other through a "ring" of inhabited systems. The Earth itself is administered—by analogy with the associative centers of the human brain—by an astronautic council and an economic council which tallies all plans with existing possibilities; their specialized research academies correspond to man's sensory centers. Within this framework of the body politic, Yefremov is primarily interested in the development of a disalienated man and new ethical relationships. For all the theatrical loftiness of his characters, whose emotions are rarely less sublime than full satisfaction and confidence (only an occasional melodramatic villain feels

fear or hate), they can learn through painful mistakes and failures, as distinct from the desperado and superman clichés of
"socialist realism" or much American SF after Gernsback.

The reexhumation of socialist utopianism brought back into
Soviet fiction whole reaches of the SF tradition: the philosophical
story and romantic *étude*, classic sociological and modern cosmological utopianism. Yet in Yefremov's novel the strong narrative sweep full of adventurous actions, from a fistfight to an
encounter with electrical predators and a robot-spaceship from
the Andromeda nebula, is imbued with the joy and romance of
cognition. This certainly embraces an understanding of, and intervening into, the outside world of modern cosmology and
evolutionist biology. But Yefremov's strong anthropocentric bent
places the highest value on creativity, a simultaneous adventure
of deed, thought, and feeling resulting in physical and ethical
(body and mind being indissolubly connected in this materialist
writer) beauty. His utopian anthropology is evident even in the
symbolic title: the Andromeda nebula recalls the chained Greek
beauty rescued from a monster (class egotism and violence, personified in the novel as a bull and often bearing hallmarks of
Stalinism) by a flying hero aided by superior science. Astronautics thus do not evolve into a new uncritical cult but are claimed
as a humanist discipline, in one of the most signifiant cross-
connections among physical sciences, social sciences, ethics, and
art that Yefremov establishes as the norm for his new people.
Even the novel structure, oscillating between cosmic and terrestrial chapters, emphasizes this connection. Furthermore, this future is not an arrested, pseudo-perfect end of history—the bane
of optimistic utopianism from Plato and More to Bellamy. Freed
from economic and power worries, people must still redeem
time, which is unequal on Earth and in space, through a
humanist dialectics of personal creativity and societal teamwork
mediated—in a clear harking back to the ideals of the 1920s—by
the artistic and scientific beauty of functionality (Dar listening to
the cosmic symphony, or the Tibetan experiment). Creativity is
always countered by entropy, and self-realization paid for in effort and even suffering. In fact, several very interesting approaches to a Marxist "optimistic tragedy" can be found in the
book (for example, in the Mven Mass "happy Fall" motif). Finally, the accent on beauty and responsible freedom places

Chernyshevskian female heroines in the center of the novel, interacting with the heroes and contributing to the emotional motivation of new utopian ethics, in complete contrast to contemporary American SF (with which Yefremov was obviously in a well-informed polemical dialogue).

How difficult it is for an SF writer to portray basically different, even if philosophically already sketched human relations, can be seen from some places where the novel's dialogue, motivation, and tone flag, so that it falls back on pathos and preaching, which slow down its rhythm. Yefremov's characters tend to be statuesque and monolithic in a kind of neoclassic way, and his incidents often exploit the quantitatively grandiose: Mven blows up a satellite and half a mountain, Veda loses the greatest anthropological find ever, and to think of the manly Erg blushing or the pure Nisa stepping into, say, offensive jellyfish offal on the iron-star planet is practically blasphemous. Most of this can be explained by *Andromeda*'s having had to achieve several aims at once: it was the first work to burst open the floodgates closed for 25 years, and it overflowed into clogged channels. One feels in it the presence of a reader unused to fast orientation in new perspectives and, as Yefremov himself wrote, "still attracted to the externals, decorations, and theatrical effects of the genre." But it cannot be denied that some aspects of Yefremov's ethics and aesthetics, such as the erotic and generally intimate interpersonal relations—though understandable enough in the context of the social taboos obvious to a Soviet Russian scientist of an older generation—are curiously old-fashioned for a sweeping SF glance. His limitations are more clearly manifested in the later long story *Cor Serpentis*, where Terrans meeting a fluorine-based mankind put an end to its loneliness by promising to transmute fluorine into oxygen. This story—an explicit counterblast to the US story "First Contact" (by Murray Leinster), with its bellicose and acquisitive presuppositions—might be a legitimate pacifist-socialist allegory for changing American capitalist meritocrats into Russian socialist ones, yet such an ethnocentric view precludes a full development of imaginative SF vistas, the point of which is unity in variety. But again any further discussion of such vistas in Soviet SF was made possible by Yefremov's pioneering effort. *Andromeda*'s polyphonic scope, with its large number of protagonists, is

Tolstoian rather than Flaubertian. Not being limited to the consciousness of the central hero, it is perhaps, together with Lem's
Magellan Nebula in Poland, the first utopia in world literature
which successfully shows new characters creating and being
created by a new society, that is, *the personal working out of a
collective utopia* (analogous to what Scott did for the historical
novel). Yefremov's basic device of unfolding the narration as if
the anticipated future were already a normative present unites
the classic "looking backward" of utopian anticipations with the
modern Einsteinian conception of different coordinate systems
with autonomous norms; twentieth-century science and the age-
old dreams of a just and happy society meet in his novel. This
meeting made it the nodal point of the Russian and socialist
tradition examined in this chapter. And this is also why the novel
was able to usher in the new era of Soviet SF—an era which
seems to have closed with the 1960s.

Subsequent developments and differentiations within Soviet
SF can be fully appreciated only from this perspective. In the
dozen years of its second flowering, mastering new themes and
approaches, it has produced a considerable body of significant
works. It has assembled about 50 habitual (though not full-time)
writers, an insatiable reading public, an expectation of literary
clarity and careful craftsmanship, and it has avoided being confused with fantasy, gangster novels, horror thrillers, and cloak-
and-dagger adventures, though not with the more deeply rooted
national tradition of the folktale. Perhaps most important for
understanding it is the fact of its leading writers having opted
for a *hope* that grows out of the central position of functionally
clear human figures. They have, in other words, developed the
basic philosophical and literary tradition of socialism—utopianism, equated here with the open horizons of anticipated humanizing potentialities.

The "Yefremov era" in Soviet SF is now fast receding into
history. But the failure of the original utopian confidence from
the mid-1960s on, to which Yefremov's own later works also
testify both in overt ideological profiles and in their reduced
significance, is in the practice of significant subsequent Soviet
SF—in the cases of the Strugatsky brothers, of Varshavsky or
Shefner—itself measured and judged by the values of that utopian and dealienating horizon that is its permanent hallmark.

12

Karel Čapek,
or the Aliens Amongst Us

1. There is both irony and poetic justice in the fact that Karel Čapek is today, at least outside the Slavic countries, remembered mainly as the creator of the word *robot*. A first irony is that this neologism—from the archaic Czech *robota*, meaning "drudgery" with strong feudal connotations of the serf's compulsory work on the master's property—was coined by Karel's brother Josef, a prominent painter and writer with whom he collaborated on a number of early works, including the plays *From the Life of the Insects* and *Adam the Creator*, and who himself wrote a symbolistic SF play (*Land of Many Names*, 1923). A second irony is that Karel Čapek's eight plays are, despite the world popularity of some among them (including *Rossum's Universal Robots*, or *R.U.R.*), the weakest part of his opus, which comprises about fifty books of stories, essays, travelogues, novels, and articles. The poetic justice, however, stems from the fact that a quite central preoccupation of his was with the potentials and actualizations of inhumanity in twentieth-century people, and that this preoccupation was throughout his whole opus translated into the image of the Natural Man versus the Unnatural Pseudo-Man. This manlike, reasonable but unfeeling being is in Čapek's work represented by a number of approximations, one of the first among which were the robots of *R.U.R.*

Josef Čapek's happy coinage, with its blend of psychophysiological and political meanings, hits thus the bull's-eye of what his brother was trying to get at. For all of Karel's menacing, inhuman beings are associated with and rendered possible by capitalist industrial technology with its accompanying social extremes of the upper-class tycoon and the working-class multitude. The criterion of naturalness is for Čapek drawn from the middle class, and his heroes range from small employees and craftsmen to doctors and engineers. Born in 1890, he himself grew up as the son of a physician in a rural district, in a home which he characterized "like thousands of other homes in the bourgeois world of that time," and in a semi-colonial state which made of the Czechs "on the whole, a nation of petty bourgeois." Čapek's grandparents were peasants, and some of his most stubborn values and prejudices can be traced back to the traditional peasant confidence in the immediately available, secure, everyday things and relationships of the little people, as opposed to the *hubris* of the hustling and bustling modern industry and the swift changes it brings about. In the plays, this attitude is openly expressed by his small people who act as ideological arbiters, such as Nana in *R.U.R.* or Kristina in *The Makropoulos Secret*; in the novels, it is implied by strategic collocations of key actions, such as the return to normality at the endings of *Krakatit* and *The Factory for the Absolute*; but as a rule, it pervades all of Čapek's works. On the other hand, he was "enchanted and terrified" by the world of factories and technology—the workers' districts of Prague and the miners of his childhood days—as well as the "pride, power, wealth" of the capitalists such as the emblematic Mr. Bondy from both the symbolically named *The Factory for the Absolute* and *War With the Newts*. Čapek's SF was written to deal with "great social interests and collective spiritual problems" arising out of "the leading ideas of science, guesses about the future, feats of technology"—that is, to deal with the destructive menaces which the irruption of modern mass production brings to the little man.[1]

Therefore, in Čapek's first SF phase, which extends through the decade following World War I, there is a basic tension between the "natural," average little people, representative of the audience he was writing for, and the catastrophic forces of inhuman violence amid which they have to live, suffer, and die. For Čapek, inhuman, large-scale technology and industry lead in politics logically to international and civil warfare. A fatal ambiguity between the menace to Man as such and the menace to the middle-class man vitiates this whole phase of his work, its

---

1. All these quotations are from Karel Čapek as cited in Alexander Matushka (Bibliography VII)—the first from p. 78, the second from p. 94, the third and fourth from p. 230, and the last two from p. 93.

qualities lying in what he managed to do in spite of and on the margins of such an ideological muddle. For the menace to Man's existence arises from aliens created and abetted by large industry and its capitalist masters and engineering managers; but the menace to middle-class life arises from the workers, who had in Russia just seized power in the Bolshevik revolution. The "robots" of R.U.R. (1920), synthetic androids outwardly indistinguishable from men, are mass-produced for the express purpose of being "workers with the minimum amount of requirements" (act 1), improved producers with a machinelike precision but without the nonexploitable qualities of emotion, sex, art, and the like. In their first story "System" (1908) the Čapek brothers had in fact dealt with a workers' revolt in such circumstances. The machine-men of R.U.R, each of whom replaces two and a half workers, are a technolgical variant of the workers from "System" or of the Morlocks, Wells's workers of the future who also became the new lords of the creation. But in Čapek robots are not only stand-ins for workers but also—in an ideological mystification which brought him instant fame because it corresponded to deep needs for self-delusion in his audience—inhuman aliens "without history" (R.U.R., act 1). Thus their creation does not lead to Domin's engineering utopia of total abundance and leisure which would breed Nietzschean supermen, but to a genocidal revolt of the submen against humans. The only surviving man is the Tolstoian pacifist Alquist, an architect who had dealt in construction rather than in the blasphemous progress of the robots' producers. But at the end of the play, the robots again grow more like a new human order than like inhuman aliens, more like workers than machines; reacquiring pain, feelings, and love, they usher in a new cycle of creation or civilization. For all the interest inherent in the basic concept and the theater tricks of Čapek's, this fundamental oscillation between mutually incompatible ways of envisaging the robots—which also means an oscillation between old-fashioned psychological and modern "collective" drama—has by now dated this play.

In *From the Life of the Insects* (1921, also translated as *The Insect Play* or *Comedy; The World We Live In*; and *And So Ad Infinitum*) human moral concepts and social behaviors are personified as insects: the flighty erotics of the butterflies are a takeoff on the upper-class "golden youth" of postwar Middle Europe, the dung-beetle and cricket families on the acquisitive and sentimen-tal petty bourgeoisie, and the ants on robotlike militarism and chauvinist nationalism of the masses and their leaders. The ani-mal fable is used for a "surprising and cruel analogy" and bitter satire of the "insect selfishness" of human individuals and collec-tives,[2] for a Morality play which is the Čapeks' best stage product. Especially memorable is the ants' act, with its portrayal of the war-machine collective, which progresses from Taylorism trans-ferred wholesale from industrial to military behavior to a death-lust racism. On the contrary, both the biblical Expressionism of *Adam the Creator* (1927) and the psychological detection of *The Makropoulos Secret* (1922, about the elixir of longevity and very similar to Godwin's *St. Leon*) are very shakily allied to a defeatist humanism, and make for Čapek's feeblest SF plays.

Čapek's real strength as an SF writer lies in his novels. *The Factory for the Absolute* (1922, also translated as *The Manufacture of the Absolute* and *The Absolute at Large*) is a revue-novel (Čapek called it a "column-novel") based on another destructive inven-tion which was supposed to usher in a utopia. It is the Absolute or God, mass-produced as a by-product of atomic fission in "kar-burators" that rapidly take over as the cheap suppliers of the world's energy. The concept is a fortunate one, combining wildly hilarious with weighty philosophical possibilities. And the novel is chock-full of irony and satire on the uses and abuses of the Absolute by church and state, corporations and individuals, academics and journalists. It bears out the cynical Catholic bishop who declares that mankind cannot cope with "a real and active God": both the economic system, when faced with bound-lessly cheap overproduction but no adequate distribution, and the personal relationships, when faced with the Absolute work-ing within variously oriented individual consciences, simply col-lapse. Sectarian and national fanaticism multiplies when the Absolute gets control of the two greatest powers in the world, "industry and the masses." This leads to a final "Greatest War," recapitulating the experiences from the Thirty Years' War through Napoleon to World War I, which peters out only after all "atomotors" have been destroyed and most people killed.

---

2. Čapek's formulation, cited in Matushka, p. 298.

However, it is not clear why the "mystical Communism" of the Absolute must bend itself to the capitalist forms of economic organization and to individualist competitive psychology, which are illogically assumed to be stronger than even an absolute power. Further, the disparate workings of the Absolute in things (overproduction of industrial goods only, not of farm produce or communications) and in people (destructiveness to match the overproduction) do not follow any consistent pattern either. Thus, instead of being a true Absolute, the power which is unleashed by the atomotors is for Čapek simply a chaotic magnification of the antagonisms inherent in acquisitive economics and psychology. This makes for brilliant if spotty social satire, but hardly for consistent SF conceptualization. That is why by the middle of the novel Čapek has to substitute for logical explanations a dazzling display of chronicle overviews alternating with hyperbolic and grotesque snapshots. The only people who retain a tightfisted "normality" are the farmers, and the final chapter culminates in a typically Czech beer-and-sausage feast of the little people, which is consecrated as the highest achievable form of tolerance and everyday happiness. As already seen in *R.U.R.*, any highminded idea leads necessarily to huge disasters, and one should stick to the pragmatic immediacy of people believing in other people. Not even the Absolute can improve men, religions, or the bourgeois institutions: the paradoxes of this creed explain but do not cancel out the inconsistencies of the novel.

The parallel of men and matter is carried forward in Čapek's most unjustly neglected work of SF, the novel *Krakatit* (1924, also transalted as *An Atomic Phantasy*). Different from his earlier works, it has a romantic hero—Prokop, the naive inventor-genius who pierces the secret of explosiveness (atomic fission). But such "destructive chemistry" is also taking place in humans, and this bulky novel is as full of Dostoevskian fevered dreams and nightmares, dissociations of memory, and explosive human encounters as of physical explosions, fights, and escapes. The plot traces Prokop's development from a solitary "value-free" scientist caring only about matter to a wiser human being who has painfully learned about the primacy of human relationships: "His hair stood on end in horror at the nature of the forces among which we live." Čapek has in *Krakatit* made a conscious and significant attempt to integrate popular paraliterature—in particular the detective story and the epic adventure from Homer through the folktale to pulp thrillers—into sophisticated, poetic SF dealing with central questions of modern life. He wanted to fuse the "love and heroism" of a sensational newspaper story or a "novel for serving-maids"[3] with a psychological narrative, and the overtones of countercreation inherent in a mad scientist story with a sympathetic, suffering and relatively complex hero whose education advances through a series of erotic-cum-political temptations. For once, Čapek's hero rejects not only the militarist temptation of established power and the nihilist temptation of new, personal power (since the explosive force of power necessarily leads to violence), but also the small-town idyll or island of repose. He is left with a resolve to achieve useful warmth instead of destructive explosions: "He whose thoughts are full of the highest turns his eyes away from the people. Instead you will serve them. . . ," Prokop is told by the mysterious Grandfather he meets at the end. From the fog of suffering and yearning, the hero has finally emerged into the clarity of moderation: his earth-shaking invention will be refunctioned. Though the novel has not quite succeeded in fusing realism and allegory, because it has not quite solved how to fuse ethical moderation with the certainties of the folktale, it is a largely successful first try at transcending the sterile opposition between scientific progress and human happiness which has haunted science fiction from Swift and Voltaire (Čapek's teachers) to the present day. For the first and last time in Čapek's SF, a believable hero fights successfully back at the destructive forces within himself and society.

2. The second phase of Čapek's SF was the result of the rise of Nazism, which threatened directly both his native land and his basic values. It comprises a few minor stories on the margins of SF, satire, and fantasy, as well as the novel *War With the Newts* (1936), and the *The White Sickness* (1937, also translated as *The White Plague* or *Scourge*, and *The Power and the Glory*). By this time Čapek had shed many of his illusions, in particular his prejudice in favor of the little man's instinctual rightness and of everybody having his own truth. In *R.U.R.*, for example, all figures—from the Nietzschean utopist Domin through his various director col-

---

3. Eva Strohsová (Bibliography VII), p. 131.

leagues to the robots themselves—were right in their own way; the same is true in *The Factory for the Absolute*. But already in *Krakatit* this relativism was waning, and after the rise of Hitler, Čapek reconsidered the role of the intellect which he satirized earlier (for example, in the name of the robots' inventor, which translates as Mr. Reasson). Now he wrote sharply against an intellect that is giving up its rights "in favor of irrationalism and daimonism, be it the cult of will, of the land, of the subconscious, of the mass instincts, or of the violence of the powerful—that is a decadent intellect because it tends toward its own downfall."[4] A limit was found beyond which the pseudo-human became clearly evil; that limit is reached when the new creatures in *War With the Newts* grow into an analogy to the Nazi aggressors. That is why in his final SF novel Čapek's satire is most clearly focused, the development of the novum most consistent, and there is no conciliatory happy ending. "This is not a speculation about something in the future," Čapek said about it, "but a mirroring of what exists and amid what we live."[5] Let us briefly analyze the development of this remarkable novel.

War With the Newts (properly *War With the Salamanders*) is divided into three "books," the first of which, "Andrias Scheuchzeri," shows, beneath its ironically neutral, scientific name, the Salamanders entering the life of mankind on the wrong foot, as it were—that is, under a cloud of delusions and misperceptions. The satire is aimed at the fictions of mankind which prevent it from seeing the rise of a catastrophic menace. The first five chapters are an increasingly ironic counterfeit of the exotic adventure tale associated with the names of Sindbad, Kipling, Conrad, London, and others. It shows how the Salamanders are led to an independence (confirmed by the ironic dates of July 3 and 13 instead of the proper US and French liberation dates of July 4 and 14) from their biological and geographical barriers. This is possible because first Captain van Toch and then the business tycoon Bondy see in them a juvenile romantic adventure, in which the misanthropic captain with the baby-blue eyes plays the role of a Salamander culture-hero, and the businessman that of a merchant-adventurer's financier. In the dou-

4. Čapek's article in the newspaper *Přitomnost*, No. 29 (1934).
5. See Čapek's book *Poznámky o tvorbě* (Prague, 1959), p. 110.

ble chapter 6–7 the Salamanders are recognized by the world through its two most virulent illusion industries—capitalist movies and sensational tabloid newspapers oriented toward erotic and exotic clichés. The Hollywood way of apprehending the world in terms of platinum blondes, exotic monsters, and native treasures is mercilessly satirized because it screens from mankind the reality of human, social, and biological events both by suppression of episodes that do not fit the clichés and by an inability to think outside such clichés (Abe and Li). Thus the rise of the Salamanders is interwoven with a satire of human obfuscations, in particular of the means of communication. This satire is most intimately woven into the very composition and texture of Čapek's novel, since its various segments debunk the various genres and conventions of informational transmission. After the exotic, basically juvenile adventure story, the tabloid sensations, and the South Sea movie (to which will later be added the pseudo-historical movie of the *Henry VIII* type), in chapters 8–11 the pseudo-scientific way of data collecting and dissemination from observations in zoos, interviews, and newspaper popularizations is taken to task. It is made clear that it is as charlatanic as the interpolated country-fair show of a false "Captain van Toch and his trained lizards." (It is worth noticing that the exotic names of both the captain and the movie star Lily Valley mask the prosaic Czech names of Vantoch and Nowak.) Professional scientists and academics are shown to be as myopic, timid, and ideologically limited—especially in their nationalistic subservience to the powers that be—as the public at large; in the Hitler decade Čapek noted with a sinking heart but firm glance that the treason of the intellectuals to their humanist calling was proceeding apace. But the real political villains were the capitalists who financed the menace to humanity (Nazis as well as Newts); and the fulcrum of the novel's first part is chapter 12, the formation of the Salamander Syndicate, which moves from the fairy tale and juvenile-epic mode of dealing with the Salamanders to an industrial utopianism, a "hymn of construction" satirized in Čapek's minutes of a corporation meeting. At this point, the Salamanders—who began as exotic monstrosities or pets, and in chapters 9 and 10 demonstrated that they were psychologically and physically no more monstrous than the average human (the newspaper-reading Englishman or the Czech fat lady)—begin to be treated as an "extremely cheap labor force," "toilers of the sea" halfway between expendable undermen and a new trained subproletariat. Čapek thus gives us a shortened genesis of capitalism. Beginning as a competitive colonial merchant-buccaneering, it is in this chapter qualitatively transformed to a global, monopolistic, and exploitative corporation aiming at a new Atlantis, at remodeling the Earth; eventually, it will end as Atlantis did, unable to control the globally destructive forces it has unleashed for exploitation but never really understood. "Do I know what a Newt is like? What good is that to me?" says the wistful tycoon Bondy, echoing Brecht's famous "Song of the Commodity":

> What is in fact rice?
> Do I know what rice is?
> Do I know who knows that?!
> I don't know what rice is,
> I know only its price.
>   [*The Measures Taken*]

From this point on, the global scale and technologicoeconomical acceleration of Salamandrism will necessitate a larger and brisker overview. There is just time, in the first part, to insert an appendix on the Salamanders' sexual life, as a clue that the Salamander Syndicate's utopia is the greatest illusion of them all. The Salamanders' ominous, Nazi-like "Collective Male" horde, capable of politics and technics but not of real sociability, testifies that the Syndicate has misunderstood the basic nature of the demon it has let out of the bottle.

The second book of *War With the Newts* is titled "Along the Steps of Civilization"—which, bitterly, means along the steps to war. The Salamanders "progress" from animals first to slaves, then to an increasingly powerful alternative society with class differentiation, industry, economic and military power. At the same time they remain barbarians with a perverted intellect and with languages "rationalized into [their] simplest and most rudimentary form." Equal in power to humans, they are in fact a robotic or absolutistic caricature of mankind, a mankind deprived of human qualities. On the other hand, in a brilliant use of satire, it is mankind that not only abets them but also teaches them the inhuman combination of slavery and stock-market, warlike aggression and ideological propaganda—in brief, the corruption of reason for violent purposes.

In the third book, the Salamanders begin their warfare upon a very corrupt mankind. Čapek's satire is here most bitter and topical, though no less precise. Briefly but impressively, the nodal points of defeatism in face of rising Salamandrism (read fascism) are passed in review, from the Spenglerian philosopher Meynert, through "Salamandrist" fashions in art and entertainment, to the secret deals of the bourgeois states with it and the public hypocrisy of international conferences. The military successes of the Salamanders run parallel to the failures of reason and humanism among men. In a startling maturation for Čapek, even his beloved small Czech people are found guilty of neutralist complacency in the person of Povondra, the only character to be found in all parts of the novel.

In a way, the satire of literary, journalistic, and essayistic forms in *War With the Newts* is also a critique of past and (unintentionally) of subsequent SF. The history of the Salamanders starts with an echo of H. G. Wells' *Island of Dr. Moreau*, as well as of Arthur Conan Doyle's *Lost World* and of the animal fable from Aesop to Pierre MacOrlan's story "The Conquering Beast." It proceeds with a global overview which latches onto Wells's later SF, from *The World Set Free* to *The Shape of Things To Come*, as well as onto Anatole France's ironic *Penguin Island*. It ends with havoc-wreaking aliens out of *The War of the Worlds* or "In the Abyss." But instead of Wells's alternatively pessimistic and optimistic outcomes, Čapek's end is, much more realistically, an open question. The final chapter, where the author's two inner voices debate the possible outcome, is to my mind much more mature than the facile extremes of, on the one hand, the a priori optimism of Bellamy and the feebler Wells (later picked up by writers such as Robert Heinlein, Isaac Asimov, and others) or, on the other, the despair of Aldous Huxley's *Brave New World* or the Spenglerian pessimism criticized in Wolf Meynert (and later picked up by James Blish, A. E. Van Vogt, and others). Čapek is much superior to ordinary SF mystifications: "No cosmic catastrophe, nothing but state, official, economic, and other causes. . . ." He is therefore much more activistic: the menace could be (or could have been) stopped—all depends on men organizing to fight it. But instead:

"Do you know who it is that is feverishly working day and night in the laboratories to invent still more efficient machines and materials for annihilating the world? Do you know who lends [the Newts] money, do you know who finances this End of the World, all this New Flood?"

"Yes, I do. All the factories. All the banks. All the different states."

Such writing makes of Čapek the pioneer of all anti-fascist and anti-militarist SF in the world, from the later Wells and Sinclair Lewis to the postwar American and Slavic writers. And he is still one of the best among them.

The enduring power of *War With the Newts* (and to a smaller degree of *The Factory for the Absolute*) is due to Čapek's mastery of stylistic strategies for building up his vision. In the first part of this mosaic the events are introduced and refracted in comically conflicting, individual though typical, points of view. As the focus of the action widens, impersonal points of view from articles and documents become more and more important, and the third part is mainly a kind of historicophilosophical essay emotionally strengthened by what one could call a tragic lampoon. The traditional individualist psychology is used in a masterly—though mainly comical and abbreviated—fashion where necessary, but it has been found insufficient for events of a global character. As in all modern literature, from James Joyce and John Dos Passos on, traditionally "nonfictional" forms are re-functioned for fictional use, resulting in a far richer and wider view than any combination of merely individual points of view could have effected. In this way, Čapek is—together with Evgeniy Zamyatin—the most significant world SF writer between the World Wars. Though three or four English-language writers of that epoch have had a much greater influence on the development of postwar SF, more complex preoccupations have again resulted in a return to Čapek's cognitive polyphony in writers such as Stanislaw Lem (clearly influenced by him), John Brunner, or Ursula Le Guin.

This is not to say that even *War With the Newts* is perfect. Čapek did not quite manage to overcome his permanent ambiguity of the inhumans being on the one hand a wronged inferior race or class (at the beginning) and on the other a menacing embodiment of the worst in modern humanity—both Nazis and robotized masses. It is indicative that in a novel published in 1936 and supposed to take place in the immediate future, Russia is represented as a tsarist state. Čapek wrote for twenty years a column in an anti-communist paper and was a friend of President Masaryk, and yet he had a considerable ambiguity toward communism. On the one hand it represented the wronged, on the other an abstract idea allied to modern masses, a large state, and large industry. Therefore, he defined himself as a kind of ethical socialist: "I believe in the socialization of means of production, in the limitation of private property, in an organization of production and consumption, in the end of capitalism, in the right of each to life, work, sufficiency and freedom of mind, I believe in peace, solidarity and equality of the peoples, I believe in humaneness and democracy, and in man, Amen."[6] That is why he felt once compelled to write an article "Why I am Not a Communist," and why he felt unable to deal not only with socialism but also with any positive radical novelty in his major works. Thus he dealt in catastrophes; and at the time of the rise of Nazism, when Czechs looked to the USSR for a counterpoise, he concentrated his fire almost entirely (except for a silly proclamation by the Third International to the Salamanders) on bourgeois society. Conversely, this strange love-hate relationship led the communist bureaucracy in Czechoslovakia to neglect him in the early 1950s, although he has since been rehabilitated.

Čapek's evolution is by no means simple. The work that is to my mind as significant as *War With the Newts*, *Krakatit*, was written early in his career. And his final SF play, *The White Sickness*, fits well into an ideational development toward an active anti-fascism, a critique of militarism, chauvinism, and subservient medical science as well as of the "neutral" petty bourgeoisie, yet it is a second-rate work reposing upon misleading allegory. Perhaps it would not be fair to analyze it too thoroughly: as he said after the Munich agreement, after his beloved England had left the Czechs to Hitler, "the world I believed in has fallen apart."[7] He died at the end of 1938 having lost the will to live—if

6. Čapek, *O věcech obecných čili Zoon politikon* (Prague, 1932), pp. 136–37.
7. Čapek's formulation, cited in Halina Janaszek-Ivaničková (Bibliography VII), p. 244.

you will, of a broken heart. His writings were forbidden by the
Nazis, and his brother Josef died returning from Bergen-Belsen.
But in a few works, such as *War With the Newts* he has left us a
precious legacy. It may not be as significant as that of his coun-
trymen Franz Kafka or Jaroslav Hašek; but these are the highest standards applicable. And for SF at least, he—rather than
Edgar Rice Burroughs or Hugo Gernsback—is the missing link
between H. G. Wells and a literature which will be both entertaining (which means popular) and cognitively (which means also
formally) avantgardist. He took the adventure novel and the
melodramatic thriller, the legacy of French and British SF as well
as of German fantasy from the Romantics to the Expressionists
(Hoffmann, Meyrink, Kaiser), and infused all this with the prospects of modern poetry, painting, and movies, with an eager and
constant interest in societal relationships, in natural and physical
sciences, and above all in the richly humorous and idiomatic
language of the street and the little people. In that way, he is the
most "American" of the often elitist European SF writers; and
yet he is also not only intensely Czech, but a "European local
patriot" for whom Europe meant culture and humanism. When
they were betrayed, the Salamanders had arrived. In order to
defend them, in order to understand what was happening, he
wrote literature:

> Discovery—what a great and insatiable passion. I am con-
> vinced that I write for that reason, to discover. . . . I am
> interested in everything there is. That is why I cannot be-
> come anything more than just a writer.[8]

That is also why, in particular, he wrote SF. As he said about his
SF plays:

> . . . it would be easier to say [much about human lives] more
> pointedly, with fewer words, preparations, demonstrations,
> and proofs, in short more effectively than in a play in which
> humans only would be portrayed.
> . . . [the dramatist] must include in his play those great
> forces that determine human life, forces that are revealed to
> us step by step by biology, sociology, economics. . . . the

8. Cited in Matushka, pp. 66–67.

poet of our day must master facts as yet unknown, complex and exciting problems, glowing and terrible dreams. He can make use of collective psychology as well as individual, and he can *study the heroism of ideas as well as inner simplicity*.[9]

The part I italicize seems to me an excellent definition of significant science fiction—and of Čapek.

9. Both quotations cited in Matushka, the first on pp. 73–74, the second on p. 372.

Bibliography

Students of various matters discussed in this book will recognize my very large debts to other scholars and critics, far too numerous to acknowledge properly in the notes. I hope the following checklist may suffice to indicate them, though it had to be confined to a strongly curtailed selection from a much longer list which I hope at some future time to publish separately as an annotated bibliographic guide, and to which the Žantovská-Suvin item from Section I is an introduction. In the initial work on such a bibliography, without which this list could not have been compiled, I gratefully acknowledge a Québec Ministry of Education FCAC grant given to a team headed by Professor Marc Angenot and myself at McGill University.

However, the following lists are also intended to be fairly complete surveys of the indispensable secondary literature from the major European languages (excluding dissertations) a graduate student or scholar would need for further independent research in all but the minutest details of the fields indicated by the section titles (and even such details, could, I believe, be pursued with help of the bibliographies and notes in the items listed). Striving for finiteness and practicality, I have as a rule also excluded handbooks, biographies, general bibliographies, and general surveys of periods or authors, however useful they often might be. In order not to let this selection grow into a Frankensteinian creation, I have after much reluctance decided to exclude the introductory category of "methodological landmarks," for which I refer the curious reader to "Bibliographie φ" in my *Pour une poétique de la science-fiction* (Montréal: Presses de l'Université du Québec, 1977), as well as to Marc Angenot's annotated bibliography of the sociology of literature in *Science-Fiction Studies*, No. 13 (1977). As a rule, I have listed books and articles by their short titles and the most accessible edition which I took to be an English-language one wherever it exists; for texts in languages other than English and French I have also used the French version whenever possible. Articles from periodicals have been listed only if I found them of fundamental significance or if my argument was—by agreement or disagreement—more or less directly indebted to them. In my experience, to find an article in a periodical it has proved sufficient to know the year of publication plus the volume or issue number, and I have here too opted for practicality rather than bibliographic orthodoxy. The bibliography has been taken to 1976, but it shares the perennial open-endedness of all encompassing attempts: a few items from 1976 and indeed much earlier years have proved stubbornly unfindable, and a few items from 1977 and 1978 have also been included. (B) indicates that the item either is a bibliography or contains a larger one.

The following abbreviations have been used in titles of periodicals:

Ass.	Association	*Proc.*	Proceedings
Bull.	Bulletin	*Pub(b)l.*	Pub(b)lications
Ges.	Gesellschaft(liche)	*R.*	Review or Revue
Gesch.	Geschichte	*Trans.*	Transactions
J.	Journal	*Wiss.*	Wissenschaft(liche)
Lit(t).	Literature or Literary (various languages)	*Z.*	Zeitschrift

I. Theory and General History of SF After Wells

For Russian SF see Bibliography VI, and for Čapek Bibliography VII. See also Biesterfeld, Clarke (1966), Ruyer, and Schwonke in Bibliography II, III A, and IV B.

Aldiss, Brian W. *Billion Year Spree*. London, 1975.

Amis, Kingsley. *New Maps of Hell*. New York, 1975.

Atheling, William, Jr. (pseud. of James Blish). *The Issue at Hand*. Chicago, 1964.

———. *More Issues at Hand*. Chicago, 1970.

Bailey, J. O. *Pilgrims Through Space and Time*. Westport, CT, 1972 (B).

Barmeyer, Eike, ed. *Science Fiction*. Munich, 1972 (B by Franz Rottensteiner).

Barron, Neil, ed. *Anatomy of Wonder*. New York, 1976 (B).

Baudin, Henri. *La Science-fiction*. Paris, 1971.

Baxter, John. *Science Fiction in the Cinema*. New York, 1970.

Bretnor, Reginald, ed. *Modern Science Fiction*. New York, 1953.

———. *Science Fiction, Today and Tomorrow*. Baltimore, 1975.

Bridenne, Jean-Jacques. *La Littérature française d'imagination scientifique*. Paris, 1950.

Caillois, Roger. *Images, images. . . .* Paris, 1966.

Chauvin, Cy, ed. *A Multitude of Visions*. Baltimore, 1976.

Cinéma d'aujourd'hui, N.S. No. 7 (1976).

Clareson, Thomas. *Science Fiction Criticism*. Kent, OH, 1972 (B).

Clareson, Thomas D., ed. *Many Futures, Many Worlds*. Kent, OH, 1977.

———, ed. *SF: The Other Side of Realism*. Bowling Green, OH, s.a. [1971].

———, ed. *Voices for the Future*. Bowling Green, OH, 1976.

Clarke, Ian. *The Tale of the Future*. London, 1972 (B).
Davenport, Basil, ed. *The Science Fiction Novel*. Chicago, 1969.
Eco, Umberto. *Apocalittici e integrati*. Milan, 1973.
Europe, 55 (Aug.-Sept. 1977) (B).
Ferrini, Franco. *Che cosa è la fantascienza*. Milan, 1970.
Gerber, Richard. *Utopian Fantasy*. New York, 1973 (B).
Gunn, James E. *Alternate Worlds*. Englewood Cliffs, NJ, 1975.
Gurevich, Georgii. *Karta Strany Fantazii*. Moscow, 1967.
Handke, Ryszard. *Polska proza fantastyczno-naukowa*. Wroclaw, 1969.
Harrison, Harry, and Brian Aldiss, eds. *SF Horizons*. New York, 1975.
Hienger, Jörg. *Literarische Zukunftsphantastik*. Göttingen, 1972.
Hillegas, Mark R. *The Future as Nightmare*. Carbondale, IL, 1974.
Johnson, William, ed. *Focus on the Science Fiction Film*. Englewood Cliffs, NJ, 1972.
Kagarlitskii, Iu. *Chto takoe fantastika?*. Moscow, 1974 (Kagarlizki, *Was ist Phantastik?*. [East] Berlin, 1976).
Ketterer, David. *New Worlds for Old*. New York, 1974.
Klein, Klaus-Peter. *Zukunft zwischen Trauma und Mythos: Science Fiction*. Stuttgart, 1976.
Knight, Damon. *In Search of Wonder*. Chicago, 1967.
Konstantinova, Elka. *Fantastika i beletristika*. Sofia, 1973.
Krysmanski, Hans-Jürgen. *Die utopische Methode*. Cologne, 1967.
Lem, Stanislaw. *Fantastyka i futurologia*, I-II. Cracow, 1973.
Lewis, C. S. *Of Other Worlds*. New York, 1967.
Moskowitz, Sam. *Explorers of the Infinite*. Westport, CT, 1974.
———. *Seekers of Tomorrow*. Westport, CT, 1974.
———. *Strange Horizons*. New York, 1976.
Mullen, R. D., and Darko Suvin, eds. *Science-Fiction Studies: Selected Articles . . . 1973-1975*. Boston, 1976.
Nagl, Manfred. *Science Fiction in Deutschland*. Tübingen, 1972 (B).
Pagetti, Carlo. *Il Senso del Futuro*. Rome, 1970.
Pehlke, Michael, and Norbert Lingfeld. *Roboter und Gartenlaube*. Munich, 1970.
Rose, Mark, ed. *Science Fiction*. Englewood Cliffs, NJ, 1976.
Rottensteiner, Franz. *The Science Fiction Book*. New York, 1975.
Sadoul, Jacques. *Histoire de la Science Fiction moderne*, I-II. Paris, 1975.
Samuelson, David N. *Visions of Tomorrow*. New York, 1975.
Scholes, Robert. *Structural Fabulation*. London, 1975.
———, and Eric S. Rabkin. *Science Fiction: History—Science—Vision*. New York, 1977.
Tuck, Donald H. *The Encyclopedia of Science Fiction and Fantasy*, I. Chicago, 1974.
Van Herp, Jacques. *Panorama de la science fiction*. Verviers, 1973.

Versins, Pierre. *Encyclopédie de l'utopie, de la science-fiction et des voyages extraordinaires*. Lausanne, 1972.

Wessels, Dieter. *Welt im Chaos*. Frankfurt, 1974.

Žantovská-Murray, Irena, and Darko Suvin. "A Bibliography of General Bibliographies of SF Literature." *Science-Fiction Studies* 5 (1978) (B).

See also the journals:

Algol, ed. Andrew Porter, POB 4175, New York City 17, USA.

Extrapolation, ed. Thomas D. Clareson, Wooster College, Wooster, OH, USA.

Foundation, ed. Malcolm Edwards, North East London Polytechnic, Dagenham, Essex, G. Britain.

Quarber Merkur, ed. Franz Rottensteiner, Felsenstr. 20, Miesenbach, Austria.

Science-Fiction Studies, eds. Marc Angenot, Charles Elkins, Robert M. Philmus, and Darko Suvin, English Dept., McGill University, Montreal, Qué., Canada H3A 2T6.

Science-Fiction Times, eds. Hans Joachim Alpers and Ronald M. Hahn, Weissenburger Str. 6, 2850 Bremerhaven 1, W. Germany.

Most SF magazines publish current book reviews; see for the USA, H. W. Hall. *Science Fiction Book Review Index, 1923-1973*. Detroit, 1975, continued by the compiler on a yearly basis from Bryan, TX; and for France, the magazine *Fiction*.

II.   THEORY OF THE FICTIONAL UTOPIA

Bakhtin, Mikhail. *Rabelais and His World*. Cambridge, MA, 1968.

Baldissera, Alberto. "Il concetto di utopia," in Gianni Giannotti, ed. *Concezione e previsione del futuro*. Bologna, 1971.

Barthes, Roland. *Sade, Fourier, Loyola*. New York, 1976.

Berneri, Marie-Louise. *Journey Through Utopia*. New York, 1971.

Bloch, Ernst. *Das Prinzip Hoffnung*, I–II. Frankfurt, 1959 (*Le Principe espérance*. Paris, 1976–).

Boas, George. *Essays on Primitivism and Related Ideas in the Middle Ages*. New York, 1966.

Brüggemann, Fritz. *Utopie und Robinsonade*. Weimar, 1914.

Buber, Martin. *Paths in Utopia*. Boston, 1949.

Cioranescu, Alexandre. *L'Avenir du passé*. Paris, 1972.

Coli, Edoardo. *Il Paradiso Terrestre dantesco*. Florence, 1896.

Dubois, Claude-Gilbert. *Problèmes de l'utopie*. Paris, 1968.

Elliott, Robert C. *The Shape of Utopia*. Chicago, 1970.

Extrapolation 19 (1977) (B).

Giamatti, A. Bartlett. *The Earthly Paradise and the Renaissance Epic*. Princeton, 1966.

Graf, Arturo. *Miti, leggende e superstizioni del Medio Evo*, I. Bologna, 1965.

Herbrüggen, Hubertus Schulte. *Utopie und Anti-Utopie*. Bochum, 1969.

Hertzler, Joyce Oramel. *The History of Utopian Thought*. New York, 1965.

Kerényi, Karl. "Ursinn und Sinnwandel des Utopischen," in Adolf Portmann, ed., *Vom Sinn der Utopie. Eranos-Jahrbuch 1963*. Zurich, 1964.

Krysmanski, Hans-Jürgen. *Die utopische Methode*. Cologne, 1963.

Lalande, André. "Utopie," in his *Vocabulaire technique et critique de la philosophie*. Paris, 1968.

Lovejoy, Arthur O., and George Boas. *Primitivism and Related Ideas in Antiquity*. New York, 1965.

Mannheim, Karl. *Ideology and Utopia*. New York, 1966.

Manuel, Frank E., ed. *Utopias and Utopian Thought*. Boston, 1967.

Marin, Louis. *Utopiques*. Paris, 1973.

Morton, A. L. *The English Utopia*. London, 1969.

Negley, Glenn, and J. Max Patrick. *The Quest for Utopia*. College Park, MD, 1971.

Neusüss, Arnhelm, ed. *Utopie*. Berlin, 1968 (B).

Patch, Howard Rollin. *The Other World*. New York, 1970.

Revue des sciences humaines, No. 155 (1974).

Ruyer, Raymond. *L'Utopie et les utopies*. Paris, 1950.

Sauer, Gerda-Karla. *Kindliche Utopien*. Berlin, 1954.

Schwonke, Martin. *Vom Staatsroman zur Science Fiction*. Stuttgart, 1957.

Tillich, Paul. *Politische Bedeutung der Utopie für das Leben der Völker*. Berlin, 1951.

Villgradter, Rudolf, and Friedrich Krey, eds. *Der utopische Roman*. Darmstadt, 1973.

Voigt, Andreas. *Die sozialen Utopien*. Leipzig, 1906.

Walsh, Chad. *From Utopia to Nightmare*. Westport, CT, 1972.

III. HISTORY OF SF TO THE EIGHTEENTH CENTURY

A.   General (including the general history of fictional utopia).

See also Bibliography I and II—in particular Bakhtin, Barron, ed., Barthes, Berneri, Bloch (1959), Elliott, *Extrapolation*, Marin, Morton, Negley-Patrick, Patch, *RSH*, Ruyer, Schwonke, Walsh, and Žantovská-Suvin.

Beauchamp, Gorman. "Themes and Uses of Fictional Utopias." *Science-Fiction Studies* 4 (1977) (B).

Beer, Max. *The General History of Socialism and Social Struggles*, I–II. New York, 1957.

Biesterfeld, Wolfgang. *Die literarische Utopie*. Stuttgart, 1974 (B).

Cawley, Robert Ralston. *Unpathed Waters*. London, 1967.

Ceserani, Gian Paolo. *I falsi Adami*. Milan, 1969.

Cohen, John. *Human Robots in Myth and Science*. London, 1966.

Duveau, Georges. *Sociologie de l'utopie*. Paris, 1961.

Ehrmann, Jacques. "Le dedans et le dehors." *Poétique*, No. 9 (1972).

Eurich, Nell. *Science in Utopia*. Cambridge, MA, 1967.

Gibson, R. W., and J. Max Patrick. "Utopias and Dystopias, 1500–1750," in R. W. Gibson, *St. Thomas More*. New Haven, 1961 (B).

Gove, Philip Babcock. *The Imaginary Voyage in Prose Fiction*. New York, 1975 (B).

Mucchielli, Roger. *Le Mythe de la cité idéale*. Paris, 1960.

Mumford, Lewis. *The Story of Utopias*. New York, 1966.

Nicolson, Marjorie. *Science and Imagination*. Ithaca, NY, 1962.

Patai, Daphne. "Utopia for Whom." *Aphra*, No. 5 (1974).

Philmus, Robert M. *Into the Unknown*. Berkeley, 1970.

Sargent, Lyman Tower. "Themes in Utopian Fiction in English Before Wells." *Science-Fiction Studies* 3 (1976) (B).

Schlanger, Judith E. "Power and Weakness of the Utopian Imagination." *Diogenes*, No. 84 (1973).

Seeber, Hans Ulrich. *Wandlungen der Form in der literarischen Utopie*. Göppingen, 1970.

Simon, Heinrich. "Arabische Utopien im Mittelalter." *Wiss. Z. der Humboldt-Univ. Berlin, Ges.-Sprachwiss. Reihe* 12 (1963).

Trousson, Raymond. *Voyages aux pays de nulle part*. Bruxelless, 1975.

Tuveson, Ernest Lee. *Millennium and Utopia*. Berkeley, 1949.

B. Extra-European, Antique, Medieval

See also Bibliography II, III C, and III F—in particular Beger, Bloch (1959), Boas, Brunner, Cioranescu, Coli, Förster, Graf, Lovejoy-Boas, Morton, Patch, Seibt, Süssmuth, Villgradter-Krey, ed., and Volgin (1975)—and Bibliography III A.

Ackermann, Elfriede Marie. *"Das Schlaraffenland" in German Literature and Folksong*. Chicago, 1944.

Baldry, H. C. *Ancient Utopias*. Southampton, 1956.

Barker, Ernest. *The Political Thought of Plato and Aristotle*. London, 1959.

Bauer, Wolfgang. *China und die Hoffnung auf Glück*. Munich, 1971.

Bompaire, J. *Lucien écrivain*. Paris, 1959.

Bonner, Campbell. "Dionysiac Magic and the Greek Land of Cockaigne." *Trans. & Proc. American Philological Ass.* 41 (1910).

Chesneaux, Jean. "Egalitarianism and Utopian Traditions in the East." *Diogenes*, No. 62 (1968).

Cornford, Francis Macdonald. *Plato's Cosmology*. London, 1956.

Curtius, Ernst Robert. *European Literature and the Latin Middle Ages*. New York, 1963.

Ferguson, John. *Utopias of the Classical World*. New York, 1975.

Finley, M. I. "Utopianism Ancient and Modern," in Kurt H. Wolff and Barrington Moore, Jr., eds., *The Critical Spirit*. Boston, 1967.

Fredericks, S. C. "Lucian's True History as SF." *Science-Fiction Studies* 3 (1976).

Gatz, Bodo. *Weltalter, Goldene Zeit und sinnverwandte Vorstellungen*. *Spudasmata* XVI. Hildesheim, 1967.

Graus, F. "Social Utopias in the Middle Ages." *Past and Present*, No. 38 (1967).

Gronau, Karl. *Der Staat der Zukunft von Platon bis Dante*. Braunschweig, 1933.

Machovcová, Marketa, and Milan Machovec. *Utopie blouznivců a sektářů*. Prague, 1960.

Manuel, Frank E., and Fritzie P. Manuel. "Sketch for a Natural History of Paradise." *Daedalus* 101 (1972).

Merkelbach, Reinhold. *Roman und Mysterium in der Antike*. Munich, 1962.

Nuita, Seiji. "Traditional Utopias in Japan and the West," in David W. Plath, ed. *Aware of Utopia*. Urbana, IL, 1971.

Nutt, Alfred. "The Happy Otherworld in the Mythico-Romantic Literature of the Irish," in Kuno Meyer, ed., *The Voyage of Bran . . .* , I. New York, 1972.

Peters, Elizabeth. *Quellen und Charakter der Paradiesesvorstellungen in der deutschen Dictung vom 9. bis 12. Jahrhundert*. Breslau, 1915.

Pöhlmann, Robert von. *Geschichte der sozialen Frage und des Sozialismus in der antiken Welt*, I–II. Munich, 1925.

Rohde, Erwin. *Der griechische Roman und seine Vorläufer*. Berlin, 1960.

Salin, Edgar. *Platon und die griechische Utopie*. Munich, 1921.

Schuhl, Pierre-Maxime. *La Fabulation platonicienne*. Paris, 1968.

Swanson, Roy Arthur. "The True, the False, and the Truly False: Lucian's Philosophical SF." *Science-Fiction Studies* 3 (1976).

Vallauri, Giovanna. *Evemero di Messene. Univ. di Torino: Pubbl. della facoltá di lettere e filosofia* 8, No. 3 (1956).

Westropp, Thomas Johnson. "Brazil and the Legendary Islands of the North Atlantic." *Proc. Royal Irish Academy* 30 (1912).

Winston, David. "Iambulus' *Islands of the Sun* and Hellenistic Literary Utopias." *Science-Fiction Studies* 3 (1976) (B).

C. Renaissance Utopias

See also Bibliography I, II, III E, and III F—in particular Bakhtin, Berneri, Bloch (1959), Brunner, Dubois, Elliott (*Shape*), Giamatti, Marin, Morton, Patch, Sainéan, Schwonke, Tuveson, ed., Vickers, and Villgradter-Krey, eds., and Žantovská-Suvin—and Bibliography III A.

1. GENERAL AND THOMAS MORE

Adams, Robert P. "The Philosophic Unity of More's *Utopia*." *Studies in Philology* 38 (1941).

———. "The Social Responsibilities of Science in *Utopia*, *New Atlantis* and After," in P. O. Kristeller and P. P. Wiener, eds., *Renaissance Essays*. New York, 1968.

Ames, Russell. *Citizen Thomas More and his Utopia*. Princeton, 1952.

Beger, Lina. "Thomas Morus und Plato." *Z. für die gesamte Staatswiss*. 35 (1879).

Chambers, R. W. *Thomas More*. Ann Arbor, 1968.

Dermenghem, E. *Thomas Morus et les Utopistes de la Renaissance*. Paris, 1927.

Donner, H. W. *Introduction to Utopia*. New York, 1969.

Dudok, G. *Sir Thomas More and his Utopia*. Amsterdam, 1923.

Dupont, V. *L'Utopie et le Roman Utopique dans la Littérature Anglaise*. Toulouse, 1941.

Förster, Richard. "Lucian in der Renaissance." *Archiv für Literaturgesch*. 14 (1937).

Gallagher, Ligeia, ed. *More's Utopia and its Critics*. Chicago, 1964.

Heiserman, A. R. "Satire in the *Utopia*." *PMLA* 78 (1963).

Hexter, J. H. *More's "Utopia"*. New York, 1965.

Massó, Gildo. *Education in Utopia*. New York, 1972.

Miles, Leland. "The Literary Artistry of Thomas More." *Studies in English Lit*. 6 (1966).

Morris, William. "Introduction" to Thomas More, *Utopia*. London, 1893 (rpt. in *Science-Fiction Studies* 3 [1976]).

Nelson, William, ed. *Twentieth Century Interpretations of "Utopia"*. Englewood Cliffs, NJ, 1968.

Pons, Emile. "Les Langues Imaginaires dans le voyage utopique: . . . Thomas Morus." *R. de litt. comparée* 10 (1930).

Rebhorn, Wayne A. "Thomas More's Enclosed Garden." *English Lit. Renaissance* 6 (1976).

Reiss, Timothy. "*Utopia* and Process." *Sub-Stance*, No. 8 (1974).

Sanderlin, George. "The Meaning of Thomas More's *Utopia*." *College English* 12 (1950).

Seibt, Ferdinand. "Utopie im Mittelalter." *Historische Z*. 208 (1969).

Surtz, Edward L., S. J. *The Praise of Pleasure*. Cambridge, MA, 1957.
——. *The Praise of Wisdom*. Chicago, 1957.
——, and J. H. Hexter. "Introduction" to *The Complete Works of St. Thomas More*, 4. New Haven, 1965.
Süssmuth, Hans. *Studien zur Utopia des Thomas Morus*. Münster, 1967.
Sylvester, R. S., and G. P. Marc'hadour, eds. *Essential Articles for the Study of Thomas More*. Hamden, CT, 1977.
L'Utopie à la Renaissance. Brussels, 1963.
Volgin, V. P. *Ocherki istorii sotsialisticheskikh idei s drevnosti do kontsa XVIII v.*. Moscow, 1975.

2. OTHER UTOPOGRAPHERS

Auerbach, Erich. *Mimesis*. Garden City, NY, 1957.
Badaloni, Nicola. *Tommaso Campanella*. Milan, 1965.
Beaujour, Michel. *Le Jeu de Rabelais*. Paris, 1969.
Bierman, Judah. "Science and Society in the *New Atlantis* and Other Renaissance Utopias." *PMLA* 78 (1963).
Blodgett, Eleanor Dickinson. "Bacon's *New Atlantis* and Campanella's *Civitas Solis*." *PMLA* 46 (1931).
Bock, Gisela. *Thomas Campanella*. Tübingen, 1974.
Diéguez, Manuel de. *Rabelais par lui-même*. Paris, 1960.
Doren, Alfred. "Campanella als Chiliast und Utopist," in *Kultur- und Universalgeschichte: Walter Goetz zu seinem 60. Geburtstag. . . .* Leipzig, 1927.
Farrington, Benjamin. *The "New Atlantis" of Francis Bacon*. Richmond Hill, 1965.
François Rabelais: IVe Centenaire de sa Mort. Geneva, 1953.
Gorfunkel, A. *Tomazo Kampanela*. Moscow, 1969.
Greene, Thomas M. *Rabelais*. Englewood Cliffs, NJ, 1970.
Grendler, Paul F. "Utopia in Renaissance Italy: Doni's *New World*." *J. of the History of Ideas* 26 (1965).
Kaiser, Walter. *Praisers of Folly*. Cambridge, MA, 1963.
Knights, L. C. *Explorations*. Westport, CT, 1975.
Lefebvre, Henri. *Rabelais*. Paris, 1955.
Lefranc, Abel. *Les Navigations de Pantagruel*. Geneva, 1967.
Marin, Louis. "Les Corps utopiques rabelaisiens." *Littérature*, No. 21 (1976).
Paris, Jean. *Rabelais au futur*. Paris, 1970.
Reiss, Timothy J. "Structure and Mind in Two Seventeenth-Century Utopias: Campanella and Bacon." *Yale French Studies* 49 (1973).
Sainéan, Lazare. *La Langue de Rabelais*, I–II. Paris, 1922-23.
Saulnier, V.-L. *Le Dessein de Rabelais*. Paris, 1957.
Scholtz, Harald. *Evangelischer Utopismus bei J. V. Andreae*. Stuttgart, 1957.

Spitzer, Leo. *Romanische Stil- und Literaturstudien*. Marburg, 1931.
———. "Ancora sul prologo al *Gargantua* di Rabelais." *Studi francesi* 27 (1965).
White, Howard B. *Peace Among the Willows: The Political Philosophy of Francis Bacon*. The Hague, 1968.
Wiener, Harvey S. " 'Science or Providence': Toward Knowledge in Bacon's *New Atlantis*." *Enlightenment Essays* 3 (1972).

3. SHAKESPEARE

Allen, Don Cameron. *Image and Meaning*. Baltimore, 1960.
Kermode, Frank. "Introduction," to *The Tempest. Arden edn. of the Works of William Shakespeare*. London, 1963.
Kott, Jan. *Shakespeare Our Contemporary*. Garden City, NY, 1966.
Langbaum, Robert, ed. *The Tempest. Signet Classic Shakespeare*. New York, 1964.
Leech, Clifford. *Shakespeare's Tragedies*. London, 1950.
Lovejoy, A. O. *Essays in the History of Ideas*. New York, 1960.
Palmer, D. J., ed. *Shakespeare: "The Tempest."* London, 1968.

D. The "Planetary Novel" and Cyrano

See also Bibliography II, III B, III C, III E, and III F—in particular Atkinson, Bakhtin, Cornelius, Eddy, Graf, Paris, Rozanova, Schwonke, Toldo, and Tuzet—and Bibliography III A.

Alcover, Madeleine. *La Pensée philosophique et scientifique de Cyrano de Bergerac*. Geneva, 1970.
Blanchot, Maurice. "Cyrano de Bergerac," in A. Adamov, et al. *Tableau de la littérature française*, I. Paris, 1962.
Boas, George. *The Happy Beast*. New York, 1966.
Brandwajn, Rachmiel. *Cyrano de Bergerac*. Warsaw, 1960.
Chambers, Ross. "*L'Autre Monde*, ou le mythe du libertin." *Essays in French Lit.* 8 (1971).
Dunlop, Alexander. "The Narrative Function of Ideas in Cyrano's *Estats et empires de la lune*." *Romance Notes* 13 (1971).
Harth, Erica. *Cyrano de Bergerac and the Polemics of Modernity*. New York, 1970.
Harvey, Howard G. "Cyrano de Bergerac and the Question of Human Liberties." *Symposium* 4 (1950).
Laugaa, Maurice. "Introduction" to Cyrano de Bergerac, *Voyage dans la Lune*. Paris, 1970.
———. "Lune, ou l'Autre." *Poétique*, No. 3 (1970).
Lavers, A. "La Croyance à l'unité de la science dans *L'Autre Monde* de Cyrano de Bergerac." *Cahiers du Sud* 45 (1959).

Lear, John. "Introduction and Interpretation," in *Kepler's Dream*. Berkeley, 1965.

Liger, Christian. "Les cinq envols de Cyrano." *Nouvelle R. française* 13 (1965).

Mongrédien, Georges. *Cyrano de Bergerac*. Paris, 1964.

Nicolson, Marjorie Hope. *Voyages to the Moon*. Havertown, PA, 1973.

Pintard, René. *Le Libertinage érudit dans la première moitié du XVIIe siècle*. Paris, 1943.

Ridgely, Beverly S. "A Sixteenth-Century French Cosmic Voyage: *Nouvelles des Regions de la Lune*." *Studies in the Renaissance* 4 (1957).

Rosenfield, Leonora Cohen. *From Beast-Machine to Man-Machine*. New York, 1968.

Spink, John Stephenson. "Form and Structure: Cyrano de Bergerac's Atomistic Conception of Metamorphosis," in *Literature and Science: Proc. of the 6th Congress of IFMLL*. Oxford, 1955.

——. *French Free-Thought From Gassendi to Voltaire*. New York, 1969.

Thibaudet, Albert. "Réflexion sur la littérature: le roman de l'aventure." *Nouvelle R. française* 13 (1919).

Van Baelen, Jacqueline. "Reality and Illusion in *L'Autre Monde*." *Yale French Studies* 49 (1973).

Weber, H. "Introduction" to Cyrano de Bergerac, *L'Autre Monde*. Paris, 1959.

E.   *"Gulliver's Travels"*

See also Bibliography I, II, III D, and III F—in particular Adams (1962), Boas (*Happy Beast*), Elliott (*Shape*), Kagarlitskii, Negley-Patrick, Nicolson (1973), and *RSH*—and Bibliography III A.

Atkinson, Geoffroy. *The Extraordinary Voyage in French Literature*, I–II. New York, 1969.

Bonner, William H. *Captain William Dampier*. London, 1934.

Brady, Frank, ed. *Twentieth Century Interpretations of "Gulliver's Travels."* Englewood Cliffs, NJ, 1968.

Brunetti, Giuseppe. "Swift e la satira della scienza," in Mario Praz, ed., *English Miscellany* 24. Rome, 1973–74.

Carnochan, W. B. *Lemuel Gulliver's Mirror for Man*. Berkeley, 1968.

Case, Arthur E. *Four Essays on "Gulliver's Travels."* Gloucester, MA, 1958.

Donoghue, Denis, ed. *Jonathan Swift*. Harmondsworth, 1971.

Eddy, William. *Gulliver's Travels*. New York, 1963.

Elliott, Robert C. *The Power of Satire*. Princeton, 1970.

Forrester, Kent. "They Shoot Horses, Don't They?" *Kentucky Philological Ass. Bull.* (1974).

Foster, Milton P., ed. *A Casebook on Gulliver among the Houyhnhnms*. New York, 1961.

Frantz, R. W. "Swift's Yahoos and the Voyagers." *Modern Philology* 29 (1931).

Greenberg, Robert A., ed. *Gulliver's Travels*. New York, 1970 (B).

Jeffares, A. Norman, ed. *Fair Liberty was all his Cry*. London, 1967.

———, ed. *Swift*. London, 1968.

Kiernan, Colin. "Swift and Science." *Historical J.* 14 (1971).

Price, Martin. *Swift's Rhetorical Art*. Carbondale, IL, 1973.

Quintana, Ricardo. *Swift*. London, 1962.

Sacks, Sheldon. *"Fiction" and the Shape of Belief*. Berkeley, 1966.

Stanzel, Franz. *"Gulliver's Travels*: Satire, Utopie, Dystopie." *Moderne Sprachen* 7 (1963).

Sutherland, John H. "A Reconsideration of Gulliver's Third Voyage." *Studies in Philology* 54 (1957).

Sutherland, W. O. S., Jr. *The Art of the Satirist*. Austin, 1965.

Toldo, Pietro. *Les Voyages merveilleux de Cyrano de Bergerac et de Swift et leur rapports avec l'oeuvre de Rabelais*. Paris, 1907.

Tuveson, Ernest, ed. *Swift*. Englewood Cliffs, NJ, 1964.

Vickers, Brian. *The Satiric Structure of "Gulliver's Travels" & More's "Utopia."* Oxford, 1968.

———, ed. *The World of Jonathan Swift*. Oxford, 1968.

Voigt, Milton. *Swift and the Twentieth Century*. Detroit, 1964.

Williams, Kathleen. *Jonathan Swift and the Age of Compromise*. Lawrence, KS, 1958.

F.   Other Works of the Seventeenth and Eighteenth Centuries

See also Bibliography I, II, III C, III D, III E, and VI—in particular Atkinson, Bailey, Barthes (1976), Berneri, Bloch (1959), Brüggemann, Chistov, Cioranescu, Clarke, Dupont, Fedosov, Herbrüggen, Kagarlitskii, Kizevetter, Morton, Nicolson (1973), *RSH*, Ruyer, Schwonke, Sipovskii (1909-10), Sipovskii (1924), Spink (1969), Suvin (1976), Sviatlovskii, Thibaudet, and Volgin (1975)—and Bibliography III A.

Adams, Percy G. *Travelers and Travel Liars, 1660-1800*. Berkeley, 1962.

Baczko, B. "Lumières et utopie." *Annales* 26 (1971).

Belaval, Yvon. "Le Conte philosophique," in W. H. Barber, et al., eds., *The Age of Enlightenment*. Edinburgh, 1967.

Blitzer, Charles. *An Immortal Commonwealth: The Political Thought of James Harrington*. Hamden, CT, 1970.

Brunner, Horst. *Die poetische Insel*. Stuttgart, 1967.

Chérel, Albert. *De Télémaque à Candide*. Paris, 1958.

Chinard, Gilbert. *L'Amérique et le rêve exotique dans la littérature française au XVIIe et au XVIIIe siécle*. Geneva, 1970.

Coe, Richard N. *Morelly*. [East] Berlin, 1961.

Cornelius, Paul. *Languages in Seventeenth- and Early Eighteenth-Century Imaginary Voyages*. Geneva, 1965.

Coste, B. *Mably*. Paris, 1975.

Courbin, J.-Cl. *Le Monde de Restif*. Paris, 1962.

Dalnekoff, Donna Isaacs. "The Meaning of Eldorado: Utopia and Satire in *Candide*." *Studies on Voltaire and the Eighteenth Century*, No. 127 (1974).

Dédéyan, Charles. *Le Télémaque de Fénelon*. Paris, 1967.

Elliott, Robert C. "The Costs of utopia." *Studies on Voltaire and the Eighteenth Century*, No. 151 (1976).

Ellison, Lee Monroe. "Gaudentio di Lucca." *PMLA* 50 (1935).

Girsberger, Hans. *Der utopische Sozialismus des 18. Jahrhunderts in Frankreich*. Wiesbaden, 1973.

Gordon, L. S. "Zabytyi utopist XVIIIogo veka Tifèn de Larosh," in *Istoriia sotsialisticheskikh uchenii*. Moscow, 1962.

Hafter, Monroe Z. "Toward a History of Spanish Imaginary Voyages." *Eighteenth Century Studies* 8 (1975).

Heuvel, J. Van den. *Voltaire dans ses contes*. Paris, 1967.

Hinterhäuser, Hans. *Utopie und Wirklichkeit bei Diderot*. Heidelberg, 1957.

Hohendahl, Peter Uwe. "Zum Erzählproblem des utopischen Romans im 18. Jahrhundert," in Helmut Kreuzer, ed., *Gestaltungsgeschichte und Gesellschaftsgeschichte*. Stuttgart, 1969.

Ioannisian, A. R. "Restif de la Bretonne et le communisme utopique." *La Pensée* (March-April 1958).

Krauss, Werner. *Fontenelle und die Aufklärung*. Munich, 1969.

Lachèvre, Frédéric. *Les Successeurs de Cyrano de Bergerac*. Paris, 1922.

Lanson, Gustave. "Les Origines et les premières manifestations—" and "Formation et développement—de l'esprit philosophique dans la littérature française." *R. des cours et conférences* 16-18 (1907–10).

Le Breton, A. *Le Roman au XVIIIe siècle*. Geneva, 1970.

Le Flamanc, Auguste. *Les Utopies prérevolutionnaires et la philosophie du XVIIIe siècle*. Paris, 1934.

Lichtenberger, André. *Le Socialisme au XVIIIe siècle*. Osnabrück, 1970.

Mayer, Hans. "Die alte und neue epische Form," in his *Von Lessing bis Thomas Mann*. Pfullingen, 1959.

McNelis, James I., Jr. "Introduction" to Ludvig Holberg, *The Journey of Niels Klim to the World Underground*. Lincoln, NE, 1960.

Messac, Régis. "Voyages modernes au centre de la terre." *R. de litt. comparée* 9 (1929).

Mühll, Emanuel von der. *Denis Veiras et son "Histoire des Sévarambes" (1677-1679)*. Paris, 1938.

Nerval, Gérard de. *Les Illuminés*. Verviers, 1973.

Paludan, Julius. *Om Holbergs Niels Klim*. Copenhagen, 1878.

Patrick, J. Max. "A Consideration of *La Terre Australe Connue* by Gabriel de Foigny." *PMLA* 61 (1946).

Pons, Emile. 'Le 'Voyage,' genre littéraire au XVIIIe siècle." *Bull. faculté des lettres de Strasbourg* 4 (1925-26).

―――. "Les Langues imaginaires dans le voyage utopique: . . . Vairasse et Foigny." *R. de litt. comparée* 12 (1932).

Poster, Mark. *The Utopian Thought of Restif de la Bretonne*. New York, 1971.

Rihs, Charles. *Les Philosophes utopistes*. Paris, 1970.

Rozanova, A. A. *Sotsial'naia i nauchnaia fantastika v klassicheskoi frantsuzkoi literature XVI–XIX vv.*. Kiev, 1974.

Sainéan, Lazare. *L'Influence et la réputation de Rabelais*. Paris, 1930.

Sareil, Jean. *Essai sur "Candide."* Geneva, 1967.

Schmidt, Arno. *Dya Na Sore*. Karlsruhe, 1959.

Tuzet, Hélene. *Cosmos et imagination*. Paris, 1965.

Venturi, Franco. *Utopia e riforma nell'Illuminismo*. Turin, 1970.

Volgin, V. P. *Frantsuzkii utopicheskii kommunizm*. Moscow, 1960.

Wade, Ira O. *Voltaire's "Micromégas"*. Princeton, 1950.

Wijngaarden, Nicolaas van. *Les Odyssées philosophiques en France entre 1616 et 1789*. Haarlem, 1932.

IV.   HISTORY OF SF FROM THE FRENCH REVOLUTION TO H. G. WELLS

A.   Radical Rhapsody and Romantic Recoil

See also Bibliography I, II, III A, III C, and III F, in particular Aldiss, Bailey, Barron, ed., Barthes, Beer, Berneri, Bloch, Clarke, Cohen, Dupont, Elliott (*Shape*), Ketterer, Marin (1973), Morton, Mumford, Negley-Patrick, Nicolson, Philmus, Sargent, Schwonke, Tuzet, and Žantovská-Suvin.

1.   IN FRANCE

Angenot, Marc. "Science Fiction in France Before Verne." *Science-Fiction Studies* 5 (1978).

Ansart, Pierre. *Sociologie de Saint-Simon*. Paris, 1970.

Béclard, Léon. *Sébastien Mercier*. Paris, 1903.

Cole, G. D. H. *A History of Socialist Thought*, I–V. New York, 1953-58.

Debout Oleskiewicz, Simone. "Introduction" to *Oeuvres complètes de Charles Fourier*, I. Paris, 1966.

———. "Préface" to *Oeuvres complètes de Charles Fourier*, VII. Paris, 1967.
Desanti, Dominique. *Les Socialistes de l'utopie*. Paris, 1970.
Desroche, Henri. *La Société festive*. Paris, 1975.
Durkheim, Emile. *Socialism and Saint-Simon*. Yellow Springs, OH, 1958.
Engels, Friedrich. "Socialism: Utopian and Scientific," in Karl Marx and Friedrich Engels, *Selected Works In One Volume*. New York, 1968.
Lehouck, Emile. *Fourier, aujourd'hui*. Paris, 1966.
Leroy, Maxime. *Histoire des idées sociales en France*, I–III. Paris, 1947-54.
Majewski, Henry F. "Grainville's *Le Dernier Homme*." *Symposium* 17 (1963).
Manuel, Frank. *The New World of Henri Saint-Simon*. Cambridge, MA, 1956.
———. *The Prophets of Paris*. New York, 1965.
Riasanovsky, Nicholas V. *The Teaching of Charles Fourier*. Berkeley, 1969.
Volgin, V. P. *Sen-Simon i sen-simonizm*. Moscow, 1961.

2. GENERAL AND IN ENGLAND

Auden, W. H. *The Enchaféd Flood*. New York, 1967.
Ault, Donald D. *Visionary Physics*. Chicago, 1974.
Bloom, Harold. *The Ringers in the Tower*. Chicago, 1971.
Brailsford, H. N. *Shelley, Godwin and Their Circle*. London, 1954.
Bronowski, Jacob. *William Blake and the Age of Revolution*. London, 1972.
Buchen, Irving H. "*Frankenstein* and the Alchemy of Creation and Evolution." *The Wordsworth Circle* 8 (1977).
Cameron, Kenneth Neill. *The Young Shelley*. New York, 1973.
Curran, Stuart, and Joseph Anthony Wittreich, Jr., eds. *Blake's Sublime Allegory*. Madison, 1973.
DiSalvo, Jackie. "Blake Encountering Milton," in Joseph Anthony Wittreich, Jr., ed., *Milton and the Line of Vision*. Madison, 1975.
Erdman, David V. *Blake: Prophet Against Empire*. Princeton, 1969.
Fisher, Peter F. *The Valley of Vision*. Toronto, 1961.
Frye, Northrop. *Fearful Symmetry*. Princeton, 1969.
Goldberg, M.A. "Moral and Myth in Mrs. Shelley's *Frankenstein*." *Keats-Shelley J.* 8 (1959).
Grabo, Carl H. *A Newton Among Poets*. New York, 1968.
Hughes, A. M. D. *The Nascent Mind of Shelley*. Oxford, 1971.
Joseph, M. K. "Introduction" to Mary W. Shelley, *Frankenstein or the Modern Prometheus*. London, 1971.
Kayser, Wolfgang. *The Grotesque in Art and Literature*. Gloucester, MA, 1963.
Kreutz, Christian. *Das Prometheussymbol in der Dichtung der englischen Romantik*. *Palaestra* Bd. 236. Göttingen, 1963.

Levine, George. "*Frankenstein* and the Tradition of Realism." *Novel* 7 (1973).

Lewis, C. S. *Rehabilitations*. London, 1939.

Massey, Irving. *The Gaping Pig*. Berkeley, 1976.

McNeice, Gerald. *Shelley and the Revolutionary Idea*. Cambridge, MA, 1969.

Morton, A. L. *The Everlasting Gospel*. Folcroft, PA, 1974.

Mumford, Lewis. *Technics and Civilization*. New York, 1963.

Palacio, Jean de. *Mary Shelley dans son oeuvre*. Paris, 1969.

Pollin, Burton R. "Philosophical and Literary Sources of *Frankenstein*." *Comparative Lit.* 17 (1965).

Ridenour, George M., ed. *Shelley*. Englewood Cliffs, NJ, 1965.

Rieger, James. *The Mutiny Within*. New York, 1967.

Rubenstein, Marc A. " 'My Accursed Origin': The Search for the Mother in *Frankenstein*." *Studies in Romanticism* 15 (1976).

Sambrook, A. J. "A Romantic Theme: The Last Man." *Forum for Modern Language Studies* 2 (1966).

Schorer, Mark. *William Blake: The Politics of Vision*. New York, 1959.

Sir Walter Scott on Novelists and Fiction. Ed. I. Williams. London, 1968.

Small, Christopher. *Mary Shelley's "Frankenstein."* Pittsburgh, 1973.

Smith, Elton E., and Esther G. Smith. *William Godwin*. New York, 1966.

Walling, William A. *Mary Shelley*. New York, 1972.

Ward, Aileen. "The Forging of Orc: Blake and the Idea of Revolution." *Triquarterly*, No. 23/24 (1972).

Wasserman, Earl R. *Shelley's "Prometheus Unbound."* Baltimore, 1965.

Wilner, Eleanor. *Gathering the Winds*. Baltimore, 1975.

Woodings, R. B., ed. *Shelley*. London, 1968.

3. IN THE UNITED STATES

Adams, Richard P. "Hawthorne." *Tulane Studies in English* 8 (1958).

Bailey, J. O. "Sources of Poe's *Arthur Gordon Pym*, 'Hans Pfaal' and Other Pieces." *PMLA* 57 (1942).

Beaver, Harold. "Introduction" and "Commentary," in idem, ed., *The Science Fiction of Edgar Allan Poe*. Harmondsworth, 1976 (B).

Carlson, Eric W., ed. *The Recognition of Edgar Allan Poe*. Ann Arbor, 1966.

Chase, Richard. *Herman Melville*. New York, 1949.

Davidson, Edward H. *Poe*. Cambridge, MA, 1957.

Davis, Merrell R. *Melville's Mardi*. New Haven, 1952.

Falk, Doris V. "Poe and the Power of Animal Magnetism." *PMLA* 84 (1969).

Fiedler, Leslie. *Love and Death in the American Novel*. London, 1967.

Fogle, Richard Harter. *Hawthorne's Fiction*. Norman, OK, 1964.

Franklin, H. Bruce. *The Wake of the Gods*. Stanford, 1963.
———. *Future Perfect*. New York, 1968.
Halliburton, David. *Edgar Allan Poe*. Princeton, 1973.
Howarth, William, ed. *Twentieth Century Interpretations of Poe's Tales*. Englewood Cliffs, NJ, 1971.
Kaul, A. N. *The American Vision*. New Haven, 1963.
Ketterer, David. "The S-F Element in the Work of Poe." *Science-Fiction Studies* 1 (1974) (B).
Levin, Harry. *The Power of Blackness*. New York, 1960.
Lynen, John. *The Design of the Present*. New Haven, 1969.
Matthiessen, F. O. *American Renaissance*. New York, 1941.
Parrington, Vernon Louis. *Main Currents in American Thought*, I–III. New York, 1958.
Pollin, Burton R. "*Rappaccini's Daughter*—Sources and Names." *Names* 14 (1966).
Vernon, John. "Melville's *The Bell Tower*." *Studies in Short Fiction* 7 (1970).

B.   *Verne and the Space-Binding Machines*

See also Bibliography I, II, III A, III F, and IV A, in particular Aldiss, Angenot, Auden, Bailey, Barron, ed., Beer, Bloch (1959), Bridenne, Cohen, Elliott (1970), Gove, Lem, Messac, Moskowitz (*Explorers*), Mumford (*Story*), Nagl, Nicolson (1973), Philmus, Sargent, Scholes-Rabkin, Schwonke, and Žantovská-Suvin, as well as the three bibliographic surveys on Verne cited in note 3 to chap. 7.

1.   VERNE

Allott, Kenneth. *Jules Verne*. Port Washington, NY, 1974.
Allotte de la Fuÿe, Marguerite. *Jules Verne*. Paris, 1966.
Andreev, Kirill. *Tri zhizni Zhiulia Verna*. Moscow, 1960.
L'Arc, No. 29 (1966).
Barthes, Roland. "Par où commencer?" *Poétique*, No. 1 (1970).
———. "The *Nautilus* and the Drunken Boat," in his *Mythologies*. St. Albans, Herts., 1973.
Butor, Michel. "Le Point suprême et l'âge d'or à travers quelques oeuvres de Jules Verne," in his *Essais sur les modernes*. Paris, 1964.
Cahiers de l'Herne, No. 25 (1974).
Chesneaux, Jean. *The Political and Social Ideas of Jules Verne*. London, 1972.
Cohen, M. "Remarques à propos de la manière d'écrire de Jules Verne," in *Im Dienste der Sprache: Festschrift V. Klemperer*. Halle, 1958.
Compère, Daniel. *Approche de l'île chez Jules Verne*. Paris, 1977.

Diesbach, Ghislain de. *Le Tour de Jules Verne en quatre-vingt livres*. Paris, 1969.

Escaich, René. *Voyage au monde de Jules Verne*. Paris, 1955.

Europe, No. 112/113 (1955).

Huet, Marie-Thérèse. *L'Histoire des "Voyages extraordinaires"*. Paris, 1973.

Jules-Verne, Jean. *Jules Verne*. Paris, 1973.

Macherey, Pierre. "Jules Verne ou le récit en défaut," in his *Pour une théorie de la production littéraire*. Paris, 1966.

Martin, C.-N. *Jules Verne et son oeuvre*. Lausanne, 1971.

Moré, Marcel. *Le très curieux Jules Verne*. Paris, 1960.

———. *Nouvelles explorations de Jules Verne*. Paris, 1963.

Parménie, A., and C. Bonnier de la Chapelle. *Histoire d'un éditeur et de ses auteurs: P. J. Hetzel*. Paris, 1953.

Portuondo, José Antonio. "Jules Verne's America." *Américas* 9 (1957).

Poulet, Georges. *Metamorphoses of the Circle*. Baltimore, 1966.

Serres, Michel. *Jouvences sur Jules Verne*. Paris, 1974.

Vierne, Simone. *L'Ile mystèrieuse de Jules Verne*. Paris, 1973.

———. *Jules Verne et le roman initiatique*. Paris, 1974.

2. OTHERS

Amis, Kingsley. "Afterword" to Samuel Butler, *Erewhon*. New York, 1960.

Christensen, Allan Conrad. *Edward Bulwer-Lytton*. Athens, GA, 1976.

Clarke, I. F. "The Nineteenth-Century Utopia." *The Quarterly R.* 296 (1958).

———. *Voices Prophesying War 1763-1984* [*sic*]. London, 1966 (B).

Cole, G. D. H. *Samuel Butler*. London, 1961.

Deenen, Maria. *Le Merveilleux dans l'oeuvre de Villiers de l'Isle Adam*. Paris, 1939.

Holt, Lee E. *Samuel Butler*. New York, 1964.

Parks, M. G. "Strange to Strangers Only." *Canadian Lit.*, No. 70 (1976).

Schepelmann, Wolfgang. *Die englische Utopie im Uebergang: von Bulwer-Lytton bis H. G. Wells*. Vienna, 1975.

Schlösser, Anselm. "Der viktorianische Gulliver." *Z. für Anglistik und Amerikanistik* 9 (1961).

Seeber, Hans Ulrich. "Gegenutopie und Roman: Bulwer-Lytton's *The Coming Race* (1871)." *Deutsche Vierteljahresschrift für Lit.wiss. und Geistesgesch.* 45 (1971).

Sussman, Herbert L. *Victorians and the Machine*. Cambridge, MA., 1968.

Willey, Basil. *Darwin and Butler*. London, 1960.

Woodcock, George. "De Mille and the Utopian Vision." *J. of Canadian Fiction* 2 (1973).

C. Anticipating the Sunburst

See also Bibliography I, II, III A, III C, III F, IV A, and IV B, in particular Bailey (1972), Barron, ed., Beauchamp, Beer, Bloch (1959), Bridenne, Dupont, Elliott (1970), Elliott (1976), *Extrapolation* (1977), Franklin (1968), Kaul, Ketterer (*New Worlds*), Lewis (1939), Morton (1969), Mumford (1963), Mumford (1966), Parrington, Patai, Sargent, Schepelmann, and Žantovská-Suvin.

1. GENERAL AND THE UTOPOGRAPHERS

Aaron, Daniel. *Men of Good Hope*. New York, 1961.

Bleich, David. "Eros and Bellamy." *American Quarterly* 16 (1964).

Bowman, Sylvia E. *The Year 2000*. New York, 1958.

———, et al. *Edward Bellamy Abroad*. New York, 1962.

Brantlinger, Patrick. "News From Nowhere." *Victorian Studies* 19 (1975).

Brooks, Van Wyck. *New England: Indian Summer*. New York, 1950.

Calhoun, Blue. *The Pastoral Vision of William Morris*. Athens, GA, 1975.

Cole, G. D. H. "Introduction" to William Morris, *Selected Writings*. London, 1948.

Cornet, Robert J. "Rhetorical Strategies in *Looking Backward*." *Markham R.* 4 (1974).

Forbes, Allyn B. "The Literary Quest for Utopia, 1880-1900." *J. of Social Forces* 6 (1927/28).

Goode, John. "William Morris and the Dream of Revolution," in John Lucas, ed., *Literature and Politics in the Nineteenth Century*. London, 1971.

Henderson, Harry B., III. *Visions of the Past*. New York, 1974.

Hicks, Granville. *Figures of Transition*. Westport, CT, 1969.

Hofstadter, Richard. *Social Darwinism in American Thought*. New York, 1959.

Howells, W. D. "Edward Bellamy," in Edward Bellamy, *The Blindman's World*. London, [1898].

Jaher, Frederic Cople. *Doubters and Dissenters*. Glencoe, IL, 1964.

Kasson, J. F. *Civilizing the Machine*. New York, 1976.

Kocmanová, Jessie. "Two Uses of the Dream Form as a Means of Confronting the Present With the Past." *Brno Studies in English* 2 (1960).

Lewis, Arthur O. "Introduction," in idem, ed., *American Utopias*. New York, 1971.

Lindsay, Jack. *William Morris, Writer*. London, 1961.

Lokke, Virgil. "The American Utopian Anti-Novel," in Ray Browne et al, eds., *Frontiers of American Culture*. Lafayette, IN, 1968.

Martin, Jay. *Harvests of Change*. Englewood Cliffs, NJ, 1967.

Meier, Paul. *La Pensée utopique de William Morris*. Paris, 1972.

Middlebro', Tom. "Brief Thoughts on News From Nowhere." *J. of the William Morris Society* 2 (1970).

Parrinder, Patrick. *"News From Nowhere, The Time Machine*, and the Break-Up of Classical Realism." *Science-Fiction Studies* 3 (1976).

Parrington, Vernon L., Jr. *American Dreams*. New York, 1964 (B).

Poli, Bernard. *Le Roman américain 1865-1917*. Paris, 1972.

Redmond, James. "Introduction" to William Morris, *News From Nowhere*. London, 1970.

Ridge, Martin. *Ignatius Donnelly*. Chicago, 1962.

Roemer, Kenneth N. *The Obsolete Necessity*. Kent, OH, 1976 (B).

Sadler, Elizabeth. "One Book's Influence." *New England Quarterly* 17 (1944).

Saxton, Alexander. "Caesar's Column." *American Quarterly* 19 (1967).

Schiffman, Joseph. "Edward Bellamy's Altruistic Man." *American Quarterly* 6 (1954).

———. "Edward Bellamy and the Social Gospel," in Cushing Strout, ed., *Intellectual History in America*, I. New York, 1968.

Shurter, Robert L. "The Literary Work of Edward Bellamy." *American Lit.* 5 (1933).

Taylor, Walter F. *The Economic Novel in America*. New York, 1964.

Thomas, John L. "Introduction" to Edward Bellamy, *Looking Backward, 2000–1887*. Cambridge, MA, 1967.

Thompson, E. P. *William Morris, Romantic to Revolutionary*. New York, 1977.

Towers, Tom H. "The Insomnia of Julian West." *American Lit.* 47 (1975).

Williams, Raymond. *Culture and Society 1780-1950*. Harmondsworth, 1966.

———. *The Country and the City*. New York, 1973.

2. TWAIN AND OTHERS

Budd, Louis. *Mark Twain: Social Philosopher*. Port Washington, NY, 1973.

Cox, James M. *Mark Twain: The Fate of Humor*. Princeton, 1966.

Foner, Philip S. *Mark Twain: Social Critic*. New York, 1966.

Griffin, Martin I. J. *Frank R. Stockton*. Port Washington, NY, 1965.

Griffith, Clark. "Merlin's Grin." *New England Quarterly* 48 (1975).

Kaplan, Justin. "Introduction" to Mark Twain, *A Connecticut Yankee in King Arthur's Court*. Harmondsworth, 1971.

Long, E. Hudson. *Mark Twain Handbook*. New York, 1957.

Salomon, Roger B. *Twain and the Image of History*. New Haven, 1961.

Smith, Henry, Nash. *Mark Twain's Fable of Progress*. New Brunswick, 1964.

————. *Mark Twain: The Development of A Writer*. New York, 1972.
Taylor, Walter Fuller. "Mark Twain and the Machine Age." *The South Atlantic Quarterly* 37 (1938).

V.   H.G. WELLS AND HIS SF CONTEXT

See also Bibliography I, II, III A, III D, III F, IV B, and IV C, in particular Aldiss, Bailey, Barron, ed., Bloch (1959), Clareson, ed. (1971), Clarke (1966), Hillegas, Kagarlitskii, Morton, Moskowitz (1976), Mumford (1966), Nagl, Nicolson (1973), Parrinder (1976), Philmus, Schepelmann, Scholes-Rabkin, Schwonke, Tuzet, and the notes to chap. 10.

Bellamy, William. *The Novels of Wells, Bennett and Galsworthy: 1890–1910*. London, 1971.
Bergonzi, Bernard. *The Early H. G. Wells*. Manchester, 1969.
————. "Wells, Fiction and Politics," in his *The Turn of a Century*. New York, 1973.
————, ed. *H. G. Wells*. Englewood Cliffs N.J., 1976.
Borges, J. L. "The Flower of Coleridge" and "The First Wells," in his *Other Inquisitions 1937-1952*. New York, 1968.
Brooks, Van Wyck. *The World of H. G. Wells*. St. Clair Shores MI, 1970.
Cantril, Hadley. *The Invasion from Mars*. New York, 1966.
Caudwell, Christopher. "H. G. Wells: A Study in Utopianism," in his *Studies and Further Studies in a Dying Culture*. New York, 1971.
Hammond, J. R. *Herbert George Wells*. New York, 1977 (B).
Hillegas, Mark R. "Cosmic Pessimism in H. G. Wells's Scientific Romances." *Papers of the Michigan Academy of Sciences, Arts, and Letters* 46 (1961).
————. "Introduction" to H. G. Wells, *A Modern Utopia*. Lincoln, NE, 1967.
————. "Martians and Mythmakers," in Ray B. Browne et al., eds., *Challenges in American Culture*. Bowling Green, OH, 1970.
————. "Victorian 'Extraterrestrials'," in Jerome H. Buckley, ed., *The Worlds of Victorian Fiction*. Harvard English Studies 6. Cambridge, MA, 1975.
Hughes, David Y. "*The War of the Worlds* in the Yellow Press." *Journalism Quarterly* 43 (1966).
Kagarlitski, Julius. *The Life and Thought of H. G. Wells*. London, 1966; augmented edn. *H. G. Wells: La vita e le opere*. Milan, 1974.
Locke, George. "Wells in Three Volumes?" *Science-Fiction Studies* 3 (1976).
Lodge, David. *The Novelist at the Crossroads*. Ithaca, 1971.

MacKenzie, Norman and Jeanne. *The Time Traveller*. London, 1973; in USA as *H. G. Wells: A Biography*. New York, n.d. [1973].

Morton, Peter R. "Biological Degeneration." *Southern R.*, No. 9 (1976).

Moskowitz, Sam. "George Griffith," in George Griffith, *The Raid of "Le Vengeur.*" London, 1974.

Nicholson, Norman. *H. G. Wells*. Folcroft, PA, 1973.

Parrinder, Patrick, ed. *H. G. Wells: The Critical Heritage*. London, 1972.

——. *H. G. Wells*. New York, 1977.

Philmus, Robert M. "Revisions of the Future: *The Time Machine*." *J. of General Education* 28 (1976).

Philmus, Robert M., and David Y. Hughes, eds. *Early Writings in Science and Science Fiction by H. G. Wells*. Berkeley, 1975.

Platzner, Robert L. "H. G. Wells's 'Jungle Book': The Influence of Kipling on *The Island of Dr. Moreau*." *Victorian Newsletter* 36 (1969).

Pritchett, V. S. *The Living Novel*. London, 1960.

Raknem, Ingvald. *H. G. Wells and His Critics*. Oslo, 1962.

Suvin, Darko, with Robert M. Philmus, eds. *H. G. Wells and Modern Science Fiction*. Lewisburg, PA, 1977 (B).

Vernier, Jean-Pierre. *H. G. Wells et son temps*. Rouen, 1971 (B).

——. *Wells at the Turn of the Century*. *Wells Society Occasional Papers*. London, 1973.

Wagar, W. Warren. *H. G. Wells and the World State*. Freeport, NY, 1971.

West, Geoffrey. *H. G. Wells*. Folcroft, PA, 1973.

Woodcock, George. "The Darkness Violated by Light." *Malahat R.* 26 (1973).

Zamyatin, Yevgeny. "H. G. Wells," in Mirra Ginsburg, ed., *A Soviet Heretic*. Chicago, 1970.

VI.   Russian SF to 1958

See also Bibliography I, II, III A, III C, and V, in particular Barmeyer, ed., Beer, Bowman et al, Elliott, Gurevich, Hillegas, Kagarlitskii, Scholes-Rabkin, Suvin-Philmus, eds., Villgradter-Krey, eds. and Žantovská-Suvin. For a more detailed bibliography that goes to 1974, see Suvin (1976) in the present section. In view of the widespread Russian publishing practice of using only the first initial of the author's given name, I have standardized this for all Russian items in this section.

Bel'chikov, N. *Dostoevskii v protsesse petrashevtsev*. Leningrad, 1936.

——. " 'Zolotoi vek' v predstavlenii F. M. Dostoevskogo," in V. Kuleshov et al., eds., *Problemy teorii i istorii literatury*. Moscow, 1971.

Brandis, E., and V. Dmitrevskii. *Cherez gory vremeni*. Moscow, 1963.
————. "Problemy izobrazheniia budushchego v svete leninskikh predvidenii," in *O literature dlia detei*, issue 15. Leningrad, 1970.
Britikov, A. *Russkii sovetskii nauchno-fantasticheskii roman*. Leningrad, 1970 (B by B. Liapunov).
————. [sub-chapters III/14-16, IV/17 and VIII/8-9] in *Russkii sovetskii rasskaz*. Leningrad, 1970.
Chistov, K. *Russkie narodnye sotsial'no-utopicheskie legendy XVI-XIX vekov*. Moscow, 1967.
Collins, Christopher. *Evgenij Zamjatin*. The Hague, 1973.
Fedosov, I. *Iz istorii russkoi obshchestvennoi mysli XVIII stoletiia: M. M. Shcherbatov*. Moscow, 1967.
Flaker, Aleksandar. *Heretici i sanjari*. Zagreb, 1958.
Gregg, R. A. "Two Adams and Eve in the Crystal Palace." *Slavic R*. 24 (1965).
Grille, D. *Lenins Rivale*. Cologne, 1966.
Gromova, A. "Dvoinoi lik griadushchego," in *NF: Al'manakh nauchnoi fantastiki*. Moscow, 1964.
————. "Introduction: At the Frontier of the Present Age," in C. G. Bearne, ed. *Vortex*. London, 1971.
Jackson, Robert L. *Dostoevskij's Underground Man in Russian Literature*. The Hague, 1958.
Kizevetter, A. "Russkaia utopiia XVIII st.," in his *Istoricheskie ocherki*. The Hague, 1967.
Liapunov, B. *Aleksandr Beliaev*. Moscow, 1967.
————. *V mire fantastiki*. Moscow, 1975 (B).
Maksimov, D. *Briusov*. Leningrad, 1969.
Miliavskii, B. *Satirik i vremia*. Moscow, 1963.
Mochulskii, K. *Valerii Briusov*. Paris, 1962.
Naumova, N. *Roman N. G. Chernyshevskogo "Chto delat'?"*. Leningrad, 1972.
Nazirov, R. "Vladimir Odoevskii i Dostoevskii." *Russkaia lit.*, No. 3 (1974).
Nudelman, R. "Conversation in a Railway Compartment." *Science-Fiction Studies* 5 (1978).
————. "Fantastika, rozhdennaia revoliutsiei," in *Fantastika 1966*, issue 3. Moscow, 1967.
Pil'nen'kii, Sergii. *Kriz' desiatilittia*. Kiev, 1973.
Poliak, L. *Aleksei Tolstoi—khudozhnik*. Moscow, 1964.
Richards, D. J. *Zamyatin*. London, 1962.
Ripellino, Angelo Maria. *Majakovski et le théâtre russe d'avant-garde*. Paris, 1965.

Riurikov, Iu. *Cherez 100 i 1000 let*. Moscow, 1961.

Rullkötter, Bernd. *Die Wissenschaftliche Phantastik der Sowjetunion*. Bern, 1974.

Rynin, N. *Interplanetary Flight and Communication*. Springfield, VA, 1972 (B).

Sakulin, P. *Iz istorii russkogo idealizma: Kniaz V. F. Odoevskii*. Moscow, 1913.

————. *Russkaia literatura i sotsializm*, I. Moscow, 1924.

Shane, Alex M. *The Life and Works of Evgenij Zamjatin*. Berkeley, 1968 (B).

Siniavskii, A. "Sovremennyi nauchno-fantasticheskii roman," in *Puti razvitiia sovremennogo sovetskogo romana*. Moscow, 1961.

Sipovskii, V. *Ocherki iz istorii russkogo romana*, I-II. St. Petersburg, 1909-10.

————. *Etapy russkoi mysli*. Petrograd, 1924.

Skaftymov, A. *Nravstvennye iskaniia russkikh pisatelei*. Moscow, 1972.

Smelkov, Iu. *Fantastika—o chem ona?*. Moscow, 1974.

Suvin, Darko. *Russian Science Fiction 1956-1974*. Elizabethtown NY, 1976 (B).

Sviatlovskii, V. *Russkii utopicheskii roman*. Petersburg, 1922 (B).

Trotsky, Leon. *Literature and Revolution*. Ann Arbor, 1966.

Veksler, N. *Aleksei Nikolaevich Tolstoi*. Moscow, 1948.

Vorob'ev, B. "Nauchnaia fantastika v trudakh K. E. Tsiolkovskogo," in K. Tsiolkovskii, *Put' k zvezdam*. Moscow, 1960 (French in C. Tsiolkowski, *Le Chemin des étoiles*. Moscow, 1963).

Voronskii, A. "Evgeny Zamyatin." *Russian Lit. Triquarterly*, No. 2 (1972).

VII.   KAREL ČAPEK AND HIS SF

See also Hillegas, Philmus, and Small in Bibliography I, III A, and IV A.

Bernshtein, I. A. *Karel Chapek*. Moscow, 1969.

Burianek, František. "Předmluva," in Karel Čapek, *Valka s mloky*. Prague, 1955.

Harkins, William E. *Karel Čapek*. New York, 1962.

Janaszek-Ivaničková, Halina. *Karol Čapek*. Warsaw, 1962.

Klíma, Ivan. *Karel Čapek*. Prague, 1962.

Malevič, Oleg. "Tovarna na Absolutno po 40 letech . . . ." *Česka lit.*, No. 3 (1962).

Malevich, O. *Karel Chapek*. Moscow, 1968.

Matushka, Alexander. *Karel Čapek*. Prague and London, 1964.

Mukařovský, Jan. *Kapitoly z česke poetiky*, II. Prague, 1948.

————. "O Karlu Čapkovi i jeho Krakatitu," in Karel Čapek, *Krakatit*. Prague, 1948.

Nikol'skii, S. *Roman K. Chapeka "Voina s salamandrami"*. Moscow, 1968.

————. *Karel Chapek—fantast i satirik*. Moscow, 1973.

Piša, A. M. *Směry a cíle*. Prague, 1927.

Strohsová, Eva. "Román pro služky a Čapkovo směřovani k epičnosti," in *Struktura a smysl literárního díla*. Prague, 1966.

Wellek, René. "Karel Čapek," in his *Essays on Czech Literature*. The Hague, 1963.

Index

Only proper names of non-imaginary persons have been retained; also excluded are names in prefatory matter and Bibliography, names cited only in notes referring to the Bibliography, names in titles of literary works, and names of editors of works by other authors.